LATINO/A BIBLICAL HERMENEUTICS

SBL

Society of Biblical Literature

Semeia Studies

Gerald O. West, General Editor

Editorial Board
Pablo Andiñach
Fiona Black
Denise K. Buell
Gay L. Byron
Steed V. Davidson
Jennifer L. Koosed
Monica Jyotsna Melanchthon
Yak-Hwee Tan

Number 68

LATINO/A BIBLICAL HERMENEUTICS

PROBLEMATICS, OBJECTIVES, STRATEGIES

Edited by
Francisco Lozada Jr. and Fernando F. Segovia

SBL Press
Atlanta

Copyright © 2014 by SBL Press

All rights reserved. No part of this work may be reproduced or transmitted in any form or by any means, electronic or mechanical, including photocopying and recording, or by means of any information storage or retrieval system, except as may be expressly permitted by the 1976 Copyright Act or in writing from the publisher. Requests for permission should be addressed in writing to the Rights and Permissions Office, SBL Press, 825 Houston Mill Road, Atlanta, GA 30329 USA.

Library of Congress Cataloging-in-Publication Data

Latino/a biblical hermeneutics : problematics, objectives, strategies / edited by Francisco Lozada, Jr. and Fernando F. Segovia.
    p. cm. — (Society of Biblical Literature. Semeia studies ; number 68)
 Includes bibliographical references.
 ISBN 978-1-58983-654-9 (paper binding : alk. paper) — ISBN 978-1-58983-655-6 (electronic format) — ISBN 978-1-58983-927-4 (hardcover binding : alk. paper)
 1. Bible—Hermeneutics. 2. Bible—Criticism, interpretation, etc.—Latin America. I. Lozada, Francisco, 1965– II. Segovia, Fernando F. III. Title: Latino biblical hermeneutics. IV. Title: Latina biblical hermeneutics.
 BS476.L36 2014
 220.6089'68—dc23   2014039646

Printed on acid-free, recycled paper conforming to
ANSI/NISO Z39.48-1992 (R1997) and ISO 9706:1994
standards for paper permanence.

Contents

Acknowledgments ix
Abbreviations xi

Introduction: Approaching Latino/a Biblical Criticism:
   A Trajectory of Visions and Missions
   Fernando F. Segovia 1

Addressing the Problematic:
What Does It Mean to Be a Latino/a Critic?

What Does It Mean to Be a Latino/a Biblical Critic? A Latino
   Pentecostal Perspective, with Reflections on the Future
   Efrain Agosto 45

Rethinking Latino Hermeneutics: An Atheist Perspective
   Hector Avalos 59

Reexamining Ethnicity: Latina/os, Race, and the Bible
   Eric D. Barreto 73

Position Reversal and Hope for the Oppressed
   Aída Besançon Spencer 95

What Does It Mean to Be a Latino Biblical Critic? A Brief Essay
   Alejandro F. Botta 107

Forgotten Forebears in the History of North American Biblical
   Scholarship
   Gregory Cuellar 121

The Challenges of Latino/a Biblical Criticism
    Rubén R. Dupertuis 133

Latino/a Biblical Hermeneutics: Problematic, Objectives, Strategies
    Cristina García-Alfonso 151

Reading from No Place: Toward a Hybrid and Ambivalent Study of Scriptures
    Jacqueline M. Hidalgo 165

Toward Latino/a Biblical Studies: Foregrounding Identities and Transforming Communities
    Francisco Lozada Jr. 187

Toward a Latino/a Vision/Optic for Biblical Hermeneutics
    Rubén Muñoz-Larrondo 203

A Latina Biblical Critic and Intellectual: At the Intersection of Ethnicity, Gender, Hermeneutics, and Faith
    Ahida Calderón Pilarski 231

Interpretive World Making: Formulating a Space for a Critical Latino/a Cultural and Biblical Discourse
    David Arturo Sánchez 249

How Did You Get to Be a Latino Biblical Scholar? Scholarly Identity and Biblical Scholarship
    Timothy J. Sandoval 263

El Sur También Existe: A Proposal for Dialogue between Latin American and Latino/a Hermeneutics
    Osvaldo D. Vena 297

Conclusion

Advancing Latino/a Biblical Criticism: Visions and Missions for the Future
    Fernando F. Segovia 323

Latino/a Biblical Interpretation: A Question of Being and/or
  Practice?
    Francisco Lozada Jr. 365

Contributors..371

Acknowledgments

This volume has been made possible due to the assistance and support of a good number of people, to whom we are deeply indebted and most thankful. First and foremost, to all those who took part in the project, for their gracious acceptance of our invitation and fine contributions. Second, to Mr. Luis Menéndez Antuña, who, as a doctoral student in New Testament and Early Christianity within the Graduate Department of Religion at Vanderbilt University, served as editorial assistant for the project, for his keen editing of the manuscript. Third, to the Editorial Board of Semeia Studies, for their kind acceptance of the volume for publication in the series, and to its Editor, Gerald L. West, for his excellent work in shepherding the volume toward publication. Finally, to the entire publications staff of SBL Press, for its impeccable assistance throughout the process of publication.

Abbreviations

AB	Anchor Bible
BDB	Francis Brown, S. R. Driver, and Charles A. Briggs, *The Brown-Driver-Briggs Hebrew and English Lexicon with an Appendix Containing the Biblical Aramaic*. 1907. Repr., Peabody, MA.: Hendrickson, 2001.
BibInt	*Biblical Interpretation*
BTB	*Biblical Theology Bulletin*
CBQ	*Catholic Biblical Quarterly*
HSM	Harvard Semitic Monographs
HTR	*Harvard Theological Review*
JBL	*Journal of Biblical Literature*
JHLT	*Journal of Hispanic/Latino Theology*
JJS	*Journal of Jewish Studies*
JSJ	*Journal for the Study of Judaism*
JSNT	*Journal for the Study of the New Testament*
JSOTSup	Journal for the Study of the Old Testament: Supplement Series
NIGTC	New International Greek Testament Commentary
NRSV	New Revised Standard Version
RSV	Revised Standard Version
SBLSymS	Society of Biblical Literature Symposium Series
SemeiaSt	Semeia Studies
TNIV	Today's New International Version
WUNT	Wissenschaftliche Untersuchungen zum Neuen Testament
WW	*Word and World*
ZAW	*Zeitschrift für die alttestamentliche Wissenschaft*

Introduction:
Approaching Latino/a Biblical Criticism:
A Trajectory of Visions and Missions

Fernando F. Segovia

This project on the identity and role of the Latino/a biblical critic constitutes an exercise in racial-ethnic criticism in general and minority biblical criticism in particular. To express it otherwise: just as minority biblical criticism represents a variation of racial-ethnic criticism, so does an analysis of the critical task as envisioned by minority critics represent a variation of minority biblical criticism. To explain what this variation signifies and entails, it is imperative to conceptualize and formulate its placement within both critical frameworks. Toward this end, I draw on previous reflections, offered as part of a study of the poetics of minority biblical criticism, on the interdisciplinary character of these endeavors (Segovia 2009). These reflections will allow me to capture and convey the nature, objective, and approach of the project.

Racial-ethnic biblical criticism brings together two fields of study, biblical studies and racial-ethnic studies, with important academic-scholarly features in common: both possess long-standing and well-established traditions of scholarship; both embrace an expansive sense of scope, with manifold areas of interest brought under the lens of analysis; and both reveal a complex, shifting, and conflicted trajectory of critical discussions on any area of analysis. Biblical studies involves the problematic of scriptural interpretation: the study of biblical texts and contexts in terms of production and reception, understood broadly in both respects. Racial-ethnic studies has to do with the problematic of race and ethnicity: the study of the representations of Other and Self—in primarily somatic or cultural terms, respectively—that emerge as a result of processes of migration and encounter between population groups. A bringing together of these fields requires, therefore, pointed focalization of the concrete problematic to be addressed—exposition of its design (*what*), its rationale (*why*), and its mode (*how*)—as well as active engagement with the literature in both fields regarding such focalization.

Minority biblical criticism brings together specific components from each field of study: from racial-ethnic studies, it foregrounds the set of formations and relations involving minority groups within a state; from biblical studies, it highlights the principles and practices of interpretation at work among critics from such minority groups. This it does for the sake of analyzing such principles and practices in relation to the practices and principles operative among critics from the dominant group. Such analysis can proceed in any number of directions. From the point of view of biblical studies, it can highlight any dimension of the field: the texts and contexts of antiquity; the interpretations of such texts and contexts, and their contexts; the interpreters behind such interpretations, and their contexts. This it can do in terms of any tradition of reading, not just the academic-scholarly. From the point of view of minority studies, it can foreground any individual group, any combination of groups, or the set of such groups as a whole. In so doing, it can pursue any aspect of the process of minoritization and its ramifications. An exercise in minority biblical criticism demands, consequently, a closely targeted and properly informed focalization of the concrete interdisciplinary problematic to be examined.

As a variation of minority criticism, the present project seeks to analyze the vision of the critical task espoused by Latino/a critics. With respect to design, the project places the following components from each field in dialogue: from biblical studies, the mission of the critic as critic, and hence a focus on interpreters and their approach to the craft of interpretation—a dimension of criticism that is hardly ever discussed, much less theorized; from minority studies, an individual minoritized group within the United States—the Latino/a American formation, and thus the Latino/a circle of critics. In terms of rationale, the project seeks to ascertain how such critics approach their vocation as critics in the light of their identity as members of the Latino/a experience and reality—howsoever they define the social-cultural situation of the group and their own affiliation within it. With respect to mode of correlation, the project proceeds by asking a variety of critics—representing a broad spectrum of the Latino/a American formation, along various axes of identity—to address the problematic in whatever way they deem appropriate: What does it mean to be a Latino/a critic?

A further reflection is in order. Behind any exercise in minority criticism in general and minority biblical criticism in particular lies, I have argued, a desire for self-assertion and self-introjection, in the light of the practices of marginalization and erasure that govern their reality and experience in society and culture. In effect, the axis of relations between dominant and minority formations within a state constitutes a variation among many of unequal or differential relations of power, exercised through a dialectical process of minoritization. Thus when I use the term *minority* I mean *minoritized*, and from now on I shall use the latter term. Any such exercise, therefore, partakes in such a desire, as I put it at the time (Segovia 2009, 285), "to break through the gaze-patrol of dominant culture and society," interrupting thereby the dialectics of minoritization by transgressing established ways of thinking and doing set up and maintained by such a process.

The present project does this in at least two regards. I have noted above that theorization of the critical task has been mostly ignored in the scholarly-academic tradition of reading. Further, contextualization of the critic in social and cultural terms has been largely bypassed in the field as well. A foregrounding of critical mission from the minoritized perspective of Latino/a criticism constitutes, therefore, a serious interruption in dominant biblical discourse by way of problematizing a critical component that remains invariably taken for granted. A further dimension of this move renders it more serious still. The force of the argument leads, logically and inexorably, to a similar problematization within the dominant tradition itself.

Lastly, a word about the presentation of the project is also in order. In this work we have adopted a threefold division. The first part, represented by this introductory study, traces the path of Latino/a biblical criticism up to this point by way of recent definitions of the approach. The second part consists of the various studies addressing the problematic of critical identity and role for Latino/a criticism. These have been arranged in alphabetical order. There are two reasons for such a choice: first, given the freedom of approach allowed the contributors, without any set of categories or areas of any sort; second, in light of the complex character of the proposals advanced, which do not fall easily into any distinctive pattern of organization. The third part involves two concluding studies. The first begins by examining in detail the dynamics and mechanics of each study and then goes on to a critical comparison of such findings, all in the light of the critical trajectory of definitions regarding Latino/a criticism outlined in the first part. The second study brings the volume to an end by pointing forward, imagining the contours for the next phase of Latino/a criticism in its ongoing trajectory.

Tracing the Trajectory of Latino/a Biblical Criticism

This project is not without a trajectory, and this trajectory is very much worth tracing. In recent years a number of major proposals—five in all—have appeared from the ranks of Latino/a critics and scholars toward a vision and a program for Latino/a biblical interpretation. Such a development is a sign of growth in numbers within the movement, as more and more Latino/as join the circle of biblical criticism. It is also a sign of growth in sophistication, as more and more attempts at self-reflection take place. In what follows I should like to examine such proposals by way of setting the stage for the project. In so doing, I activate rhetorical dynamics outlined in the study on the poetics, the formal features of emplacement and argumentation, deployed by minoritized biblical criticism. In other words, this study is also an exercise in minoritized criticism.

What I do here adopts the strategy of interruptive stocktaking, which I have described as "the self-conscious problematization of the established grounds and practices of criticism itself by way of rethinking and revisioning" (Segovia 2009, 286). This involves a turning of criticism upon itself, toward development of alternative visions of the critical task. This it does by looking at questions of identity (background and motivation) and questions of critical role (procedure and objective). Thus I want to examine, in sustained and systematic fashion, how this recent trajectory has envisioned the path ahead for Latino/a biblical interpretation. In so doing, moreover, I adopt the tactic of "taking a personal turn," looking at how these scholars approach the critical task "not only as members of minority groups but also as distinct members within such groups" in terms of individual location as well as agenda. I examine, therefore, various aspects of each proposal—context of publication, personal background, critical stance, and resultant vision. In thus turning Latino/a criticism upon itself, my aim is to chart a trajectory of social-cultural as well as academic-scholarly assertion and introjection. Toward this end, I proceed in chronological fashion.

Luis Rivera Rodriguez (2007)—Reading from and for the Diaspora

With the proliferation of method and theory in biblical criticism since the 1970s, the discipline of biblical studies has expanded beyond its traditional historical moorings and approach, drawing on a growing number of disciplines, established as well as emerging, for its work and becoming increasingly thereby a field of study.[1] In this process of transformation, biblical studies was by no means alone, but followed rather the path of the disciplinary spectrum as a whole, including historiography itself. While always interdisciplinary in character, discursive interaction became ever more diverse and sophisticated. Such development has generated any number of projects that have sought to bring biblical criticism in dialogue with other fields of study.

One such interaction has involved, within the umbrella field of Christian studies, the conjunction of ethical studies and biblical studies, for which the volume *Bible and Ethics in the Christian Life*, by Bruce Birch and Larry Rasmussen, may be seen as a point of origins in the modern period (1976). In the mid-1990s, within the context of the joint annual meetings of the American Academy of Religion and the Society of Biblical Literature, a sustained effort in this regard was launched by way of a program unit on character ethics and biblical interpretation. The project brought together critics and ethicists to examine the role of Scripture in the process of moral formation and identity—the realm of character ethics—within Christian communities. In so doing, the project took into account both the world of production and the world of reception of the biblical texts—the communities that forged the texts and the communities that are forged by the texts. The project has generated a series of volumes, including *Character Ethics and the Old Testament*, the venue for this first model for Latino/a biblical criticism, advanced by Luis Rivera Rodriguez.[2]

Its editors, M. Daniel Carroll R. and Jacqueline Lapsley, set a twofold context for the volume, religious-theological as well as social-cultural (2007). On the one hand, they point to the major transformation at work in Christianity, away from Western Christendom and toward global Christianity—a process seen as marked by disorientation among Christian communities regarding identity and formation. On the other hand,

---

1. The results were to be expected: its object turned less unified and more expansive; its method, less set and more varied; its body of work, less coherent and more multidirectional; and its objective, less consensual and more problematized.

2. The first was *Character and Scripture*, edited by William P. Brown (2002). This was followed by *Character Ethics and the New Testament*, edited by Robert L. Brawley (2007); and *Character Ethics and the Old Testament*, edited by M. Daniel Carroll R. and Jacqueline Lapsley (2007).

they cite the multiple, severe, and interrelated crises affecting the world—a scenario viewed as marked by multidimensional violence (engendered by wars, terrorism, and drugs) and economic devastation (the ramifications of economic globalization). Such a context, they argue, presents many pressing challenges for Christian communities: (1) the global crises demand a response on their part; (2) this demand highlights the problematic of any response, given the diversity of communities and processes of moral formation and identity; (3) this problematic has given rise to a renewed focus on Scripture as a key moral resource for all communities. The volume thus sets out to advance, in the academic-scholarly realm, this appeal to Scripture in the midst of such a complex and urgent scenario.

The volume is thus profoundly theological and resolutely social in orientation. All contributors are said to subscribe to the notion that Scripture "has shaped and continues to shape those committed to God's justice and the desire that all might thrive" (xviii)—a high regard for scriptural authority and normativity, with a focus on justice for all. Further, such commitment is said to involve, above all, "those who lie outside the walls of the more privileged sectors of society" (xviii)—an explicit solidarity with the marginalized, within its embrace of justice for all. Its design is twofold. A first part, involving critics, deals with formation and identity in the texts—it is expansive and canonically comprehensive. The second part, involving theologians, reflects on formation and identity in present-day contexts by way of the texts—it is circumscribed and globally selective. Four such frameworks are represented, all having to do with nonprivileged communities: two from North America (United States: diasporic Latino/a Americans throughout; migrant workers and prisoners in the Northwest), one from Africa (South Africa), and one from Latin America (Guatemala). It is in this section that one finds Rivera Rodriguez's piece, "Toward a Diaspora Hermeneutics."

His choice for this task is on point—materially as well as discursively. Materially, Rivera Rodriguez is a member of the Latin American and Caribbean diaspora in the United States. He presents himself within it as a native of Puerto Rico, in itself a unique case: formally, a commonwealth in association with the United States, a self-governing unincorporated territory, since 1952; however, this status is largely perceived as colonial by its inhabitants. Consequently, he describes himself as a citizen by birth but an immigrant by choice. First, he came to the United States for doctoral studies at Harvard University (1979–1986); later on, he opted for long-term residency as a member of the theological academy (1995–). As such, he represents "a first-order diasporan": someone who has gone through the "experience of translocality"—the process of "exiting, traveling, entering, and settling in countries other than their own native lands" (2007, 170). Discursively, Rivera Rodriguez is at work on a hermeneutical model of the diaspora. He identifies his aim, as a Latino theologian, as the development of a theological hermeneutics that is grounded in the context and informed by the interests of Latino/a diasporans—primarily of the first order, his own experience.[3]

The model is unpacked in four steps. The first three deal with diasporic experience in general. Rivera Rodriguez begins with a definition of diaspora formations: the process of migration leads to the development of diaspora groups and communities. The latter, the focus of attention, are distinguished by way of identity and behavior. Communities are more settled: "stable and organized conglomerates of immigrant families and groups, and their descendants, who have established a long-term residency in a host country." They are also more complex: they "carry out their social action and cultural existence through their own networks and within the power networks of three fundamental social fields: the diaspora community itself, the host land, and the homeland" (171–72). Then he analyzes the character of such communities by way of a grid of components derived from the social sciences. Thereupon, in the light of such analysis, he outlines a set of reading strategies for such communities. The final step turns to religious-theological diasporic experience in particular. Here, with diasporic communities in mind, specifically Christian, he unfolds a framework for the theological interpretation of religious texts and traditions.

From a religious-theological point of view, Rivera Rodriguez lies at the center of this reading tradition of the biblical texts. As noted, not only does he describe himself as a Latino theologian interested in a theological hermeneutics of and for the diaspora, but the proposal also forms part of a Christian biblical-ethical project designed to further the renewed turn to Scripture in the midst of Christian diversity and global crises. Further, the model is advanced as a dialogical contribution to an ongoing project on the part of Latino/a scholars and ministers who take diaspora as a fundamental "point of reference" (169) in the theological interpretation of religious and biblical traditions, as they seek "to live out their faith and

---

3. The model, it is intimated, may well find resonance among second-order Latino/a diasporans, but this is not pursued.

politics as members of diasporic communities and congregations" in the country (183). As such, it is presented as an option, a way of providing further stimulus to the project.

In this envisioned theological reading of "sacred texts and traditions" (179) by Christian Latino/a religious communities of the diaspora, three interrelated dimensions are outlined. The first involves the religious character of the diaspora as represented in the texts or experienced by readers: How is diaspora "interpreted in connection to the divine" (179)? The second concerns the diasporic character of the religious life as represented in the texts or experienced by readers: How are the divine realm and the religious life "represented and interpreted through the symbolics of diaspora" (180)? The third involves the appropriation of the religious texts and traditions in the light of new diasporic situations: What new insights or orientations are brought to bear on "the divine, the human, and the religious life" (180)? Two principles clearly underlie such a reading: on the one hand, the biblical texts are seen as bearing witness to the experience of migration and diaspora; on the other hand, the interpretation of such experience by real readers who have themselves undergone such an experience is foregrounded. The model is thus religious-theological to the core. Although the authority and normativity of Scripture are not addressed as such, it is clear that both constitute key components of theological diasporic interpretation.

From a theoretical-methodological angle, the model emerges as thoroughly interdisciplinary and as yielding a distinctive way of reading. Rivera Rodriguez calls for critical dialogue with fields of studies having to do with the phenomenon of diasporas. Only then, he argues, can diasporic communities—and hence religious diasporic communities and congregations—be properly analyzed and addressed in full, as "social formations and locations in their variety, complexity, conflicts, identities, politics, and dynamics" (170). In his own case, four major elements are appropriated from social analysis of diasporas: constitutive dynamics, political strategies, identity constructions, and socioreligious functions. On the basis of such analytical dissection, he sets forth three reading strategies, described as carried out "simultaneously" (177), for the interpretation of biblical texts by religious communities.

The first, reading through diaspora, focuses on the inscription of diaspora in texts and readers. Three angles are noted: (1) the process of emigration (translocality); (2) the process of immigration and its effects on community (communality), identity (ethnogenesis), and relation to host country (marginality); and (3) the strategies deployed for action in the in-between situation of diaspora (transnationality). The second strategy, reading from diaspora, centers on the diaspora as a human condition. Its focus is on how texts and readers assess the meaning and consequences of life in the diaspora. Such a focus attends to the visions of self and community, ethnic and generational identities, and power struggles and conflict in communities. The final strategy, reading for diaspora, addresses diaspora as a vocation. It examines ideal visions and corresponding praxis proposed for the diaspora. In all three cases, it should be noted, the goal is explanatory as well as evaluative: laying out and passing judgment on all aspects of diaspora—inscriptions, conditions, visions—in texts and readers, both other readers and oneself.

From a social-cultural point of view, the model constitutes an exercise in "theopolitical hermeneutics" (183). For Rivera Rodriguez, its foundation lies in "identification with the struggles of immigrant communities" in the country, and its objective is to move toward "a pastoral and theological response of advocacy toward immigrants" (185 n. 4). What such advocacy entails is pointedly outlined: the aim is to "inspire and mobilize members of diaspora communities and congregations in their struggles for the survival, safety, recognition, freedom, and flourishing in this country" (183). All three reading strategies have such advocacy in mind, as their joint descriptive and critical dimensions make clear.

A further point is in order here: while Rivera Rodriguez has the Latino/a diaspora foremost in mind, a more expansive agenda is identified as well. His interest extends to other minoritized first-order diasporas, such as the Asian Americans. Consequently, his work is very much in league with that of Asian American critics and theologians who are engaged in the development of a theological diaspora hermeneutics. Indeed, he faults both Anglo-European and African American scholars for failing to pay, for the most part, due attention to the work of their Latino/a and Asian American colleagues in this regard. This is a theopolitical project writ large, therefore.

In this vision of Latino/a criticism, the critic emerges, first of all, as at once restricted and expanded. The proposal comes from and concerns critics who are first-order diasporans and who have first-order diasporic communities and congregations in sight. In addition, the relevance of the model for critics and communities that are removed from a first-order diasporic experience of diaspora is not considered. At the same time, such critics can and should make common cause with first-order diasporan critics who hail from and address other first-order minority communities and congregations. The critic also emerges as at once united with and separate from their diasporic communities and congregations. This becomes readily apparent in the description of their role. First, it is to foreground the experience of diaspora in its totality and hence in its full diversity—in texts, in readers of texts, and in one's own reading of the texts. Second, it is to pass judgment on all such representations of the diaspora. Third, it is to focus on visions of life in diaspora that have the concerns and interests in mind of the diaspora. In all such endeavors, critics, set apart by learning and sophistication, work for the sake of the people in the Christian communities, so that they too learn to deploy a theological hermeneutics of the diaspora and move toward a better understanding of their situation and a better resolution for the future. In sum, their critical expertise and mission are to be placed at the service of the community, for the sake of conscientization and mobilization, with a better life in mind—one of justice for all, especially the nonprivileged.

Efrain Agosto (2010)—Reading through Latino/a Eyes

With the transition of biblical studies from a discipline to a field of studies and with the rise in interdisciplinary work, a new genre makes its appearance in the scholarly literature—introductions to critical approaches. The aim of this type of volume is to provide an overview of methodological strategies and corresponding theoretical frameworks at work in the field. Such overviews address, with variations, a fairly standard set of topics: (1) the mechanics, its methodological procedures (*how*), and the dynamics, its theoretical foundations (*why*), of the approach; (2) its relation to other approaches in biblical criticism; the developing tradition of interpretation generated by the approach in biblical criticism; (3) its relation to other fields of studies in the academy, its interdisciplinary configurations; and (4) analysis of units or sections of a text by way of illustration. It is in one such introduction, *Hearing the New Testament: Strategies for Interpretation,* edited by Joel Green, that the second model to be considered, by Efrain Agosto (2010), is to be found.[4] This is the first time, to the best

---

4. This was the second edition of this volume, published fifteen years after the first (Green 1995). Interestingly enough, there were no studies on Latino/a American and African American criticism in the first volume.

of my knowledge, that Latino/a biblical criticism is included in this type of publication.

The volume itself, which consists of sixteen studies altogether, is quite expansive in scope, yet decidedly unbalanced in representation, especially in the light of its date of publication. The emphasis lies clearly on historical and literary approaches, which together account for eleven essays in all; remarkably, there is a total absence of sociocultural approaches. Of the five essays that move beyond such parameters, two deal with the religious-theological tradition of reading, while the other three take up ideological readings. The piece by Agosto, "Latino/a Hermeneutics" (2010), is one of two on racial-ethnic criticism, alongside African American criticism; the other is devoted to feminist criticism. Given the overall choice of entries for the volume, especially the limited apportionment of essays assigned to the ideological paradigm, the inclusion of Latino/a biblical criticism is most surprising, though most welcome.

At the time of writing, Agosto was professor of New Testament at Hartford Seminary and a senior figure in the movement, active in it from the start. Materially, he is both of Puerto Rican descent, the product of the U.S. imperial-colonial framework in the Caribbean (1898), and born in the United States, a product of the massive Puerto Rican migration to the mainland devised and promoted by the federal government through Operation Bootstrap (1948). He is thus a Latino by birth, a child of territorial expansion by the United States, and a Nuyorican in particular, a child of the Puerto Rican diaspora that settled in the large cities of the Northeast, with New York as the classic example, and created the barrios in the process. Discursively, Agosto brought to doctoral studies, which focused on the Pauline corpus and the early Christian communities behind the letters, the travails and concerns of the barrios: the problematic of social-cultural as well as religious-ecclesial marginalization and the development of alternative modes of leadership within the Christian communities of the barrios. He was thus an ideal choice for the assignment: a Latino scholar deeply embedded in Latino/a life, with profound concientization regarding such reality and experience, and an extensive, sustained, and sophisticated trajectory in biblical criticism in general and Latino/a criticism in particular.

The piece follows a highly focused development: an overall introduction to the proposed vision of Latino/a hermeneutics; a critical analysis of two models in this vein advanced by Latino scholars, Justo González and myself; and application of the model to two units from 1 Cor 11.

In dialogue with such earlier proposals for Latino/a biblical criticism, Agosto lays out the foundations for intercultural criticism, or a reading "through Latino eyes." The project foregrounds and problematizes the element of the reader, as real reader, in the process of interpretation. As a result, reading—its contexts, its ways, and its findings—becomes a major part of the object of inquiry, alongside the texts and contexts of antiquity. All readers are to be highlighted and analyzed—hence Latino/a readers as well.

The approach opposes, therefore, a passive, restrictive notion of the reader: a neutral, professional agent who examines the texts—historical documents from very different social and cultural circumstances—through a variety of critical methods, which are taken to assure proper deciphering and recovery of textual meaning as well as contextual framework. Instead, the approach favors an active, expansive concept of the reader: a creative, popular or professional, agent who analyzes the texts—social and cultural documents from a quite different historical period—through an array of contemporary social-cultural filters, which, regardless of method, are seen as leaving their imprint on any process of unveiling and retrieving, whether in the reconstruction of textual meaning or the recreation of contextual framework. For Agosto, therefore, the role of Latino/as in reading the Bible, along with the social-cultural circumstances for such reading, emerges as of paramount importance in criticism.

In terms of religious-theological position, Agosto stands solidly within such a tradition of reading. While not addressing the question directly, it is clear that he affirms the authority of Scripture for Latino/a readers, but with a major twist. Thus, while he adopts a broad view of the social-cultural circumstances of the Latino/a community, it is the religious-theological dimension that he highlights above all. In his reading of 1 Corinthians, for example, all the insights from the Latino/a community brought to bear on the text are taken from this perspective. It is the Latino/a Christian communities that he has foremost in mind. At the same time, his position regarding such authority—and here is the twist—is a critical one, which situates the project decidedly toward the minimizing pole of the interpretive spectrum. Scriptural authority has to be weighed in the light of community needs and concerns, a process that sometimes will lead to affirmation and at other times to rejection of the text. Scripture, therefore, emerges as authoritative not because it represents the Word of God, valid for all times and places, but rather because it provides fundamental and guiding parameters for Christian life, parameters that are ultimately subject to critical evaluation in terms of their liberative or limiting character for the readers in question.

As far as theoretical-methodological position is concerned, Agosto does advance a way of reading for intercultural criticism and does relate such a way to discussions regarding meaning-construction in literary studies, though in general rather than detailed fashion in both regards. First of all, reading "through Latino eyes" uses the context of Latino/a readers as point of entry into the text, insofar as all readers are said to approach the texts from their respective contexts and to find in the text what such contexts are looking for. This is evident in the reading of 1 Cor 11, as insights from the Latino/a community are brought to bear on communal issues identified among the Corinthian community. Such insights are said to shed a different light on the text. Second, such a way of reading, with its emphasis on the agency of Latino/a readers, is described as a construction of the text in interpretation in the light of the readers' location and ideology.

This position constitutes a variation of reader-response criticism, toward the reader-dominant side of the spectrum. For Agosto, the reader does not so much activate different dimensions of the text but constructs a new "text" in the process of engagement. It is not clear, however, how much significance is allotted to the text in the process. This is not an unimportant question, for the more active the role of construction, the more fragile the notion of scriptural authority becomes. Agosto himself is keenly aware of the ramifications of his position. Intercultural criticism, he argues, is not well received among those who insist on historicizing reconstruction and recreation as "not only possible but necessary" (352). In the end, however, for him, as a Latino scholar, the introduction of the real reader in interpretation trumps any such reaction.

In terms of social-cultural position, Agosto stands in full agreement with the assessment of the Latino/a community offered by previous proposals. On the one hand, the negative dimensions may be summarized as across the board marginalization, racial-ethnic othering, and national-political bifurcation and ambiguity. On the other hand, the positive dimensions may be outlined as emphasis on communal-familial solidarity and the presence of radical diversity. It is such features that serve as both points of entry into the biblical texts and norms of judgment in the evaluation of such texts as liberative or limiting. This can be readily seen in the reading of 1 Cor 11. Some insights yield affirmation of Paul. For example, Agosto points to a feel for the "fluid complexity" of traditions in the community's search for "identity" in "new and changing settings" on the part of "the relatively young immigrant population represented by many Latino groups" (366). In addition, he cites a ready connection with the "mistreatment" involving different formations of power within the community in light of the "'otherness' of the Latino immigrant experience" (369). Other insights result in critique. Thus Agosto refers to the determination to overcome the gender limitations imposed on women in church and society alike by Latinas, who have "suffered the brunt" of patriarchal interpretation and "the cultural burden of *machismo*" (367). Similarly, he mentions the distrust for any call to "community unity in 'spiritual matters'" among Latino/as, who know all too well what it means not only to receive "the 'leftovers' of economic prosperity in U.S. society" but also to do so as "generous apportionments" (370). "Latino/a experience today," Agosto concludes, "illuminates both the liberating and limiting aspects of these Pauline texts in 1 Corinthians" (370).

Within this vision of Latino/a criticism, the role of the critic, not pursued as such, emerges as at once no different from and different from that of Latino/a readers in general. In engaging the biblical texts, the critic produces, as in the case of any other Latino/a reader, a construction of that text. Insofar as Latino/a readers, including the critic, work from a context that exhibits a number of distinctive social-cultural features, which mark the community as community, the critic brings more or less the same points of entry into the text. Further, the critic does this for the same purpose as other readers: to assess the liberative or limiting potential of the text. Yet, in such engagement, the critic stands apart as well. First, as an individual reader, the critic produces a construct of his/her own, as does any other Latino/a reader, especially given the stress on the diversity of the community. Second, as a professional reader, the critic also possesses superior expertise in comparison to Latino/a readers at large in analyzing the text as a historical document and assessing its character as authoritative for the community. These two aspects of the Latino/a critic, homogeneity and difference, remain ultimately unresolved within the vision. To put it differently, in a democratizing view of reading the Bible and evaluating its authority, what difference does the professional critic make?

Justo González (2010)—Reading with the Latino/a Community

A variation of the new genre of introductions to critical approaches, described above in the discussion of Agosto's model, begins to surface as well in the scholarly literature—introductions to particular writings by way of readings from a variety of critical approaches. The objective is to provide a sense of interpretive diversity when different critical lenses, different methodological strategies and underlying theoretical frameworks, are brought to bear on the same text.

The overview of the various approaches follows, again with variations, the pattern of topics set by the general introductions: (1) a description of the approach, both in terms of mechanics or procedures and dynamics or foundations; (2) comparative references to other approaches, especially those represented in the volume; (3) an account of the interpretive trajectory of the approach as applied to the writing in question; (4) attention to the interdisciplinary dimensions of the approach, its discursive sources and critical conversations; and (5) analysis of texts from the writing under examination. The importance given to the various topics undergoes change in the process, as one would expect: (1) the delineation of the approach as such is not as expansive; (2) the focus of inquiry becomes more pointed throughout, given the delimitation of the object of research; and (3) the analysis of texts becomes more extensive.

The third model to be analyzed, from the pen of Justo González, appears in one such collection of critical approaches on a Gospel, *Methods for Luke*, also edited by Joel Green (2010c). This too is the first time, to the best of my knowledge, that Latino/a biblical criticism is included in this type of collection.

The volume, which forms part of a series, Methods in Biblical Interpretation, includes four studies in all: one on historical criticism, one on literary criticism (narrative), and two devoted to ideological readings: feminist criticism and racial-ethnic criticism. The essay by González, "A Latino Perspective" (2010), constitutes the sole entry in this last category. The collection is thus fairly narrow in scope as well as in representation, as a comparison with its companion volume on Matthew in the series readily shows.[5] Most striking in this regard, again, is the absence of any contribution from a sociocultural perspective. Green's introduction (2010a) is to the point here. First, he explains that by *method* he means not technique or procedure but rather "the sensibilities and commitments by which

---

5. The volume (Powell 2009) includes six essays: two on historical criticism; one each on literary and sociocultural approaches, and two on ideological approaches. There is, however, no overview of racial-ethnic studies in general and thus no essay on Latino/a criticism.

we engage texts" (5)[6]—that is, the mode and aim of criticism. Second, he argues that, given the "veritable smorgasbord of interpretive methods" available today, the essays chosen are, "in their own ways," "representative of major currents in the field" (6)—that is, major sensibilities and commitments.

In the case of González, Green points to the use of biography—both individual and communal—as context for and point of entry into the reading of the text. This strategy he identifies as an explicit marker of contemporary criticism: the stance that what a reader finds in a text is very much dependent on context (where that reader stands) and purpose (what that reader is seeking). Such interpretive practices and interests, he adds, parallel those adopted by other interpretive communities, by which he means, given the examples adduced, ethnic-racial or global-continental formations—African American, African, Asian American (8). Any one of these could have served, therefore, as an example for this critical category and approach. Given the limited selection of entries, above all the restricted number of contributions allotted to the ideological paradigm and the representative nature of such contributions, the choice of Latino/a biblical criticism proves again entirely unexpected, although also most welcome.

The invitation extended to González for this task is at once understandable and peculiar. It can be readily comprehended, certainly, insofar as he had already addressed the question of biblical interpretation among Latino/as in one of the early works of the Latino/a religious-theological movement and discourse, *Santa Biblia: The Bible through Hispanic Eyes* (1996). It is odd, nonetheless, insofar as he is not a biblical critic by training but rather a church historian, and hence not altogether at home in the discursive discussions within the field since the 1970s. The choice is thus both incisive and intriguing. Two other comments are in order. González—an independent scholar for most of his life, except for a couple of early appointments at the Seminario Evangélico de Puerto Rico and Emory University—is a sharp and prolific scholar, with a distinguished

---

6. Such sensibilities and commitments involve such issues as the following: the central assumptions about meaning; the aims behind such an approach to interpretation; and the protocols of interpretation to be followed. The position is summarized as follows: "I am referring both to one's willingness and ability to show how this reading was achieved, and to the openness of interpreters to have their approach to interpretation and the results of their reading queried in relation to their coherence with the text being read" (6).

list of publications to his name, including a number of writings on biblical interpretation. Further, he has also been an activist on behalf of the Latino/a community in religious-ecclesial and academic-theological circles, with broad knowledge of the community. These various aspects of his life and work come across in this vision of Latino/a biblical criticism.

Indeed, such aspects are in evidence from the start, as he explains why he finds the protocol for development of the study problematic. This protocol calls for a threefold structure: explication of the method, discussion regarding application to the Gospel of Luke in general, and illustrative application by way of a text. Such a structure, he points out, embodies two assumptions: first, the priority of method over reading in interpretation, corresponding to a similar priority of the theoretical over the practical in theological education; second, the absence of the biographical dimension in interpretation, personal-psychological as well as social-cultural. Both assumptions, he explains, are at odds with the actual practices of Latino/a religious-ecclesial communities. To begin with, Latino/as start by doing interpretation and ministry on their own, and then move on to formal theological education and critical study of method and theory. In addition, Latino/as on interpretation on their own by drawing upon their biographical reality and experience. This critique of the protocol González deftly uses to turn the first phase on method upside down. What he does, in effect, is to theorize such actual practices as a method for interpretation, thus observing while subverting the protocol.

With respect to religious-theological stance, the model stands squarely within this tradition of reading, displaying a high, though nuanced, view of the authority of Scripture. This is evident in his theorization of the biographical dimension. This component González unpacks in terms of three factors identified as key in his own trajectory as a reader of the biblical texts: generation, denomination, and gender. All three are clearly personal-psychological in nature, but they are also deeply rooted in the social-cultural realm.

The generational element emerges as primary. González, a Cuban American, draws on national origins and immigrant status. First, as a Protestant born and raised in a dominant and preconciliar Catholic context, Scripture served a twofold role: a guide for the life of the church (worship, belief, practice) and a weapon for debate with non-Protestants. Subsequently, as an immigrant, ethnic-cultural minority in the United States, Scripture took on another role: a weapon against marginalization by the dominant society and culture. As a result, reading Scripture is described, first, as a most serious exercise, "not just an academic or hermeneutical exercise" (116); and, second, as a charter in the struggle against marginalization, as something "contrary to the word of God" (117). At the same time, from all three factors a measure of distantiation comes to the fore. The generational factor leads to an acknowledgment that many Latino/as native to the United States, who have experienced the use of Scripture against them, are more open to seeing biblical passages as problematic and looking elsewhere for authority.

The denominational factor brings to mind the view of Scripture among Catholic Latino/as as one of several sources for theology, who thus find themselves more comfortable in critiquing difficult passages. The generic factor leads to an admission of bias in Scripture against women, a move that brings about consternation regarding its authority, but also rejoicing through the discovery of countervailing texts (such as Luke-Acts). All such reservations, which circumscribe his strong sense of scriptural authority, come across as decidedly reluctant but utterly genuine. In the end, the model may be described as one of guarded hermeneutical affirmation—Scripture, absolutely, but not blindly so.

With regard to theoretical-methodological position, González outlines a way of reading in his theorization of the practical dimension. This approach to Scripture has two components: the experiential and the communitarian. The experiential angle involves a process encompassing a number of phases (118–25). Such development is described as "spiral," insofar as each phase in the process represents an expansion of the previous one(s). The communitarian angle presents this process as community-based throughout. The two components are thus closely interrelated.

The process has six steps: (1) "naive reading": interpreting Scripture along the lines interpreted by others; (2) initial "suspicion": awareness that a text may have different interpretations; (3) crucial insight: not only the production of a different reading of the text, but also a sense that such a reading comes about as a result of one's identity and context; (4) expansion of insight: a realization that other texts may yield a similar reading, giving rise to a "conscious quest" for a new method; (5) formalization of insight: reflection on such a way of reading as a way of reading; and (6) ongoing development: refinement of such a way of reading in the light of "amplifications and corrections" derived from actual application of the method. This process takes place within a context of community gatherings and readings, carried out in the light of its experiences and in the face of its struggles (125–26). Within this communal process, some members receive and assume the task of "bringing the community into the task of interpretation" by way of formal approaches and critical tools, but only to return to the community and continue the process of interpretation *en conjunto*.

González further delineates this way of reading by way of comparison. On the one side, it is not to be confused with fundamentalism. The naive reading of Latino/a communities lacks the agonistic edge of the fundamental reading. It does tend toward a literal reading of the text, but not by way of reaction to an enemy, liberalism. As such, it is said to constitute a source for "some of our best, most creative, and most radical readings" (119). On the other side, such a reading should be seen as close to the interpretive proposals from Latin America associated with the movement of liberation. In general terms, it is in accord with the notion of a hermeneutical circle, with its emphasis on praxis, on the reality and experience of actual practices, as leading to reflection. More particularly, it is similar to the process of seeing-judging-acting when applied to Scripture as a whole: analysis of the text in context; analysis of the text from the perspective of the community, in context; and action in context, in the light of the previous analysis, at which point the process begins again, in spiraling fashion.

For the Latino/a way of reading, therefore, fundamentalism stands as an alien intrusion, while liberation represents a kindred spirit. The key difference is the regard for context and praxis, with method growing out of context. At no time, it should be noted, does González undertake a theoretical grounding for the method outside the religious-ecclesial realm. From an academic-scholarly perspective, the method represents, to my mind, an exercise in reader-response criticism, very much within the text-dominant pole of the spectrum. Meaning lies in the text, but it is accessed differently by different readers. Thus extratextual readers, such as Latino/as, call forth, as a result of their related social-cultural and personal-psychological contexts, certain distinctive aspects of the text. It is not clear how the difference in readings produced by the different contexts would be addressed.

With respect to social-cultural stance, the model foregrounds the elements of marginalization in and justice for the community, as the theorization of both the biographical and the practical dimension shows. From a personal-psychological perspective, González reveals how he himself moved, in reading the biblical texts, from one optic of marginalization to another—from ethnic-racial, to economic, to gender, and so on. From an experiential-communitarian perspective, he points out how the focus on praxis involves not only emphasis on doing but also a grounding for such doing "on a commitment to love and justice" (123). Then, in the middle section on application of the method to the Gospel of Luke, González lays out in greater detail the context of the Latino/a community and its ramifications for interpretation. In effect, given their multidimensional experience of marginalization (economic, cultural, racial), "Hispanic readers of Scripture," he states, "are prompt to see economic, social, and racial-ethnic issues—often all mixed into one" (127). With regard to Luke, then, he points out how attractive the Gospel proves for Latino/as, given "its subversiveness, questioning the existing order and announcing a better one" (127). For González, such subversiveness, what Lukan scholarship has referred to traditionally as the great reversal, becomes a central theme in the whole of Luke-Acts and the focus of his own reading, for which he has recourse throughout to insights from the Latino/a community.

The task of Latino/a critics is at once straightforward and ambiguous. It is straightforward insofar as the critic is embedded in the community. As a member of the community, who shares in the fate of the community, the critic works for the community. Emerging out of and living within the community, the critic brings the community's perspective of marginalization and justice to the reading of Scripture—a perspective forged in the history and context of the community, marked by marginalization and a search for justice. The critic does this with a view of Scripture as authoritative and in conversation with the methods and tools of criticism. Following such critical engagement with Scripture, the critic returns to the community for practical action in the light of marginalization.

At the same time, the task is ambiguous, insofar as a variety of critics, and communities, is posited. There are critics for whom Scripture is not the sole source of authority—Catholic Latino/as as well as Latino/as born in the United States. There are also critics for whom Scripture is not as authoritative, or even downright problematic—Latino/as native to the United States, for whom Scripture has been deployed as a tool of oppression, or Latinas, for whom Scripture bears a decidedly patriarchal strain. Such differences, however, are not theorized into the overall vision of Latino/a hermeneutics, so that, in the end, the Latino/a community is represented as one, as is the reading of Scripture associated with it.

Jean-Pierre Ruiz (2011)—Reading in, with, and for the
Latino/a Community

A fourth model for Latino/a biblical criticism has been put forth by Jean-Pierre Ruiz. The proposal, in contradistinction to the others, forms part of a full-fledged volume on the relationship between the biblical texts and the Latino/a communities. The work, however, is not a monograph as such—unified, progressive, and teleological from beginning to end. It is, rather, a focused collection of studies—independent in their own right, yet integrated as a whole, by way of an overarching agenda. Thus the collection sets forth a model for interpretation (chs. 1–3) and offers demonstrations of its application (chs. 4–9). The model is taken up in the first part on matters of method and theory ("Reading Strategies"). The application is developed in a second part devoted to analysis of various texts ("Looking to the Texts"), mostly biblical (four from the Hebrew Scriptures and one from the Christian Scriptures) but also one instance of historical interpretation.

The title, *Readings from the Edges: The Bible and People on the Move*, captures the endeavor well. The subtitle looks to the community side of the relationship, conveying a central vision of the Latino/a experience—a "people on the move." The title proper picks up the textual side, introducing a fundamental strategy for approaching the Bible from the perspective of a "people on the move"—a reading "from the edges." As a whole, therefore, the title conveys both a negative sense of difference and marginality and a positive sense of distinctiveness and insight.

For the pursuit of this project, Jean-Pierre Ruiz is eminently qualified. To begin with, as a "Nuyorican" (7)—an individual of Puerto Rican descent born in the city of New York, a member of the diaspora as a result of emigration to the United States—he forms part of the Latino/a community. He bears the legacy of a "people on the move" and possesses his own story within it. Further, as an "academic" (7)— associate professor of biblical studies and senior research fellow of the Vincentian Center for Teaching and Learning Theology at St. John's University of New York—he is a critic by training and profession. He has extensive and sophisticated knowledge of the field as conceptualized and practiced today. Finally, as a Latino critic, he places the Latino/a community at the center of his work. This he does on both social-cultural grounds, pointing to the shared stories with the Latino/a community, and academic-scholarly ones, citing a view of scholarship as calling for "engagement with and not flight from experience" (2). The result is a closely linked vision of community and texts from an inside voice with profound investment in both regards.

The designation "people on the move" functions as the defining marker of the Latino/a experience, in light of the massive migration of Latin Americans to the United States. Its signification is expansive: the way of being of Latino/a communities in general; the character of Latino/a religious communities in particular; and, most concretely, the lives, concerns, and interests of Latino/a religious-theological scholars. In unpacking this vision, Ruiz argues, one must attend to both the "big picture" and the "little stories," with the former element actually entailing two levels of analysis (1). First, one must view the Latino/a migration as one of many such phenomena unleashed by the dynamics of mechanics of globalization—the many-sided and multidirectional processes of emigration, travel, and immigration at work throughout all continents of the globe. Second, and more important, one must examine it, as with all other variations, in terms of its particular context and local features. Third, and more important still, in such analysis one must pay attention to the countless "little stories" of the people caught up in such a process, so that those "at the edges of society" suffer no further marginalization, as their voices and faces disappear and are represented by others.

The designation "reading from the edges" signals a move beyond traditional strategies for bringing the Bible to bear on Latino/a migration: appealing to texts that deal directly, in one way or another, with migration; approaching the Bible as the unitary and unambiguous Word of God and hence as normative foundation for Christian thought and action on all matters related to migration. The strategy proposed, Ruiz explains, takes up a different path. First, it looks at texts "that are rarely marshaled in service of arguments on behalf of people on the move or of public policy reform regarding immigrants and refugees" (6)—the "little stories." Second, it examines texts by way of critical dialogue, with emphasis on diversity of meaning and with justice and dignity as driving principles—a reading "around the edges" (6).

In analyzing the Latino/a experience of a "people on the move," therefore, the critic must keep in mind the comparative dimension of migration as global, the particular dimension of the Latino/a migration as local, and the personal dimension of Latino/as at the margins. Further, in analyzing biblical texts "from the edges," the critic must look at texts of all sorts, eschewing in so doing any adherence to a view of the Bible as presenting "a *single* voice" (7) and subscribing instead to a vision of "complex negotiation" throughout (8). Both sides of the relationship communities-texts are thus closely related. The emphasis on the "little stories" of the community, produced by the "edges of society," corresponds to the emphasis on the "little stories" of the Bible, to be approached by reading "around the edges." The focus throughout is thus on restoration from marginalization and foregrounding of diversity.

From a religious-theological angle, Ruiz's proposal shows deep roots in this tradition of reading. First, he identifies himself as a member of the circle of "Latino/a theologians and biblical scholars," and, indeed, it is with them that he engages in critical conversation throughout. This circle reveals a very prominent Catholic dimension, but it is ecumenical in reach as well. Such engagement he situates within the tradition of a *teología de conjunto* (doing constructive theology in common), for which it is not the individual thinker but the community of scholars that matters. It is a tradition marked, as he puts it, by "the shared energy of intense discussions and of the sort of in-depth analysis that is only possible in an atmosphere of deep trust and shared commitment" (ix). Second, he characterizes the work of critical and theological scholarship in general, and that of the Latino/a circle in particular, in terms of "ecclesial vocation" (8, 23). Such work is placed thereby at the intersection of church and academy, indeed, "at the heart of the church for the sake of its mission to witness to the goodness and the justice of God in the world" (x). Lastly, in keeping with his self-identification, he views such work as perforce interdisciplinary, although *intra muros*, with a model of the various theological disciplines as working together on issues and projects having to do with the Latino/a community. Further, such collaboration means leaving behind a traditional view of criticism as providing raw data, toward "constructive self-critical discourse" across disciplinary boundaries—in effect, ideological analysis of the different disciplinary discourses, assumptions and findings alike, by all on all sides.

Despite such explicit and thorough foundations within a broad religious-theological framework, and the importance assigned to the biblical texts and their interpretation therein, the view of the Bible that underlies the proposal is considerably diminished. It is not that the Bible ceases to be authoritative and normative, for it so remains. The problematic is, rather, that what the Bible has to say cannot be determined in and of itself: its meaning is neither self-evident nor stable. As such, it cannot be invoked and deployed without a sense of ambiguity or a duty to pass judgment. Such a weakening turn of biblical authority and normativity is a direct result of the critical position adopted.

In terms of theoretical-methodological point of view, the proposal is quite forthcoming. Its central tenets have already been noted: diversity of meaning and need for critical dialogue. These are duly unpacked. Ruiz dispenses with any notion of criticism as critical search: exclusive orientation toward the texts, belief in unitary and unambiguous meaning in the Bible as the Word of God, a stance of unquestioned acceptance of such meaning. Instead, he opts for a view of criticism as critical encounter: concerned with both texts and readers; a vision of meaning in the Bible as not only diverse in and of itself but also multidimensional, given the agency attributed to readers as well as the role attributed to context in such agency; a stance of critical evaluation regarding texts and readers alike, taking into consideration context and perspective throughout.

The strategy of reading "from the edges" emerges, therefore, as a process of "complex negotiation" with texts and readers, "mapping relationships between texts and their contexts, between readers and their contexts, and between texts and readers across contexts" (8). Ruiz characterizes it as a reading *with* others or aloud, *en voz alta* (50–53). It regards no one interpretation as ultimate, attends to all interpretations with a mixture of respect and discernment, and remains always open to revision. It clearly lies toward the reader-dominant pole of reader response, given its strong emphasis on construction, contextualization, and ideology.

From a social-cultural angle, Ruiz's position is decidedly activist. Its central principle has already been pointed out as well: the invocation of justice and dignity as guiding principles. This foundation is well developed. To begin with, its origins are traced to the early influence of liberation theology upon him, which has led to the conviction that "theology can make a difference when it is deeply engaged in the lived daily reality of ordinary people, including those on the margins of society" (ix). In addition, its mode is shaped and mandated by the reality of the Latino/a community as a "people on the move," especially the experiences of its countless "little voices." For this situation he makes the words of Arturo Bañuelas, a fellow member of the Latino/a circle of critics and theologians, his own.[7] On the one hand, the reasons for being "on the move" are unsparingly outlined: extreme poverty, unemployment, political and military corruption, government instability—for all of which the United States is said to bear much responsibility. On the other hand, the consequence of being "on the move" is named outright: an attack on the *Latinidad* of all Latino/as. Finally, its élan is described as openly political, driven by the conviction that theological discourse must appropriate, in the public sphere, "the concerns of our

---

7. Bañuelas is a pastor-activist in El Paso, Texas, and a constructive theologian with whom Ruiz crossed paths in Rome during the course of doctoral studies at the Gregorian University. This encounter of two Latinos "on the move" he offers as the moment of conception for the volume—"a ¡Sí, se puede! moment" (1).

brothers and sisters on the move" (4). It is such solidarity with the community that drives the critical process of "complex negotiations" involving texts and readers and forms the core of the religious-theological optic.

In all this the legacy of liberation theology is evident; at the same time, a critique is offered. First, while the principle of the preferential option for the poor and the strategy of reading the Bible with the people are lauded, liberation, Ruiz argues, has tended to reify both the poor, as a dichotomous Other, and the biblical texts, as the sole and unambiguous sources of liberation. Reading "from the edges" seeks to move beyond both perceived limitations. With respect to the former, the flattening of the poor, the strategy emphasizes the "lived daily experience" of the "little voices"— "always situated, always specific, always concrete" (33). With respect to the latter, the exclusivity and flattening of the Scriptures, the strategy makes a twofold move. To get beyond biblicism, it argues for popular religion as a source—the religion of the poor, especially, as "the 'canon' of the Word-made-flesh" (33). To move past homogenization, it argues for leaving behind the initial models of correlation and correspondence, whereby present and past are simplistically related to one another—the former, by ignoring the problematic of production ("the complexity of its generative matrix"); the latter, by bypassing the problematic of reception ("imposing *one* reading ... as normative).

Within this vision of Latino/a criticism, the role of the critic is directly entertained. The critic is called upon to be a public intellectual. There are actually two dimensions to this role. One is to move beyond an overriding or exclusive concentration on the world of the texts, the world of antiquity, and the study of this world in formalist and apolitical fashion— what Ruiz calls an "academic esotericism that fetishizes texts and reduces biblical scholars to irrelevance as 'tribal theologians'" (52). The aim is an approach to the texts as imbricated, in complex and conflicted fashion, in society and culture, both in terms of production and reception. The other is to shun the sort of engagement that focuses on self-promotion and self-enrichment—what Ruiz characterizes as "star quality ... engaging in high profile (and high-profit) popularization" (35). The goal is to embody an engagement that is marked by political awareness and responsibility and guided by an interventionist agenda of justice for all in society and culture, transhistorically and cross-culturally. For the Latino/a critic, this call demands a sense of grounding in, conversation with, and commitment to the Latino/a community. Such grounding demands, in turn, taking on and addressing the problematic of the community as a "people on the move," in local and global fashion, with attention to all voices, especially those of the people. Such addressing entails, in turn, a religious-theological and intertheological reading of the Bible that foregrounds the diversity of the texts, the multidimensional character of interpretation, and the ideological critique of texts and interpretations alike.

M. Daniel Carroll R[odas] (2013)—Reading in and from the Hispanic Diaspora

The most recent model for Latino/a biblical criticism is offered by M. Daniel Carroll R., who is Distinguished Professor of Old Testament at Denver Seminary in Littleton, Colorado, and adjunct professor at El Seminario Teológico Centroamericano (SETECA) in Ciudad de Guatemala (Guatemala City), the capital of Guatemala. The model was formulated within the framework of a project on global hermeneutics sponsored by the Institute of Biblical Research. The institute is a learned organization, formally launched in 1973, for evangelical Christian scholars in biblical studies (OT studies and NT studies) and related fields of study. It holds an annual meeting, scheduled immediately prior to the annual meeting of the Society of Biblical Literature, with a program organized around a central theme. In 2011 the topic chosen was "Global Readings," with a focus on the advent and spread of biblical criticism on a worldwide scale. The proceedings were subsequently published in *Global Voices: Reading the Bible in the Majority World*, edited by Craig Keener and Carroll R. (2013a).

In the introduction, the editors lay out the objective, rationale, and background for the project (2013b). The aim was to bring biblical scholarship from outside the West—Africa, Asia, and Latin America—to the attention of scholars in and of the West. The reason for so doing was to raise the awareness of Western scholars regarding the existence of such production and perspectives, given their continued focus on their own ecclesial and critical concerns, to the neglect of "the needs of the global church" (1). The context was explained in terms of two developments. First, the editors point to the sharp expansion of Christianity outside the West over the course of the twentieth century: non-Western Christians in general now account for close to 65 percent of the global church; evangelicals in particular outside the West now outnumber their counterparts in the West by four to five times. Second, the editors refer to the importance of the insights brought to bear by such scholarship on the biblical texts: unfolding dimensions of meaning bypassed, downplayed, or spiritualized by traditional scholarship. In the end, the editors set forth a vision for the future: bringing together scholars from throughout the world, from both the West and the "Majority World," to engage in "fruitful work and constructive conversations" in reading the Bible (3).

Toward this end, invitations were issued to scholars from across these continents, and from a variety of Christian traditions, to serve as presenters and respondents—ten in all, five in each category. Among the presenters was Carroll R., who also served as the keynote speaker for the gathering. As such, his study, "Reading the Bible through Other Lenses: New Vistas from a Hispanic Diaspora Perspective" (2013), has a twofold dimension. On the one hand, as keynote speaker, he addresses the issue of and need for "multiethnic readings" of the Bible in the light of contemporary global realities. On the other hand, as continental representative, he brings the voice of Latin America to the project. With regard to global realities, Carroll R. moves beyond the question of growth outside the West, duly emphasized nonetheless, to introduce the problematic of such growth inside the West, the result of massive migration from the Global South to the Global North and the consequent establishment of diaspora communities throughout the world. It is this development, he specifies, that constitutes the focus of his essay (7).[8] With regard to Latin America, it is the optic of its diasporic trajectory to and presence in the United States that he brings to the fore, and hence the voice of Hispanic or Latino/a Americans.

This is a task for which Carroll R. is eminently suited, given his own diasporic experience, his explicit self-designation as "half-Guatemalan" (2), and his recourse to and integration of such experience and self-identification in his scholarship. This political-ethnic context he lays out in an earlier volume on immigration and the church (Carroll R. 2008) and is worth summarizing here.

To begin with, he presents his familial-personal background: a child of a mother from Guatemala and a father from the United States, who is born and grows up in the United States but who spends summers in Guatemala, with his maternal relatives, through childhood and adolescence. Then he turns to his initial professional experience: a long tenure as professor of Old Testament at the Seminario Teológico Centroamericano (SETECA) in Ciudad de Guatemala (1982–1996). He sets these years in

---

8. On this development, Carroll R. cites the ongoing research of Philip Jenkins (2011).

broad social-cultural perspective. This was a time of crisis in Guatemala, and indeed throughout all of Central America, caught as it was in the struggle between East and West through their surrogates in the region. It was therefore a time of devastation, violence, and displacement. Lastly, he describes his subsequent professional career: a professor of Old Testament at Denver Seminary from 1996 on, while continuing to spend time and teach in Guatemala on a regular basis.

Carroll R. thus portrays himself as deeply immersed in the diaspora of Latin America. On the one hand, he is a product of it: a "hybrid" individual, bilingual and bicultural, who strides "the majority culture and the Hispanic culture," with "care for both" yet with "deepest longings for my Guatemalan roots" (2008, 19). On the other hand, he is a witness to it: a firsthand observer, on both sides of the border, of massive migration and the systemic-structural causes behind such a process of emigration and immigration.

At the heart of the model, there lies, to begin with, a vision of the Christian faith as diasporic (16). Such a vision is grounded in the Bible itself. First, it is "forged" in diaspora. Thus Genesis represents Abraham, "the father of our faith," as a migrant from Ur to Canaan, where he becomes a "perpetual outsider in that landless existence." Second, it describes, metaphorically, "the life of all Christians." Thus 1 Peter represents believers as "strangers in a strange land." Such a vision also captures, materially, the life of Christians in diasporic communities today, marked as it is by similar "vulnerability and dependence" in all realms of existence. Such realities and experiences, Carroll R. argues, open up distinctive dimensions of and insights into the Bible.

In addition, the model also constitutes a thoroughly interdisciplinary exercise. A variety of discursive resources are invoked, which provide solid theorization—literary testimonies, social attitudes, theoretical frameworks. For example, accounts involving radical situations of survival, penned by migrants who have crossed the border, are viewed as shedding light on the deception involving Abram and Sarai in Egypt, where they have migrated as a result of famine (Gen 12:10–20). Similarly, the bilingual and bicultural practices of migrants in the United States, as experienced by many Latino/as in the country, are seen as bringing a revealing perspective on the figure of Joseph in Egypt, a "bilingual, cultural hybrid" within the plan of God for the people of God. Finally, he perceives the coping mechanisms of immigrants in new cultural contexts, as outlined by assimilation theory, as shedding light on various dimensions of the character of Ruth the Moabite. Thus the dynamics and mechanics of contemporary migration, through the eyes of Latinos and Latinas, can open up such forces in the biblical texts as well. In so doing, Carroll R. declares, "because the text lives, so can we," for "the text walks with us in our pilgrimage of faith" (26).

In terms of religious-theological stance, it is clear that the model lies very much within this tradition of interpretation. This is evident from Carroll R.'s personal as well as professional context: this is a model grounded and forged in the ambit of evangelical Christianity. First, the host project, as detailed above, emanates from and is directed at the circles of evangelical Christian biblical scholarship. Further, both professional affiliations have been at evangelical institutions: SETECA is associated with the Evangelical Association of Theological Education for Latin America (AETAL), while Denver Seminary is a nondenominational evangelical seminary that subscribes to the Statements of Faith of the National Association of Evangelicals. Lastly, a recent outline of attitudes toward the Bible among majority world Christians, both at home and in the diaspora, is cited with approval: a high view of scriptural authority; an embrace of supernatural events, such as miracles and visions; and a close identification with the political and economic realities of the Hebrew Bible.[9] Such working principles, he argues, "bring different and valid insights into the biblical text that deserve to be heard" (2013, 7). As such, the model itself subscribes to a high view of scriptural authority: a reading of the Bible, as the introduction puts it, with "a common commitment to Scripture's unique role in communicating God's message," while allowing for and insisting on the need for "different lenses" in the discernment of that message (Keener and Carroll R. 2013b, 3).

Such a stance is sharply differentiated from another approach to Scripture with a focus on diaspora, postcolonial biblical criticism. Such criticism, Carroll R. argues, problematizes the biblical texts themselves, foregrounding what are perceived as "inherent ideological shortcomings" in the texts or challenging the "hegemonic status" of the texts for Christian communities (2013, 9–10). Although such an approach is acknowledged as raising "challenging questions," it is not what he has in mind, given its "problematic" "philosophical underpinnings" (11). What the model seeks to problematize involves, rather, the reading and reception

---

9. Here again the work of Philip Jenkins (2006) is cited.

of the biblical texts: the contribution that multiethnic readings, including those of the diaspora, make to biblical criticism and the appropriation of the texts in such communities. What one finds, therefore, is a hermeneutics of affirmation, the unquestioned and unquestionable authority of Scripture, modified by way of imperative expansion in terms of the provenance, the faces and voices, of critics approaching Scripture in search of God's message.

With respect to theoretical-methodological position, the model does not elaborate an explicit theoretical grounding. What it does espouse may be described, I would argue, as a variation of reader-response criticism within the text-dominant pole. Concerning the reader, the model highlights the agency of extratextual readers in the process of interpretation, with emphasis on the social-cultural location of such readers. Carroll R. explicitly dismisses, as an evangelical, any claims to a view of criticism as "objective observation"—"detached from and unaffected by social standing, economic status, ethnicity, culture, and gender" (2013, 11). Contextualization of readers is thus of the essence in interpretation. Concerning the text, the model asserts the priority of the text as the repository of meaning, with a view of such meaning as multidimensional, so that various dimensions of it are perceived and activated by different readers in the light of their different social-cultural locations. Contextualization of texts is hence of the essence in interpretation as well. Such contextualization, however, will assume different dimensions by virtue of the different reader contextualizations brought upon it.

From this perspective, it follows that scholars from outside the West will call forth and deploy different readings than their colleagues inside the West. It follows as well, given the novelty of such non-Western readings and the ever-greater number of critics behind them, that Western critics should become aware of such expanding production and varying perspectives. From the religious-theological perspective outlined above, it follows likewise that non-Western scholars are calling forth and deploying new and significant insights into the unique communication of God's message in the Bible. It follows as well that the desideratum should be—beyond greater awareness—a truly global dialogue among Christians involving multiethnic readings of the Bible, toward an ever-richer discernment of the message of God.

In terms of social-cultural stance, the model allows in principle for any number of topics to be pursued by way of multiethnic readings of the Bible, while settling on the phenomenon of migration as a foremost problematic of our times, especially given its significance for Latin America and its diaspora in the United States. Global migration is presented as the result of the forces of economic globalization, which, whether looked upon as a positive or negative development overall, has brought about the dislocation and relocation of millions of people both within and across nation-states. Such diaspora communities are characterized as "needy" and "marginalized" (9). This has been the experience of millions of Latin Americans as well, who have left their respective homelands and settled throughout the United States. Carroll R. thus focuses on a particular sector, though quite large, of the Latino/a population, those who have arrived in the country—with or without documentation—over the last few decades of spreading globalization, and the particular markers of this population, their situation of poverty and peripherization.

Such migrants, he points out, have already brought about crucial changes in the country, especially in terms of demographics. A great many of them, moreover, are Christian and have already brought about significant developments as well within their respective ecclesial bodies. In both regards, they shall continue to do so in unremitting fashion, raising a host of challenges, widespread and far-reaching, in the process, which neither the country nor the church can afford to ignore. For Carroll R., one such challenge involves biblical interpretation: the attention to the appropriation and reading of the Bible by such communities, in the face of their location in the social-cultural periphery. Thus, he asks, "What is it like to read the OT from a Hispanic diaspora perspective?" (2013, 16). In other words, what insights into God's message does such a diasporic location uncover and activate in the Bible? Such is precisely what the model is designed to bring forth.

Such, then, is the task envisioned for Latino/a critics. Such a task must be carried out in a spirit of collaboration and dialogue at all levels: with fields of studies across the religious-theological spectrum, with fields of studies across the scholarly-academic world at large, and with churches across the religious-ecclesial spectrum. Such a task also makes demands on traditional critics. It calls for a spirit of "hermeneutical charity" (14) toward the project of multiethnic reading of the Bible made imperative by global Christianity: respect for and patience toward Latino/a interpretations—and, ultimately, all readings of the global majority, at home or in the diaspora—by way of genuine hospitality and active engagement. It is, after all, a "serious academic exercise" that opens up the message of God.

Critical Comparison of the Proposals: Dimensions and Implications

The preceding trajectory of introjection and assertion reveals the increasing presence, activity, and recognition of Latino/a biblical criticism in the field of studies. It brings out the variety of faces and voices among Latino/a critics, a diversity that makes itself felt in every aspect of analysis: from context of publication, through personal background and critical stance, to critical mission. It also brings out the similarities that exist among such voices and faces in the conceptualization and articulation of critical stance and mission, as they look toward the future. By way of conclusion, I should like to summarize, as a critical mapping for the future, the similarities and the diversity that emerge from the ongoing trajectory thus far. I shall do so by comparing the religious-theological, theoretical-methodological, and social-cultural dimensions and implications of the various proposals.

A comment is imperative here. There is one absence in this trajectory that is striking, especially at this particular point in time in the field of studies: the faces and voices of Latina scholars. For some time now, the persistent dearth of Latina critics has been noted and regretted within the circle of Latino/a critics as a whole. Such absence is particularly felt at a moment when visions for the future are sought and elaborated. This is a lacuna that must be remedied, but one that will not be at all easy to reverse, given the many factors that militate against it, whether it be in the field of studies as such, in the Latino/a communities themselves, or in the dominant society-culture at large. It is a lacuna that this project has sought, in its own limited way, to address.

Critical Stance and Mission: Religious-Theological Dimension

All proposals are grounded, howsoever expressed, in the religious-ecclesial tradition of Christianity and subscribe to a religious-theological reading of the Bible. They all have in mind the Latino/a religious communities, which they regard—implicitly or explicitly—as reflections of the Latino/a communities, and they all view the biblical texts as authoritative, as Scripture, for such communities. At the same time, a spectrum of positions on the nature of biblical authority is evident: toward one side, a heightened view of the Bible as the Word of God; toward the other, a lessened view of the Bible as a constitutive yet problematic component of the Christian tradition. All proposals adopt the rhetorical tactic of retrieving the religious-theological dimension, a variation of the strategy of interpretive contextualization in minority poetics (Segovia 2009, 293–94).

At the strong end, I would place Carroll R. Here Scripture is viewed as the message of God for the world—a message beyond fault or challenge—and hence as the foundation for Christian beliefs and practices. Different individuals or groups in different times and places, however, grasp this message of God, rich beyond measure as it is, in different ways. These different insights into and appropriations of the Word of God are to be sought and treasured. At the soft end, I would situate Agosto and Ruiz. Here Scripture is viewed as subject to critical analysis by its readers, a process that can yield affirmation or rejection. For Agosto it is community concerns and needs that ultimately determine authority; for Ruiz it is the process of evaluation required of critical readers.

I see both González and Rivera Rodriguez as occupying the middle of the spectrum. González leans toward the strong end, with a view of the Bible as the guide for the whole of ecclesial life, but with reservations. These come as a result of his bow to the sensitivities of various formations of Latino/a Christian readers: those who, as the target of attacks based on the Bible, problematize such authority; those who accept Scripture as one among several sources of Christian theology; and those who have highlighted the bias against women present in the texts. Rivera Rodriguez leans toward the milder pole, given its emphasis on readers. The diasporic filter of reading brought to bear on the texts searches for diaspora in the Bible and appropriates such findings in the light of contemporary situations of diaspora, giving diasporic readers leeway in this process of discernment and integration.

Critical Stance and Mission: Theoretical-Methodological Dimension

All proposals offer a way of reading the Bible, but not all outline the mechanics involved in such a way of reading. Not all proposals, moreover, provide an explicit and informed exposition of such a reading in terms of a theory of interpretation, pursuing the relationship between the past and the present, the ancient texts and contexts and the contemporary readers and contexts. Sufficient information is given, however, to allow for a fair description of the different models. Approaching it from the perspective of text-reader interaction and the creation of meaning, a spectrum of opinion readily emerges. Toward one side, the text is viewed as dominant, with readers as receivers, actively engaged in the process; toward the other side, the reader is seen as dominant, with texts as indeterminate sources, actively constructed by readers. Throughout, the Latino/a religious communities function as point of entry, thus exemplifying the rhetorical tactic of appealing to contextual enlightenment, within the strategy of interpretive contextualization (Segovia 2009, 292–93).

At the objectivist pole, I would locate Carroll R. as well as González. Neither advances a theoretical grounding in academic-scholarly terms. While both outline a way of reading, González does so in greater detail, along biographical rather than formalist lines. The two positions are quite close. While Carroll R. speaks in collective terms, González introduces a strong personal dimension within the collective.

For Carroll R. the Bible functions as the conveyor of God's message to the world, to be received and embraced by readers. Readers attain different glimpses into God's message, given different social-cultural contexts. The result is a view of meaning as virtually inexhaustible, as God speaks to readers across time and culture. What Latino/a readers bring to this message is a situation of diaspora, which they access through a variety of means drawn from their repertoire—testimonies, practices, mechanisms. For González the Bible serves as the guide for the church, to be hearkened to and appropriated by readers. Readers derive different directions from God's guide, given different religious-ecclesial contexts, within which they stand as individuals in community. It is here that González introduces his biographical-developmental method of reading: the emergence, expansion, and formalization of personal insight into the biblical texts, in the light of varying personal-communitarian trajectories and exigencies. The result is also a view of meaning emerges as virtually inexhaustible, since it is a guide for churches across time and culture. What Latino/a readers bring to this guide is their situation of marginalization, which they access as individuals in community.

At the subjectivist pole, I would locate Agosto and Ruiz. Both present a theoretical grounding with reference to academic-scholarly criticism. Both also outline a way of reading. In both regards Ruiz proves more expansive. The two positions are quite close. While Agosto refrains from commenting on the text as text, Ruiz does, stressing the multidimensionality of meaning in texts. Further, while Agosto does not pursue the question of dealing with other readings, Ruiz does.

For Agosto, readers play a key role in interpretation, leaving behind in their readings the filters of their respective social-cultural contexts. This is true of all readers, professional or popular. It is thus true of Latino/a readers as well. Meaning, therefore, involves construction on the part of readers. Latino/a readers, coming from situations of marginalization, bring such issues as entries into the text. For Ruiz, readers play no less crucial role in interpretation, yielding a multitude of readings that reflect the influence of context and perspective. This applies to all readers, including Latino/a readers, be they professional or popular. There is no meaning outside interpretation. Latino/a readers produce meaning, as individuals, from the overall perspective of a situation of migration. Such diversity of interpretation calls for critical dialogue with other readers and readings at all times.

Lastly, I regard Rivera Rodriguez as standing at the center of the spectrum, closer to the subjectivist end. He does have recourse to an academic-theoretical grounding, although not to a theory of interpretation as such, but rather to the discourse of the diaspora. From the optic of the diaspora, then, he outlines a specific way of reading. Since Latino/a religious communities share a situation of diaspora, he advances a set of corresponding reading strategies of the Bible, to be applied to both texts and readers. Latino/a readers are to examine and evaluate representations of the process of diaspora, assessments of life in the diaspora, and ideal visions of the diaspora. Such reading strategies imply a diversity of opinions and critique, thus bringing him closer to the reader-dominant pole.

Critical Stance and Mission: Social-Cultural Dimension

All proposals—as already noted in the theoretical-methodological summary—tie biblical criticism directly to the Latino/a religious communities, both by way of social-cultural location and ideological-political agenda. In terms of context, first of all, criticism is not viewed as just an individualist affair, nor is it construed as a strictly academic-scholarly one. It is always, in some way, a venture tied to the community—carried out from within the community and in dialogue with the community. Similarly, in terms of agenda, criticism is not seen as simply a formalist or idealist affair. It is always, in some way, conceived as an activist, materialist endeavor—carried out on behalf of the community. The various positions are quite similar in both regards. A spectrum of positions can be drawn nonetheless with regard to the scope of criticism: from the expansive to the circumscribed.

This sense of community embeddedness and commitment constitute a rhetorical strategy of minority criticism that I failed to name and theorize in my analysis of its poetics. While akin to interpretive contextualization, it goes beyond it. While not unlike interruptive stocktaking, it goes beyond it as well. It might be characterized as materialist commitment: engaging worlds. Such strategy has to do with the mission and vocation of the critic in the various religious-ecclesial, political-national, and geopolitical-systemic realms or worlds of context and activity.

Toward the more encompassing end, I would situate Rivera Rodriguez and Ruiz. Both view the Latino/a communities in the light of global developments; both also espouse a highly engaged position for criticism in society and culture. Rivera Rodriguez sees the Latino/a religious congregations, like the Latino/a diasporic communities, as the result of a massive global migration brought about by the dynamics of violence and economics. They constitute communities of the nonprivileged, who undergo all the struggles of marginalization. Within such circumstances, the role of criticism involves comparative analysis of diaspora and communal advocacy, with justice and well-being as a goal. Ruiz views the Latino/a communities, including the churches, as one example of the multiple processes of migration at work in the world, unleashed by the forces of economic globalization. These are caused by profound social travails and lead to keen marginalization. Against this background, the role of criticism entails multidimensional analysis of migration and the pursuit of justice and dignity for the communities, above all for those at the edge. While calling for critical attention to the global framework, neither charts a path for so doing, although Rivera Rodriguez does advocate joining hands with similar endeavors among other diasporic communities in the country.

Toward the more focused end I would place Agosto and González. Neither stresses the global dimension behind the presence of the Latino/a communities in the country; both do adopt a highly engaged position for criticism in society and culture. Agosto emphasizes the twofold character of the communities: on the one hand, marginalization as others within the country; on the other hand, diversity and solidarity within the community. Given such a situation, the role of criticism is to bring these features of communal life to bear on the texts, in order to determine, with the betterment of the community in mind, what bears adopting and what bears leaving behind. González stresses the experience of the communities: sites of multidimensional marginalization and, as such, venues for the exercise of love and justice. Given such conditions, the role of criticism is to search the texts with marginalization and justice in mind. How such a task relates to the world in general or to other marginalized communities is not pursued.

At the center, I see Carroll R., with a clear tilt toward the encompassing side. The Latino/a communities, within which are to be found the religious communities, are placed against the background of global migration in general and Latin American migration in particular, set off by the dynamics of economic globalization. Their situation in the country is also viewed as marked by poverty and marginalization. Within such circumstances, the role of criticism, while activist in nature, is seen as focusing on the religious-ecclesial realm. It calls for attention to the insights that such communities discover in the Bible, with their ramifications for interpretation and church alike. Criticism thus inserts the needs and insights of migrants—the vulnerable and the dependent—into the global church and its pilgrimage with the Bible. A connection to the global framework behind migration in social-cultural terms is not pursued.

A Final Comment

The similarities shared by these visions of and projects for Latino/a criticism are evident; no less evident is the diversity that prevails among such similarities. All proposals embrace the religious-theological tradition of reading the Bible, but they do so with varying views of biblical authority. All ascribe a role to readers in interpreting the Bible, but they do so with differing degrees of agency. All posit the community as the foundation, optic, and objective of interpretation—imbued by an overriding awareness of marginalization, a clarion call for solidarity and liberation, and an unwavering appeal to ideals of social justice—but they do so with varying shades of attention to the social-cultural imbrications of the community in the world. A critical mapping for the future is thus well laid out.

In the end, this mapping also yields a vision of the Latino/a critic as a public figure not only in the Latino/a community but also beyond it—in the religious-ecclesial realm, the academic-scholarly field of studies, and the social-cultural world at large. In so doing, the mapping further yields a vision of how minoritized critics approach biblical interpretation as a discursive framework, among others, within the overall dialectical framework of dominant-minority formations and relations and the process of minoritization in the country.

Works Cited

Agosto, Efrain. 2010. Latino/a Hermeneutics. Pages 350–71 in *Hearing the New Testament: Strategies for Interpretation*. Edited by Joel B. Green. 2nd ed. Grand Rapids: Eerdmans.

Birch, Bruce C., and Larry L. Rasmussen. 1976. *Bible and Ethics in the Christian Life*. Minneapolis: Augsburg.

Brawley, Robert L. 2007. *Character Ethics and the New Testament: Moral Dimensions of Scripture*. Louisville: Westminster John Knox.

Brown, William P., ed. 2002. *Character and Scripture: Moral Formation, Community, and Biblical Interpretation*. Grand Rapids: Eerdmans.

Carroll R., M. Daniel. 2008. *Christians at the Border: Immigration, the Church, and the Bible*. Grand Rapids: Baker.

―――. 2013. Reading the Bible through Other Lenses: New Vistas from a Hispanic Diaspora Perspective. Pages 5–26 in Keener and Carroll R. 2013a.

Carroll R., M. Daniel, and Jacqueline E. Lapsley, eds. 2007. *Character Ethics and the Old Testament: Moral Dimensions of Scripture*. Louisville: Westminster John Knox.

González, Justo L. 1996. *Santa Biblia: The Bible through Hispanic Eyes*. Nashville: Abingdon.

―――. 2010. A Latino Perspective. Pages 113–43 in *Methods for Luke*. Edited by Joel B. Green. Methods in Biblical Interpretation. Cambridge: Cambridge University Press.

Green, Joel B., ed. 1995. *Hearing the New Testament: Strategies for Interpretation*. Grand Rapids: Eerdmans.

―――. 2010a. The Challenge of Hearing the New Testament. Pages 1–14 in *Hearing the New Testament: Strategies for Interpretation*. Edited by Joel B. Green. 2nd ed. Grand Rapids: Eerdmans.

―――, ed. 2010b. *Hearing the New Testament: Strategies for Interpretation*. 2nd ed. Grand Rapids: Eerdmans.

―――, ed. 2010c. *Methods for Luke*. Methods in Biblical Interpretation. Cambridge: Cambridge University Press.

Jenkins, Philip. 2006. *The New Faces of Christianity: Believing the Bible in the Global South*. Oxford: Oxford University Press.

―――. 2011. *The Next Christendom: The Coming of Global Christianity*. Oxford: Oxford University Press.

Keener, Craig, and M. Daniel Carroll R., eds. 2013a. *Global Voices: Reading the Bible in the Majority World*. Peabody, Mass.: Hendrickson.

Keener, Craig, and M. Daniel Carroll R. 2013b. Introduction. Pages 1–4 in *Global Voices: Reading the Bible in the Majority World*. Edited by Craig S. Keener and M. Daniel Carroll R. Peabody, Mass.: Hendrickson.

Powell, Mark Allan, ed. 2009. *Methods for Matthew*. Methods in Biblical Interpretation. Cambridge: Cambridge University Press.

Rivera Rodriguez, Luis. 2007. "Toward a Diaspora Hermeneutics (Hispanic North America)." Pages 169–89 in Carroll R. and Lapsley 2007.

Ruiz, Jean-Pierre. 2011. *Readings from the Edges: The Bible and People on the Move*. Maryknoll, N.Y.: Orbis.

Segovia, Fernando F. 2009. Poetics of Minority Biblical Criticism: Identification and Theorization. Pages 279–311 in *Prejudice and Christian Beginnings: Investigating Race, Gender, and Ethnicity in Early Christian Studies*. Edited by Laura Nasrallah and Elisabeth Schüssler Fiorenza. Minneapolis: Fortress.

Addressing the Problematic:
What Does It Mean to Be a Latino/a Critic

What Does It Mean to Be a Latino/a Biblical Critic? A Latino Pentecostal Perspective, with Reflections on the Future

Efrain Agosto

"I have been teaching the Bible since I was fifteen years old." So began the personal essay to both my application for theological school thirty-five years ago and that for graduate school over thirty years ago. This sentence reflected a couple of matters that I would like to point out at the outset of this study.

First, at an early age in the Latino/a Pentecostal church in which I grew up, a love for the Bible was instilled, including a sense of its authority, guidance, and literary beauty, but also of its challenges, abuses, and confusion about interpretation for our economically poor, but culturally and spiritually rich, urban Latino/a community in New York City. Upon graduating from the junior high school Sunday school class and the departure of its teacher, my pastor—the late, great Reverend Miguel Angel Rivera, who saw something of that love of Scripture in me but also was short of options—appointed me, for bad and for good, the teacher of this class. This was bad for the kids because of my inexperience, but good for me in terms of my early development as a Bible teacher.

This rather odd appointment—after all, how much can be expected from a fifteen-year-old teaching twelve-to-fourteen-year-olds, who have to suffer through this novice teacher?—exemplifies my second point. Besides the early love for and experience with the Bible and teaching the Bible for one who is now a senior Latino biblical critic, there is the matter of the nature of the Pentecostal Hispanic experience and how that might impact the hermeneutics of a Latino/a biblical critic. This was a community that lacked sufficient resources for a professionalized religious education program, and for many of its leadership roles and programs, for that matter.

Nonetheless, the opportunities for leadership that ensued as a result of these limited resources empowered a generally poor community—"the least of these," to cite the Gospel saying—to develop and exercise significant leadership within a community organization in the inner city in ways that, for the most part, the dominant society did not allow in systems and structures outside the community.

There we were, then, at a young age, doing biblical interpretation and teaching, struggling with the text, teaching theologies often imposed on us by the dominant, white denominational structures, but nonetheless reflecting on these together and questioning them, sometimes more unconsciously than consciously. Engaging the text early and often brought some of us to the table of academic biblical criticism, slowly but surely. For that, I will always be grateful to the Latino/a Pentecostal church, even though I am no longer an official member of it.

Latino/a Biblical Criticism in Light of the Pentecostal Experience

What happens to biblical interpretation when one is nurtured in such an ecclesial or religious setting of marginalization, both religiously and socioeconomically? I would like to suggest two things in this study. First, one becomes a biblical critic intensely tied to the importance of *experience* and the relationship of one's experience, in my case as a New Testament biblical critic, to the experience of the earliest followers of Jesus represented in the New Testament documents. In other words, I am interested in the religious experience of the earliest Christian believers because of the impact my particular religious experience has had on my life and career. Second, when one has an opportunity to reflect on the task of biblical criticism, as I do here, the urban Latino/a Pentecostal experience per se becomes a conversation partner in developing a Latino/a biblical hermeneutic. I would like to illustrate these two related but somewhat distinct strands, the second broader than the first, by an example from my own work and then brief examples from the work of two Latino Pentecostal scholars.

From Grassroots Leadership to New Testament Leadership

At the beginning of my monograph *Servant Leadership: Jesus and Paul* (2005), I offer various motivations for this study of leadership and social status in the Jesus movement and Pauline Christianity. One entailed the issue of the experience of grassroots religious leaders in Latino/a communities as a resource for investigating similar concerns in the New Testament text. I wrote as follows (1–2):

> [A]s a Puerto Rican raised in New York City, I know persons, especially in the storefront Pentecostal churches of my youth, who lacked access to traditional opportunities for training and leadership. Nonetheless, they exercised significant leadership roles within the Latino Christian church, as well as other community institutions of the city. After seminary, I began to work on the theological education of such individuals, and I also pursued graduate studies in New Testament. I became intrigued by the question: Is there a biblical perspective relative to the issue of access to and opportunity for leadership. Thus in my graduate studies and beyond I have explored the question of who became leaders in the churches founded by Paul and what was the social status of those leaders with respect to the strict, hierarchical social structure of Greco-Roman society. I hoped to make a biblical-theological contribution to the work of urban theological education, including the preparation of Latino and Latina church leaders in our communities. I strongly believe that such a motivation and line of inquiry contributes to leadership issues in churches of all races and denominations.

Deconstructing this paragraph, I see an emerging Latino biblical critic who does not shy away from engagement of personal experience in the historical questioning of ancient texts, because, as Fernando Segovia and others have taught us, this is the reality of biblical interpretation whether interpreters state the case or not. All biblical interpretation engages a kind of intercultural studies—an encounter between the cultures of today, be they Latino/a or otherwise, and the cultures of the ancient world, including those represented in the texts of the New Testament.[1]

However, I make a second kind of move in this statement of purpose at the outset of my study, and that is to suggest an agenda in the historical exercise of biblical interpretation. I explore, however briefly, the history of the Latino/a church in the United States and then make a statement about what this implies for this experience as a resource of Latino/a biblical hermeneutics. Allow me, therefore, to quote a second paragraph from *Servant Leadership*:

---

1. See Segovia's seminal essay detailing the need for intercultural studies and not just historical, literary, or even "cultural" biblical criticism (1995).

> Although some of this is changing, historically many U.S. Latino churches, especially in urban areas, have been led by charismatic grassroots leaders who often lacked the academic credentials expected in the North American society. For example, the history of the Hispanic Pentecostal church includes stories of many indigenous leaders who, having in material possessions or social status sacrificed much for the good of the gospel, grew large, vital congregations in a relatively short span of time. In addition, many of these Latino churches have also produced a significant cadre of community leaders, both ministerial and lay. (2005, 2)

I go on to suggest that we can learn from the historical experience of Latino/a indigenous churches for the practice of ministry today and, more pertinent to the purpose of this study, for the exercise of a biblical criticism that is in dialogue with both the ancient text and the "text" of readers today, one that seeks out avenues of a liberating leadership, both in the past and in the present—that is, a leadership that has the agenda of liberation for church and community.

I find in these two statements of my modus operandi in a previous study an example of the kind of agenda that I think informs the work of many, if not all, Latino/a biblical critics. What can we learn from our exploration of the history of earliest Christianity in light of our—the interpreter's—history for the necessary liberationist agenda of biblical interpretation and theology? What in the text, both its positive and negative aspects, nourishes us, teaches us, infuriates us, and galvanizes us for the agenda of liberation that is fundamental to the Latino/a biblical critic's vocational agenda?

A Latino/a Pentecostal Hermeneutic: Two Examples

Given these two signposts of my New Testament hermeneutic as a Latino biblical critic, experience as a legitimate guide for research and liberation as an ultimate goal for our vocation as biblical critics, I would like to offer reflections on two Latino/a Pentecostal theologians as a further affirmation of these inclinations.

First, Eldin Villafañe, a Latino Pentecostal social ethicist—best known for his work *The Liberating Spirit: Toward an Hispanic American Pentecostal Social Ethic* (1993)—asserts that Pentecostalism has its roots in the "left wing of the Reformation," which has significant implications "because of its constituency—the poor and the oppressed" (123). Latino/a Pentecostalism, he adds, also subscribes to the Reformation teaching about the internal witness of the Holy Spirit. He states, "implicitly Hispanic Pentecostals subscribe to a view of revelation that is dynamic and continuous in nature," reading the Bible in an "existential-spiritual manner" (205–6). In other words, experience is central to Latino/a Pentecostal biblical interpretation, asserts Villafañe, and he sees its practice throughout his study of the Latino/a Pentecostal church in the United States.

Samuel Solivan, a Latino Pentecostal systematic theologian, elaborates further the importance of experience in Latino/a biblical and theological constructions, as he explores a Latino/a theology of suffering from the perspective of U.S. Hispanic Pentecostals in his work, *The Spirit, Pathos and Liberation* (1998). His theological concept of "orthopathos"—redemptive suffering—is "informed fundamentally but not exclusively by the Scriptures of the Hebrew Bible, the New Testament and the person of Jesus Christ as Savior." Along with these scriptural resources, Solivan argues that "we must place tradition, reason and critical reflection on our present situation." We must include "modern critical scholarship which appropriates the text and the sociopolitical situation" from which one reads the text. Such an approach "demonstrates a high regard for the authority of Scripture," an important principle for many Pentecostals, including Latino/as, but also exhibits "a keen insight into the sociopolitical issues of the day, a great sensitivity to the needs of lay people and a wise use of critical biblical scholarship" (72).

Moreover, Latino/a Pentecostal readings of the Bible, posits Solivan, help engender a focus on justice and community. Solivan asserts that Latino/a biblical interpretation as practiced by Latino/a Pentecostals owes its roots to its "ancestor," Methodism, with its "quadrilateral principle of Scripture, experience, reason and tradition." In practice, "of these four, Scripture as illuminated by the Holy Spirit and experience as guided by the Holy Spirit, … possess the greatest weight" for Latino/a Pentecostal biblical interpreters. Thus Solivan claims that in Latino/a Pentecostalism "what lends authority to the Scriptures is not its authors or preciseness of its claims but the internal witness of the Holy Spirit in our hearts and minds which bears fruit in our transformation" (93 n. 1). Once again, I would say, the personal experience of the reader is key to constructing Pentecostal biblical interpretation.

In addition, there is a socioeconomic dimension to such a view of biblical interpretation by Latino/a Pentecostals. Pentecostalism as a whole, he states, "was and continues to be rooted in the life of the poor." Solivan cites the reality of religious experience, transformed lives, and liberative praxis as a criterion in authentic biblical interpretation: "Transformation, both personal and collective, [was] the canon against which questions of authority were to be determined. The verification of Scripture's claims was not to be found in the internal claims made by Scriptures themselves, but in the external power of the Holy Spirit transforming people's lives in light of those claims" (93 n. 1).

Experiencing God through healing and transformation made the Bible come alive and gave it its authority. However, healing and transformation that included liberation from destructive patterns that alienate neighbor from neighbor are the ultimate agenda in Latino/a Pentecostal biblical criticism. These too "point to Scripture's authority" (93 n. 1). Justice and community come to the fore as the critical aspects of authentic biblical interpretation as understood by Latino/a Pentecostals.

Thus Latino/a Pentecostals like Solivan argue that one needs statements about the Bible that recognize the impact of social status and cultural background in its interpretation. Culture becomes a partner in the liberating enterprise of biblical criticism, rather than having an "approach that amalgamates the cultural perspectives, reducing it all to some common denominator, usually under the definitional power of the dominant culture" (93 n. 1). Solivan concludes that Latino/a Pentecostalism has learned to read the Bible from the perspective of the nondominant, the poor, who often eschew the focus on literary aspects of the biblical text. Poor, nonliterate cultures have taught us to experience the Bible as Scripture—not just to study it for its own sake or to make static claims about it. He states, "When the Scriptures are reduced to a literary genre entrapped in history, the results are similar—a dead, lifeless word, far from the living creative Word of God spoken of by the prophets and experienced by the apostles and the church of the poor" (96–97).

Thus in Latino/a Pentecostalism, as understood by Solivan, the notion of "Scripture" has an expansive understanding, which encompasses the written text, a community's experience and living interpretation of that text, and its ultimate goal of personal and community transformation. Moreover, the poor lead the way toward such a liberating perspective on the interpretation and authority of the Bible.

Highlighting the Experience of the Poor in Latino/a Biblical Criticism

I have shared perspectives from two Latino Pentecostal scholars—one, an ethicist; the other, a systematic theologian—to complement my own perspective as a Latino biblical critic, so that I might thereby affirm that role of *experience*, especially the experience of the poor, in biblical criticism. Such an experience, both in terms of living it and using it, has guided me to this point in my career as a senior biblical critic. In many ways, I agree with a statement from the important volume *They Were All Together in One Place? Toward Minority Biblical Criticism*: "the ways in which people have been treated in the U.S. become the hermeneutical frame for interpreting the text" (Bailey et al. 2009, 22).

In my case, the experience of marginalization in a small, urban Latino/a Pentecostal community became the starting point for a lifetime of research, reflection, teaching, and writing on the role of the Bible in our lives as Hispanic/Latino/as in the United States. I am a biblical critic because of that experience; I am marked by it; and I write from it. For me, to be a Latino biblical critic means to write from the margins to the empire and to inch forward with each successive engagement toward the center to disarm it and claim a voice—a Hispanic/Latino, community-oriented, liberating voice with and over against texts that bear a measure of authority in these communities. So often, especially through means of particular interpretations, these same texts continue to marginalize communities of color. It is time to bring the community voice forward, firmly entrench it in the center of the conversation, without losing where we have been. Latina/o biblical criticism must always assist in this endeavor.

The Future of Latino/a Biblical Criticism: Further Reflections of a Senior Biblical Critic

In the light of this focus on experience and culture, I would like to suggest a number of future directions for Latino/a biblical criticism, as I look forward to the next ten to fifteen years of work, in this latter part of my career: placing biblical texts and contemporary Latino/a communities in conversation; placing Paul and Latino/a cultural studies in conversation; and addressing the question of pedagogy in biblical criticism.

Placing Biblical Texts and Latino/a Communities in Conversation

To begin with, I would like to see those of us who have engaged in critical work on the hermeneutics of Latino/a biblical criticism—that is, thinking more theoretically about the project—engage specific texts of the Bible in more systematic ways. Thus, for example, in New Testament studies, my specific area of criticism, I am particularly interested in engaging the Pauline Letters from the perspective of a Latino critic who cares about the experience and faith of the Latino/a community today. I am of the opinion that our community desires to see Latino/a biblical criticism look closely at specific texts.

One such example might be the Letter to the Romans on the topic of justification by faith. What does justification by faith look like for the U.S. Latino/a person of faith today, or even for someone who has no religious ties, who wants to know what the God of justice, and the people that profess that God, has to say about the social, political, and economic situation of the Latino/a community?[2] Another might be the Letter to the Philippians, which exhibits themes that resonate with U.S. Latino/a reality today—dealing with unjust imprisonment and conflict; the necessity for creative, grassroots leadership; community unity; and economic concerns. Other examples might include: the Letter to the Galatians and the discussion of what "freedom in Christ" means in everyday life, or the Letter to Philemon and its carefully nuanced approach to what seems to be a request for manumission of a slave to the slave owner. The list of topics with a bearing on social justice available for such conversations between ancient texts and Latino/a communities can be readily expanded. These conversations between the first-century missives of an itinerant religious leader and his localized, urban constituents (many of them immigrants themselves, facing an unjust imperial order) and our minoritized, marginalized U.S. racial and ethnic communities today (including the largely immigrant population that constitutes Latino/as in the United States) would make for very fruitful engagement indeed.

The reason we care about such engagement across centuries is that these texts still continue to bear a measure of authority and thus have important impact on our Latino/a religious communities, including Pentecostal and other communions. Why not engage in a critical analysis of these texts that resonates with the social and economic needs of the Latino/a community rather than let interpretations that come from other, usually more spiritualized, less politically concrete, corners rule the day?

---

2. Latin American biblical scholar Elsa Tamez has explored this topic with regard to the meaning of Paul's discussion of justification in his letters, especially Romans and Galatians, in light of the socioeconomic context of Latin America. Her readings of Paul's letters would be helpful to us in the U.S. Latino/a context (1993).

A recent national research project on the use of Scriptures in U.S. communities of color—conducted under the auspices of Claremont Graduate University's Institute of Signifying Scriptures and institute director, Professor Vincent Wimbush—demonstrated the wide regard that African American, Arab American, Asian American, Latino American, and Native American religious groups of all types held for their scriptures.[3] This included a study on Latino/a Pentecostal churches (as well as a Latino/a Roman Catholic parish and a Latino/a Muslim group), in which it became clear that the Bible still has major, some might say exorbitant, importance in these communities.[4] Yet the study showed that there is often a disconnect between long-held doctrinal ideas about the Bible as the "Word of God" and the search for social justice that these communities undertake with or without traditional interpretations of their scriptures to help them.

It behooves the Latino/a biblical interpreter to make available his or her critical approaches to the Bible, including interpretations of specific texts of the Bible, to grassroots Latino/a communities of faith, so that the relevance of their Scriptures continues to make sense, especially since they continue to give the Bible so much authority in their lives. For example, I continue to be interested in my own work on how the apostle Paul and his letters relate to issues of leadership, ministry, and justice in his own day as well as in Christian congregations, including Latino/a congregations, today.[5]

Placing Paul and Latino/a Cultural Studies in Conversation

Second, I would like to put Paul in conversation with critical Latino/a cultural studies today. As Fernando Segovia suggests, "it is crucial for Latino/a biblical criticism, as an exercise in Latino/a criticism, to stay in close con-

---

3. See the description of conference and research studies that came from this research project to date at the website for the Institute for Signifying Scriptures: http://www.cgu.edu/pages/7393.asp.

4. The specific Latino/a community report of the ISS research project on Scriptures was titled "Seeking Guidance from the Word: U.S. Latino/a Religious Communities and Their Scriptures," written by Efrain Agosto, Brian Clark, Elizabeth Conde-Frazier, and Jacqueline Hidalgo. For the final analysis of the study, see Agosto 2013.

5. My current research projects include a book on "Reading Paul through the Eyes of Ministry," with which I hope to introduce Paul's Letters *latinamente*, with issues of ministry, community, and justice in the forefront.

tact with the analysis of race and ethnicity at a variety of levels: most concretely, Latino/a studies; more generally, minority studies; most broadly, ethnic-racial studies" (2009, 221). Thus, besides attention to Latino/a religion and minority biblical studies in general, the Latino/a biblical critic should be in contact with the broader, interdisciplinary fields of ethnic studies and Latino/a studies as conversation partners for our work in biblical studies.

For example, one of the great heroes of Puerto Rican history and the struggle for Puerto Rican independence is Pedro Albizu Campos, who died in 1965, shortly after his release from prison, after some fifteen years in captivity. He was a long-time advocate for a free and independent Puerto Rican nation, starting as leader of the Independence Party in the 1920s, through his arrest in the 1940s by U.S. authorities, with time in a federal prison in Atlanta, and arrest again in the 1950s. He was a highly educated lawyer and great orator. His speeches are readily available for study, but his correspondence from prison seems less accessible. Albizu Campos has been called "the apostle of Puerto Rican independence." An intercultural and interdisciplinary study of these two figures, the "apostle to the Gentiles" of the first-century CE Jesus movement, Paul and his letters, and this "apostle of independence" from twentieth-century Puerto Rican history and struggle, would be a most attractive example of this envisioned conversation between biblical studies and ethnic studies. Both were imprisoned for political reasons by an imperial power, and both wrote letters and speeches in defense of their movements and leadership. Such a conversation would illustrate the struggle of freedom from oppression across the centuries.[6]

I agree, therefore, with Fernando Segovia and others that Latino/a biblical critics, and indeed all biblical critics, are called to take bold, interdisciplinary, cross-cultural, and liberationist projects as part of our work as critics.

---

6. I first suggested this Paul-Campos comparative project in an essay I wrote on Paul's Letter to the Philippians as an example of the anti-imperial agenda in Pauline Christianity and the need to engage postcolonial conversations across texts and contexts (2007). The project remains on the agenda for this Latino/Puerto Rican biblical critic.

Addressing the Question of Pedagogy in Biblical Criticism

Finally, I would like to offer a word about the agenda of pedagogy in Latino/a biblical criticism, as we look toward the future of our enterprise. How do we teach a biblical criticism that takes seriously the context of Latino/a reality in the United States as an exemplum for academic, theological, and religious/ministerial work that brings justice and liberation to needy communities across the land and the world? This question of biblical pedagogy has, of course, been given consideration previously, including the third volume in the 1990s series on *Reading from This Place*, titled *Teaching the Bible: The Discourses and Politics of Biblical Pedagogy*, edited by Fernando F. Segovia and Mary Ann Tolbert (1998).

In his opening essay for that volume, Segovia reminds us that historical criticism, literary criticism, and cultural criticism all rely on the expertise of an omniscient "teacher-critic" (1998, e.g., 6). Such a critic must train readers in complex and comprehensive methodologies in order for them to provide adequate biblical interpretation—"objectively" historical, appropriately in tune with literary theory and/or as fully cognizant as possible of the social reality of the ancient world, albeit two millennia removed. These methodologies, while helpful in part, each in their own way, lack consideration of the social locations of current readers or real "flesh-and-blood" readers—their diverse backgrounds, cultures, and socioeconomic status and needs—as tools for (or obstacles to) interpretation. Moreover, insisting on the importance of diverse readers and not just the right methods, whether historical, literary, or sociological, assures the presence of the so-called margins in both the task of biblical interpretation and the task of teaching biblical interpretation. Two other contributors to the volume discuss Latino/a considerations of biblical pedagogy: Jean-Pierre Ruiz and Francisco García-Treto.

Ruiz argues that a good theologian involved in theological education learns from the Bible (1998). With regard to John, the object of analysis, he outlines several such models. To begin with, a good theological educator learns to be prophetic like John the Baptist, who comes from the wilderness—the margins—to call for transformation, as well as to be a good disciple like the woman at the well who encounters Jesus (John 4), tells others from her community what she has learned, and continues to draw on that "well" of knowledge even beyond her initial encounter. Likewise, a good theologian as educator is like Mary Magdalene, who not only encountered an empty tomb and a risen Lord who healed her doubts and restored her faith (John 19) but also told others. She was a theologian as "evangelizer," a bringer of good news. Finally, a good theological educator is a visionary like John of Patmos, who sees beyond the present to a hopeful future. Good theologians, posits Ruiz, teach a mode of interpretation that is inclusive, inviting, prophetic, and forward-looking.

Ruiz's proposal is not as explicit as what I am about to suggest, but his Johannine models of good theologians for good theological education provide a worthy framework for Latino/a biblical pedagogy, insofar as it seeks to teach from the margins to the center and draws continually on our community's diverse founts of information and life, both as a faith community and a cultural community—writers and artists, scholars and ministers, laborers and family members, and so on.

We need educators who "evangelize" like Mary Magdalene, in the sense that they want their charges to take the Bible as a tool for engendering the good news of justice and liberation for needy communities. When the Bible fails to deliver in such ways, they are not afraid to call that out, so that what we teach keeps the news of liberation and justice on the front burner, even when the biblical narrative puts it on the back burner or seems to propose the opposite. We need educators who are visionaries like John of Patmos in the book of Revelation, who saw his community suffering at the hands of the Roman Empire and dared to declare that the empire's word was not the last word. They include those conversant with postcolonial theory who call our community to embrace an anti-imperial message wherever it is to be found in the Bible and condemn imperial injustice wherever it manifests itself today, as John of Patmos did twenty centuries ago.[7]

García-Treto challenges biblical pedagogy on three fronts: critical engagement with "the other" in dialogue, attention to the experience of exile and otherness, and the primacy of the values of justice and dignity (1998).

First, like the actions of the three figures of the Hebrew Bible he studies (Cain, Abraham, Ezekiel), the biblical pedagogue needs to engage "the other" in dialogue and be willing to question and be questioned. García-Treto demonstrates how each of these three individuals engages God in dialogue, questions God's actions on matters pertinent to their life and

---

7. On postcolonial theory as an appropriate "optic" for biblical interpretation and biblical pedagogy, because it focuses on understanding imperial aspects of the ancient world, the history of interpretation, and the sociopolitical reality of interpreters today, who are the "children of colonialism," see Segovia 2000.

faith, and actually alters God's plans or requests for them. Similarly, a good biblical pedagogue teaches a critical engagement that does not shy away from questioning positions taken by the Bible, whether by divine figures or so-called heroic figures of the biblical narratives, especially since many of these heroes—and even some "villains" as well—challenge God to better alternatives, which God often accepts.

Second, García-Treto reminds us that the Hebrew Bible emerges from "a culture massively influenced by exile" (106–7). Each of the three biblical figures highlighted is an exile in one form or another, and their responses to God's plans or requests of God on their behalf are pleas for justice and human dignity, given their difficult exilic situation. Exile, as a fact and symbol of the human experience, including the experiences of many Latino/as who live in the United States today, remains a part of what we teach when we teach the Bible as well as a part of what many readers, including Latino/a readers, bring to the table of biblical interpretation and teaching. For example, when confronted with the need to "embrace the other" in biblical interpretation and teaching, critics who know something of the exilic experience from personal or family history "have this perception [of otherness] forced upon them, since what is customary in one society may be illegal in another; in other words, the hierarchy of values is different in different cultures, and the concrete forms of expression given to those values may be radically different across the border" (106–7). Thus, pedagogically, the Latino/a biblical critic resonates with Hebrew or Christian Scriptures that rely on the experience of exile and otherness to convey the message of justice and liberation. Such an experience becomes part and parcel of our biblical pedagogy.

Third, even as individuals in the biblical story cross borders, as we ourselves do, there are certain lines that are not crossed. In the case of each individual in these stories, lines of human dignity and justice are not crossed. Cain, as the murderer of his brother, merits punishment, but his exile will not be total. He asks God not to exile him so far away that he cannot even commune with God, and God listens, softening the blow. Similarly, Abraham pleads on behalf of Sodom, where punishment is due for their wickedness. Yet, he asks, does not God's justice extend to the righteous in Sodom? Would God's punishment wipe out both the wicked *and* the righteous? As a result, because God has taught Abraham that justice above all is the standard by which God will conduct God's dealings with humanity, especially humanity on the move (as in the case of Abraham and his family, something about which Abraham reminds God), Sodom and Gomorrah are spared, at least for a time. As García-Treto points out, the important lesson to learn "is that the human/divine dialogue concerning what is just always remains open," especially for those who cross borders and experience new rules and values (111). One value, God promises, does not change, and that is the nature of justice. Another is that of human dignity. When Ezekiel pleads with God not to let him eat something that is abhorrent to his humanity, just to prove the point of the need for flexibility in exile, God relents and again softens the blow, allowing Ezekiel to eat something less abhorrent but still proving the point—when in exile, the rules change, and one must be ready for such change.

Biblical pedagogies that embrace change, cross borders, and invite new ways of reading and interpretation must be welcomed in what lies before us as Latino/a biblical critics. Yet some things must never change, and among these are the concern for justice and human dignity for all in what we teach, how we teach, and whom we teach and are taught by. García-Treto is right: even God is taught something new in dialogue with the faithful. So must we as biblical critics.

Conclusion

For sure, the concerns of biblical pedagogy from the perspectives of Latino/a biblical critics are an important part of what lies ahead for us in the years to come. For example, I myself have pursued for a number of years now a research project on the question of teaching New Testament introduction, seeking to know how such a course offering is taught by Latino/a biblical critics around the country. With a grant from the Wabash Center for Teaching and Learning in Theology and Religion, I have interviewed and visited various professors of New Testament studies at their schools and discussed with them the question of teaching the New Testament in general and this introductory course in particular *latinamente*. In so doing, I have posed such questions as the following: How does being a Latino/a biblical critic influence what we read, how we teach, and how our students engage the New Testament text, especially as they are being introduced to it early in their theological education? More such work is needed. How we keep the needs and concerns of our growing U.S. Latino/a constituents on the forefront of our studies constitutes another important part of the task ahead. This we will do by doing what we do best—studying the biblical text with all the resources at our disposal. In particular, we should do this in conversation with our cohorts in other fields, especially Latino/a studies in particular and ethnic/minority studies in general. This we will also do by having a clear agenda—justice and liberation for all, especially, as Jesus taught us, for "the least of these."

WORKS CITED

Agosto, Efrain. 2005. *Servant Leadership: Jesus and Paul*. St. Louis: Chalice.
———. 2007. The Letter to the Philippians. Pages 281–93 in *A Postcolonial Commentary on the New Testament Writings*. Edited by Fernando F. Segovia and R. S. Sugirtharajah. London: T&T Clark.
———. 2013. Reading the Word in America: U.S. Latino/a Religious Communities and Their Scriptures. Pages 188–255 in *MisReading America: Scriptures and Difference*. Edited by Vincent L. Wimbush, with Lalruatkima and Melissa Renee Reid. Oxford: Oxford University Press.
Bailey, Randall C., Tat-siong Benny Liew, and Fernando F. Segovia. 2009. Toward Minority Biblical Criticism: Framework, Contours, Dynamics. Pages 3–43 in *They Were All Together in One Place? Toward Minority Biblical Criticism*. Edited by Randall C. Bailey, Tat-siong Benny Liew, and Fernando F. Segovia. SemeiaSt 57. Atlanta: Society of Biblical Literature.
Garcia-Treto, Francisco. 1998. Crossing the Line: Three Scenes of Divine-Human Engagement in the Hebrew Bible. Pages 105–16 in *Teaching the Bible: The Discourses and Politics of Biblical Pedagogy*. Edited by Fernando F. Segovia and Mary Ann Tolbert. Minneapolis: Fortress.
Ruiz, Jean Pierre. 1998. Four Faces of Theology: Four Johannine Conversations. Pages 86–101 in *Teaching the Bible: The Discourses and Politics of Biblical Pedagogy*. Edited by Fernando F. Segovia and Mary Ann Tolbert. Minneapolis: Fortress.
Segovia, Fernando F. 1995. "And They Began to Speak in Other Tongues": Competing Modes of Discourse in Contemporary Biblical Criticism. Pages 1–32 in *Social Location and Biblical Interpretation in the United States*. Vol. 1 of *Reading from This Place*. Edited by Fernando F. Segovia and Mary Ann Tolbert. Minneapolis: Fortress.
———. 1998. Introduction: Pedagogical Discourse and Practices in Contemporary Biblical Criticism: Toward a Contextual Biblical Pedagogy. Pages 1–28 in *Teaching the Bible: The Discourses and Politics of Biblical Pedagogy*. Edited by Fernando F. Segovia and Mary Ann Tolbert. Minneapolis: Fortress.
———. 2000. Biblical Criticism and Postcolonial Studies: Toward a Post-

colonial Optic. Pages 119–32 in *Decolonizing Biblical Studies: A View from the Margins*. Maryknoll, N.Y.: Orbis.

———. 2009. Toward Latino/a American Biblical Criticism: Latin(o/a)ness as Problematic. Pages 193–223 in *They Were All Together in One Place? Toward Minority Biblical Criticism*. Edited by Randall C. Bailey, Tat-siong Benny Liew, and Fernando F. Segovia. SemeiaSt 57. Atlanta: Society of Biblical Literature.

Solivan, Samuel. 1998. *The Spirit, Pathos and Liberation: Toward an Hispanic Pentecostal Theology*. Sheffield: Sheffield Academic Press.

Tamez, Elsa. 1993. *The Amnesty of Grace: Justification by Faith from a Latin American Perspective*. Translated by Sharon Ringe. Nashville: Abingdon.

———. Carta a los Gálatas. 2003. Pages 894–912 in *Comentario Bíblico Latinoamericano: Nuevo Testamento*. Edited by Armando Levoratti, Elsa Tamez, and Pablo Richard. Estella [Navarra]: Verbo Divino.

Villafañe, Eldin. 1993. *The Liberating Spirit: Toward an Hispanic American Pentecostal Social Ethic*. Grand Rapids: Eerdmans.

Rethinking Latino Hermeneutics: An Atheist Perspective

Hector Avalos

I am not a Latino biblical scholar. I am a biblical scholar who happens to be Latino. I make this distinction for a number of subtle but significant reasons. While my upbringing as a Mexican American Pentecostal Protestant rendered me intimately acquainted with the Bible, my secularist stance has an even larger influence on the topics and approaches I use in biblical scholarship. In fact, I would say that my experience with a chronic illness (Wegener's Granulomatosis) explains more of my publications as a biblical scholar than my Latino identity (Avalos 1995, 1999, 2007).

However, in this chapter I will concentrate on how being an openly atheist biblical scholar affects my hermeneutics. First, I certainly do not subscribe to religionist approaches to the Bible. By "religionist" I refer to any approach that sees religion as an essentially good and valuable phenomenon that should be supported and maintained in human society. Divesting myself of religionist views of the Bible means that I see most of biblical scholarship, whether practiced by openly confessional or self-described "historical-critical" scholars, as partly apologetics. Biblical scholarship is often meant to mitigate any negative views of the Bible and to maintain the cultural and ethical superiority of the Bible in modern society.

Accordingly, some of my publications have focused on deconstructing the principal hermeneutical strategies used by most biblical scholars, especially when they address ethical issues in the Bible. Here I focus on two of these hermeneutical strategies: representativism and reinterpretation. I will also demonstrate how these hermeneutical strategies are used in Latino liberatory readings of the Bible. In contrast to most Latino biblical scholars, I will argue that much of what is called Latino "liberatory" hermeneutics does not go far enough in liberating the modern world from the authority of ancient imperialistic and violent texts.

Principal Hermeneutical Strategies

Representativism

Representativism affirms that a particular view in the Bible is "representative," while others (usually bad ones, like slavery and genocide) are unrepresentative. Walter Brueggemann (1997, 144) provides an instance when he claims that Israel's God, "full of sovereign power and committed in solidarity to the needy, and especially to Israel in need—dominates the narrative of Israel's liturgy and imagination (cf. Deut 10:12–22)." Brueggemann tells us, "It is important to accent that something like 'God's preferential option for the poor' is deeply rooted in Israel's testimony, so deeply rooted as to be characteristic and definitional for Israel's speech about God."

The first problem is that Brueggemann, much like almost every other biblical theologian, never establishes criteria for what is "characteristic and definitional." Is it a statistical criterion? That is, is it the number of times a specific concept or term is repeated? Or is it qualitative? That is, is it something said to be the most important concept, regardless of how many times others are repeated? If it is qualitative, then is a representative teaching one that the biblical authors say is representative, or is it something a modern scholar is retrojecting into the biblical text?

If we appeal to statistics to find out what is "characteristic," we soon encounter a very complex and confusing situation. Brueggemann quotes Deut 10 to support the idea that a characteristic of God is his concern for the poor. Now Deut 10:12–22 is part of a larger work scholars usually denominate as the Deuteronomistic History, stretching from Joshua through 2 Kings (except Ruth) in Protestant Bibles. Yet Frank Frick's study of the terminology of poverty in the Deuteronomistic History concludes that this work is the least concerned with poverty compared to other biblical corpora. For example, he points out, Job has twenty instances of poverty terminology, while the Deuteronomistic History has eleven (1995, 84).

If we use a "qualitative" criterion, we also do not make much progress in finding what is "characteristic and definitional," because "quality" can be very subjective and selective. Indeed, we may come to a very different conclusion about what is "characteristic and definitional" by reading the text Brueggemann cites, Deut 10:12–22:

> And now, Israel, what does the LORD your God require of you, but to fear the LORD your God, to walk in all his ways, to love him, to serve the LORD your God with all your heart and with all your soul, and to keep the commandments and statutes of the LORD, which I command you this day for your good? Behold, to the LORD your God belong heaven and the heaven of heavens, the earth with all that is in it; yet the LORD set his heart in love upon your fathers and chose their descendants after them, you above all peoples, as at this day. Circumcise therefore the foreskin of your heart, and be no longer stubborn. For the LORD your God is God of gods and Lord of lords, the great, the mighty, and the terrible God, who is not partial and takes no bribe. He executes justice for the fatherless and the widow, and loves the sojourner, giving him food and clothing. Love the sojourner therefore; for you were sojourners in the land of Egypt. You shall fear the LORD your God; you shall serve him and cleave to him, and by his name you shall swear. He is your praise; he is your God, who has done for you these great and terrible things which your eyes have seen. Your fathers went down to Egypt seventy persons; and now the LORD your God has made you as the stars of heaven for multitude.

True enough, the text speaks about how Yahweh cares about justice for the widow, and how he loves the stranger. However, the text also repeatedly emphasizes how Israelites should "fear" and "serve" and "love" Yahweh with all their souls. Verbs commanding obligation toward Yahweh outnumber any commandments to be kind to widows or strangers. Statistically, we could argue that this passage makes Israel's slavery to Yahweh "characteristic and definitional." Verse 14 speaks of how the earth belongs to Yahweh, and so Yahweh's imperialism might be "characteristic and definitional," not some preferential option for the poor.

And how does loving and caring for strangers coincide with the genocide of the Canaanites that is also commanded in Deut 7:1–5 and 20:17–18? Why is genocide of any stranger not favored by Yahweh "characteristic and definitional"? To explain genocide, Brueggemann lapses back into a technique well known among fundamentalists, who also pick and choose what to take literally and what to take figuratively. Brueggemann tells us that such genocidal texts are really "a theological construct without any historical base" (1997, 497). This, of course, assumes that talk about "justice" is also not "a theological construct without any historical base."

All of this illustrates that seeking the representative message of the Bible is a failure. However, it is a failure not because there is not a core message, but because the core message is assumed to be benign (e.g., justice, love, mercy). What if the "characteristic and definitional" message of the Bible is something we would regard as negative—namely, intolerance of other religions? Actually, intolerance of other religions can be easily supported as a consistent message in the Bible, whether in the Hebrew or Christian canons. The authors of the Bible advocated only the worship of Yahweh, and so it follows that any other religions cannot be tolerated.

Intolerance of other religions explains much more of the content and actions prescribed in biblical literature than "mercy" and "love." Religious intolerance is enshrined in the first commandment in Exod 20:3 ("You shall have no other gods before me"). Intolerance, not love and mercy, better explains the genocide of the Canaanites for following their religious traditions. Intolerance explains the anger of the prophets against the worship of other gods. Intolerance explains Paul's warnings not to follow other gospels (Gal 1:8).

Indeed, intolerance of other religions is one of the innovations that I see in the Bible relative to other Near Eastern cultures. Yet you will hardly ever see any biblical scholar phrase it in those terms. I suggest that the reluctance to see "the characteristic and definitional" aspects of the Bible in negative terms is part of the religionism I see permeating the field of biblical studies, and especially what is called "biblical theology."

Reinterpretation: Does Original Intent Matter?

By far, the most common strategy to explain undesirable aspects in the Bible is reinterpretation. Reinterpretation means that a modern biblical scholar allows the original meaning of the text to be erased or changed to fit a later or modern context.

In a much-cited article in *The Interpreter's Dictionary of the Bible*, Krister Stendahl argued that scholars should distinguish "what it meant and what it means" (1962, 420). The premise of Stendahl's distinction is that the Bible is so alien to our culture that only reinterpretation could keep it alive. Note Stendahl's own remarks: "This understanding leads to the puzzling insight that in the living religious traditions continuity is affirmed and achieved by discontinuity. Authority is affirmed and relevance asserted by reinterpretation" (1970, 31). Stendahl claimed that reinterpretation, even when it means disregarding the "original" sense of a text, was an essential function of Scriptures, as evidenced by this statement: "From a historical point of view, Paul did not mean what Augustine heard him to say. ... For better or worse that is how Scriptures function, and if so, we had better take note thereof in our treatment of the history of ideas" (1970, 31). For Stendahl, it is the nature of Scripture to be reinterpreted. Stendahl echoed the ideas of Hans-Georg Gadamer, who asserted that readers were always recreating meaning to the extent that it did not much matter what an author meant. In essence, Stendahl champions the legitimacy of "recontextualization" and "reappropriation," which claims that a text can and should mean whatever a faith community needs it to mean to keep that text or the community alive.

Biblical scholars usually do not very thoroughly address the philosophical and ethical problems with reinterpretation. Such ethical and philosophical problems can be seen more clearly if we realize that two positions can be identified for those who believe there is even such a thing as authorial intent: (1) authorial intent is the only one that matters; (2) authorial intent is not the only one that matters.

If one chooses the former position, then reinterpretation would be as unethical as reinterpreting my words to mean something other than what I intended, at least insofar as my intentions are clearly expressed by my words. Reinterpretation really becomes a game of "let's pretend the Bible now says something else." If one chooses the latter position, then the only result is chaos and relativism that renders moot and superfluous all research into the ancient sociohistorical context and philology of the Bible. Why bother finding out what a text meant, if we are allowed to reinterpret it anyway? Reinterpretation in that sense is really the rejection of an original meaning. As such, we cannot say that any reinterpretation is biblical any more than my original intentions could be called mine if they were reinterpreted in the future.

Latino/a Liberationist Theologies

Given the previous comments about how nonreligionism affects my biblical hermeneutics, my view of liberationist hermeneutics is very different from most Latino/a biblical scholars I know. There are now numerous liberation theologies, and their related postcolonial versions, that suit various ethnic or underempowered groups (see, e.g., Moore and Segovia 2005). For our purposes, we can show that, despite their differences with traditional theologies, liberation hermeneutics are founded on traditional "representativist" and "reinterpretive" strategies.

To illustrate this point, let us consider the prevalent use of the biblical prophets as the paradigms of liberationist messages in liberation theologies (see Tamez 1982; Croatto 1981; Carroll 1992). The use of the prophets is advertised in the titles of a number of books, such as *Hispanic Women: Prophetic Voice in the Church* by Ada María Isasi-Díaz and Yolanda Tarango (1992), or *Prophesy Deliverance* by Cornel West (2002). We have commentaries from a liberation theology perspective, as in the case of Carol Dempsey's *The Prophets: A Liberation-Critical Reading* (2000). Guillermo Meléndez offers an explanation for choosing the prophets as paradigms:

> We have chosen to call this church born from the people "prophetic" because this model recovers the biblical tradition of the prophets' cry for justice for the downtrodden and their trust in God's requirement that the covenant community care especially for the poor. This model of the church is prophetic also because it looks to God's promise of "a future and a hope" (Jeremiah 29:11) and the people's call to participate in establishing God's Reign of justice, mercy, and peace. (1990, 7–8)

Similarly, Fernando Segovia, in his perceptive study of Hispanic American theologies, describes one Latino liberatory approach to the Bible as follows: "Such an entrée to the liberating power of the Bible calls for a specific way of reading the Bible ... a prophetic reading from the perspective of the oppressed that reappropriates the basic story of the Bible, vis-à-vis a royal reading from the position of imperial authority that obfuscates and distorts the basic story" (1992, 48). Francisco Garcia-Treto is among the few Latino/a biblical scholars who have pointed out the problems of applying the prophets to modern liberationist readings: "As I have suggested, a monologic reading of the Bible is neither the only nor best one possible, and the assumption that the prophetic paradigm of communication is the only one present in the biblical text is likewise flawed and limiting" (1996, 84).

If one inspects the stated values of most of these Hispanic theologians, one finds at least three commonalities: (1) A valuing of multiracial/ethnic identities; (2) acceptance and celebration of the mixture of Christian and indigenous religious traditions; and (3) claimed opposition to imperialistic hegemonies. However, upon closer inspection, one can show that the biblical prophets were opposed to all of these major features and could be seen as agents of imperialism themselves.

For example, if one looks for biblical figures who valued multiculturalism, then it was certainly not the prophets. Rather, it was the kings often labeled as "evil" or otherwise chastised for their multiculturalism (Thiel 2004). Solomon is one example discussed in 1 Kgs 11:1–6:

> King Solomon loved many foreign women along with the daughter of Pharaoh: Moabite, Ammonite, Edomite, Sidonian, and Hittite women, from the nations concerning which the LORD had said to the Israelites, "You shall not enter into marriage with them, neither shall they with you; for they will surely incline your heart to follow their gods." … when Solomon was old, his wives turned away his heart after other gods. … For Solomon followed Astarte the goddess of the Sidonians, and Milcom the abomination of the Ammonites. So Solomon did what was evil in the sight of the LORD.

Later we are told how Josiah was regarded as good because he destroyed the religious pluralism that Solomon advocated:

> The king [Josiah] defiled the high places that were east of Jerusalem, to the south of the Mount of Destruction, which King Solomon of Israel had built for Astarte the abomination of the Sidonians, for Chemosh the abomination of Moab, and for Milcom the abomination of the Ammonites. (2 Kgs 23:13)

Similarly, Ahab, regarded as perhaps the most evil king of all ancient Israel, was famed for his ethnic and religious pluralism:

> Ahab son of Omri did evil in the sight of the LORD more than all who were before him. And as if it had been a light thing for him to walk in the sins of Jeroboam son of Nebat, he took as his wife Jezebel daughter of King Ethbaal of the Sidonians, and went and served Baal, and worshiped him. He erected an altar for Baal in the house of Baal, which he built in Samaria. Ahab also made a sacred pole. Ahab did more to provoke the anger of the LORD, the God of Israel, than had all the kings of Israel who were before him. (1 Kgs 16:30–33)

Most of the prophets were definitely against any sort of ethnic and religious pluralism. For instance, Ezek 44:22 says that a priest "shall not marry a widow, or a divorced woman, but only a virgin of the stock of the house of Israel, or a widow who is the widow of a priest." And Jer 11:13 laments: "For your gods have become as many as your cities, O Judah; and as many as the streets of Jerusalem are the altars you have set up to shame, altars to make offerings to Baal." Elijah goes so far as to slaughter the priests of the god Baal (1 Kgs 18:40).

Despite such biblical examples of intolerance, we find liberation theologians who seem oblivious to how the prophetic messages promote injustice toward other ethnic groups and religions. Gustavo Gutiérrez, a founding father of liberation theology, says: "The prophets announce a reign of peace. But peace presupposes the establishment of justice: 'The product of justice shall be peace, and the fruit of equity, perpetual security' (Isa 32:17; cf. also Ps 85)" (1987, 224).[1]

Overall, the appeal to the prophets as champions of justice rests on the most uncritical readings of these books. To understand this problem, let us consider two statements about the government response to Hurricane Katrina, which struck New Orleans on August 29, 2005.

Statement 1
Our priorities are clear: We will complete the evacuation as quickly and safely as possible. We will not let criminals prey on the vulnerable, and we will not allow bureaucracy to get in the way of saving lives.[2]

Statement 2
We have been fighting for assistance to spur the Gulf Coast's economy and get help to those in need. But too many in Washington have stood in the way.[3]

From just reading these statements, one could infer that these are critics of the government and champions of the people of New Orleans. Statement 1 promises help and seems to be criticizing the bureaucracy. Statement 2 also speaks about efforts to assist and speaks about many in Washington standing in the way.

Yet both statements are by Washington insiders and bureaucrats. Statement 1 is by President George W. Bush, and statement 2 was issued by the office of Senator John F. Kerry (D-Massachusetts), the Democratic

---

1. "Los profetas anuncian un reino de paz. Pero la paz supone el establecimiento de la justicia; 'El producto de las justicia será la paz, el fruto de la equidad, una seguridad perpetua (Is 32, 17; cf. tambien Sal 85)" (my trans.).

2. Speech by President George W. Bush on September 3, 2005, available at http://georgewbush-whitehouse.archives.gov/news/releases/2005/09/20050903.html.

3. Statement on the official site of John F. Kerry issued on August 29, 2006, on the one-year anniversary of Katrina, now available at http://votesmart.org/public-statement/204525/kerry-on-katrina-anniversary-one-year-later-miles-to-go#.VD_2lW9LpKF.

opponent of President Bush in the 2004 elections. If one reads enough of these political statements, one learns that each side will accuse the other of injustice, mismanagement, theft, lying, and so on. That is normal political rhetoric, in which the truth of the accusation is not always so obvious.

Likewise, it is unjust to accept uncritically the accusations of the prophets against the kings. The prophets may not always be correct, and we do not have any responses from supposedly evil kings. These prophets, if they were literate, were already probably part of the elite, and they often showed themselves to be lackeys of foreign imperialists, such as Cyrus or Nebuchadnezzar. Any prophetic accusations or championing of the downtrodden cannot be taken at face value any more than the rhetoric and characterizations that flow every day from Republicans against Democrats, and vice versa (see Marcus 1995).

Although most liberation theologians see themselves as fighting against Eurocentric perspectives on the Bible, the use of the prophets as a paradigm of liberation continues a very Eurocentric tradition. Such a tradition is exemplified by Julius Wellhausen (1844–1918), the German scholar who is widely regarded as a principal synthesizer of modern critical scholarship. Wellhausen himself observed: "It was Amos, Hosea, and Isaiah who introduced a movement against the old popular worship of the high places; in doing so they are not in the least actuated by a deep-rooted preference for the temple of Jerusalem, *but by ethical motives*" (1983, 47; italics mine). Likewise, William G. Dever, who, as a critic of multiculturalism and defender of the "Western cultural tradition," appears to have no commonalities with Latin American liberationists, shares a bibliolatrous respect for the prophets when he exclaims: "But the portentous historical situation and the real life theological crises of the Assyrian and Babylonian era produced an eloquent call for reform—for social justice—that is found nowhere else in the literature of the ancient Near East. In that sense, the prophets were indeed 'inspired,' and their message remains vital today" (2001, 285).[4] And for all the proclamations against imperialism, liberation theologians seem blissfully oblivious to the brutal imperialism endorsed, accepted, or promoted by many prophets.[5] Consider this example from Isaiah, the very prophet cited by Gutiérrez as a promoter of liberation:

---

4. See Dever (2006) for his recent defense of the "western cultural tradition."
5. For similar criticisms of liberation theology, see Levenson 1993, 127-59.

> Thus says the Lord to his anointed, to Cyrus, whose right hand I have grasped to subdue nations before him and strip kings of their robes, to open doors before him and the gates shall not be closed: I will go before you and level the mountains, I will break in pieces the doors of bronze and cut through the bars of iron, I will give you the treasures of darkness and riches hidden in secret places, so that you may know that it is I, the Lord, the God of Israel, who call you by your name. (Isa 45:1–3)

Here it is clear that Yahweh endorses the empire of Cyrus, the Persian king, who even becomes even a messianic figure (Isa 45:1). People should be Cyrus's vassals. The thought is not of liberation for all. Consider also this example in Jer 27:6–8:

> Now I have given all these lands into the hand of King Nebuchadnezzar of Babylon, my servant, and I have given him even the wild animals of the field to serve him. All the nations shall serve him and his son and his grandson, until the time of his own land comes; then many nations and great kings shall make him their slave.
>
> But if any nation or kingdom will not serve this king, Nebuchadnezzar of Babylon, and put its neck under the yoke of the king of Babylon, then I will punish that nation with the sword, with famine, and with pestilence, says the Lord, until I have completed its destruction by his hand.

Far from advocating liberation from the Babylonian Empire, the prophet Jeremiah says that it is Yahweh's will that all people be servants of Nebuchadnezzar. There is no thought of liberation here—it is just the opposite. Imperialism and servitude are part of God's plan. Jeremiah is Nebuchadnezzar's lackey, not some courageous foe of an imperialist.

Perhaps most importantly, these liberationist theologians miss the fact that Yahweh himself is the ultimate imperialist in the prophets. Indeed, this is a feature common to all monotheistic religions, because they suppose the existence of one god who created the world and therefore owns it. These prophets actively celebrate Yahweh's empire, as is clear in Isaiah:

> It shall come to pass in the latter days that the mountain of the house of the Lord shall be established as the highest of the mountains, and shall be raised above the hills; and all the nations shall flow to it, and many peoples shall come, and say: "Come, let us go up to the mountain of the Lord, to the house of the God of Jacob; that he may teach us his ways and that we may walk in his paths." For out of Zion shall go forth the law, and the word of the Lord from Jerusalem. He shall judge between the nations, and shall

decide for many peoples; and they shall beat their swords into plowshares, and their spears into pruning hooks; nation shall not lift up sword against nation, neither shall they learn war any more. (Isa 2:2–4)

Liberation theologians are uncritical about the nature of "peace" envisioned by these prophets. As I have noted elsewhere, the Hebrew word *šālôm*, usually translated "peace," can be viewed as a thoroughly imperialistic term (2005, 169–70). As used in the Hebrew Bible, it really refers to a state of affairs favorable to Yahweh. Peace means no more war only insofar as Yahweh has destroyed his opponents or he has successfully beaten them into utter submission. Note this example from Isaiah:

> But the LORD will have compassion on Jacob and will gain choose Israel, and will set them in their own land; and aliens will join them and attach themselves to the house of Jacob. And the peoples will take them and bring them to their place, and the house of Israel will possess them in the LORD's land as male and female slaves; they will take captive those who were their captors, and rule over those who oppressed them. (Isa 14:1–2)

To be fair, many of these liberation theologians might argue that "prophetic" is a metaphor or that they have simply recontextualized the prophets. Yet such recontextualization is as meaningless as using other promoters of imperialism as paradigms of the opposite. No one thinks of using the works of the Spanish conqueror Hernán Cortés as a paradigm of liberation, and with good reason. Further, just as liberation theologians are prepared to repudiate Cortés completely for his genocidal and imperialist thoughts, liberation theologians should be willing to repudiate completely all prophetic literature that endorses genocide and Yahwistic imperialism.

Conclusion

My Latino identity explains very little about how I approach biblical hermeneutics. My thorough secularism explains a lot more. With many Latinos, I share the goal of liberation of the oppressed, but I see the Bible as a thoroughly imperialist text. However, I cannot call myself antihegemonic or anti-imperialist, because everyone is pursuing hegemony. As Hans Morgenthau, the famed political realist explains, everyone who works against an empire is simply trying to replace that empire with another one. Thus even those who think of themselves as religious pluralists will eventually seek to make religious pluralism the reigning hegemony.

So what I am against is religious empires, including the Christian empire, and I see most biblical scholarship as an agent of that empire. Biblical scholarship often seeks to retain the superior value of the Bible as a cultural authority. Accordingly, liberation, for me, means liberation from the very idea that any ancient text should be an authority in the modern world. For me, equality entails leveling the authority and influence of the Bible in the modern world to the level of the *Iliad* or *Popol Vuh*. Equality means that I do not privilege the Bible at the expense of many other texts that are silenced because we devote so much time to the Bible. As an atheist biblical scholar who happens to be Latino, my primary act of altruism is to deconstruct the religionist and imperialist bibliolatry that lies at the core of my profession.

Works Cited

Avalos, Hector. 1995. *Illness and Health Care in the Ancient Near East: The Role of the Temple in Greece, Mesopotamia, and Israel*. HSM 54. Atlanta: Scholars Press.

———. 1999. *Health Care and the Rise of Christianity*. Peabody, Mass.: Hendrickson.

———. 2005. *Fighting Words: The Origins of Religious Violence*. Amherst, N.Y.: Prometheus.

———. 2007. *The End of Biblical Studies*. Amherst, N.Y.: Prometheus.

Avalos, Hector, Sarah J. Melcher, and Jeremy Schipper, eds. 2007. *This Abled Body: Rethinking Disabilities in Biblical Studies*. SemeiaSt 55. Atlanta: Society of Biblical Literature.

Brueggemann, Walter. 1997. *Theology of the Old Testament: Testimony, Dispute, Advocacy*. Minneapolis: Fortress.

Carroll R., M. Daniel. 1992. *Contexts for Amos: Prophetic Poetics in Latin American Perspective*. JSOTSup 132. Sheffield: Sheffield Academic Press.

Croatto, J. Severino. 1981. *Exodus: A Hermeneutics of Freedom*. Maryknoll, N.Y.: Orbis.

De La Torre, Miguel A., and Edwin David Aponte. 2001. *Introducing Latino/a Theologies*. Maryknoll, N.Y.: Orbis.

Dempsey, Carol J. 2000. *The Prophets: A Liberation-Critical Reading*. Minneapolis: Fortress.

Dever, William G. 2001. *What Did the Biblical Writers Know and When*

Did They Know It? What Archaeology Can Tell Us about the Reality of Ancient Israel. Grand Rapids: Eerdmans.

———. 2006. The Western Cultural Tradition Is at Risk. *Biblical Archaeology Review* 32, no. 2:26, 76.

Frick, Frank S. 1995. *Cui Bono?*—History in the Service of Political Nationalism: The Deuteronomistic History as Political Propaganda. *Semeia* 66:79–92.

Gadamer, Hans-Georg. 1989. *Truth and Method.* Translated by Joel Weinsheimer and Donald G. Marshall. 2nd rev. ed. New York: Crossroad.

García-Treto, Francisco O. 1996. The Lesson of the Gibeonites: A Proposal for Dialogic Attention as a Strategy for Reading the Bible. Pages 73–85 in *Hispanic/Latino Theology: Challenge and Promise.* Edited by Ada María Isasi-Díaz and Fernando F. Segovia. Minneapolis: Fortress.

Gutiérrez, Gustavo. 1987. *Teología de la liberación: Perspectivas.* 13th ed. Salamanca: Sígueme.

Isasi-Díaz, Ada María, and Yolanda Tarango. 1992. *Hispanic Women: Prophetic Voice in the Church.* Minneapolis: Fortress.

Levenson, Jon D. 1993. *The Hebrew Bible, the Old Testament, and Historical Criticism: Jews and Christians in Biblical Studies.* Louisville: Westminster John Knox.

Marcus, David. 1995. *From Balaam to Jonah: Anti-prophetic Satire in the Hebrew Bible.* Brown Judaic Studies 301. Atlanta: Scholars Press.

Meléndez, Guillermo. 1990. *Seeds of Promise: The Prophetic Church in Central America.* New York: Friendship.

Moore, Stephen D., and Fernando F. Segovia, eds. 2005. *Postcolonial Biblical Criticism: Interdisciplinary Intersections.* London: T&T Clark.

Morgenthau, Hans J. 1993. *Politics among Nations: The Struggle for Power and Peace.* Revised by Kenneth W. Thompson. New York: McGraw-Hill.

Segovia, Fernando F. 1992. Hispanic American Theology and the Bible. Pages 21–49 in *We Are a People! Initiatives in Hispanic American Theology.* Edited by Roberto S. Goizueta. Minneapolis: Fortress.

Stendahl, Krister. 1962. Biblical Theology, Contemporary. Pages 418–32 in vol. 1 of *The Interpreter's Dictionary of the Bible.* Edited by George A. Buttrick. 4 vols. Nashville: Abingdon.

———. 1970. Biblical Studies. Pages 23–39 in *The Study of Religion in Colleges and Universities.* Edited by Paul Ramsey and John F. Wilson. Princeton: Princeton University Press.

Tamez, Elsa. 1982. *Bible of the Oppressed*. Translated by Matthew J. O'Connell. Maryknoll, N.Y.: Orbis.

Thiel, Winfried. 2004. Evil in the Book of Kings. Pages 2–13 in *The Problem of Evil and Its Symbols in Jewish and Christian Tradition*. Edited by Henning Graf Reventlow and Yair Hoffman. JSOTSup 366. London: T&T Clark.

Wellhausen, Julius. 1983. *Prolegomena to the History of Ancient Israel*. 1883. Repr., Gloucester, Mass.: Peter Smith.

West, Cornel. 2002. *Prophesy Deliverance: An Afro-American Revolutionary Christianity*. Louisville: Westminster John Knox.

Reexamining Ethnicity:
Latina/os, Race, and the Bible

Eric D. Barreto

The run-up to the 2008 presidential election evoked a great deal of reflection in the U.S. media about the state of race relations in the country. That Barack Obama was eventually victorious suggested to many that the country had now entered a "post-race" era. Even though some problems still lingered, some reasoned that the election of America's first African American president represented a critical step forward, an epochal hinge leading inexorably toward the decimation of the specter of racism. At least, this was one perspective.

A few months prior to the November election, Jorge Ramos, a news anchor at Univision, hosted a panel of Latin American journalists on his Sunday morning political talk show to discuss how South and Central Americans were perceiving the U.S. election. Two political pundits working in both the United States and Latin America argued that race was front and center in the political contest. Though usually dismissed by American journalists as an important factor in the campaign, these political observers noted that Obama's race—especially his complex ethnic origins—was the central narrative of this political season. Living in a culture that has construed race and ethnicity differently than the United States, these journalists could name the difficulties that North American reporters faced in discussing these difficult notions.

The spoken and unspoken narratives that were weaved during and in the wake of the 2008 election reveal several basic but vital insights. Race and ethnicity continue to reside in the eye of the beholder. Race and ethnicity are constructed identities, not biologically guaranteed or genetically inherited realities. Our local and national narratives fundamentally shape our views of race and ethnicity. Also true is that our views of race and ethnicity fundamentally shape our local and national narratives.

Latina/o biblical and theological scholarship has always necessarily functioned within the bounds of a particular ethnic discourse.[1] The organizing principle of such scholarship has always placed ethnic identity squarely at the center of theological reflection, helpfully decentering the misguided notion that the rigors of scholarship required the eschewing of particularity and the appeal to the universal. Latina/o scholars, in alliance with other readers from the "margins," have helped puncture the myth of scholarly objectivity and demonstrated the persuasiveness and power of contextual theologies and readings. It was the particularity of a people and the prioritization of that perspective that produced these leaps.

However, while reflections *from* an ethnic place are increasingly common, reflections *on* our ethnic places are far less so. The very notion of a Latina/o ethnicity is itself a powerful but ambiguous category, rife with historical problematics. The heirs and agents of various colonialisms, Latina/os are living intersections of the cultural, political, imperial, racial, and ethnic forces that have shaped contemporary life. That we are both heirs and agents of these diffuse yet intermingled legacies introduces a profound complexity into our ethnic identities but also provides a privileged hermeneutical ground for biblical, theological, and ethnic reflection.

Latina/o scholarly encounters with the texts of Scripture ought to continue grappling with the constructed nature of race and ethnicity along with the pervasiveness of these notions today and in antiquity.[2] This is a vital project not just because a central component of Latina/o theological reflection may remain underscrutinized but also because Latina/o historical particularity provides a great deal of potential leverage to understand the nature and function of ethnic discourse.

---

1. By "discourse" I mean the internal logic, the organizational principles of ideas and ideology of a social structure like ethnicity; see Jones 1997, 55.

2. To be sure, the many ways in which racial and ethnic notions infuse daily life and discourse means that such efforts will always be in need of revision and refreshment. My argument in this essay is that specific theoretical attention to the nature and function of racial and ethnic discourse is a critical desideratum in Latina/o biblical scholarship. Much has already been done by a number of Latina/o theological scholars to highlight the importance of racial and ethnic identities and experiences in theological reflection and biblical exegesis. What is needed is an interrogation of how these discourses shape and sometimes misshape contemporary life and thought.

What, then, does it mean to be Latina/o biblical critic? For me, defining features of this inherently hybrid identity include: a recognition of the complexities of ethnic discourse in our cultures, our scholarship, and the Bible; an incisive critique of unexamined or underexamined notions about the fluid categories of ethnic identity; and a constructive theological imagination around ethnicity.

In this essay, I pursue these various facets of scholarship in three parts. First, I explore further the complexities, promise, and contradictions already present in Latina/o ethnic discourses. Second, I recount how Latina/o biblical scholarship has engaged these discourses. Finally, I suggest what exegetical and theoretical guidelines might reshape a Latina/o reading of both biblical as well as contemporary ethnic discourses.

Ultimately, I contend that race and ethnicity are plastic notions, amenable to shifting contexts and discursive spaces. At the very same time, ethnic discourse tends to treat racial and ethnic identities as inherent, inborn, immutable classifications (Barreto 2010, 27–59). This is the fundamental tension that defines ethnic discourse; this tension is also a central feature of Latino/a identity. Latina/o biblical scholarship should and can ably reflect on these lived realities in order to open up new interpretive possibilities and potentially transformative theological imaginations around the disputed territories of personal and communal identity.

Race, Ethnicity, and Latina/os

The particular terminology of a "Hispanic" ethnicity is a relatively recent invention, initially imposed and only later fully embraced by Latina/os themselves.[3] "Hispanic" was a demographic innovation of the U.S. Census in 1970 and an effort to encapsulate a growing number of people who were not adequately covered by the previously standard racial categories of White, Black, Native American, Asian American, and so on (Nobles 2000, 79–84). At core, the invention of the term *Hispanic* was an outgrowth of

---

3. Whether the term *Hispanic* or *Latina/o* best encapsulates those descendants of Latin Americans now living in the United States is itself controversial. "Hispanic" is still widely used in politics and the media. "Latino" has also been used more frequently recently. This gendered term, however, proves limiting, so I opt for "Latina/o." See De La Torre and Aponte 2001, 15–16; Martínez 2009, 289–94, esp. the bibliography on 294; Nanko-Fernández 2010, xvi, 34–37, who advocates "Latin@" with an accent over the @ symbol.

ethnic anxiety. When a growing number of Latina/os complicated the relatively straightforward assignments of racial identity, a new "ethnic" category—a category meant to stand alongside established American racial categories—proved requisite. On census forms, Latina/os are asked to locate themselves within constructed but long-established racial categorizations. In the end, the underlying ethnic discourse of the U.S. census assumes that Latina/os will identify themselves as "Hispanics" ethnically but as white or black racially.[4]

Such ethnic negotiations begin to reveal the generally indiscriminate or at least inconsistent ways terms like *race* and *ethnicity* are often deployed in popular, governmental, demographic, and scholarly discourses alike.[5] In the case of the census, demography treats racial and ethnic categories as distinct in the case of exactly one population: Latina/os.[6] Why is this distinction made in the case of Latina/os but not, for example, Arab Americans?[7] What differentiates "Hispanic" as an ethnicity as opposed to a race? To be sure, there are underlying sociological and demographic distinctions in play, but the underlying discourse reveals the contingent, constructed, and often fragile negotiations of difference that have characterized the complex tableau of U.S. racial and ethnic negotiations.

Race was the preferred terminology of the academy for most of modern history, fading from much of the scholarly lexicon in favor of *ethnicity* after World War II (Buell 2005, 17–18). Motivated by the disastrous conclusions of racial thinking in Germany, scholars eschewed the notion that "race" was a natural, biological, and genetic reality. In contrast, "ethnicity" purported to point to a cultural, subjective phenomenon. That is, ethnicity is an act of cultural fiction. And yet the discourses of ethnicity have not completely overtaken racial language and perhaps for good reason. Both "race" and "ethnicity" ultimately point to the same underlying phenomena of drawing upon myths of origins, homelands, physical difference, and, more comprehensively, notions of "fictive kinship" (Hall 1997) to group peoples and organize difference.

---

4. Of course, such an assumption excludes Latina/os who would identify themselves as descendants of Asians or Native Americans.
5. For a discussion of the slippery use of "race" and "ethnicity" in the study of early Christianity, see Buell 2005, 13–21; Barreto 2010, 29–31.
6. 2010 U.S. Census data is available online: http://2010.census.gov/2010census/index.php.
7. See Padgett 2010.

Therefore, I tend to use the terms interchangeably and am in agreement with Denise Kimber Buell:

> Because our interpretive models for studying the ancient past have been formulated and revised within racist cultures, we need to keep the term [*race*] active so as to be able to examine how our interpretive models encode, and thus perpetuate, particular notions about race. By using the terms race and ethnicity interchangeably I signal my view that neither term has a one-to-one counterpart in antiquity; moreover, this choice indicates that these terms cannot be neatly distinguished even in modern parlance. I also want to keep modern readers alert to the contemporary stakes of historical work. By excluding the category of race from work on classical antiquity, we risk implying that our modern legacy of racial thinking can be shut off when we examine ancient texts and that our versions of ancient history are either irrelevant or alien to the ways that we handle questions of human sameness and difference in the present. (2005, 21)

Moreover, using the terms interchangeably and in tandem suggests something about their tenuousness. That is, these terms reflect flexible, negotiable notions. Even when codified on a census form, racial and ethnic discourses are not absolute or fixed. Instead, these notions are in constant and rapid flux.

In these complex webs of ethnic discourse, we see not only the vicissitudes of U.S. American racial thinking but also the interstitial ethnic locations Latina/os call home. In the United States, the Atlantic slave trade and the incipient colonial enterprise of gradual but inexorable westward expansion required a clear, purportedly objective systemization of racial and ethnic difference. The ethnic ambiguities embodied by Latina/os evaded easy racial categorization. In one fell demographic swoop, however, a significant swath of overlapping but distinct cultures received a single sociological categorization.[8] The contours of a common Latina/o identity remain contentious but important. That is, the diversity of experiences grouped together as Hispanic or Latina/o remains incredibly diffuse. At the same time, demographic growth means that Hispanics and/or Latina/os are increasingly alluded to in political and cultural discourse.[9]

---

8. For a description of the panoply of experiences amongst Latina/os and an attempt to "forge a panethnic Latino/a identity," see Valentín 2002, 5–37.

9. Demographics and power are not concomitant. Increased attention by politicians and the media does not necessarily result in political, economic, or cultural influence.

Not only are the descendants of the ethnic hodgepodge of Latin America incredibly diverse, but the racial and ethnic discourses of Latin America differ from one another, but most strikingly from U.S. systemizations of racial and ethnic difference (Graham 1990; Wade 1997; Findlay 1999; Ferrer 1999; Sansone 2003; Stepan 1991). Whereas racial identity in the United States tends to revolve around the "one-drop rule," anxieties over miscegenation, and clear delineations between ethnic identities, Latin American ethnic discourse tends to work on complex and wide gradations of racial identity.

For example, one study of race and ethnicity in Puerto Rico has recorded at least nineteen gradations of racial identity ranging from *blanco* to *negro* (see both Duany 2002, 236–39, and Haslip-Viera 2001). Furthermore, these identities are pliable according to shifting discursive contexts. That this range of racial and ethnic identities is influenced by ideology and perception as much as phenotype is evident in demographic shifts not attributable to changes in population but revisions in self-perception. For example, the number of self-identified "whites" in Puerto Rico expanded consistently from 1899 to 1950 and once again in 2000 (Duany 2002, 236–39). These significant shifts reflected not physical changes but ideological ones. Perceptions of race and ethnicity changed, not the genetic composition of Puerto Ricans. Such flexibility in ethnic and racial identity is not unique to Puerto Rico. In nations like Cuba and Brazil as well, social processes of *blanqueamiento* or "whitening" have functioned as cultural pressure-relief valves allowing for social ascendancy (Skidmore 1993).

In other words, racial and ethnic ambiguities as well as the flexibility of boundaries around them are a commonplace in Latin American ethnic discourse. Indeed, they too are relatively common in U.S. racial and ethnic discourse, but the strategies for coping with these porous boundaries vary significantly between Latin America and the United States. Ultimately, Latina/os in the United States are cultural heirs of very different systems of racial and ethnic categorization than the prevalent categorization found in the United States. Latina/os once again find themselves living between two worlds, two rather different ways of classifying and organizing the peoples of the world.

Of course, such differences in racial and ethnic thinking are not qualitative. That is, neither the United States nor Latin American patterns of ethnic discourse are better or more accurate. Both, of course, are powerful social fictions. Both, of course, function within certain cultural logics. Both, of course, are liable to degenerate into base racisms and prejudices.

However, whether direct or indirect, exposure to these more liminal ethnic discourses does give Latina/os certain critical and theological leverage points. Living between and into these realities does grant Latina/os valuable critical ground within which to engage questions of ethnic identity and its inherently flexible boundaries. Latina/os experience a cultural reality in which ethnic and racial identities are both fictional and real, social constructions yet powerful cultural ciphers. In what ways, then, have these cultural and theological insights informed Latina/o biblical scholarship? In what ways might this scholarship more fully engage these contentious but indispensable notions?

Race, Ethnicity, and Latina/o New Testament Scholarship

A pair of scholarly exempla will highlight both the critical opportunities afforded by Latina/o biblical scholarship as well as the critical work that remains to be done. I have selected two seminal works to focus on: Virgilio Elizondo's *Galilean Journey* (see also Medina 2010, 26–35) and Justo González's *Santa Biblia* (see also Medina 2010, 14–15). To be sure, I could have turned to a number of other scholarly efforts (see bibliography in Agosto 2009, 647–56). However, as early efforts, both of these works helped establish the agenda of Latina/o biblical scholarship and as a pair represent its ecumenical scope. In both cases, notions of *mestizaje* and/or *mulatez* are the primary orienting point for reflection on ethnic identity, whether ancient or modern. In both cases, however, this central feature of Latina/o identity, biblical studies, and theology can be further developed by dealing more directly with the complexity of ethnic discourse, critiquing underdeveloped notions around race and ethnicity, and then engaging in constructive theological reflection on contexts both ancient and modern.

Virgilio Elizondo

Elizondo's *Galilean Journey: The Mexican-American Promise* signaled the advent of Latina/o biblical scholarship and has provided critical foundations for Latina/o theological reflection. Originally published in 1983, this book marked an innovative step in the development of a distinct Latina/o theology. The work was one of the first to read Scripture and engage in constructive theology through the cultural lens of Mexican American experience. Most innovative was Elizondo's appropriation of and reflection upon *mestizaje* as a crucial historical and theological locus. Juxtaposing the experience of Jesus as a Galilean Jew and that of Mexican Americans living on the geographical and cultural margins of the borderlands, Elizondo credits Mexican Americans with a unique theological privilege: "Even though the Mexican-Americans have been despised by both parent cultures, nevertheless it is they who have been culturally prepared to be, in God's grace, the liberators of and the bearers of peace to both parent groups. God has chosen them to be his historical agents of a new unity—not a new North American conquest, but truly a new creation" (102). This is the primary thesis of his work and the center around which all his theological and exegetical reflection moves.

Galilean Journey has three main parts, which themselves reflect Elizondo's underlying method. Part 1 focuses on "The Mexican-American Experience," part 2 turns to "The Gospel Matrix," and part 3 synthesizes both into a series of three principles entitled "From Margination to New Creation." Thus he moves from the contemporary to the biblical world and then brings the two together in a productive theological conversation (xvii).

Part 1 unfurls the implications of two different, but inextricable, conquests of Mexico. The first was the Spanish colonization of the Americas, which produced Mexicans; the second was the American invasion of Mexico and the creation of the border, which produced Mexican Americans. In both cases, the genesis of "a new ethnos" accompanied the oppressive dimensions of military conquest (1). Elizondo contends that once again the borderlands are giving birth to a new people today.

Elizondo's historical review begins in the momentous year 1492, during which the Crusades closed, "the first religiously inspired racial legislation was passed in Europe," and Columbus stumbled upon the American continents. These three historical movements together left a profound scar on world history (7). Born with the power of "scientific" rigor, racism gained an objective edge that lingers still today.

The other by-product of Latin American colonialism is also related to race, but its legacy is far more convoluted. *Mestizaje*, according to Elizondo, is the process by which a "new ethnos" emerges from two peoples; it is a lingering reminder of the dual conquests of Mexico as well as the promising prospect of a new people, a promise from which Elizondo will draw his most encompassing theological conclusions. Having moved "from cultural birth to maturity, … the Mexican-American people [are] not afraid of suffering and death—it has been its lot for centuries—but it is finding a new meaning in this suffering and death: that it is the passage to a new existence. The *raza* is the promise of the future being born today" (31).

The book's second main part turns to the ancient world and the geographical centers of Galilee and Jerusalem. For Elizondo, Jesus' cultural location in Galilee is not incidental to the message of the gospel; it is also not incidental to the Gospel writers. Their frequent mention of Galilee contrasts with the cultural image of Galilee as a political, intellectual, and cultural backwater. A multicultural crossroads, Galilee was a territory consistently contested by far-off political agents, and its people's lives were governed by political necessity in imperial centers that viewed the area as nothing more than a way to get from here to there. Jesus' choice to align with these powerless people is not incidental but a profound declaration of God's own allegiances. Ultimately, Jesus' response to these cultural and political realities cohered and challenged the prevailing Jewish expectations of God's intervention in history:

> The Galilean crisis marks one of the crucial moments of the continuity/transcendence that is so characteristic of the entire way of Jesus. In breaking with their *traditions*, Jesus does not destroy *tradition*, but *reaffirms* the strongest and most original element of it: there is only one living God and nothing can take the place of this God. By *breaking* with traditions that function as gods, he *reaffirms* the one God. (66)

In the "Galilean crisis," Jesus' acceptance of the rejected paradoxically prompts rejection by his own people.

From the backwater of Galilee, Elizondo and the Gospel writers bring Jesus to Jerusalem, which Elizondo labels a "symbol of established power." Reacting to their fractured history, according to Elizondo, the Jews had established a rigid religious dogma that provided their identity and purpose in life in an uncertain political situation. Elizondo details, "By the time of Jesus, tradition had been absolutized and dogmatized in such a way that it then functioned more as an imposition, as a heavy burden, and even as a curse" (68). Jerusalem represents the focal point of this exclusivistic religion: "Jerusalem can be seen as a symbol of the structural absolutism that sacralizes division, rejection of others, and even hatred and murder—all in the name of God" (70). The conflict between Jesus and Jerusalem ultimately represents the eternal conflict between spirit and establishment, freedom and rigidity, acceptance and rejection, nonviolence and unchecked power. Thus with the tearing of the temple veil faith has changed dramatically, and the ultimate standard of truth is crucified for the whole world to see.

Elizondo concludes, "The other characteristic of Jesus that comes from his intimacy with God-*Abba* is his unlimited freedom. He allowed no person, tradition, or law to stand in his way of doing good to others, of loving them to the extreme, and of thus living out his mission from the Father" (59). Jesus transcends the narrow strictures of his time by critiquing directly the religious authorities of the time, condemning their stultifying form of religiosity. Yet Jesus' critique in Elizondo's depiction resembles far more that of an objective outsider than an interested participant. The vision is revolutionary far more than reformatory. Elizondo exploits the similarities between the experiences of Jesus and Mexican Americans—thus stressing their correspondence—rarely emphasizing or even noting where their paths diverge. Construed this way, Jesus fits in where necessary; but were his cultural roots in the first century stressed without a concomitant sense of detachment and transcendence, the comparison between Galilee and the borderlands would be far more strained.

In the end, a number of critical questions can be posed in light of Elizondo's important work. First is how he grapples with the complex cultural and ethnic realities of first-century Galilee, especially in the sharp but problematic contrast Elizondo draws between Jesus and Judaism as well as between Galilean and Jerusalem religiosity. Second, instead of a negotiated sense of identity, ethnicity for Elizondo seems to be an objectively verifiable object with an existence independent of contextual construction. Thereby, it is not entirely evident whether *mestizaje* is a biological, cultural, historical, and/or theological reality. In other words, is *mestizaje* a genetic reality rooted in nature and blood? Or is it a cultural identification, a way for a culture to incorporate a troubling past? Or is it a theological reality for Elizondo, a discursive space from which to engage in theological reflection? I will return to these questions at the close of this essay.

Justo González

González's *Santa Biblia* provides a Protestant companion to Elizondo's work. His approach is focused less on the juxtaposition and analogizing of ancient and modern contexts. Instead, González opts for a thematic analysis of the overlap between biblical themes and central facets of contemporary Latina/o life. One of those critical facets is the centrality of "perspective." González argues that perspective requires viewing our reading of the Bible as a "dialogue" between the largely irretrievable ancient culture that produced the biblical texts and modern individuals and communities looking to be transformed by these same texts (1996, 13–15). Perspective is neither optional nor detachable; it is neither an exegetical burden to be shed nor a theological impediment. Instead, perspective in an ineluctable reality in which we all live but also a gift, for while it may sometimes lead to "fragmentation," the basic acknowledgment of the contextualization of *all* exegesis and *all* theology frees us from the hegemony of purported objectivity and the power that comes from being able to claim and enforce that objectivity (17–21).

González is also careful to couch his reading "through Hispanic eyes" within the panoply of Latina/o experiences. That is, he is explicit that this text provides not *the* Latina/o approach to Scripture but *an* approach. The peoples called Latina/o are too diverse, their faith too complex, to encapsulate so simply. Instead, he explains, "What we mean by 'Hispanic eyes' is the perspective of those who claim their Hispanic identity as part of their hermeneutical baggage, and who also read the Scripture within the context of a commitment to the Latino struggle to become all that God wants us and all of the world to be—in other words, the struggle for salvation/liberation" (28–29). Therefore, González isolates five motifs, themes, or hermeneutical lenses that he finds representative of such a Latina/o reading: marginality, poverty, *mestizaje* and *mulatez*, exiles and aliens, and solidarity.

Of particular interest in this study is the third chapter wherein the notions of *mestizaje* and *mulatez* are teased out.[10] This chapter not only provides a link to Elizondo's work,[11] but it also centers González's efforts on Latina/o ethnic hybridity.[12]

---

10. *Mestizaje* receives most of González's attention in his analysis, at least partly because of Elizondo's profound influence on the field, but also because *mestizaje* has tended to be the preferred terminology of ethnic hybridity in Latina/o theological scholarship. Increasingly, the terms *mestizaje* and *mulatez* are used side by side even as their differences are acknowledged. See Valentín 2002, 50–51 n. 20.

11. A debt González (78–79) acknowledges.

12. Theoretical reflections in postcolonial studies on the notion of hybridity are numerous. Increasingly, biblical scholars are drawing upon hybridity as a hermeneutical lens for reading the texts of Scripture and other ancient texts (see Charles 2009; Jervis 2004; Marshall 2008; Racine 2004; Sals 2008). For a summary and introduction to such studies, see Barreto 2010, 45–53.

González notes that the disparaging tenor of the terms *mestiza/o* and *mulatta/o* started changing in the wake of the Mexican Revolution and that "the worldwide movement promoting pride in 'negritude' played a similar role for the black and the mulatto" (77). Adding to the hybrid posture *mestiza/os* indwell, González observes that a cultural cleavage comes along with the melding of ethnic identities: "There is always a sense of belonging and yet not belonging, of being both fish and fowl, and therefore fowl to the fish, and fish to the fowl; but also able to understand the fish as no fowl can, and the fowl as no fish can" (80). Latina/os are ambassadors of an interstitial cultural place, neither here nor there, neither native nor foreigner and yet both at one and the same time.

The exegetical consequences of a life lived as *mestiza/o* or *mulatta/o* are significant, according to González. Latina/o experiences teach that ethnic purity is a mere myth, propagated by those who would most benefit by eliding their complex ethnic compositions, whose power would be most threatened by acknowledging the messy ways in which ethnic boundaries are drawn, broached, and redrawn once again. In the end, González proposes that the portrayal of Paul in Acts invites a Latina/o reading of Scripture with significant theological implications: "To me all of this is a cue that Paul can do what he does because he is a cultural *mestizo*; **and** that the entire book of Acts can be read as the progressive *mestizaje* of the church; **and** that the process and the goal of Christian mission may be interpreted as the progressive *mestizaje* of the church and the faith" (84).

For González, therefore, the church's ecclesial and missional efforts occur naturally at "borders," at those porous divisions of difference where "two realities, two worldviews, two cultures, meet and interact" (86). It is at these cultural borders where *mestiza/os* like Jesus, Paul, and the earliest Christians in Acts expose the ways in which power is invested in keeping peoples apart, whether figuratively or spatially.

González presents a powerful portrait of a Latina/o contribution to the reading of the texts of Scripture. His reading of Acts as a growing *mestizaje* is compelling, particularly for those of us striving toward a greater embrace of difference and a rejection of racism and prejudice. At the same time, Latina/o biblical scholarship ought to reassess the complexities and pitfalls of the application of such ethnic discourse to the Bible.

For example, when speaking of Paul's liminal existence in the book of Acts, González argues, "From the point of view of the good Jews in Jerusalem, Hellenistic Jews such as this Saul 'of Tarsus' were cultural *mestizos* who constantly had to prove themselves to be true, pure, Orthodox Jews. Persecuting other Hellenistic Jews who had embraced 'heterodoxy' such as Stephen was one of the ways in which these *mestizo* Jews could prove themselves to be true Jews" (82). Unfortunately, González—like Elizondo before him—falls into a problematic binary of ethnically obsessed dogmatic Jews in contrast to libertine, more ethnically conscious (*mestizo*) Christ-followers. The contrast benefits Christians, even as it denigrates ancient Jews. The contrast stresses Paul's "in-betweenness" along with the liminal experience of the earliest Christ-followers but does not address the many ways in which he and they were firmly rooted in a Jewish ethnic milieu.

A Concluding Comment

In the case of both these important scholarly efforts, racial and ethnicity identities play a central role in exegesis and theology, but in both cases these identities tend to be asserted rather than fully constructed or theorized. This is particularly true in the reconstruction of ancient Jewish religiosity and identity. To be sure, both authors helpfully complicate the notion that clear, rigid boundaries differentiate one people from another. The flexibility of ethnic identities is, of course, an important starting point for reflections on the nature and function of race and ethnicity. While a requisite development in scholarship, it yet remains an incipient step, one that requires additional reflection and the application of new theory and insight.

(Re)configuring Race and Ethnicity in
Latina/o Biblical Scholarship

What, then, might biblical interpretation shaped by the liminal and hybrid experiences of Latina/os as well as influenced by recent insights into the construction and function of ethnic identity look like going forward? What cultural and theological insights might emerge at the critical intersection of ethnic discourse and Latina/o biblical studies?

Several recent works in New Testament scholarship have already started to ask critical questions about the nature and function of ancient ethnicity as well as how modern constructions of race and ethnicity have influenced and even misshaped modern biblical scholarship (Barreto 2010, 2011; Brett 1996; Buell 2001, 453; 2005; Buell and Hodge 2004;

Cosgrove 2006; Duling 2005).[13] Similarly, recent Latina/o scholarship has broached anew questions about the theological dimensions of ethnic identity (González 2010; Guardiola-Sáenz 2002; Medina 2010; Mejido 2003; Valentín 2002). Moreover, a number of cultural, political, and social developments are drawing scholars to ask difficult questions about how we have imagined, constructed, and interpreted ethnic identity. In other words, the time is ripe for a reassessment of the function and role of ethnic and racial identities in Latina/o biblical scholarship.

As I noted earlier, defining features of the inherently hybrid identity of Latina/o biblical scholarship include a recognition of the complexities of ethnic discourse in our cultures, our scholarship, and the Bible; an incisive critique of unexamined or underexamined notions about the fluid categories of ethnic identity; and a constructive theological imagination around ethnicity. I will turn to each facet in order.

Recognizing the Complexities of Ethnic Discourse

First is the surprisingly difficult task of uncovering and helping others recognize the complexities of our racial and ethnic discourses. In many ways, racial and ethnic identities are like the air we breathe. Though breathing sustains life, it is something we largely do instinctively. In similar ways, racial and ethnic discourse organizes, structures, and sustains life as we know it. Like breathing, the construction of ethnic identities is largely reflexive. That is, we are acculturated from our earliest days into ethnic and racial systems of thought and practice. Only rarely do we take a step back to reflect on what appears utterly natural and inherent. The ease with which so many of us engage in ethnic discourse actually belies its complexity and its constructed nature. Concomitant to the sense that racial and ethnic identities are merely natural is the frequently unquestioned notion that the boundaries between ethnic peoples are rigid, unchangeable, and impermeable.

In fact, ethnic and racial identities exhibit fluid boundaries. They shift as situations demand emendation. Moreover, they are not absolute; individuals and communities alike can shift from identity to identity or even inhabit the liminal spaces between them. Finally, ethnic discourse

---

13. For two recent theological explorations of race and ethnicity, see Carter 2008; Jennings 2010. For a fuller bibliography, see Barreto 2010, 195–99.

carries with it the potential for *both* ill and good. Scholarship that has sought to extend Christian theology's expansive grasp has tended to prioritize the former in order to highlight how ethnic and racial discourse can tear people apart. This happens, of course. Yet ethnic discourse can also frame and organize the many loose ends of diverse human cultures. Ethnic experiences can and should inform our reading of biblical texts and our theology. Ethnicity is not solely an obstacle to greater harmony among us or a diversion on the road to fine scholarship. It is only when racial and ethnic discourse is injected with notions of superiority or prejudice that this discourse becomes a detriment. What Latina/o biblical scholarship can contribute is not a way around ethnic particularity but a full engagement with the complexities of race and ethnicity, so that we may be fully aware of their contingency but also their incredible power to tear us apart but also to bring us together.

Latina/o biblical scholarship has already started harvesting such fertile theological ground. What work remains to be done is a sharpening of our understanding of Latina/o and ancient ethnic discourses. For example, a wholesale reexamination of the application of the hermeneutical lenses of *mestizaje* and *mulatez* in the reading of Scripture is needed. First, Latina/o biblical scholarship ought to grapple more deeply with the constructed nature of these identities. We ought to explore further how *mestizaje* and *mulatez* are inextricable in Latina/o theological scholarship, the latter too often neglected in a culture influenced in subtle ways by dreams of *blanqueamiento*.

Moreover, what are the methodological pitfalls we face in these endeavors? In what ways are the categories of *mestizaje* and *mulatez* so tied to the modern history of colonialism in Latin America that they may prove inapplicable in the study of antiquity? I think we have to be careful at this point, for while it is true that notions like *mestizaje* and *mulatez* are predominantly modern inventions, they still provide important hermeneutical lenses for uncovering new readings of ancient texts and new angles of visions for the most important scholarly questions of our day. If, however, our reconstruction of the early church relies too much on the equation of ancient and contemporary contexts, we risk that shifts in how we understand the ancient or modern worlds will undercut our work.

Furthermore, deeper study of ethnic discourse will necessarily require engaging and theorizing various forms of identity. Races and ethnicities are not formed in isolation from other ways of categorizing peoples. Instead, identity is formed at the intersection of race, ethnicity, gender, sexuality, socioeconomics, and other facets of individual and communal identities. These various components of identity are intertwined, even mutually constitutive. When it comes to questions about *mestizaje* and *mulatez*, therefore, we ought to ask in what ways gender, sexuality, and other forms of identity shape how we perceive and perform these hybrid ethnic notions (Loya 2002).

Latina/o biblical scholars are well poised to expose these complexities by contextualizing exegetical work on the texts of Scripture in wider conversations about race and ethnicity in ways that helps demystify the largely arbitrary but indispensable and powerful boundaries we draw. These efforts are of course not new. Virgilio Elizondo and Justo González among many others conducted this very work, and we ought to advance it. What biblical texts have not been explored? What complexities in Latina/o ethnic identity have not been brought to bear on the interpretation of Scripture? What unexamined assumptions about race and ethnicity are currently foreclosing theological reflection on the Bible?

Critiquing Prevailing Notions of Ethnic Discourse

Second are incisive critiques of prevailing notions of ethnic discourse. An indispensable first step in doing so is defining the cultural phenomena at hand. When we speak of race or ethnicity, what exactly do we mean?

Previous scholarly efforts to define ethnicity rested on two seemingly mutually exclusive options. On the one hand, race was in earlier times seen to be a primordial reality. Race was a natural, biological, or genetic inheritance into which an individual was born and out of which one could simply not escape. In response, instrumentalists or circumstantialists would counter that ethnicity was a social construction, a cultural fiction with enormous power. In general, the instrumentalist position has won the day in scholarship, with the primordialist position being deemed atavistic in more recent days (Barreto 2010, 33–35; Hutchinson and Smith 1996).

However, some recent scholarship suggests a more complex situation may be at play in ethnic discourse (Gil-White 1999; Barreto 2010, 27–59). The consensus remains that ethnicity is not an objective, scientifically measurable reality. It is indeed a social construction. At the same time, however, it is increasingly evident that ethnic discourse typically trades on the primordialist posture. That is, ethnicities are flexible, porous, and negotiated, but ethnic discourse posits otherwise. Even as ethnic boundaries are broached, ethnic discourse continues to advance ways in which those boundaries remain impregnable. An active tension is at play in ethnic discourse between these modes of thinking and acting. In the end, the instrumentalist and primordialist perspectives are neither equivocal nor irreconcilable; the dispute between primordialist and instrumentalist perspectives proves unavailing.

Going forward, conceptualizations of race and ethnicity will need to discern how to hold these seeming contradictions together. Furthermore, such conceptualizations will have to discern how best to hold together the various facets and sources of ethnic identity. As individual components of ethnic identity, neither language nor culture, neither religion nor geography, neither physiognomy nor artifacts are constitutive or wholly reflective of racial and ethnic identity. Instead, these various facets of identity form a dynamic and complex matrix within which race and ethnicity are consistently in negotiation and in flux.

Examining Ethnicity, Constructing Theology

The implications of a reassessment of ethnic discourse for Latina/o biblical and theological scholarship are significant. First, the flexibility of ethnic identities and the porous boundaries that define them call for a variety of exegetical approaches. I would advocate focusing on the negotiation of fluid ethnic boundaries in the biblical texts as much as, if not more than, individual instantiations of particular ethnicities. It is in the negotiation and reconfiguration of ethnic discourse that we can see most clearly its function in the biblical texts. In isolation from the wider culture, we may be able to say something about the blackness of the Ethiopian eunuch or the varied ethnic and cultural contexts that shaped a *mestizo* Jesus or Paul. But focusing on such individual instantiations may narrow our vision too much, occluding that ethnic discourse functions necessarily both on the level of the individual and the wider community to which she belongs and is fundamentally a matter of negotiation.

Second, Latina/o biblical scholarship can contribute to a burgeoning and important reconceptualization of early Christian ethnic discourse. In an effort to spur greater diversity and inclusion of difference in the church, biblical scholars have tended to construct early Christianity as a movement that eschewed difference. Under the banner of Christ, all were made one, all were made the same. Paul's declaration in Gal 3:28, "there is no longer Jew or Greek, there is no longer slave or free, there is no longer male and female," has typically been taken to mean that union with Christ erases completely these differences. As Denise Kimber Buell has concluded,

> Most historical reconstructions published in the last twenty years depict earliest Christianity as an inclusive movement that rejected ethnic or racial specificity as a condition of religious identity. "Christianity swept racial distinctions aside," proclaims Frank Snowden, Jr., a classicist whose influential scholarship has helped to reframe the way we think about race in antiquity. Similarly, Anthony Smith, writing for anthropologists as well as historians, states that earliest Christianity "helped to … transcend existing ethnic divisions." And the feminist theologian Rosemary Radford Ruether asserts that "class, ethnicity, and gender are … specifically singled out as the divisions overcome by redemption in Christ." These are only three examples, ranging across three disciplines, but they are typical in making the rejection of the relevance of race or ethnicity a defining feature of earliest Christianity. (2001, 453)

These depictions emerge from a clearly positive desire to see the end of the ethnic and racial strife that pervades our world and our shared histories. However, by denying the continued importance of racial and ethnic differences among the earliest Christians, such reconstructions advocate an inaccurate portrayal with significant impact today. In our hope to make racism a relic of the past, we may strive too quickly and move too easily into a mode of forgetfulness or denial. Unfortunately, when we are all made the same, too often those in power get to dictate the rules of unity. Homogeneity is imagined under the terms of the majority. Unity then consists of becoming more like the powerful and numerous rather than an equitable negotiation in the midst of great diversity. By denying the reality of difference, we may end up only exacerbating the problem of prejudice. By denying that the earliest Christians and Scripture embraced difference in deep and powerful ways, we tell incorrectly the story of faith.

Most pernicious is the tendency to construct a false binary between a nationalistic, ethnocentric, law-obsessed Judaism on one side, and an open, inclusive, grace-filled Christianity on the other. In these constructions, ethnicity, ideology, and doctrine are intertwined. Inseparable from notions of peoplehood is orthodoxy. This false pairing only works if Christianity is imagined as a faith that evades difference. The persuasive power of this grand narrative is evident in that it is present in all corners of biblical scholarship, in Christian proclamation, and in popular reconstructions of the earliest churches. Latina/o biblical scholarship can bring to our efforts a knowledge that all peoples engage in ethnic discourse, that every identity is rooted in wider cultures and negotiated in the midst of conflict, and that ethnic identity is not an obstacle to Christian theology and God's aims of liberation but inherent to the work of God through God's diverse people. The New Testament does not project a world in which God effaces our differences but a world in which God invites all God's people to live into the complexities, promises, and perils of our differences.

Works Cited

Agosto, Efrain. 2009. Hermeneutics. Pages 647–56 in *Hispanic American Religious Cultures*. Edited by Miguel A. De La Torre. Santa Barbara: ABC-CLIO.

Barreto, Eric D. 2010. *Ethnic Negotiations: The Function of Race and Ethnicity in Acts 16*. WUNT 2/294. Tübingen: Mohr Siebeck.

———. 2011. Negotiating Difference: Theology and Ethnicity in the Acts of the Apostles. *WW* 31:129–37.

Brett, Mark G., ed. 1996. *Ethnicity and the Bible*. Biblical Interpretation Series 19. New York: Brill.

Buell, Denise Kimber. 2001. Rethinking the Relevance of Race for Early Christian Self- Definition. *HTR* 94:449–76.

———. 2005. *Why This New Race? Ethnic Reasoning in Early Christianity*. New York: Columbia University Press.

Buell, Denise Kimber, and Caroline Johnson Hodge. 2004. The Politics of Interpretation: The Rhetoric of Race and Ethnicity in Paul. *JBL* 123:235–51.

Carter, Kameron J. 2008. *Race: A Theological Account*. Oxford: Oxford University Press.

Charles, Ronald. 2009. Hybridity and the *Letter of Aristeas*. *JSJ* 40:242–59.

Cosgrove, Charles H. 2006. Did Paul Value Ethnicity? *CBQ* 68:268–90.

De La Torre, Miguel A., and Edwin David Aponte, eds. 2001. *Introducing Latino/a Theologies*. Maryknoll, N.Y.: Orbis.

Duany, Jorge. 2002. *The Puerto Rican Nation on the Move: Identities on the Island and in the United States*. Chapel Hill: University of North Carolina Press.

Duling, Dennis C. 2005. Ethnicity, Ethnocentrism, and the Matthean Ethos. *BTB* 35:125–43.

Elizondo, Virgilio. 2002. *Galilean Journey: The Mexican-American Promise*. Maryknoll, N.Y.: Orbis.

Ferrer, Ada. 1999. *Insurgent Cuba: Race, Nation, and Revolution, 1868–1898*. Chapel Hill: University of North Carolina Press.

Findlay, Eileen. 1999. *Imposing Decency: The Politics of Sexuality and Race in Puerto Rico*. Durham, N.C.: Duke University Press.

Gil-White, Francisco J. 1999. How Thick Is Blood? The Plot Thickens … : If Ethnic Actors Are Primordialists, What Remains of the Circumstantialist/Primordialist Controversy? *Ethnic and Racial Studies* 22:789–820.

González, Justo L. 1996. *Santa Biblia: The Bible through Hispanic Eyes*. Nashville: Abingdon.

González, Michelle A. 2010. Who We Are: A Latino/a Constructive Anthropology. Pages 64–84 in *In Our Own Voices: Latino/a Renditions of Theology*. Edited by Benjamín Valentín. Maryknoll, N.Y.: Orbis.

Graham, Richard, ed. 1990. *The Idea of Race in Latin America, 1870–1940*. Austin: University of Texas Press.

Guardiola-Sáenz, Leticia A. 2002. Reading from Ourselves: Identity and Hermeneutics among Mexican-American Feminists. Pages 80–97 in *A Reader in Latina Feminist Theology: Religion and Justice*. Edited by María Pilar Aquino, Daisy L. Machado, and Jeanette Rodríguez. Austin: University of Texas Press.

Hall, Jonathan. 1997. *Ethnic Identity in Greek Antiquity*. Cambridge: University of Cambridge Press.

Haslip-Viera, Gabriel, ed. 2001. *Taíno Revival: Critical Perspectives on Puerto Rican Identity and Cultural Politics*. Princeton: Wiener.

Hutchinson, John, and Anthony D. Smith. 1996. Introduction. Pages 3–14 in *Ethnicity*. Edited by John Hutchinson and Anthony D. Smith. Oxford: Oxford University Press.

Jennings, Willie James. 2010. *The Christian Imagination: Theology and the Origins of Race*. New Haven: Yale University Press.

Jervis, Ann L. 2004. Reading Romans 7 in Conversation with Post-colonial Theory: Paul's Struggle towards a Christian Identity of Hybridity. *Theoforum* 35:173–93.

Jones, Siân. 1997. *The Archaeology of Ethnicity: Constructing Identities in the Past and the Present*. London: Routledge.

Loya, Gloria Inés. 2002. Pathways to a *Mestiza* Feminist Theology. Pages 217–40 in *A Reader in Latina Feminist Theology: Religion and Justice*. Edited by María Pilar Aquino, Daisy L. Machado, and Jeanette Rodríguez. Austin: University of Texas Press.

Marshall, John W. 2008. Hybridity and Reading Romans 13. *JSNT* 31:157–78.
Martínez, Juan Francisco. 2009. Identity (Latino/a vs. Hispanic). Pages 289–94 in *Hispanic American Religious Cultures*. Edited by Miguel A. De La Torre. Santa Barbara: ABC-CLIO.
Medina, Néstor. 2010. *Mestizaje: (Re)mapping Race, Culture, and Faith in Latina/o Catholicism*. Maryknoll, N.Y.: Orbis.
Mejido, Manuel J. 2003. The Fundamental Problematic of U.S. Hispanic Theology. Pages 163–78 in *New Horizons in Hispanic/Latino(a) Theology*. Edited by Benjamín Valentín. Cleveland: Pilgrim.
Nanko-Fernández, Carmen.2010. *Theologizing en Espanglish: Context, Community, and Ministry*. Maryknoll, N.Y.: Orbis.
Nobles, Melissa. 2000. *Shades of Citizenship: Race and the Census in Modern Politics*. Stanford: Stanford University Press.
Padgett, Tim. 2010. Still Black or White: Why the Census Misreads Hispanics. *Time*. March 29. Online: http://www.time.com/time/nation/article/0,8599,1975883,00.html.
Racine, Jean-François. 2004. L'hybridité des personnages: Une stratégie d'inclusion des gentils dans les Actes des Apôtres. Pages 599–66 in *Analyse narrative et bible: Deuxième Colloque international du RRENAB, Louvain-la-Neuve, avril 2004*. Edited by Camille Focant and André Wénin. Bibliotheca ephemeridum theologicarum lovaniensium 191. Leuven: Leuven University Press.
Sals, Ulrike. 2008. The Hybrid Story of Balaam (Numbers 22–24): Theology for the Diaspora in the Torah. *BibInt* 16:315–35.
Sansone, Livio. 2003. *Blackness without Ethnicity: Constructing Race in Brazil*. New York: Palgrave Macmillan.
Skidmore, Thomas E. 1993. *Black into White: Race and Nationality in Brazilian Thought*. Durham, N.C.: Duke University Press.
Stepan, Nancy Leys. 1991. *"The Hour of Eugenics": Race, Gender, and Nation in Latin America*. Ithaca, N.Y.: Cornell University Press.
Valentín, Benjamín. 2002. *Mapping Public Theology: Beyond Culture, Identity, and Difference*. Harrisburg, Pa.: Trinity Press International.
Wade, Peter. 1997. *Race and Ethnicity in Latin America*. Chicago: Pluto.

Position Reversal and Hope for the Oppressed

Aída Besançon Spencer

Not until I kept teaching the Gospel of Luke in light of its overall purpose did I notice to what extent Mary's Magnificat was similar to Jesus' own call and primary message. What I discovered is that Mary, as his mother, affected Jesus' message by reinforcing God's concern for the oppressed. Why is this significant?

Two reasons come readily to mind. The first has to do with certain not-always-stated beliefs that women do not affect the world of thought. For example, Thomas De Quincey writes: "Woman, sister, there are some things which you do not execute as well as your brother, man; no, nor ever will. Pardon me if I doubt whether you will ever produce a great poet from your chairs, or a Mozart, or a Phidias, or a Michael Angelo, or a great philosopher, or a great scholar" (1938, 151). De Quincey, like others, presupposes that women have lesser intellects. Mary's message, however, was "magnificent." The second is that this message has particular significance to the Latin American community in the United States today. Traditionally, Spanish-speaking Roman Catholics have tended to elevate Mary, while Protestants have tended to avoid her. In the United States, although the Spanish community is slowly growing, it is still a minority community with resulting difficulties. Hispanics are often ignored in practice, having a lower standard of living and provided with a lesser education. In the Latino Christian community, sometimes women are limited in the opportunities they are encouraged to seek. Thus Mary's message about the downtrodden is particularly relevant to any who are or feel oppressed.

In what follows I should like to approach the Magnificat as a message of Mary, the mother of Jesus, about the liberation of the oppressed. I shall begin with an overview of the history of interpretation of this text; continue with an analysis of its message of liberation, focusing on the representation of God as the God of the humble as well as on the theme of reversal of positions brought about by Jesus; go on to examine the theme of reversal in the Old Testament; and conclude with a word about the relevance of the Magnificat for the Latino/a community in general and Latinas in particular.

Survey of Interpretation

How has Luke 1:46–55 been understood? While the beauty of the Magnificat has been celebrated in much song, scholars have often persisted in divesting Mary of her authorship. Many interpreters see Luke as the composer or the adapter of the Magnificat (Brown 1977, 347). Other interpreters have chosen to see the original text as reading "Elizabeth" rather than "Mary," because a few less authoritative Latin manuscripts read "Elizabeth" (Creed 1942, 22, 307–8; Marshall 1978, 77–78). Still other scholars assume that the early church community composed the Magnificat, because, as I. Howard Marshall explains, "The story could certainly be detached from the narrative about John without loss" (1978, 77). Some scholars have particularly favored the interpretation that the Magnificat was composed by Jews or Jewish Christians. William Manson, for example, suggests that either the psalm was a purely Christian creation or it came from Jewish messianic psalms (1930, 12). Raymond Brown has proposed that some Jewish Christian "poor ones" (*Anawim*), such as the later Jewish Christian community at Jerusalem, composed the psalm (1977, 350–55). About Mary as the author, Brown declares: "It is obviously unlikely that such finished poetry could have been composed on the spot by ordinary people, and today there would be no serious scholarly support for such a naïve hypothesis" (346). Yet what Brown dismisses so cavalierly is exactly what I believe and I consider to be the best scholarly hypothesis.

Mary, to whom this song of praise is attributed, was a devout woman steeped in the Old Testament and inspired by God. When ancient women did write, they often wrote poetry (Goodwater 1975, 35–52). Although Mary does not refer to Jesus as the Messiah or to events in the life of Jesus, nevertheless her song is very much "Christian" in the sense that it underlies Christ's proclamation throughout his life (Juel 1983, 21; see Marshall 1978, 79; Zorrilla 1986, 223). J. Gresham Machen, in his classic book *The Virgin Birth of Christ*, forcefully argues against Adolf von Harnack for the genuine Palestinian character of the song and supports Mary as the composer. He believes the hymn was either produced spontaneously or during the three-month visit with Elizabeth. Because of his high view of Scripture, he is able to affirm the abilities of a woman: "Why may not the mother of Jesus have been endowed with the gift of simple poetry, so that, under the immediate impression of her wonderful experience, she may have molded her store of Scripture imagery, made part of her life from childhood, into this beautiful hymn of praise? Why must the mother of Jesus of Nazareth have been a nonentity?" (1930, 95). Alvin Padilla agrees: "María, residente de una de las regiones más pobres y más oprimidas de sus días, seguramente ha experimentado en su propia vida el dolor de la opresión y la dependencia total que el pobre expresa a su Dios" (2007, 14–15).

Mary's song of praise in Luke 1:46–55 has an emphasis on the liberation of the oppressed, which we can also find throughout Jesus' ministry. This is evident in such themes as the following: (1) God as Savior; (2) the favorable position of the humble, especially the slave (in imagery), the hungry, and the poor; (3) the irony of life because God reverses positions; and (4) joy as the result.

God as Savior of the Humble

Luke 1:46–48a reads, "And Mary said: 'My soul magnifies the Lord, and my spirit is extremely joyful over God my Savior, since (he) looked at the lowly state of his slave.'"[1] God as Savior corresponds with Mary as slave. God is the one who liberates those who are oppressed or needy, in other words, a "slave" (slave vs. freeborn). The concept of slave later becomes a paradigm for all of Jesus' ministry. Today, this is a commonplace idea, but in practice it contrasts with the leader as a "person or man with a mission," set apart, therefore, receiving special treatment. Jesus says in Matt 20:28 (Mark 10:45): "The Son of Humanity came *not* to be served but to serve." What kind of service? A service to the point of full sacrifice of one's life: "and to give his life a *ransom* for many." "Ransom" (*lytron*) is the "price of release," the sum paid for manumission of a slave.

Jesus is the slave who frees other slaves, and Jesus commands us as well to follow his example: "You know that the rulers of the Gentiles lord it over them, and their great ones are tyrants over them. It will not be so among you; but whoever wishes to be great among you must be your servant, and whoever wishes to be first among you must be your slave" (Matt 20:25–27 NRSV; Luke 22:25). "The ones ruling the Gentiles" subdue

---

1. All translations are mine unless otherwise indicated.

or exercise complete dominion over (*katakyrieuō*) and "rule over, wield power" (*katexausiazō*). In contrast, the ones leading Jesus' disciples are the ones who serve, as Jesus said of himself: "I am in your midst as the one serving" (Luke 22:27). Jesus compares the person who sits at table with the one who serves: the slave, the servant, the woman.

God's irony is that God elevates the one serving to being the one with authority (Luke 22:27–30). John 12:24–26 says: "Very truly, I tell you, unless a grain of wheat falls into the earth and dies, it remains just a single grain; but if it dies, it bears much fruit. Those who love their life lose it, and those who hate their life in this world will keep it for eternal life. Whoever serves me must follow me, and where I am, there will my servant be also. Whoever serves me, the Father will honor" (NRSV). The person who wants to serve Jesus must follow him to death to receive honor from the Father. In John 13 the concept of ministry as the service of a slave is fleshed out, when Jesus washes the feet of the disciples as a slave would. Jesus uses his authority to serve others. Therefore, he concludes, you yourselves ought to wash another's feet. Even though Jesus was freeborn, "slavery" was an important image for Jesus' self-understanding.

Jesus also uses the same word family (*tapeinōsis*, "lowly") that Mary used to describe herself to describe himself: "Take my yoke upon you and learn from me, since I am gentle and *lowly* in heart, and you will find rest for your souls" (Matt 11:29). *Tapeinōsis* may literally refer to not rising far from the ground, to being low of place or of stature or size, and to persons—humbled, abased in power, pride, and so forth. Paul describes Christ with these same concepts in 2 Corinthians but himself with *tapeinos*. Thus 2 Cor 10:1 says: "I myself, Paul, exhort you through the gentleness [*praus*] and meekness [*epieikeia*] of Christ, who, on the one hand, in person was humble [*tapeinos*] among you, but, on the other hand, being absent, was bold among you"; while 2 Cor 11:7 states, "Did I commit a sin making myself *lowly* in order that you might be exalted?" Jesus taught: those who enter heaven's reign must also *humble* themselves as do children (Matt 18:4). Paul too exhorts Christians to be "lowly" because Christ is "lowly" (Phil 2:3–8). As opposed to selfishness and conceit, in humility they are to count others better than themselves. This concept is illustrated by Jesus, who "took the form of a slave," in other words, became human and "*humbled* himself, becoming obedient to death" (2:7–8). *Tapeinōsis* is also used in Isa 53:7–8 (LXX) to describe the Messiah: "He was oppressed, and he was afflicted, yet he opened not his mouth; he was led as a sheep to the slaughter, and, as a lamb before the shearer is dumb, so he opens not his mouth. In his *humiliation* his judgment was taken away ... because of the iniquities of my people he was led to death." (Acts 8:33 quotes Isa 53:7 in the passage the Ethiopian officer was reading.)

Although *tapeinōsis* occurs only occasionally, it is a key concept for Mary and Jesus, which Paul picks up and develops. *Tapeinōsis* is a significant part of Paul's central message to both the Corinthians and the Philippians. At Corinth Paul was criticized for his "lowly" leadership style, and he defends it, while the Philippians lacked unity because they lacked humility (or a proper sense of perspective). Paul describes his own ministry and trials in Acts 20:19 as "lowly." He includes "lowliness" as the way we should treat one another in Eph 4:2 and Col 3:12. In Colossians "lowliness" is misunderstood as severity to body and legalism (2:18, 23).

God Reverses Positions, Resulting in Joy

Mary announces in Luke 1:48b, 51–54a, "The Mighty One has made me great. ... He has shown strength in his arm, he scattered arrogant ones in thought of their hearts; he took down rulers from thrones, and he exalted lowly ones, hungry ones he filled with good things, and rich ones he sent away empty. He has come to the aid of Israel his child." Like Mary, Zechariah extols God's mercy and promises to ancestors, especially Abraham (1:72–78). However, Mary in her joy highlights God's liberation of the oppressed and "the irony of life" or reversibility of positions (or position reversal). In Luke 4:18–19, when Jesus reads from Isa 61:1–2 in his home synagogue at Nazareth and says, "Today this Scripture among you has been fulfilled" (4:21), he declares the central message of his ministry (which Luke is careful to record) and harks back to his mother Mary's message.

To whom is Jesus' message directed? What does he promise them? "The Spirit of the Lord is upon me because he has anointed me to preach good news to the poor, he has sent me to preach to the captives release and to the blind recovery of sight, to send the ones having been oppressed liberty, to preach an acceptable year of the Lord" (Luke 4:18–19). "Poor," "captives," and "blind," all parallel concrete terms, are summarized by the abstract term, "the ones who have been oppressed." They are promised "release," "recovery of sight," and "liberty." Jesus, like Mary, shows that God is concerned for the "lowly," the humble in spirit, and the hungry or poor. In a general sense, this message is reiterated in 6:20 ("Blessed are the poor, for yours is God's reign") and in 18:24–29, where he teaches that it is necessary to leave all for the sake of God's reign.

More specifically, Mary accentuates the irony of life and position reversal. The haughty and powerful and rich are scattered and taken down and sent away empty, while the lowly and hungry are exalted and filled. This is not verbal irony (words with an opposite meaning), but a type of dramatic irony wherein life is perceived in terms of incongruities that occur between appearance and reality. In this case, those who appear to be on top will move to the bottom, and those who appear to be on the bottom will come out on top. Elisabeth Schüssler Fiorenza calls this "eschatological reversal" (1983, 122); David Scholer, "social reversal" (1986, 218); Pedrito Maynard-Reid, "reversal of status" (1987, 38); and Allen Verhey, the "great reversal" (1984, 94). Mary's contrast between powerful and powerless, rich and poor, Jesus accentuates in Luke 4:18 (the poor, captives, and blind are oppressed and then liberated). A similar summary was given to John: "The blind receive sight, lame walk, lepers are cleansed, and deaf hear, dead are raised, poor have good news preached to them" (Luke 7:22).

The same theme of reversal of positions may be found in the Sermon on the Plain: "Blessed are the poor, for yours is the reign of God. Blessed are the ones hungering now, for you shall be satisfied. Blessed are the ones weeping now, for you shall laugh. ... But woe to you, the ones who are rich, for you have received your consolation. Woe to you, who are full now, for you shall hunger. Woe to you, the ones laughing now, for you shall mourn and weep" (Luke 6:20–21, 24–25 RSV). Also, upon the return of the seventy-two disciples, it is stated, "In that hour Jesus was extremely joyful [*angaliaō*, the same word Mary used in 1:47] in the Holy Spirit and said: 'I publicly praise you, Father, Lord of the heaven and the earth, that you have hidden these things from wise and intelligent people, and have revealed them to babies; yes, Father, that such a choice was pleasing to you'" (Luke 10:21). Jesus, like Mary his mother, is extremely joyful when the powerless—"the babies"—receive God's salvation (similar to the low estate of a slave). The lowly are like those without the world's idea of wisdom and intelligence. Knowledge of God's concern for the meek (and participation in God's work) results in great joy and public praise.

Also, Jesus teaches, "whenever you give a feast, invite the poor, maimed, lame, blind" (14:13). That same position reversal is found in Matt 23:12 in regard to the Pharisees who act to be seen by others versus the servant who acts to serve: "Whoever exalts himself will be humbled, and whoever humbles himself will be exalted [*tapenoō*]." That same teaching is found in other parables: Luke 14:11 (those who seek and do not seek a place of honor) and Luke 18:14 (tax collector and Pharisee reverse positions). The rich ungenerous end up in torment, while poor Lazarus ends up blessed (Luke 16:19–25). Jesus appropriated God's concern for the oppressed to the extent of identifying so totally with the oppressed that he became oppressed himself. He knows that he himself is to suffer and has no place to call home (Luke 9:51, 58).[2]

If Mary influenced Jesus, did she also affect his brothers? The terms *tapeinōsis* and *tapeinos* are also cited and highlighted by James, as is position reversal and the emphasis on the poor versus the rich: "Let the lowly brother boast in his exaltation, but the rich in his humiliation, because, like a flower of grass, he will pass away" (Jas 1:9–10). James emphasizes not showing partiality. He is against the rich being given a seat and special treatment, while the poor are simply told to stand: "Has not God chosen the poor in the world to be rich in faith and heirs of the kingdom?" (2:1–5), "God opposes the proud, but gives grace to the humble [*tapeinos*]," and "Humble yourselves before the Lord and he will exalt you" (4:6, 10). The same idea is in 1 Pet 5:5–6: "Toward one another clothe yourselves with humility since God opposes the proud, but gives grace to the humble. Therefore, humble yourselves under the mighty hand of God, that he may exalt you in due time."

In summary, the theme of God's concern for the oppressed—the poor, the humble, the enslaved, and the powerless—and action to reverse their position with the rich, haughty, and powerful are accentuated by Mary, as well by Jesus and James. They also became a central aspect of Paul's leadership style and exhortation to the church. Mary's Magnificat highlights both specific words and concepts central to Jesus' message: (1) God is a Savior who liberates the slaves, those who are not free. The concept of slave became a paradigm in Jesus' ministry. (2) Lowliness, *tapeinōsis*, is used by both Mary and Jesus to describe themselves. And (3) Mary and Jesus have extreme joy when they perceive that God does liberate the poor, captive, blind, and humble in spirit and that God will reverse their positions with

---

2. I do not think Mary fully understood the crucifixion, since she probably did not comprehend that Jesus was God until after the resurrection. Although Mary certainly was present at Jesus' crucifixion, we are told that Jesus' brothers and sisters did not believe in Jesus (John 7:5) and that Jesus' family went to seize him because people said he was "beside himself" (Mark 3:21), Jesus also told Mary, "My hour has not yet come" (John 2:4).

the rich and proud. Mary, as a thinking believer and Jesus' human parent, influenced him for good.³

Biblical Background for Reversal of Positions

Does this mean that Jesus' own message was not direct revelation? No, because even as Elizabeth and Zechariah were filled with the Holy Spirit (Luke 1:41, 67), so too we can conclude that Mary's wisdom came from God: she was "filled by the Holy Spirit" (Luke 1:35). In addition, the angel's conversation with her suggests some elements of position reversal. She, a simple woman, a "handmaiden," was now a "favored one," and her son would be "great," "Son of the Most High." This message is reinforced by Elizabeth (Luke 1:28–33, 35, 42–43).

Moreover, the Old Testament records similar ideas. Mary's message of reversal of positions is close to the prayer of her matriarch Hannah in 1 Sam 2:1–8 (vv. 1–5 my trans.; vv. 6–8 NRSV):

> ¹ My heart rejoices in the Lord,
> my horn becomes exalted in the Lord,
> my mouth is wide open to my enemies
> because I am glad in your salvation.
> ² None is holy as the Lord
> because there is none besides you
> as there is no Rock as our God.
> ³ Don't increase talking very haughtily
> nor [don't let] arrogance go forth from your mouth,
> because a God of wisdom is the Lord
> and by him actions are weighed.
> ⁴ The bows of the mighty are broken,
> and they that stumbled are girded with strength.
> ⁵ They that were full have hired themselves for bread;
> and they that were hungry have ceased;
> while the barren hath borne seven,
> she that had many children hath languished.
> ⁶ The Lord kills and brings to life;
> he brings down to Sheol and raises up.
> ⁷ The Lord makes poor and makes rich;
> he brings low, he also exalts.

---

3. Luke describes Mary with the word *symballō*—"to think about, consider; to bring together in one's mind, confer with oneself" (2:19).

⁸ He raises up the poor from the dust;
he lifts the needy from the ash heap,
to make them sit with princes
and inherit a seat of honor.
For the pillars of the earth are the Lord's,
and on them he has set the world.

Here again the position of the strong is reversed with the weak, while the poor and hungry are reversed with the rich. (Hannah, of course, has a different context from Mary, since she is oppressed by the second wife, Peninnah, because Hannah had no children; 1 Sam 1:4–7.)

Position reversal between God's people, the Jews, and their Persian oppressors is dramatically illustrated by Esther and Mordecai. Esther is affirmed in her request before King Ahasuerus, and Mordecai is honored with the honor that Haman had desired, while Haman is first shamed and eventually killed on the gallows that he had prepared for Mordecai (Esth 5–7). Israel is promised that it "will take captive those who were their captors, and rule over those who oppressed them" (Isa 14:2 NRSV). The psalmist repeats, "It is God who executes judgment, putting down one and lifting up another" (Ps 75:7 NRSV), and "Great is our Lord, and abundant in power; his understanding is beyond measure. The Lord lifts up the downtrodden; he casts the wicked to the ground" (Ps 147:5–6). Youth are warned not to "envy the violent" because "The Lord's curse is on the house of the wicked, but he blesses the home of the righteous. He mocks proud mockers but shows favor to the humble and oppressed. The wise inherit honor, but fools get only shame" (Prov 3:33–35 TNIV). This position reversal is also found in Ezekiel to describe a time of complete and final punishment: "Remove the turban, take off the crown; things shall not remain as they are. Exalt that which is low, abase that which is high" (Ezek 21:26 NRSV).[4] The ability to reverse people's position is a quality of a powerful and great God: "All the trees of the field shall know that I am the Lord. I bring low the high tree, I make high the low tree; I dry up the green tree and make the dry tree flourish" (Ezek 17:24). Similar to the situation of Ezekiel, the advent of Jesus is the commencement of a time when life's traditional values are reversed.

---

4. See also Eccl 10:14; Psalms of Solomon 2:31; 3:11–12; 4:23–24; 9:5; 12:6; 13:11; 15:13; 16:5.

Ultimately, the manner in which God chose a poor, humble woman as the means for God's incarnation is a synecdoche of Jesus' ministry, which was presaged in Isaiah 52–53. The Lord's servant would be "exalted and lifted up," and "very high," having "a portion with the great," only after being "marred" in appearance, without "form or majesty" to impress: "He was despised and rejected by others; a man of suffering and acquainted with infirmity; and as one from whom others hide their faces he was despised, and we held him of no account" (53:3). "By a perversion of justice he was taken away. Who could have imagined his future?" (53:8). Jesus himself lives out the dramatic irony of position reversal. The great God is born as a child in a poor home, and, after suffering in behalf of others, he is again exalted: "While being in (the) form of God, he did not regard equality with God as something to be retained, but he emptied himself, taking (the) form of a slave ... therefore, God also highly exalted him and gave him the name, the one above every name" (Phil 2:6–7, 9).

Conclusion

A foundational theology in the New Testament is revealed by God to a woman, and Jesus builds his self-understanding as a servant in agreement with this theology because Mary's wisdom is one with Old Testament roots. Luke's whole Gospel accentuates this theme, because in it Luke challenges Theophilus to follow God, who has come in the person of Jesus, empowered by the Spirit, and with authority to liberate all oppressed people. Luke's central message is also proclaimed by Mary. Luke was careful to record her words of praise. Therefore, in the church, seminary, institutions, and scholarly societies, we need to encourage participation by women and to listen to the thoughts and wisdom of devout women. At Jesus' inaugural sermon, the people were baffled by Jesus' wisdom and asked: Is not this Joseph's son? They should also have exclaimed: Here certainly is Mary's son! Her song of praise was fulfilled in the child the Lord gave her.

The role of Mary presents a difficult problem for ministry in Latin America. Do we emphasize her so much that she becomes our intercessor, or do we ignore her so as not to confuse anyone? As we consider the necessity for models of shared ministry, God's action toward Mary and her response remind us of our great loss if we ignore her—in model and in teaching calling us to pay attention to those who look least significant. They may very well be God's channels of work and the cornerstones of God's work and models for all of us.

Mary in her Magnificat, and Jesus and Paul and James and others in the Old and New Testaments, teach that God is concerned for the oppressed. Many Hispanics are oppressed in the United States. Hispanic women, in particular, may be oppressed. Like Mary, at times, Hispanics are not recognized for what they accomplish. Hispanics can both affirm a Christian message that relies on an authoritative and reliable Bible, while also affirming a Christian message that has social ramifications for people in need. God is a liberator of the oppressed or needy, a redeemer of the enslaved. God elevates the servant to the master. The message of social reversal that relies on a powerful Savior can offer hope to the Christian Spanish community that feels limited and humbled. Alvin Padilla phrases it this way: "Lo que Dios ha hecho con María es como el Poderoso trata a todos los le temen" (2007, 14). Position reversal is also a terrifying message, an act of God's dramatic reversals. Thus all of us humbly and prayerfully need to work on remaining in God's grace. At the same time, Jesus models the need to serve and free others as one has been served and freed by God. Jesus' teachings on leadership should affect the Latino leadership style. The joy of pleasing a merciful but powerful God will be the result.

The Latino/a community has many positive models. As we too seek to study the Bible, we need to keep in mind the importance of a biblical hermeneutic that is fleshed out in life. Archbishop Oscar Romero reflected much of position reversal in his own life and teachings. As a man who need not have suffered, he took Luke 4:18 as his motto: "to bring good news to the poor, to heal the contrite of heart." He discovered that defending the poor in El Salvador resulted in serious conflict with the powerful: "Sin killed the Son of God, and sin is what goes on killing the children of God" (1985, 183). Yet he could pray that he was "happy and confident" that in Jesus was his life and his death, and he could place his trust in Jesus and not be disappointed, and expected others, after his death, to carry on the work of the church (1993, 11). Now Archbishop Romero is honored by many for his perseverance in behalf of others.

Works Cited

Brown, Raymond E. 1977. *The Birth of the Messiah: A Commentary on the Infancy Narratives in Matthew and Luke.* Garden City, N.Y.: Doubleday.

Creed, John Martin. 1942. *The Gospel According to St. Luke.* London: Macmillan.

De Quincey, Thomas. 1938. Joan of Arc. Pages 129–57 in *Selected Nineteenth Century Essays*. Edited by Clyde Kenneth Hyder and John Erskine Hankins. New York: Crofts.

Goodwater, Leanna. 1975. *Women in Antiquity: An Annotated Bibliography*. Metuchen, N.J.: Scarecrow.

Juel, Donald. 1983. *Luke-Acts: The Promise of History*. Atlanta: John Knox.

Machen, J. Gresham. 1930. *The Virgin Birth of Christ*. Grand Rapids: Baker.

Manson, William. 1930. *The Gospel of Luke*. Moffatt New Testament Commentary. London: Hodder & Stoughton.

Marshall, I. Howard. 1978. *The Gospel of Luke: A Commentary on the Greek Text*. NIGTC. Grand Rapids: Eerdmans.

Maynard-Reid, Pedrito U. 1987. *Poverty and Wealth in James*. Maryknoll, N.Y.: Orbis.

Padilla, Alvin. 2007. *Lucas*. Conozca su Biblia. Minneapolis: Augsburg Fortress.

Romero, Archbishop Oscar. 1985. *Voice of the Voiceless: The Four Pastoral Letters and Other Statements*. Translated by Michael J. Walsh. Maryknoll, N.Y.: Orbis.

———. 1993. *A Shepherd's Diary*. Translated by Irene B. Hodgson. Cincinnati: St. Anthony Messenger.

Scholer, David M. 1986. The Magnificat (Luke 1:46–55): Reflections on Its Hermeneutical History. Pages 210–19 in *Conflict and Context: Hermeneutics in the Americas*. Edited by Mark Lau Branson and C. René Padilla. Grand Rapids: Eerdmans.

Schüssler Fiorenza, Elisabeth. 1983. *In Memory of Her: A Feminist Theological Reconstruction of Christian Origins*. New York: Crossroad.

Spencer, Aida Besançon Spencer. 2014. From Artemis to Mary: Misplaced Veneration versus True Worship of Jesus in the Latino/a Context. Pages 123–40 in *Jesus without Borders: Christology in Global Context*. Edited by Gene Green and K. K. Yao. Grand Rapids: Eerdmans.

Verhey, Allen. 1984. *The Great Reversal: Ethics and the New Testament*. Grand Rapids: Eerdmans.

Zorrilla, Hugo C. 1986. The Magnificat: Song of Justice. Pages 220–37 in *Conflict and Context: Hermeneutics in the Americas*. Edited by Mark Lau Branson and C. René Padilla. Grand Rapids: Eerdmans.

What Does It Mean to Be a Latino Biblical Critic? A Brief Essay*

Alejandro F. Botta

In this essay I am attempting a self-definition, which has proven to be a much more difficult task than I ever expected. Perhaps it is because my reluctant metamorphosis to USian[1] Latino is still unfinished, or perhaps because every attempt at self-definition is an attempt to capture just a moment of our continuous identity flow. As Fernando Segovia has stated, "The concept of Latin(o/a)ness ... is neither self-evident nor determinate—self-contained and unchanging; readily accessible to and intelligible by all; bearing the same force throughout, regardless of historical situation or social-cultural formation. It is rather a construct" (2009, 199). Segovia continues by describing the concept of Latino critic as having a "twofold semantic dimension," described "as a sense of identity and locus, of historical experience and present reality, and a sense of praxis and agenda, or appropriation and engagement" (200). In order to explore what it means *for me* to be classified as a U.S. Latino biblical critic, I will begin with a brief autobiographical consideration to provide the necessary context (my "historical experience") for understanding how I grew into this particular perspective (my "present reality") of reading texts. I will follow up with a strong criticism of our acceptance of U.S. racial classification as a useful tool in our struggle for *Tikkum Olam*, to repair the world, and to eliminate racism

---

* My thanks to Cristian De La Rosa for commenting on a draft of this paper.

1. USian: "A demonym, used especially in internet based writing, used to indicate that someone or something is of the United States of America. This is contrasted with 'American,' which technically means someone or something belonging to North or South America, including such disparate places as Guyana, Mexico, and Canada" (Urban Dictionary; online: http://www.urbandictionary.com/define.php?term=USian.

from U.S. society. I am aware, however, that every member of a so-called minority (actually, "minoritized") group living in the United States comes to realize sooner or later that even when racial classification is an artificial way of discrimination, it has become a very material and influential component of our living in this country. It has become incarnated in a multiplicity of social practices and perceptions. It is an inescapable umbrella that covers us all, and it has become an integral part of our identity as readers of texts in the United States. Finally, I will conclude with a few examples of what could be considered my "Latino" reading of a few biblical texts.

Autobiographical Reflections on Context

> Autobiographical biblical criticism is simply one attempt among many today that seeks to deal seriously with the "interested" nature of biblical critics and their "situatedness" as real readers in the physical world. (Staley 2002, 15)

As an emigrant worker in the United States, my present "situatedness" cannot be understood unless several factors from my past are taken into consideration. Some of these that I consider relevant for my self-understanding as a "Latino biblical critic" I enumerate and briefly explain in what follows.

One such factor is my Italian ancestry. I grew up in a small town a few miles south of Buenos Aires in a family of dominant Italian ancestry (three of my grandparents had emigrated from northern Italy to Argentina during the early 1900s). The food, the music, the songs, the neighborhood, the making of wine from bare grapes in our backyard, the long-lost European home, the mixed Italian-Spanish of my grandparents—all had a melancholic Italian flavor.

Another factor is that I have always seen myself as belonging to the working class. My consciousness as a worker began to develop quite early in my life. Like many of my friends, I began to work part-time when I was twelve years old, full-time since I was seventeen, and I continued working full-time through my high school and college years. Participating in strikes for better wages and in demonstrations for workers' rights was part of our identity as workers. It is still hard for me to understand how much of the USian work force is not unionized and how most people lack a clear understanding that, as workers, we are not "us" with our employers, but are only "us" with our coworkers.

Also, I must take into account my Latin American culturalization. It is a common dictum among Latin Americans that the *porteños* from Buenos Aires think of themselves as being more Europeans than anything else, and there is some truth to it. I "learned" to be Latin American when I began to study theology at the Instituto Bíblico Buenos Aires (IBBA) and the Instituto Superior Evangélico de Estudios Teológicos (ISEDET), and philosophy (which afterward turned into history) at the University of Buenos Aires. It was during those early years that I became familiar with Latin American history, theology, and Marxist thought.

At that time, Argentina was emerging from a bloody military dictatorship (1976–1982), which—with the support and encouragement of the Roman Catholic Church, the country's elite, and the military (trained by the United States) (Gill, 2004)—made thirty thousand of our men, women, and children disappear (i.e., they were violently murdered).[2] The democracy that arrived in 1983 opened the door for a political class who, after being elected, would multiply their personal fortunes by mismanaging public funds or engaging in corrupt practices.

A class conscience developed during those years of study and traveling in Latin America, along with the awareness that the Marxist understanding of society was a good explanation for the realities I encountered in Argentina and throughout our continent.[3] At the same time, I utterly rejected "socialist paradises" like Cuba and the Soviet Union, which obliterated individual freedoms, and Marxist terrorist organizations like Sendero Luminoso and others, which brought chaos and despair to our region. I still vividly remember the events reported by one of the delegations participating at the Meeting of the Latin-American Theological Fraternity in Quito, Ecuador, in December 1989. A Sendero Luminoso unit had shown up at their village, picked up a man accused of collaborating with the government, and forced the members of the village to line up and, under threat of death, and push, little by little, a knife through the man's head as punishment for his cooperation with the government. Concepts such as "means of production," "plus-value," "dominant class," "hegemony," and so

---

2. See the report of the National Commission on the Disappearance of Persons, which was created to investigate the fates of those who "disappeared" during the military dictatorship of 1976–1982: http://www.desaparecidos.org/nuncamas/web/english/library/nevagain/nevagain_000.htm.

3. See Boff 1978, esp. ch. 1: "Mediação socio-analítica."

forth became an integral part of my historical analyses and my approach to the biblical text (Vilar 1980).

These basic autobiographical notes can help the reader understand why from my early adulthood I have had a great mistrust of religious institutions and their bureaucracies (i.e., the clergy), politicians, the dominant classes, the military, the police, and so forth. The god of the cathedrals, the military, and the elite, the god that justified oppression, was an image of a god that I despised. The pictures of murderers like Jorge Rafael Videla, de facto president of Argentina from 1976 to 1981, and his junta celebrating Sunday mass at the cathedral, while men, women, and children were being tortured and murdered in military bases with the knowledge and support of the Vatican and the Roman Catholic Church,[4] and while the babies of those victims were being given in adoption to their murderers, is a memory hard to forget. Nobel laureate Adolfo Pérez Esquivel, who was one of the leaders of our struggle for human rights during those years, has explained: "Priests and bishops in Argentina justified their support of the government on national security concerns, and defended the taking of children as a way to ensure they were not 'contaminated' by leftist enemies of the military."[5]

In such a context my first public lecture at a meeting of Argentine Theological Students in 1986 focused on the way the Gospel of Luke portrays Jesus' understanding of his mission (4:16–21; 7:18–23) and the implications for the mission of the communities of faith. Against all the washed-out and spiritualizing interpretations of those passages that USian publishing houses (Life Publishers, Bethany, Baptist Publishing House, etc.) were pouring on us, it was crystal clear to me that when reading Luke 4:18–19—"The Spirit of the Lord is upon me, because he has anointed me to bring good news to the poor [πτωχοῖς]. He has sent me to proclaim release to the captives and recovery of sight to the blind, to let the

---

4. See the interview with Jorge Rafael Videla published in the magazine *El Sur*: http://www.revistaelsur.com.ar/noticias/12/14/articulo/659/2012-07-15_la_confesi-n.html. It is summarized in English at: http://en.mercopress.com/2012/07/24/argentine-military-dictator-confirms-catholic-church-hierarchy-was-well-aware-of-the-disappeared.

5. Adolfo Pérez Esquivel, quoted by Alexei Barrionuevo in "Daughter of 'Dirty War,' Raised by Man Who Killed Her Parents" (http://www.nytimes.com/2011/10/09/world/americas/argentinas-daughter-of-dirty-war-raised-by-man-who-killed-her-parents.html?emc=eta).

oppressed go free, to proclaim the year of the Lord's favor"—the "poor" were the poor, are the poor, *los pobres* (those "lacking sufficient money to live at a standard considered comfortable or normal in a society"), and the good news was just for them, only for them. In a similar vein, the Magnificat proclaimed that the inversion of classes was an essential component of the biblical god's historical project of salvation—"He has brought down the powerful [δυνάστας] from their thrones, and lifted up the lowly [ταπεινούς]; he has filled the hungry with good things, and sent the rich away empty" (1:52–53).

Latin American theologians perceived very clearly that the biblical god's plan had been turned upside down by traditional theology and that it was this perception from the "reverse of history" that would finally bring the good news to those who were meant to receive it (Gutiérrez 1979; Boff and Pixley 1987, 58–67; Hanks 1982, 141–54). Good news was not for everyone, because to be brought down and sent away empty cannot in any possible way be constructed as good news for the rich and powerful, except for, perhaps, the possibility that such a new state of things could help them avoid the destiny of the unnamed rich man in Luke 16:19–31, "Child, remember that during your lifetime you received your good things, and Lazarus in like manner evil things; but now he is comforted here, and you are in agony" (16:25).

United States Racial Classification: A Critique

Acho que não sei quem sou
Só sei do que não gosto.
— Legiao Urbana, *O Teatro Dos Vampiros*

I left my family, my friends, and my country in 1992 to pursue further studies and research abroad—Jerusalem, Würzburg, and back to Jerusalem, where I had the privilege of completing a doctorate in Jewish history at the Hebrew University of Jerusalem. I felt like just another human being while living in Argentina, Israel, and Germany; however, not long after my arrival in Chicago in 1997, I realized that I had become someone different for the society with which I was interacting—a Latino/Hispanic.

It is perhaps not well known that Argentines begin almost every sentence in a dialogue (of course, in Spanish) with the negative adverb *No*. So, following the tradition of my homeland, instead of beginning with a thesis, I will move directly to an antithesis, or, to be more specific, to a critique of the attachment of the label "Latino" to the noun "critic." After the antithesis, I will attempt to present a thesis (i.e., an affirmation of such a condition), and then a more conciliatory synthesis.

I began to write these reflections at the Hebrew University of Jerusalem in Mount Scopus, and I could not help but wonder who among my colleagues and friends teaching in Jerusalem, Haifa, and Tel Aviv would understand what a Latino critic is. I asked a few; none did. I myself was completely unaware that such a thing existed before I moved to the United States. I had never heard of it in theological schools in South America, Germany, or Spain. A "Latino" critic is a category that seems to exist only within the borders of the United States. To reduce its realm of existence even further, I must say that I had never heard of a Latino approach in many other scientific or scholarly disciplines, whether in the natural sciences or in the humanities, except in literary and cultural studies. Even within other units of the Society of Biblical Literature or the American Schools of Oriental Research, like Aramaic Studies or Egyptology and Ancient Israel, the concept of a "Latino" critic is unheard of. I wonder how it would have sounded if I had added "A Latino-Critic Perspective" to the paper I delivered at the 10th International Congress of Demotic Studies in Leuven in 2008, titled "Three Additional Aramaic-Demotic Legal Formulae from Elephantine." It would not have made any sense to me or my audience. However, such pretension to universality of parochial values is quite at home in the United States, where national sport contests are labeled "world cups" and the winners of national sport competitions "world champions."

Antithesis: Rejection of Racialized Classification

Desahuciado está el que tiene que marchar a vivir a una cultura diferente.
— León Gieco, *Solo le pido a Dios*

As foreigners, we struggle with a culture that tends to assume that its national values, like racial categorization, have universal validity. Migration from Latin America to the United States adds an additional challenge, a radical change in our markers of identity. This is a mutation that for every Latin American, and even for Spaniards, implies a transition from being a citizen of our country of origin to facing a new definition of ourselves within the new social framework of U.S. society. To put it roughly, in my case it implied: from being an Argentine, three-fourths Italian and one-fourth Spaniard, to being a "Hispanic" or "Latino." This transition might seem quite natural when viewed from the perspective of the classifying dominant class or a subordinate class that internalizes that ideological classification. It is, however, far from obvious for many of us, and leads to a kind of "crisis of identity." What am I? An "Italo-South American," as my family origins and traditions would suggest; an Argentine, as it is stamped in my passport; or a Hispanic/Latino, as seems to be the way in which most people in the United States would define me?

This change of context and imposed new identity brings not a minor shift in the way we read society and, consequently, a text like the Bible, which in the United States has a disproportionate and unhealthy influence on social behavior. A most peculiar feature of this change involves having to cope with racial classification. Racial classification is a very peculiar U.S. phenomenon. When USian athletes are successful abroad, their race is hardly ever mentioned by foreign journalists. Venus and Serena Williams, for example, have won several tennis tournaments abroad, but the European media hardly ever refers to the fact that they are black—the term African American is, of course, only used in the United States; by contrast, the U.S. media highlights this as an essential components of their stories of triumph. There are, of course, "people of color" in every European country, but in none of them are they anything else but simply citizens. There is no racial classification and there are no state policies based on racial categories. The reality in the United States is quite the opposite. How, then, does one read the Bible in such a racially conditioned context? Must one accept a priori this categorization? Do we challenge these categories as ideological instruments of domination (Michaels 2006)?

This artificial, nonnatural, racial classification lays bare the question: What is the origin of racial classification in the United States? Is it a useful ideological tool in our struggle for justice and liberation? Or is it precisely the ideological framework that allows racial discrimination to continue? I contend, as previous studies have shown, that the origin of racial classification should be sought in the historical development of economic social structures and in the history of the development of economic relations among socioeconomic classes. A general survey of this problem shows that "work, especially the performance of work that was at once important to the economy of the nation and that was defined as menial and unskilled, was key to their nonwhite racial assignment" (Brodkin 2000, 55). Immigrants from Eastern Europe, who are now classified as white, were not so classified at the end of the nineteenth century, when they were mostly providing menial labor for the work force (55–76). In the particular case of California Hispanics, the Mexican *ranchero*-landowning elite that remained in the territory annexed by the United States after the Mexican-American War was initially classified as white (Almaguer 1994, 54–57), but became nonwhite after Mexicans became mass workers in low paying jobs in the California agriculture business in the late nineteenth and early twentieth century (Haney-López 2003, 56–87; Rumbaut 2006, 20–24).

In sum, one can briefly state the origins or racial classification in the United States as "initially invented to justify a brutal but profitable regime of slave labor, … and the ideological explanation it used to justify it" (Brodkin 2000, 75). I therefore tend to deny—this is an antithesis, after all—all racial labels, including the label "Latino/Hispanic," as an imposed, forced, and artificial categorization, one mostly based on the U.S. racist and discriminatory ideologies of the nineteenth century. I would suggest that accepting racial differentiation as the criteria for defining the basic contradiction of our society (Althusser 1996; esp. "Contradiction et surdétermination [notes pour une recherche," pp. 85–128) will not serve the purpose of transforming the economic structures that sustain social inequalities among us.

Thesis: Affirming "Latinicity" for Justice

I have just put forward the idea that being a Latino critic is not only a parochial scholarly dimension but also a social categorization that is the direct result of the oppressive policies of the country in the nineteenth century. I am, however, as immersed in these ideological dimensions as anyone else.

This ideological (in the neo-Marxist sense; Althusser 1970),[6] racist, socioanalytical mediation that divides people into several races was not just an illusion. It became very material for the children who were forbidden to speak Spanish under penalty of expulsion in many schools in south Texas and other places.[7] It became very real as well for those who read "No Dogs, Negroes, Mexicans"[8] posted at the entrance of restaurants in a part of U.S. territory that had been taken from their Mexican homeland after the 1848 infamous treaty of Guadalupe-Hidalgo.

---

6. See Thèse I: "L'idéologie représente le rapport imaginaire des individus à leurs conditions réelles d'existence."
7. See Thèse II: "L'idéologie a une existence matérielle."
8. See http://www.jewishhistorymuseum.org/collections/artifacts/article/54.

As Ortega y Gasset stated, "Yo soy yo y mi circunstancia y si no la salvo a ella no me salvo yo" (1964, 30). Perhaps many of us would share his understanding of the peculiar role of the context in which we are living, "Lo que yo hubiera de ser tenía que serlo en España, en la circunstancia española," declared the philosopher (2006, 348)—"What I was supposed to be, I had to be in Spain, in the circumstances of Spain." Culturally translated to my situation, such an assertion would basically mean: what I was supposed to be, I had to be in the United States, within the U.S. circumstances. However, it was under protest that this embedded racial perception became a real component of my new life in the United States. It is my *Dasein,* my *In-der-Welt-sein,* as Heidegger would describe it (1967, 52–62).[9] It is strongly so because in no other country I experienced the discrimination that I have experienced in the United States, paradoxically so in self-defined liberal academic contexts. Being a nonwhite in the United States defines one as a "minority" and, as such, one is expected to be subservient, to know one's place in the order of things. One must not dare to challenge the theological icons of white academia. One must understand that one is fortunate to be a "guest" at one's institution, and one must always remember that. As a white senior colleague once told me, "If you go to the doctor and the doctor tells you what to do, you do it." As a minoritized scholar in the United States, I had to accept that we are better off by doing always what the doctor (i.e., our white senior colleagues) tells us.

In this context, I affirm my "Latinicity," my being a Latino critic in biblical studies, because I feel part of this group that is discriminated against in almost every realm of U.S. life. I feel at home with this people. I feel that we treasure life, family, and friendship in very similar ways and that we all have a commitment to work for "a little bit of more justice," as our beloved Ada María Isasi-Díaz would say (1996).

Latino Reading: Approaching Biblical Texts

I also affirm my Latinicity by implementing the approach to biblical texts that I learned during the course of my biblical studies in Argentina, especially under the direction of José Severino Croatto,[10] Nestor Míguez

---

9. See "Das In-der-Welt-sein überhaupt als Grundverfassung des Daseins."
10. Croatto passed away in 2004. See http://www.severinocroatto.com.ar for a biography and a list of his publications.

(ISEDET), and Esteban Voth (IBBA). I was trained in what I would characterize today as a holistic historical-critical method. The difference between traditional historical-critical methods and such a holistic approach is that the latter takes seriously into consideration factors often left behind by traditional approaches, such as social class, social location, and gender. These are perhaps the three most notorious components that informed my training in Argentina, to the point that, when I was asked to teach an introduction to church history at IBBA, I did it from the perspective of women and the poor. I would not characterize such an approach as a confessional enterprise or an exercise in advocacy. I see it as scholarly: It is neither a case of *fides quaerens intellectum* or of *intellectus quaerens fidem*; it is rather, purely and exclusively, a case of *intellectus quaerens intellectum*. If such an approach were to be described as "engaged scholarship," its opposite would deserve the label of "encaged scholarship" (Levenson 2000a, 2000b; Pixley 2000, 231–38; Botta 2010).

This class-conscious and gender-conscious analysis of biblical texts expands the traditional methods by taking into consideration the social class and gender of the authors and texts that are read and analyzed. The result is an increasing awareness of how the gender and social location of the reader, in addition to the social location and gender of the author(s), factor into the results of any interpretive understanding of texts. I should highlight the incompleteness of those approaches in biblical studies that leave aside such determinant historical-critical factors as not fulfilling the scholarly goals of historical-critical disciplines.

This holistic approach leads me to perceive, for example, that when the psalmist claims, "They have all gone astray, they are all alike perverse; there is no one who does good, no, not one" (Ps 14:3), he does not mean to include the whole of humanity but only the social class of "evildoers who eat up my people as they eat bread, and do not call upon the LORD" (Ps 14:4). It also helps me understand that when the book of Isaiah claims that "the LORD has anointed me; he has sent me to bring good news to the oppressed" (Isa 61:1–2), the good news is for the social class comprising the materially oppressed only and never for the social class of the oppressors. It further suggests to me that in reading the Song of the Vineyard in Isa 5:1–7 the condemnation is directed not at all the inhabitants of the land but only the elite and royal house (Chaney 1999). It helps me to realize as well that many texts from the Hebrew Bible that are usually interpreted as a general condemnation of the people of Israel are really meant to condemn the royal house, the dominant class, and/or the elite from Jerusalem.

Lastly, this approach helps me understand, in reading the parable of the Rich Man and Lazarus in the Gospel of Luke, that the reason why the former is in hell and the other in heaven is given in plain language through the words of Abraham to the rich man, "Child, remember that during your lifetime you received your good things, and Lazarus in like manner evil things; but now he is comforted here, and you are in agony" (Luke 16:25).

Being a Latino critic in biblical studies means to attempt a correction of previous readings of the Bible that are incomplete or plainly wrong because they were produced from a context with a serious blind spot to the dynamic of socioeconomic oppression and the main responsibility of the elites/dominant classes in such a dynamic. Those who are familiar with the European colonization of the Americas might remember the popular legend concerning the encounter between Friar Vicente de Valverde (who arrived with Don Francisco Pizarro in 1531) and Atahualpa in which the former handed the latter a Christian Bible and said that it contained God's Word. The story goes that Atahualpa shook it close to his ear and asked, "Why does it not speak to me?" Atahualpa then threw the Bible to the ground, which gave Valverde and Pizarro a reason to kill him and begin the war in Cajamarca on November 16, 1532.

Being a Latino critic also implies taking away the interpretive authority of the Bible from the hands of clergy like Valverde, of genocidal figures like Pizarro, of white, Anglo-Saxon, traditional intellectuals who used it to justify racism, and of all the tyrants, kings, or democratically elected officials who were anointed to bring bad news to the oppressed. Such an approach might be identified as "Latino" as long as Latinos belong to an oppressed, minoritized, racialized group in the United States. Such an approach would easily become non-Latino if Latinos were to replace the white, Anglo-Saxon, Protestant elite of the United States and become the privileged, the elite, the oppressors. As a Latin American, an USian Latino critic now, reading the Bible within the U.S. context, as an organic intellectual along the lines of Antonio Gramsci (1971), my identification is with the oppressed, no matter what race they may be. To use a religious metaphor, the metaphorical goddess of this Latino critic is not white, black, or Hispanic—she is just poor.

Works Cited

Almaguer, Tomás. 1994. *Racial Fault Lines: The Historical Origins of White Supremacy in California*. Berkeley: University of California Press.

Althusser, Louis. 1996. *Pour Marx*. Paris: La Découverte.

———. 1970. Idéologie et appareils idéologiques d'État (notes pour une recherche). *La Pensée* 151:3–38.

Boff, Clodovis. 1978. *Teologia e prática: Teologia do político e suas mediações*. Petrópolis: Vozes.

Boff, Clodovis, and Jorge Pixley. 1987. *Opção pelos pobres*. Petrópolis: Vozes.

Botta, Alejandro. 2010. The Perils of Encaged (Biblical) Scholarship: Challenges from Latin America. Lectured delivered at the Hebrew Bible/Old Testament Scholars Boston Theological Institute Meeting. October 18.

Brodkin, Karen. 2000. *How Jews Became White Folks and What That Says about Race in America*. 1998. Repr., New Brunswick, N.J.: Rutgers University Press.

Chaney, Marvin L. 1999. Whose Sour Grapes? The Addressees of Isaiah 5:1–7 in the Light of Political Economy. *Semeia* 87:105–22.

Gill, Lesly. 2004. T*he School of the Americas: Military Training and Political Violence in the Americas*. Durham, N.C.: Duke University Press.

Gramsci, Antonio. 1971. La formazione degli intellettuali (Q. XXIX). Pages 13–16 in *Gli intellettuali*. Rome: Riuniti.

Gutiérrez, Gustavo. 1979. Teología desde el reverso de la historia. Pages 58–67 in *La fuerza histórica de los pobres*. Lima: CEP.

Haney-López, Ian F. 2003. *Racism on Trial: The Chicano Fight for Justice*. Cambridge: Belknap.

Hanks, Tomás. 1982. *Opresión, pobreza y liberación: Reflexiones bíblicas*. Miami: Caribe.

Heidegger, Martin. 1967. *Sein und Zeit*. 11th ed. Tübingen: Niemeyer.

Isasi-Díaz, Ada María. 1996. *Un poquito de justicia*—a Little Bit of Justice: A *Mujerista* Account of Justice. Pages 325–39 in *Hispanic/Latino Theology: Challenge and Promise*. Edited by Ada María Isasi-Díaz and Fernando F. Segovia. Minneapolis: Fortress.

Levenson, Jon D. 2000a. Liberation Theology and the Exodus. Pages 215–30 in *Jews, Christians and the Theology of the Hebrew Scriptures*. Edited by Alice Ogden Bellis and Joel S. Kaminsky. SBLSymS 8. Atlanta: Society of Biblical Literature.

———. 2000b. The Perils of Engaged Scholarship: A Rejoinder to Jorge Pixley. Pages 239–46 in *Jews, Christians and the Theology of the Hebrew Scriptures*. Edited by Alice Ogden Bellis and Joel S. Kaminsky. SBLSymS 8. Atlanta: Society of Biblical Literature.

Michaels, Walter Benn. 2006. The Trouble with Race. Pages 1–49 in *The Trouble with Diversity: How We Learned to Love Identity and Ignore Inequality*. New York: Holt.

Ortega y Gasset, José. 1964. *Meditaciones del Quijote*. Colección Austral. Madrid: Espasa-Calpe.

———. 2006. *Obras Completas*. Vol. 6. Madrid: Editorial Taurus/ Santillana Ediciones Generales & Fundación José Ortega y Gasset.

Pixley, Jorge. 2000. History and Particularity in Reading the Hebrew Bible: A Response to Jon D. Levenson. Pages 231–38 in *Jews, Christians and the Theology of the Hebrew Scriptures*. Edited by Alice Ogden Bellis and Joel S. Kaminsky. SBLSymS 8. Atlanta: Society of Biblical Literature.

Rumbaut, Rubén G. 2006. The Making of a People. Pages 16–65 in *Hispanics and the Future of America*. Edited by Marta Tienda and Faith Mitchell. Washington, D.C.: National Academies Press.

Segovia, Fernando F. 2009. Toward Latino/a American Biblical Criticism: Latin(o/a)ness as Problematic. Pages 193–223 in *They Were All Together in One Place? Toward Minority Biblical Criticism*. Edited by Randall C. Bailey, Tat-siong Benny Liew, and Fernando F. Segovia. SemeiaSt 57. Atlanta: Society of Biblical Literature.

Staley, Jeffrey L. 2002. What Is Critical about Autobiographical (Biblical) Criticism? Pages 12–33 in *Autobiographical Biblical Criticism: Learning to Read between Text and Self*. Edited by Ingrid Rosa Kitzberger. Dorset: Deo.

Vilar, Pierre. 1980. *Iniciación al vocabulario del análisis histórico*. Barcelona: Crítica.

Forgotten Forebears in the History of North American Biblical Scholarship

Gregory Cuellar

Within the American guild of biblical scholars, Latina/o biblical interpretation is commonly described as an "emerging hermeneutics." Conversely, this description suggests that the interpretation of the Bible by Latina/o scholars is new and, in turn, insignificant to the history of the biblical tradition in North America. Indeed, the Latina/o cultural archive reminds us that the history of biblical interpretation in the American hemisphere points back to the centuries after 1492 and the colonial enterprise of the Spanish Empire.

Almost a hundred years before the publication of the *Bay State Psalm Book* (1640) in Cambridge, Massachusetts, Juan de Zumárraga, the first archbishop of colonial Mexico, published a theological/doctrinal book (quarto volume of twelve leaves) in Tenochtitlán, Mexico, titled *Breve y más compendiosa Doctrina Cristiana en Lengua Mexicana y Castellana, que contiene las cosas más necesarias de nuestra sancta fé cathólica, para aprovechamiento destos indios naturals y salvación de sus ánimas* (Penn 1939, 303; García Icazbalceta 1886, 1). Of the several hundred copies printed, some were acquired by various ecclesiastical libraries and others accompanied friars in their spiritual conquest of the indigenous peoples of the Americas (García Icazbalceta 1897, 408). Immersed in the context of the Spanish Empire, this published religious work represents the beginning of a broader theological discourse in which Western readings of Scripture and the indigenous "Other" were paramount. More importantly, for Latina/o biblical interpretation in North America, this published text represents an early thread to a complex and violent legacy of reading the Bible.

Rather than forging a discussion on contemporary Latina/o approaches to the Bible, in this study I seek to reread the context of Bible reading in sixteenth-century colonial Mexico in an effort to reclaim such reading as an antecedent to Latina/o biblical interpretation in North America. First, I present a brief history of theological education and the Bible book trade in sixteenth-century colonial Mexico. Then, *turning from context to text, I shift the discussion to an analysis* of a subversive reading of the biblical text from the perspective of the "Jewish" other in sixteenth-century colonial Mexico. In the end, I conclude with a suggestion for opening a dialogue whereby critics of contemporary Latina/o biblical interpretation understand its *hybridity and alterity* within the context of colonization and empire.

Theological Education and Bible Book Trade in Colonial Mexico

The figure responsible for organizing the Catholic Church in colonial Mexico into a major institution of power was Juan de Zumárraga, the first bishop and archbishop of Mexico. Leaving Spain in August of 1528, Zumárraga arrived in Mexico City in early December of that year (García Icazbalceta 1886, 21). Committed to the diffusion of the Catholic faith to Mexico's indigenous population, this learned prelate founded schools and encouraged other friars and other orders to do the same. Zumárraga also sought to establish an indigenous readership of biblical texts with the cofounding of America's first theological college and academic library, El Colegio Imperial de Santa Cruz de Tlatelolco (Mathes 1985, 7; González Obregón and Gómez 1935, 481). His underlying mission for the college was to provide a theological/humanistic education for promising sons of *caciques*.

Theological Education in Sixteenth-Century Colonial Mexico

According to W. Michael Mathes, the college's inaugural class of 1536 totaled sixty students (1985, 14–15). In 1537 student enrollment increased to seventy students, followed by sixty students in 1538. By 1541 the college reached a record high of two hundred indigenous students (Estarellas 1962, 236). During their three-year residency, students were offered a curriculum based on the liberal arts, divided into the two classical groups, the *Trivium* and the *Quadrivium*. In their teaching, however, the Franciscan friars did not adhere strictly to this curriculum. The needs of their students and their indigenous social location compelled faculty to expand their course offerings (236). Hence, the students were offered courses in theology, painting, and Aztec medicine, all of which were taught in either Latin or Nahuatl (MacLachlan 1990, 126; Estarellas 1962, 237).

Although the majority of the indigenous population was prohibited from owning books, the regulation did not apply to the students. In the college library, resident indigenes had access to titles in the areas of grammar, theology, philosophy, Bible, doctrine, homiletics, and classics (Mathes 1985, 15). Based on a 1568 inventory, the college's library collection consisted of books by Erasmus, Elio Antonio de Nebrija, Saint Jerome, Saint Thomas Aquinas, Quintilian, Gabriel Biel, Cicero, Plutarch, Aesop, Pliny the Elder, Dioscorides, and, of course, multiple versions of the Latin Bible (Mathes 1985, 30). By the end of the sixteenth century, other notable titles were added, including: Nicolas Cleynaerts, *Tabulae in grammaticen Hebraeam*; Gilbert Génebrard, *Psalmi Davidis Vulgate*; Elio Antonio de Nebrija, *Introductionis in Latinam grammaticen; Nicolaus de Lyra, Textus Biblie cum Glosa ordinaria* ; and Jerónimo de Azambuja, usually known as Oleastro, *Commentaria in Mósi Pentateuchum* (Mathes 1985, 51–81; 1996, 424–25).

The college produced a number of alumni who went on to occupy distinguished posts in the colony. Some participated in the administrative offices of the school, and others taught in their own alma mater or in other theological colleges. Except for the indigenous students deemed exceptional, all the names of the alumni are tragically absent from the colonial archival record (Estarellas 1962, 238). Among the named alumni, two are frequently cited: Martín de la Cruz, a physician, and Juan Badiano of Xochimilco, a scribe. The former graduate was recognized for having initiated the development and use of indigenous grammar readers in the college (Mathes 1985, 15). The latter was lauded for his remarkable mastery of Latin, which earned him a permanent faculty position at the college (Mathes 1985, 18; Gimmel 2008, 172).

Badiano's 1552 magnum opus was the Latin translation of Martín de la Cruz's Nahuatl codex *Herbario Indígena*, which was titled *Libellus de Medicinalibus Indorum Herbis*. *From the first folio of the codex we learn that the author is one Martín de la Cruz, "an Indian doctor from the College of Santa Cruz, who did not complete any professional studies but rather was an expert by way of pure experience" (Gimmel 2008, 172). The last folio tells us that the translator, Juan Badiano, was a Latin professor at the College of Santa Cruz, who undertook the translation into Latin at the behest of the Franciscan Jacobo de Grado (172). Considered the first medical book of the New World, the codex is a striking example of the impact of the colonial enterprise on indigenous culture.* Millie Gimmel, however, states that "in spite of its European appearance, the Codex is an indigenously produced work that reflects primarily indigenous sensibilities" (186). Apart from its appropriation of the linguistic tone and style of similar herbals written in Europe, the codex embodies a pre-Hispanic theological/cosmological ethos in which the health of an individual depended on the balance of three animistic entities—the tonalli (the head), the teyolia (the heart), and the ihiyotlue (the liver/god Tezcatlipoca) (180). Gimmel reminds us that "as twenty first century readers and scholars we must recognize the hybridity of this text and treat it as the blended text it is, instead of forcing it into one category or the other" (187).

Despite Badiano's achievements, the college's founding mission would be short-lived. In 1555 the Mexican Council issued a decree prohibiting the ordination of indigenous clergy (Mathes 1985, 18). In the years following, the college would function as a center for the study of indigenous ethnography and languages (Rodríguez-Buckingham 1989, 52; Mathes 1985, 19).

The Bible Book Trade in Sixteenth-Century Colonial Mexico

Certainly, throughout the sixteenth century in colonial Mexico, the bustling book trade made Bibles increasingly accessible to an isolated readership. Expert colonialist Irving Leonard indicates that, even with heightened inquisitorial vigilance, "it was still possible for a Mexican merchant to import and sell with relative freedom in the colonies foreign as well as Spanish editions of the Holy Scriptures" (1949, 17). In 1573 no fewer than 125 Bibles were known to be circulating in Mexico City, with a considerable increase in 1576. Indeed, one particular sixteenth-century invoice covering shipments of books to colonial Mexico reveals both private and conventual interests in the philological and exegetical studies of the Bible. It contains six entries listing biblical texts in Greek or in Hebrew with or without Latin translation (Green and Leonard 1941, 3–4). Also listed are commentaries on Genesis, the Pentateuch, Joshua, Psalms, Song of Solomon, the books of Kings, and various prophetic texts (3–4).

The widespread interest in reading the Bible in colonial Mexico is further evidenced by the contemporary trial documents of the Mexican inquisition. Among the readers that emerge from the Mexican inquisitional archive are sons of *caciques,* Lutheran sympathizers, and itinerant crypto-Jews, the last of whom represented the colony's primary public enemy (Báez 1960, 141; González Obregón 2002, 608; González Obregón and Gómez, 1935, 221; Cacique of Texcoco 1910, 89).

Reading the Bible as the "Jewish" Other in Colonial Mexico

After the expulsions in Spain and Portugal, the unauthorized possession of Hebrew books was considered crucial evidence for judaizing. The incriminating danger of these books compelled many crypto-Jews to turn increasingly to orthodox Christian books from which they could glean a real or surmised Jewish content (Gitlitz 1996, 428). With numerous coerced conversions to Christianity, the sovereigns and ecclesiastical authorities of Spain became increasingly reluctant to permit the dissemination of the Bible. Indeed, major concerns in sixteenth-century Spain involved the Bible in the vernacular, versions of the Bible printed by heretics, or suspicious commentaries on the Bible (Torre Revello 1940, 95).

In 1551 the Spanish Inquisition issued its first Index of Prohibited Books, condemning Bibles in the vernacular and books in Hebrew. Following this index was the 1554 Index, which focused solely on different editions of the Latin Bible (Pérez and Lloyd 2005, 205). Central to the publication of these indexes was the view that the necessary practice of heretics was to read the Bible in their common tongue. The Spanish Inquisition believed that a vernacular Bible would cause more harm to the "ignorant" layperson than good. Unfortunately for crypto-Jews, the authorized Vulgate Bible was generally restricted to the clergy. Laypeople, especially those already suspect and those with considerable knowledge of the Hebrew Bible, courted trouble by owning or reading Scripture (Cohen 2001, 95). It was therefore common for crypto-Jewish families desperate for knowledge about Judaism to send one of their sons, preferably the oldest, to study for the priesthood (34). This subterfuge gave many crypto-Jews access to Catholic centers of theological education and their libraries.

In the fall of 1571, colonial Mexico's first official inquisitor, Dr. Moya de Contreras, initiated the prosecution of colonial residents reading prohibited books or possessing them. His office issued an edict criminalizing those who read heretical books, which was followed by an official order commanding that all such books be brought to the Holy Office of the Mexican Inquisition. By 1573 an official Index of Prohibited Books was published for all Spanish residents in colonial Mexico (Greenleaf 1969,

184). Among the groups subject to close inquisitorial scrutiny were merchants who imported books from the Iberian Peninsula to sell in colonial markets (183).

Thus, upon a fleet's arrival to the port of San Juan de Ulúa, a mandated checkpoint for all ships destined for colonial Mexico, the first duty of the general of the fleet was to notify the customs officers of the Crown ("la aduana de su Magestad"; Leonard 1964, 171). Once notified, both the customs officers and inquisitorial inspectors would pull away from shore via small government boats en route to the fleet. On board the general's ship, the inspectors summoned the shipmaster, the pilot, and one or two passengers, all of whom were forced to answer eight questions truthfully, under penalty of the severest anathema of the church (173). Apart from questions concerning passengers of Jewish, Moorish, or Turkish background, they were asked whether on board there were "any forbidden books such as the Bible in any vernacular, or any other books of the Lutheran and Calvinist sects and of other heretics, or any of those forbidden by the Holy Office of the Inquisition, or any others unregistered and concealed, or without license of the Holy Office?" (Torre Revello 1940, 105; Leonard 1964, 173). The customs officers brought all books found on board to the customs house for closer examination by the provincial inquisitor ("el comisario"). An expert in canon law and suspicious literature, the *comisario* carefully cross-referenced each book with the current indexes, registered them, and then issued a license to the owners for their use. Nevertheless, records indicate that inquisitors were only partially successful in keeping heretical books out of colonial Mexico (Greenleaf 1969, 183).

Based on a 1572 edict issued by the grand *comisario* of Mexico City, the circulation of heretical books was undeterred. The edict reveals how books contrary to the Catholic faith were constantly being introduced by way of contraband (Torre Revello 1940, 105). José Torre Revello posits that it was common for heretical books to be hidden among the clothes and merchandise in Catholic ships destined for colonial Mexico (106). Furthermore, even with heightened inquisitorial vigilance, merchants could still import and sell with relative freedom foreign as well as Spanish editions of the Bible in colonial markets (Nesvig 2009, 226–28).

In the case of the convicted crypto-Jew Luis de Carvajal ("el Mozo"), the Mexican Inquisition discovered that he had been able to purchase a Latin Vulgate Bible soon after disembarking at the port of Tampico in 1581. Based on his inquisitorial trial testimonies and memoirs, de Carvajal claimed to have purchased this Bible from a vicar named Juan Rodríguez

Moreno, for six pesos in Pánuco (González Obregón and Gómez, 1935, 47, 222). Indeed, de Carvajal was no stranger to the book trade. He had once been a resident of Medina del Campo, Spain, which Torre Revello indicates had an active book commerce with the Americas during the sixteenth and seventeenth centuries (98). In fact, Medina del Campo was famous throughout Europe for its international fairs and was considered a hub of the book trade in Spain (Griffin 2005, 119).

In 1577 de Carvajal's parents moved to Medina del Campo, where his father sold merchandise on Medina Street (González Obregón and Gómez 1935, 1, 9). Shortly after their arrival, the eleven-year-old Luis was enrolled in a local Jesuit school, completing two grades of a liberal arts education. During the first year, he concentrated on Latin grammar; during the second, on rhetoric, with readings from Virgil, Cicero, and other Latin writers (Cohen 2001, 23). Hence, the combination of a mercantile background, the Medina del Campo book trade, and a formal Latin education would have proven formative for de Carvajal's bibliophilic intelligence and skill.

In his memoirs de Carvajal shares how his dream of having access to a full-fledged theological library was fulfilled when he was given the keys to the library at the College of Santa Cruz (González Obregón and Gómez 1935, 481). Based on his trial proceedings, de Carvajal owned a small private library, which included such volumes as Fray Luis de Granada's *Guía de Pecadores* and *Introducción al Símbolo de la Fe,* Juan de Dueñas's *Espejo de consolación,* a Latin Bible, a book of the penitential psalms, and other Catholic devotional materials (Cohen 2001, 137). He also had a variety of bound manuscript books, such as his memoirs, library-research notes, a self-composed liturgical book for the Sabbath and major Jewish holidays, and a small booklet of the Decalogue in Latin, which he sewed into the lining of his hat (223). Most notable was a copy of a notebook by the crypto-Jewish erudite Dr. Manuel de Morales, which contained a Spanish translation of Deuteronomy, the Shema, and religious poetry (González Obregón and Gómez 1935, 224–26). He also spoke of copying books for eager Judaizers, which usually included a Spanish translation of the Decalogue and personal prayers (11, 145; Cohen 2001, 203). In the end, however, the Latin Vulgate Bible had primacy in shaping de Carvajal's secret Jewish identity.

The Bible quoted ubiquitously by de Carvajal in his trial testimony and personal memoirs was the Latin Vulgate of St. Jerome. In his memoirs, de Carvajal states that he read his Bible assiduously in the distant northern frontier, allowing him to discover many divine mysteries. In his trial testimonies, he told inquisitors that he searched through the Bible for Jewish religious practices. From his readings, he sought to understand all the Jewish ceremonies that "God commanded in Exodus, Leviticus, Numbers, and Deuteronomy" (González Obregón and Gómez 1935, 99). These ceremonies include: keeping the Sabbath, the Feast of Passover (Lev 23:5–14), the Feast of Unleavened Bread (Exod 12:15–28), the Feast of Firstfruits (Lev 23:15–22), the Feast of Tabernacles (Lev 23:33–44), and the Festival of Lights (1 Macc 4:56–59) (99, 223).

In reading Gen 17:14, de Carvajal applied literally the command to circumcise all males, hence circumcising himself at the banks of the Pánuco River. In his second trial testimony, he cites the following, "anima enim quem circuncisa [non] fuerit delebitur de libro viventium," which he translates in his memoirs, "l[a] anima que fuere incircuncidada sera borrada del libro de los vivientes" ("the soul/life that may be uncircumcised will be erased from the book of the living"; 222, 465). Such words, he writes,

> hit me with such fear that without delay I ran out of the house leaving the Bible open, took some dull scissors with good promise and went to a ravine at the Pánuco River where with a fighting spirit and a burning desire to be written in the book of life, which is impossible without this holy sacrament, I sealed it with him [God] and cut off almost all of the prepuce only leaving a small part to cut because of the scissors. (Liebman 1967, 57)

De Carvajal's longing to recover his Jewish past gave rise to an insatiable drive to discover his ancestral faith in the biblical text. The exigencies of the Torah were satisfied with the utmost urgency.

Yet within the context of sixteenth-century colonial Mexico, his pursuit of biblical Judaism renders his reading of biblical texts subversive and inimical to the empire. With reference to the Latin Vulgate, the 1571 Antwerp Polyglot Bible as well as the Royal Bible of Spain have Gen 17:14 read, "masculus cuius præputii caro circuncisa non fuerit, delebitur anima illa de populo suo: quia pactum meum irritum fecit" (Antwerp Gen 17:14). This is translated in the 1569 Reina-Valera Antigua as follows, "Y el varón incircunciso que no hubiere circuncidado la carne de su prepucio, aquella persona será borrada de su pueblo; ha violado mi pacto." Clearly, there are discrepancies between the Latin version of de Carvajal and that of the Latin Vulgate in the Royal Bible, which was considered the official text for the Spanish church.

The key difference lies with the phrase "delebitur anima illa de populo suo" in the Royal Bible. The verb form *delebitur* forms the future passive voice of *deleo*, which literally means "to blot out of writing." In both translations, that of de Carvajal and that of the Reina-Valera, this is rendered as "será borrada," which since colonial times refers to that act of erasing something written. In the case of the Royal Bible, the verb *delebitur* is used in connection with its general meaning, to destroy or to annihilate something. Hence in Gen 17:14 the image is the annihilation of the uncircumcised soul from his people, which aligns more closely with the original Hebrew text. On the other hand, de Carvajal employs the verb *delebitur* within the context of erasing something written, more specifically, from "the book of the living" ("de libro viventium"). Indeed, the Bible de Carvajal purchased in Pánuco was a Latin Vulgate, which suggests that he adopted an alternative reading of Gen 17:14. His reading reflects a sophisticated knowledge of both Latin terms and theological concepts.

Essentially, the literal meaning of the Latin verb *deleo*, "to erase something written," allows for his connection with the book of life. In the Hebrew Bible, the book of life is the book of God wherein all the righteous are recorded for life, and to be blotted out of it signifies death. Nevertheless, in the passages that explicitly mention the book of life, like Exod 32:33 and Ps 69:28, there is no mention of circumcision. In de Carvajal's reading, the fulfillment of the command of circumcision equals eternal salvation. For him, circumcision represents "a holy sacrament" that is necessary for one to enter into heaven. Hence underneath his reading of Gen 17:14 is a sacramental theology, which was probably informed by his public Catholic devotion. As a crypto-Jew, however, de Carvajal lived a double life, one as a public Catholic and another as a secret Jew. His polemical religious identity gave way to a hybrid theology on salvation. Similar to Catholic teaching, de Carvajal's salvation is personal and is achieved through the sacramental system. Yet for his crypto-Jewish faith the sacrament of baptism is replaced by the command of circumcision.

It is very unlikely, however, that this alternative reading of Gen 17:14 was available at the time of de Carvajal's circumcision at the Pánuco River in 1581. An adolescent at the time, he had only begun to read his Bible when he came to the command of circumcision in Gen 17. Furthermore, soon after his auto-circumcision, he left Pánuco to join his uncle Luis de Carvajal de la Cueva in the colonization of the northern frontier. During his two years in the frontier, Luis brought with him only a transcription of

4 Ezra (Cohen 2001, 105, 107). Hence it is likely that this alternative reading emerged later in his intellectual and religious development.

At his first inquisitional trial in 1589, de Carvajal testified to the purchase of a Bible in Pánuco; however, there is no word about reading Gen 17:14 and his subsequent circumcision (González Obregón and Gómez 1935, 47). He stated that his father, Francisco Rodríguez de Matos, had taught him about the command of circumcision and its importance for personal salvation (48). Nevertheless, with his father already deceased, placing the blame on his father for his knowledge of Judaism may have been a strategy to avoid incriminating himself and his living family members (165).

Following his journeys throughout the frontier, de Carvajal recovered his Bible from his family in Mexico City in 1586 (Cohen 2001, 119). It was also during this time he and his brother, Baltasar Rodríguez de Carvajal, acquired a copy of Dr. Manuel de Morales's vernacular translation of the book of Deuteronomy. During his years in Mexico City, de Carvajal was actively teaching from the Bible at Sabbath services and on Jewish holidays. As noted by Martin Cohen, a typical Shabbat service contained paraphrases from the Bible in Spanish and readings in Latin with explanations in the vernacular (135). Prior to de Carvajal's first arrest, the inquisitional records indicate that he and his family celebrated the Passover, wherein he read texts from the Latin Vulgate followed by a Spanish translation (González Obregón and Gómez 1935, 101). He would read psalms of praise and particularly the Song of Moses in Exodus 32, "because it dealt with the past of the sons of Israel through the wilderness and the Red Sea" (101). Therefore, during the time between his arrival in Mexico and his first trial, de Carvajal was an active "Judaizer" with the intellectual capacity to provide his listeners with substantive crypto-Jewish readings of the Bible.

Nevertheless, the more likely scenario is that de Carvajal acquired the necessary language and theological skills for alternative readings of the Bible during his time at the library of the Colegio de Santa Cruz. After his release from prison in 1590, Fray Pedro de Oroz, the chaplain and confessor assigned to de Carvajal's family, arranged to have him transferred from his initial duties of involuntary penance at the Hospital de los Convalescientes de San Hipólito to the Colegio de Santa Cruz. At the Colegio, de Carvajal taught Latin grammar to the sons of *caciques* and assisted Fray Oroz with his sermons and library research (Cohen 2001, 198). As Cohen comments, de Carvajal's academic work at the college enriched his teaching of Judaism (206). Both his research duties and private program of studies in the library would have elevated his skills in the Latin language and biblical interpretation to the extent that he was confident with rewording key biblical passages in accordance with his crypto-Jewish beliefs. His exposure to the biblical exegesis of Jerome de Oleastro and Nicholas de Lyra, both Hebraists and learned in rabbinic literature, would have empowered his crypto-Jewish readings of the biblical text. Indeed, his readings of Scripture are intertextual and emancipatory for the "Jewish" other. Although de Carvajal would attribute his access to theological and exegetical works as completely fortuitous, he was driven by the violent erasure of his ancestral faith.

Conclusion

The space claimed by contemporary Latina/o biblical critics in the North American guild of biblical studies is one of intrigue and alterity. Yet within this "emerging" Latina/o discourse lies the residual living presence of a violent/colonial encounter. This discourse, either consciously or unconsciously, is inscribed within a history of invasion and conquest, of conflict and bloodshed, of repression and resistance. Indeed, the Spanish colonial antecedent of Latina/o biblical interpretation has contributed to its hybrid dynamism, which is inscribed by and resistant to dominant systems of power.

Works Cited

Báez-Camargo, Gonzalo. 1960. *Protestantes enjuiciados por la Inquisición en Iberoamérica.* México: Casa Unida de Publicaciones.

Carlos, Cacique of Texcoco. 1910. *Proceso inquisitorial del cacique de Tetzcoco.* México: Eusebio Gómez de la Puente.

Cohen, Martin A. 2001. *The Martyr Luis de Carvajal: A Secret Jew in Sixteenth-Century Mexico.* Albuquerque: University of New Mexico Press.

Estarellas, Juan. 1962. The College of Tlatelolco and the Problem of Higher Education for Indians in 16th Century Mexico. *History of Education Quarterly* 2:234–43.

García Icazbalceta, José Joaquín. 1886. *Bibliografía mexicana del siglo XVI.* México: Andrade y Morales.

———. 1897. *Obras de D. J. Garcia Icazbalceta: Biografía de D. Fr. Juan de Zumárraga.* 5 vols. México: Imprenta de V. Agüeros.

Gimmel, Millie. 2008. Reading Medicine in the Codex de la Cruz Badiano. *Journal of the History of Ideas* 69:169–72.

Gitlitz, David M. 1996. *Secrecy and Deceit: The Religion of the Crypto-Jews.* Philadelphia: Jewish Publication Society.

González Obregón, Luis. 2002. *Libros y libreros en el Siglo XVI.* México: Archivo General de la Nación: Fondo de Cultura Económica.

González Obregón, Luis, and Rodolfo Gómez, eds. 1935. *Procesos de Luis de Carvajal (El Mozo).* México: Estados Unidos Mexicanos, Secretaría de Gobernación.

Green, Otis H., and Irving A. Leonard. 1941. On the Mexican Booktrade in 1600: A Chapter in Cultural History. *Hispanic Review* 9:1–40.

Greenleaf, Richard E. 1969. *The Mexican Inquisition of the Sixteenth Century.* Albuquerque: University of New Mexico Press.

Griffin, Clive. 2005. *Journeymen-Printers, Heresy, and the Inquisition in Sixteenth-Century Spain.* Oxford: Oxford University Press.

Leonard, Irving Albert. 1949. On the Mexican Book Trade, 1576. *Hispanic Review* 17:18–34.

———. 1964. *Books of the Brave: Being an Account of Books and of Men in the Spanish Conquest and Settlement of the Sixteenth-Century New World.* New York: Gordian.

Liebman, Seymour B. *The Enlightened: The Writings of Luis Carvajal El Mozo.* Coral Gables, FL: University of Miami Press, 1967.

MacLachlan, Colin M. 1990. *Forging of the Cosmic Race: A Reinterpretation of Colonial Mexico.* Berkeley: University of California Press.

Mathes, W. Michael. 1985. *The America's First Academic Library: Santa Cruz de Tlatelolco.* Sacramento: California State Library Foundation.

———. 1996. University Humanism in Sixteenth- and Seventeenth-Century Libraries of New Spain. *Catholic Historical Review* 82:412–35.

Nesvig, Martin Austin. 2009. *Ideology and Inquisition: The World of the Censors in Early Mexico.* New Haven: Yale University Press.

Penn, Dorothy. 1939. The Oldest American Book. *Hispania* 22:303–6.

Pérez, Joseph, and Janet Lloyd. 2005. *The Spanish Inquisition: A History.* New Haven: Yale University Press.

Rodríguez-Buckingham, Antonio. 1989. Monastic Libraries and Early Printing in Sixteenth-Century Spanish America. *Libraries at Times of Cultural Change* 24:33–56.

Torre Revello, José. 1940. *El libro, la imprenta y el periodismo en América durante la dominación española.* Buenos Aires: Talleres S. A. Casa Jacobo Peuser.

The Challenges of Latino/a Biblical Criticism

Rubén R. Dupertuis

The term *challenges* in the title of this essay has a number of possible references, some of which are very personal. I was in graduate school working diligently to understand the Acts of the Apostles in the context of rhetorical training and education in the larger Greco-Roman world when I encountered an essay by Fernando Segovia (1995a) in which he critiques the methods that were at the very core of what had, up to that point, been my introduction to biblical and early Christian studies. My reaction was twofold.

On the one hand, the notion that the social location of the critic shapes the interpretation of texts—a notion central to all of the essays collected in that volume—made sense as the logical extension of the project of contextualization that was my focus. It also made intuitive sense, as by this point I had lived in Mexico, the United States, Costa Rica, Spain, and France and had quite a bit of practice in negotiating shifts in culture, language, and worldview. I had also studied at Seventh-day Adventist schools in five different countries, an American (United States of America) public university, and a Methodist seminary. That social location matters in interpretation seemed self-evident, and I granted it fully.

On the other hand, I had a graduate program to complete, and I was well aware of how much I still needed to learn about how to go about doing the work of contextualization, including the use of historical critical tools. So I pressed on, largely focusing on trying to understand how education and rhetorical training worked in the Greco-Roman world in order to help me make sense of the kind of writing practices the author of Acts likely had. Issues of identity, social location, and the constructed nature of the past eventually became central to the types of questions I have been interested in, but my focus has mostly been on identity construction in the ancient world, not the roles that my social location and my identity might play in any of this.

In hindsight, I think that some of my difficulty in understanding what role the explicit, critical evaluation of the reader should have in relation to the historical and critical examination of ancient texts in their contexts had a lot to do with what I perceived as the need to make a decision between engaging social location—clearly fronting it as a part of interpretation—and making any historical judgments at all. While I now see this as a false dichotomy, I think in some ways I accurately picked up on and reflected some of the tensions and fault lines—including ways of handling them—that were part of the guild I was working hard to join. As a student trying to understand how the discipline worked, the wide range of methods and interpretive approaches Segovia helpfully maps out were evident, but so were the tensions between them (1995a). This diversity of methods and approaches was on full display in the first conferences I attended, but rarely in dialogue in the same session. The need to keep some methods and critical discourses separate from one another also appeared to be reflected by the fact that the Society of Biblical Literature (SBL) published two different journals: "the flagship journal of the field" with "scholarly articles and critical notes," and an "experimental journal devoted to the exploration of new and emergent areas and methods of biblical criticism."[1] Disagreement is, of course, vital to this or any discipline. My point is simply that the various methods and approaches available for engaging the material our particular discipline is interested in can sometimes be presented as parallel tracks or as sides between which we must choose rather than different tools available to a learning community in dialogue.

That my social location has shaped me as a reader, including the questions I bring to texts and even which early Christian texts have most interested me, I take as a given. The opportunity to reflect on what it might mean to be a "Latino/a biblical critic" has allowed me to begin to reflect critically on some of the specific ways in which the particulars of my experience and social location shape what I see in the early Christian texts in which I am interested. In what follows I focus on three issues or challenges: first, I address some of the difficulties I have encountered in locating myself in the landscape of Latin American and U.S. Latino/a identities; second, I

---

1. A description of *JBL* can be found at http://www.sbl-site.org/publications/journals_jbl_nologin.aspx. *Semeia*, which ran as a journal from 1974 to 2002, can be found at http://www.sbl-site.org/publications/Books_semeiaJ.aspx.

explore the ways in which my own sense of Latino identity—messy and unresolved as it is—may be related to some of the choices I have made in my work, especially in relation to the Acts of the Apostles; and finally, I offer some observations on some of the challenges inherent in any attempt to define what it might mean to be a Latino/a biblical critic.

Wrestling with the Hyphen: My Corner of the U.S. Latino Identity

Questions of identity are always tricky, and attempts to define Latino/a identity are no exception. The heart of the issue, as I see it, is the tension between the diversity of Latino/a communities and experiences and the need to identify common threads and shared experiences. Among the latter, and a key part of the shared consciousness identified by Latino/a theologians and biblical scholars beginning in the late 1970s, is the experience of living, as Francisco García-Treto put it, "in two worlds at once and as 'other' in both" (2000, 135). He describes his experience as a Cuban-American as a "living on the hyphen" (a phrase taken from the literary and cultural critic Gustavo Pérez-Firmat [2004]). I also resonate with Fernando Segovia's description of a diasporic experience:

> We know both worlds quite well from the inside and the outside, and this privileged knowledge of course gives us a rather unique perspective: we know that both worlds, that all worlds, are constructions. ... We know what makes each world cohere and function; we can see what is good and bad in each world and choose accordingly; we are able to offer an informed critique of each world—its vision, its values, its traditions. (1995b, 65)

This sense of belonging to more than one world at once is easily one of the core elements of Latino/a experiences, even if the language and metaphors used to describe it vary significantly. García-Treto and Segovia identify with the language of the diaspora and of exile, while others prefer the metaphors of *mestizaje* (Elizondo) or of the border or borderlands (Guardiola-Sáenz).

I thoroughly identify with this sense of belonging to more than one world at once and agree with Segovia that "biculturalism represents a fundamental and inescapable way of life, involving two essential dimensions" (1994, 171). That said, this notion, or at least the ways in which others have articulated it reflecting their own experience, can for me also be somewhat limiting. As I think will quickly become clear, the sense of belonging to just two worlds—a double consciousness—does not quite fit me.

How I personally position myself in the Latino/a landscape is complicated—or better yet, it is not something I can usually do quickly. When asked where I am from, I usually say that my family is from Argentina, but that is not enough. My family is indeed from Argentina, although my father is the only one born there and I never lived there. My mother, whose parents were born in Spain and moved to Argentina as children, was born in Costa Rica, but spent most of her formative years in California, returning to Argentina for college. I split most of my childhood between Montemorelos, Mexico, where I was born and did some of grade school as well as all of *secundaria* or junior high, and Michigan, United States of America, where I did some of grade school and all of high school and college. A clear sense of national identity has always eluded me: I am not really Argentine—the only Argentina I know outside two visits as a child and teenager is the Argentina of my parents' youth filtered through the "inevitable tango of memory and imagination" (a phrase from Patricia Hampl [1999, 204] that has struck a chord with me). I am not really Mexican—I was always the son of the Argentine professor—but Montemorelos is as much my hometown as any other place where I have lived. When we moved to the United States of America for good, I was sixteen years old, and I assimilated easily enough, largely because I could: unlike many others, I do not wear my Latino identity or connection to Latin America in my skin color, my accent, or even in my last name. My personal experience has not been one of marginalization. At the same time, though I never feel pressured to hyphenate my identity, simply "American" is insufficient.

However, if "American" is not enough, the duality inherent in most of the terms and metaphors typically used in discussions of Latino/a identity does not capture my experience either, at least not all of it. While I was born in one of the Mexican states that borders the United States of America, mine has not been a borderland experience in the way that Elizondo or Guardiola-Sáenz describe theirs. I am also not sure that I can come up with a term analogous to García-Treto's "Cuban-American." I either have to use several hyphens or add a long, clarifying footnote to the hyphen (something not likely to get past any editors). My Latino experience is a mix of several cultures and traditions that became ours, sometimes fitting together neatly, but not always. Like many bilingual and multicultural families, the humor I grew up with exploited those places where cultures and languages overlapped and jarred (when headed to the bank, my father would always announce that he was headed to the "bench"). Our humor also took advantage of gaps created by words in Spanish with different connotations in Mexico, Argentina, Costa Rica, and Spain.

As a result of all of the moving around we did, from an early age I developed a fairly good sense of the different sets of cultural rules that were in place wherever we were. I developed a clear sense that all worlds are constructions and that identity is messy. I cannot say exactly how and if the particulars of my experience led to my interest in the Acts of the Apostles, but for someone interested in what happens when cultures combine, bump, and/or clash and who is perhaps predisposed to think of identity as complex, fluid, and ambiguous, the Acts of the Apostles turns out to be a pretty good playground.

The Challenge of Acts

The scope and interests of Acts are more international, or "transcultural" as Virginia Burrus put it (2007, 133), than perhaps any other text in the New Testament. Acts is a story replete with references to culture and differences. One finds: mention of Hellenists, Hebrews, Ethiopians, Greeks, Romans, people from remote little islands like Malta; name changes (Saul to Paul); and a mixed marriage between a Roman official and a Jewish woman—to choose only a few. Indeed, in Acts Jesus' charge to his disciples is to be witnesses of the Christian message in "Jerusalem and in all Judea and Samaria and to the ends of the earth" (Acts 1:8).[2] The setting of Acts, consequently, is strikingly broad in scope, covering almost the entirety of the Mediterranean world, as the reader follows the spread of the Christian mission from Judea into Syria, Asia Minor, Greece, and, finally, to the very center of the empire, Rome.

Despite the "transcultural" setting, detailed attention to the role of cultural identity—and perhaps especially ethnic identity—has, until very recently, not been a prevalent aspect of the critical study of Acts. When ethnic particularities and differences are addressed, it is often in the context of the "universalism" of Acts, where the point is that differences are transcended as part of its inclusive vision of the new/true Israel (on ethnicity in Acts scholarship see Barreto 2010, 3–12). Even in the context of Acts' universalism, interpreters are often more interested in highlighting

---

2. English translations are from the NRSV unless otherwise noted.

nonethnic aspects of this inclusiveness, noting especially the inclusion of people from all walks of life (Johnson 1992, 16–17). In addition, the language of ethnicity in Acts can be obscured or minimized by translation preferences that privilege the theological or political meanings of terms (Barreto 2010, 73–118).

However, Acts is a complicated book when it comes to issues of cultural identities, including ethnic identities. One need not read very far into any introduction to or commentary on Acts before encountering the longstanding and still ongoing debate regarding the identity of the author—was he Jewish, a Godfearer, or a Gentile? Resolution, or better yet, agreement on this issue is not likely, precisely because Acts is slippery, if not at times extraordinarily messy, when it comes to issues of cultural identity and the use of ethnic categories.

Acts and Judaism is a case in point, as Gentiles do not have to be circumcised to belong (Acts 10–11), but a Gentile is circumcised, presumably in order to satisfy some for whom this is a requirement (16:1–5). Paul is for Gentile inclusion (9:15–16; 22:21; 26:17) but almost always approaches Jewish audiences first. In addition, despite the fact that the key leaders of the church in Acts are clearly Jewish, the repeated pattern of Jewish rejection culminates in an emphasis on the mission to Gentiles in the concluding scene of Acts, depicting the encounter between a Paul awaiting trial before the emperor and the Jewish leaders in Rome. The continued debate and pointed disagreement on whether this final scene should be read as simply a shift in the mission's focus or as a final statement in the narrative on the failure of the mission to the Jews suggests the subject's complexity (Tyson 1988, 126). Attempts to land clearly on one side of the debate risk reducing the text's complexity. An analogous issue is the question of the stance of Acts on Roman rule. Does Acts portray Roman rule as largely benevolent? Is Acts anti-imperial? Very good arguments for both sides have been made, often by privileging one set of texts over another, but in the end we are left with a narrative whose stance is "hauntingly ambiguous" (Burrus 2007, 133). Indeed, the ultimately ambiguous way in which issues of cultural and ethnic identity appear in Acts may be an important aspect of the narrative that we as readers need to hear and become comfortable with.

If the identity of the author (or authors?) of Acts has proven slippery over the years, the identities of some of the characters in Acts sit squarely on a slip-n-slide. Not unlike some of us for whom a single hyphen is not enough to signal multiple aspects of our identity, who find ourselves both in and in between multiple identities at the same time, the character of Paul is Acts' poster child for complexity. From the time he is introduced into the narrative as Saul, a young man before whom witnesses to Stephen's stoning lay their garments, to the picture of a transformed man, by now Paul, at the other end of a long and adventure-filled mission awaiting trial before the emperor, who Paul is and is not, one might reasonably argue, is one of Acts' conundrums. At the very least, questions of Paul's identity, and the perhaps irreducible complexity that marks it, sustain much of the drama of the narrative.

The sheer complexity of the characterization of Paul with regard to ethnic and civic identity is worth developing a bit further. Paul is a Jew with significant connections to Jerusalem—he studied there with Gamaliel; his sister, or at least her son, presumably lives there; and it is there that the narrative picks up his trail. Yet he was born in Tarsus and can claim both Tarsian and Roman citizenship. Interpreters often approach specific passages in Acts with a composite and presumably complete picture of Paul's identity, as does Joseph Fitzmyer when he observes regarding Saul/Paul's first appearance in the narrative in Acts 7:58: "Witnesses probably piled their cloaks at the feet of Saul, because he was known to them personally and probably attended the synagogue of the Freedmen (6:9), and because he was a Roman citizen" (1998, 394). It is significant, however, that the various aspects of Paul's identity are doled out piecemeal and usually at points strategically key for heightening narrative tension.

Paul and Silas reveal their Roman identity to Ephesian officials only after they have been beaten and imprisoned, requiring an apology from the city leaders (Acts 16:19–40). In Acts' story of Paul's arrest in Jerusalem—a sequence featuring Paul's identity as its central theme (Gaventa 2003, 305)—Paul again reveals aspects of who he is in increments (21:27–22:29). On the verge of being beaten by an irate mob, Paul is rescued by the intervention of a Roman tribune who assumes him to be a militant Egyptian revolutionary, until Paul showcases his ability to speak Greek and reveals that he is a Jew (*anthrōpos Ioudaios*) and a citizen of Tarsus (21:37–39). Paul's Jewish identity takes center stage in his address to the crowd, in Hebrew, which presumably was allowed by the tribune on the strength of his Jewish, Tarsian, and elite credentials. The angry crowd's reaction to Paul's emphasis on the Gentiles at the conclusion of the speech causes the tribune to order an interrogation by scourging; it is only at this point that Paul reveals his Roman citizenship to the tribune. Certainly, Paul's citizenship (of both Tarsus and Rome) can be seen as a literary device (Pervo

2009, 554–56). Even Paul's selective presentation of himself can be understood to have a literary function, as "oratorical handbooks recommended that different credentials were suitable for different audiences" (554). This means that Paul's identity is slippery and messy. Even setting aside its complexity, identity is something to be deployed in Acts, something that is performed differently depending on the circumstances.

In this Acts is very much a product of its time and place and can be read alongside other texts of the early Roman Empire, including Christian texts, that prominently feature multiple modes of "ethnic reasoning" in the construction of identities (Buell 2005). Eric Barreto's study (2010) of Acts 16, which builds on the work of Denise Buell, is important for highlighting how prevalent ethnic discourse is in Acts and how ambiguously ethnic identities are portrayed. Especially relevant here is his argument that the revelation of Paul's Roman credentials should not be limited to claims of citizenship. The author of Acts can and does clarify when citizenship rights are in view, but does so for Paul's Tarsian citizenship and the tribune's purchased Roman citizenship (22:27), not for Paul's claims to be a *Rhōmaios*. Furthermore, "the narrative contexts of Paul's claims in Acts 16 and 22 require that Paul's claim reach beyond mere citizenship to a wider ethnic claim" (Barreto 2010, 170). In both settings, but perhaps especially in Acts 16 where the charges leveled against Paul (and Silas) have an ethnic basis, Paul's Roman claims challenge his accusers' assumptions regarding ethnic boundaries and mark him as an irreducibly complex, "hybrid" character (39–180; see also Muñoz-Larrondo 2008).

The ambiguity with which Paul is presented in Acts is not always accepted, as interpreters have tended to downplay the language of ethnicity in Acts or even tried to limit, clarify, and/or organize the various aspects of Paul's identity. Ben Witherington III, for example, states that "Paul's sense of identity came first from his Christian faith, secondly from his Jewish heritage, and only thirdly from his Greco-Roman heritage" (1998, 501). Yet, as Barreto notes, Acts appears "little concerned with creating a hierarchy of identities for Paul, and Witherington's gradation elides ethnic and religious identities. Even worse, it oversimplifies the complicated portrayal of Paul's multiple identities in Acts by treating these three dimensions of identity as self-contained antitheses" (2010, 147). Witherington's labels are problematic in other ways as well. While Acts notes when and where the term *Christian* comes into use (Acts 11:26), it is not clear that this is a term Acts claims for the followers of Jesus in the narrative (Pervo 2006, 290–91, 414 n. 93). Further, the label *Greco-Roman* obscures the complex ways in which Greek and Roman identities, which were constantly being renegotiated and redefined, were sometimes positioned against each other.

This brings into relief another aspect of Paul's identity in Acts: Paul's Greekness. The process, raw materials, and means of constructing and contesting identity in Acts have striking analogies to Greek texts of the Second Sophistic, in which educated, elite, albeit subjugated Greeks—most of them, like Paul, Roman citizens—repositioned themselves over against the colonizing Romans by recourse to Greek *paideia* or education (Gilbert 2006; Nasrallah 2008).

Several features of the portrayal of Paul in Acts are relevant here. He is generally portrayed along elite lines, including the city affiliations he possesses as well as the people with whom he associates on his travels (Neyrey 1993). He is a consummate and effective public speaker, generally following rhetorical conventions in his speeches as well as in the hand gestures that accompany them (see Acts 21:40; Carhart 2013). In addition, the portrait of Paul in Acts appears to be modeled on the figure of Socrates to a significant extent (Alexander 1993; Dupertuis 2009). All of these features construct Paul as a *pepaideumenoi*, an educated man. Tim Whitmarsh notes, "to practise *paideia* was to strive for a very particular form of identity, a fusion of manliness, elitism, and Greekness" (2005, 15). The association of *paideia* and Greek identity meant that it could be acquired. This is the case for Lucian of Samosata and Favorinus, two important figures of the Second Sophistic who are born "barbarian" but acquire a Greek identity through education (Whitmarsh 2001, 116–30), as well as, one could argue, for the Paul of Acts. If ambiguity is a central feature of Acts, with respect to identity and ethnicity no one symbolizes that ambiguity better than Paul.

I read Acts as an attempt to carve out a space for a community in the cultural landscape of the early Roman Empire. The identities Acts creates are necessarily made from the available materials, but they are nonetheless something new. The true Israel now includes Gentiles, for whom the traditional markers of covenant membership no longer apply. Gentile Christians are in some ways no longer Greeks and Romans, nor anything else in the traditional ways these labels could be understood, in part because they now worship the one true God of Israel. Paul is clearly Jewish, as well as Roman and Greek. Acts uses, rearranges, bends, and even breaks, cultural, religious, national, and ethnic boundaries—the lines between which are fuzzy—in the process of setting up new ones. I cannot always fully identify with the particular space that Acts tries to carve out for Christians in its time, but I can identify with the complex cultural world it presents and with the need to constantly negotiate one's place within it.

The Challenges of Defining Latino/a Biblical Criticism

Debates about identity and ethnicity generally, whether they are focused on the ancient Mediterranean or our contemporary world, necessarily bring up questions of definition. Francisco Lozada nicely captures one of the key difficulties of these debates and discussions as a "tension between essentialist and non-essentialist perspectives: between the notion of identity as something given and something that is always in process" (Lozada 2003, 15). Like Lozada, I land on the latter end of this spectrum, primarily because of the diverse and evolving complexity of Latino/a identities. For this reason I prefer a focus on the Latino/a critic over against a Latino/a hermeneutic or even Latino/a criticism, in part because it allows for an answer that is descriptive, not prescriptive, thus allowing for the current diversity of Latino/a experiences.

In his important "first sortie" on describing Latino/a biblical criticism, Segovia stresses the constructed nature of "Latin(o/a)ness," describing it as always

> formulated within particular historical and social-cultural contexts and advanced from particular standpoints and agendas, from which junctures it derives a meaning or set of meanings. The concept is thus always situated and ideological—variegated and shifting, pointed and political. Such meaning, moreover, is always subject to interpretation and debate, given the situated and ideological character of all reading and research. The concept is thus always evasive and fragile as well: differently perceived and defined, enmeshed in discussion and dispute. (2009, 199–200)

This statement, which Segovia refers to as "a seemingly obvious but nonetheless fundamental point, worth reiterating at the outset" (199), is important for highlighting the contested, evolving, and always incomplete nature of such discussions. It is also significant and "worth reiterating," as he notes, because it is a point that can easily be taken for granted. However "seemingly obvious" it may be, the reality of the messiness and slipperiness of Latino/a identities has not always found expression in the welcome increase of publications by Latino/a theologians and biblical critics in the 1980s and 1990s. Some of that work, as Michelle González has noted, can overlook the distinctive histories, cultures, and experiences of the diverse peoples who are named by terms such as *Latino/a* or *Hispanic* (2006, 20–21). This is understandable and was likely necessary as part of the process of creating space for and establishing Latino/a voices within the academy, but it is something worth noting and, in my judgment, being mindful of in conversations devoted to mapping the spaces inhabited by Latino/a biblical critics.

The context of González's critique is an articulation of an Afro-Cuban theology, in which she argues that some of the ways in which Latino/a identity has been understood and defined in Latino/a theology have not allowed for some aspects of the Cuban experience, particularly with regards to race. Despite the fact that the references to the diversity of Latino/a communities abound, she finds in Latino/a theological discourse a "tension between claiming the diversity of Latino/as while at times discursively negating it" (21). The diversity is often noted and very particularly named in a scholar's self-disclosure (along the lines of what I have done above in this essay). However, she argues, "these very acts of self-definition are subjected to an overarching homogenization in the same commentary" (21).

That Latino/a experiences are usually described in language that takes the encounter of indigenous peoples with the Spanish conquerors as normative effectively flattens the diversity of Latino/as and leaves little room for the differences. González notes, for example, that the common "focus on the conquest of indigenous peoples [comes] at the expense of other dimensions of the conquest—namely the transatlantic slave trade and the colonial era in the Americas" (22). She also points out that the term *mestizaje* is often used in Latino/a theology not just in reference to people of mixed Spanish and indigenous origin but in a much more general way to name the sense of double identity that is central to the experience of most Latino/as in the United States. The term "has become equivalent of mixture and hybridity" (26). When this happens terms such as *mestizaje* and *mulatez*, which are sometimes used synonymously, are deprived of "their historical value as terms that designate indigenous/Spanish and Spanish/African mixture" (27). González does not argue for doing away with the category Latino/a, as she recognizes the importance of this and similar terms in naming an historical pan-Latino legacy and for the political power the term can give historically marginalized communities. Rather, she "propose[s] that Latino/as critically examine the consequences of

'Latino/' and 'Hispanic' as discursive categories, as well as the essentialist inclinations such categories contain" (21).

This tendency toward generalization can also be seen in discussions of Latino/a biblical and criticism, especially attempts to move from the work of individual scholars to hermeneutical models that could be described as Latino/a. Two such essays are worth looking at briefly.

In "Reading the Hyphens: An Emerging Biblical Hermeneutics for Latino/Hispanic U.S. Protestants," Francisco García-Treto begins by acknowledging the diversity of Latino/a backgrounds and identities:

> A broad diversity of group identities and cultures is included in [the] category [of Hispanic/Latino], from New Mexican Hispanos to Mexican Americans (or Chicanos) in California and Texas, to Cuban American (or Cubans) in Florida, to Puerto Ricans (or Nuyoricans) in New York, not to mention Dominicans, Salvadorians, Guatemalans, or many others. Diverse historical experience, economic factors, and political allegiances, as well as the appearance of generational differences and different degrees of assimilation to Anglo culture and facility with English complicate that diversity even more. (1999, 161)

Here García-Treto goes further than most by naming some of that diversity.[3] However, despite the fact that he is on the more careful and detailed end of the spectrum, this description is necessarily limited and cannot possibly be comprehensive. I fall, for example, under the "and many others" heading. I recognize that my little corner of the Latino/a landscape is sparsely populated, and I do not really expect any such listing to be fully comprehensive, but I think it is worth noting that lists both include and, at some level, necessarily exclude. In addition, any such listing is not likely to be able to keep up with the ways in which Latino/a identities will change and evolve in the future.

Paying attention to groups that have historically been larger and more prominent is certainly fair, as I think it is in the context of García-Treto's essay as well as in introductions to Latino/a religious experience in the United States (e.g., Avalos 2004). It is also important, however, to note the limits of categories and lists. In his discussion of two authors not typically included in lists of Chicano/a religious thinkers, Rudy Busto argues that

---

3. González (2006, 29) notes and similarly appreciates another attempt at a more detailed list by Benjamin Valentin (2002, 9).

the "predicament of catalogue and classification of what constitutes specifically Chicano(a), or even broadly, 'Latino(a)' religion(s) ... needs to be questioned for underlying essentialisms of culture, identity, and nationalisms that may in fact prohibit the understanding of the richness of our 'object' of study" (2003, 242). While not addressing Latino/a biblical criticism, Busto's concern is certainly relevant. Lists and criteria do important work so long as we are mindful of their limitations.

In that same essay García-Treto goes on to list several features of a "new, U.S. Hispanic/Latino consciousness (and culture)" (1999, 161), including the sense of "being 'a people in exile,'" a generally ecumenical approach, the reliance on and the prominence of Latin American liberation theology, and the importance of maintaining ties to both the academy and the church (162–66). This clearly describes an important and sizable interpretive community, but it is not and cannot be complete. As with the term *mestizo*, the term *exile* describes the experiences of some more accurately than others, which, to be fair, García-Treto notes elsewhere (2009, 71). The sense of connection between the academy and the church has indeed been central in Latino/a theology and biblical criticism, but I wonder if the same will be said of future generations of Latino/a scholars.[4] The ecumenical nature of the emerging Latino/a community, which García-Treto describes as "inclusive of Roman Catholics, mainline Protestants, and Pentecostals ... who are developing interpretive strategies notably free of denominational baggage" (1999, 163), also has its limits, as it does not include some Protestant denominations and groups for whom approaches to Scripture preclude some of the interpretive strategies central to liberation theology (Dupertuis 1987). In fairness, García-Treto does not claim to reflect approaches to the Bible by all Latino/as, yet it is still worth noting that the "emerging hermeneutics" to which he points very accurately describes some, but not all, Latino/a communities and Latino/a scholars.

The tendency to describe Latino/as in a homogeneous way is even stronger in Pablo Jiménez's essay, "In Search of a Hispanic Model of Biblical Interpretation." Jiménez uses similarities in the interpretive approaches to the Bible of two of the most influential Latino/a theologians, Virgilio Elizondo and Justo González, as the basis for a description

---

4. In the 2009 panel discussions that led to this volume, the importance of a commitment to the church was a much stronger theme in the comments of established scholars than it was among junior scholars.

of the "characteristic traits of Latino hermeneutics" (1995, 54), which he describes as: (1) contextual, insofar as it emphasizes "reading the text from a particular social location, namely, Latino reality" (54); (2) driven by liberation hermeneutics; and (3) postmodern in its questioning of metanarratives. Repeated references to the Latino people, to a particular social location, and to a Hispanic theology—all in the singular—leave little room for the actual diversity of Latino/a experiences. While these characteristics clearly and fairly describe the works of Elizondo and González, and likely also reflect a sizable portion of Latino/a scholars, they do not reflect everyone.

I must confess to considerable unease over my use of these two essays to illustrate what could be seen as essentialist tendencies. This is especially so in the case of García-Treto, who in his work is consistently sensitive to the diversity of Latino/a experiences and is keenly aware of the importance of providing spaces for the differences (2009, 71). I think of him as a model of how to do the work of careful and critical contextualization, both of the texts we read and of ourselves as readers.

So what does it mean to be a Latino/a biblical critic? I do not want to suggest that clear definitions are not important, useful, or necessary, but I do want to stress the importance of keeping the conversations open so as to not limit how we name our Latino/a experiences and allowing for some messiness in how we do so.

Works Cited

Alexander, Loveday C. A. 1993. Acts and Ancient Intellectual Biography. Pages 31–63 in *The Book of Acts in Its Ancient Literary Setting*. Edited by Bruce W. Winter and Andrew D. Clarke. Book of Acts in Its First Century Setting 1. Grand Rapids: Eerdmans.

Avalos, Hector, ed. 2004. *Introduction to the U.S. Latina and Latino Religious Experience*. Religion in the Americas 2. Boston: Brill.

Barreto, Eric D. 2010. *Ethnic Negotiations: The Function of Race and Ethnicity in Acts 16*. WUNT 2/294. Tübingen: Mohr Siebeck.

Buell, Denise Kimber. 2005. *Why This New Race: Ethnic Reasoning in Early Christianity*. New York: Columbia University Press.

Burrus, Virginia. 2007. The Gospel of Luke and the Acts of the Apostles. Pages 133–55 in *A Postcolonial Commentary on the New Testament Writings*. Edited by Fernando F. Segovia and R. S. Sugirtharajah. London: T&T Clark.

Busto, Rudy. 2003. The Predicament of *Nepantla*: Chicano(a) Religions in the Twenty-First Century. Pages 238–49 in *New Horizons in Hispanic/Latino(a) Theology*. Edited by Benjamín Valentín. Cleveland: Pilgrim.

Carhart, Ryan. 2013. The Second Sophistic and the Cultural Idealization of Paul. Pages 187–208 in *Engaging Early Christian History: Reading Acts in the Second Century*. Edited by Rubén René Dupertuis and Todd Penner. Sheffield: Acumen.

Dupertuis, Atilio René. 1987. *Liberation Theology: A Study in Its Soteriology*. Seminary Doctoral Dissertation Series. Berrien Springs, Mich.: Andrews University Press.

Dupertuis, Rubén René. 2009. Socratizing Paul: The Trials of Paul in the Acts of the Apostles. *The Fourth R* 22, no. 6:11–18, 28.

Elizondo, Virgilio. 2000. *Galilean Journey: The Mexican-American Promise*. Rev. ed. Maryknoll, N.Y.: Orbis.

Espinoza, Gastón. 2006. Methodological Reflections on Social Science Research on Latino Religions. Pages 13–45 in *Rethinking Latino(a) Religion and Identity*. Edited by Miguel A. De La Torre and Gastón Espinoza. Cleveland: Pilgrim.

Fitzmyer, Joseph A. 1998. *The Acts of the Apostles: A New Translation with Introduction and Commentary*. AB 31. New York: Doubleday.

García-Treto, Francisco. 1999. Reading the Hyphens: An Emerging Biblical Hermeneutics for Latino/Hispanic U.S. Protestants. Pages 160–76 in *Protestantes/Protestants: Hispanic Christianity within Mainline Traditions*. Edited by David Maldonado Jr. Nashville: Abingdon.

———. 2000. Hyphenating Joseph: A View of Genesis 39–41 from the Cuban Diaspora. Pages 134–45 in *Interpreting beyond Borders*. Edited by Fernando F. Segovia. Bible and Postcolonialism 3. Sheffield: Sheffield Academic Press.

———. 2009. Exile in the Hebrew Bible: A Postcolonial Look from the Cuban Diaspora. Pages 65–78 in *They Were All Together in One Place? Toward Minority Biblical Criticism*. Edited by Randall C. Bailey, Tat-siong Benny Liew, and Fernando F. Segovia. SemeiaSt 57. Atlanta: Society of Biblical Literature.

Gaventa, Beverly Roberts. 2003. *The Acts of the Apostles*. Abingdon New Testament Commentaries. Nashville: Abingdon.

Gilbert, Gary. 2006. Luke-Acts and Negotiation of Authority and Identity in the Roman World. Pages 83–104 in *The Multivalence of Biblical Texts and Theological Meanings*. Edited by Christine Helmer with the assistance of Charlene T. Higbe. SBLSymS 37. Atlanta: Society of Biblical Literature.

González, Michelle A. 2006. *Afro-Cuban Theology: Race, Religion, Culture and Identity*. Gainesville: University Press of Florida.

Guardiola-Sáenz, Leticia A. 1997. Borderless Women and Borderless Texts: A Cultural Reading of Matthew 15:21–28. *Semeia* 78:69–81.

Hampl, Patricia. 1999. *I Could Tell You Stories: Sojourns in the Land of Memory*. New York: Norton.

Jiménez, Pablo A. 1995. In Search of a Hispanic Model of Biblical Interpretation. *JHLT* 3, no. 2:44–64.

Johnson, Luke Timothy. 1992. *The Acts of the Apostles*. Sacra pagina 5. Collegeville, Minn.: Liturgical Press.

Lozada, Francisco, Jr. 2003. Encountering the Bible in an Age of Diversity and Globalization: Teaching toward Intercultural Criticism. Pages 13–34 in *New Horizons in Hispanic/Latino(a) Theology*. Edited by Benjamín Valentín. Cleveland: Pilgrim.

Muñoz-Larrondo, Rubén. 2008. Living in Two Worlds—A Postcolonial Reading of the Acts of the Apostles. Ph.D. diss. Vanderbilt University.

Nasrallah, Laura. 2008. The Acts of the Apostles, Greek Cities, and Hadrian's Panhellenion. *JBL* 127:533–66.

Neyrey, Jerome H. 1993. Luke's Social Location of Paul: Cultural Anthropology and the Status of Paul in Acts. Pages 251–79 in *History, Literature, and Society in the Book of Acts*. Edited by Ben Witherington III. Cambridge: Cambridge University Press.

Parsons, Mikeal C. 2009. *Acts*. Paideia Commentaries on the New Testament. Grand Rapids: Baker.

Pérez Firmat, Gustavo. 1994. *Life on the Hyphen: The Cuban-American Way*. Austin: University of Texas Press.

Pervo, Richard I. 2006. *Dating Acts: Between the Evangelists and the Apologists*. Santa Rosa, Calif.: Polebridge.

———. 2009. *Acts: A Commentary*. Hermeneia. Minneapolis: Fortress.

Segovia, Fernando F. 1994. Reading the Bible as Hispanic Americans. Pages 167–73 in vol. 1 of *The New Interpreter's Bible*. Edited by Leander E. Keck. Nashville: Abingdon.

———. 1995a. "And They Began to Speak in Other Tongues": Competing Modes of Discourse in Contemporary Biblical Criticism. Pages 1–32 in *Social Location and Biblical Interpretation in the United States*. Vol. 1 of *Reading from This Place*. Edited by Fernando F. Segovia and Mary Ann Tolbert. Minneapolis: Fortress.

———. 1995b. Toward a Hermeneutics of the Diaspora: A Hermeneutics of Otherness and Engagement. Pages 57–74 in *Social Location and Biblical Interpretation in the United States*. Vol. 1 of *Reading from This Place*. Edited by Fernando F. Segovia and Mary Ann Tolbert. Minneapolis: Fortress.

———. 2000. *Decolonizing Biblical Studies: A View from the Margins*. Maryknoll, N.Y.: Orbis.

———. 2009. Toward Latino/a American Biblical Criticism: Latin(o/a)ness as Problematic. Pages 193–225 in *They Were All Together in One Place? Toward Minority Biblical Criticism*. Edited by Randall C. Bailey, Tat-siong Benny Liew, and Fernando F. Segovia. SemeiaSt 57. Atlanta: Society of Biblical Literature.

Segovia, Fernando F., and Mary Ann Tolbert, eds. 1995. *Social Location and Biblical Interpretation in the United States*. Vol. 1 of *Reading from This Place*. Minneapolis: Fortress.

Tyson, Joseph B. 1988. The Problem of Jewish Rejection in Acts. Pages 124–37 in *Luke-Acts and the Jewish People: Eight Critical Perspectives*. Edited by Joseph B. Tyson. Minneapolis: Augsburg.

Valentín, Benjamín. 2002. *Mapping Public Theology: Beyond Culture, Identity, and Difference*. Harrisburg, Pa.: Trinity Press International.

Whitmarsh, Tim. 2001. *Greek Literature and the Roman Empire: The Politics of Imitation*. Oxford: Oxford University Press.

———. 2005. *The Second Sophistic*. Greece and Rome: New Surveys in the Classics 35. Oxford: Oxford University Press.

Witherington, Ben, III. 1998. *The Acts of the Apostles: A Socio-rhetorical Commentary*. Grand Rapids: Eerdmans.

Latino/a Biblical Hermeneutics: Problematic, Objectives, Strategies

Cristina García-Alfonso

What does it mean to be a Latino/a biblical critic is the question we have been asked to ponder in this project. Such a question is wide open, inviting the biblical critic to respond to it from any number of angles. From my perspective, the essence of what constitutes being a Latina biblical critic demands to be answered at a personal level: it is who I am that, in turn, defines me academically as a scholar of Hebrew Bible studies. In order to answer this question, therefore, I shall address the two identities, the two contexts, that shape who I am today: first, being a Latina—living in the United States as part of the Latina/o theological and biblical scene at work in the country; second, being Caribbean, specifically Cuban—a part of the Cuban context and reality that continues to influence the present and future of Cuba. Since being Latina and Cuban are intrinsically related to my own self-understanding as a feminist biblical scholar, I shall reflect on the meaning of both identities and how they shape my reading of biblical texts.

I have lived now for almost eleven years in the United States. I have the privilege of participating in the knowledge production that takes place in academic settings, part of a group that engages at sophisticated levels in critical readings of ancient texts. Along with other Latino/a biblical scholars, I am also part of the various conversations that influence the Latino/a theological and biblical landscape in the country. My silent resistance to fully becoming American reveals the identity that prevails in my life: my Cuban identity. This identity is framed not only by the fact that I was born and raised in Cuba but also by the situation in which I lived and in which my family and friends continue to live on the island. This situation shapes who I am as a person, as an intercultural feminist Hebrew Bible scholar. Cuba and the United States have become two dwelling places for me, and somehow I feel that I do not live fully in either of them, but in the center.

However, I do recognize that of these dwelling places Cuba is the one to which I feel closer. Thus my answer to the question of the meaning of being a Latina critic is constructed on the basis of my Cuban social location. Being a biblical critic for me means to engage in a hermeneutic that is corporal, feminist, and attentive to issues of survival.

A corporal hermeneutics acknowledges the human body as part of the task of biblical interpretation. In my case such a hermeneutics incorporates the human corporal reality that is so much a part of my Cuban roots: emotions, body language, lively expressions that influence my experience of God's mystery. This corporal reality becomes a lens through which I read the Hebrew Bible. When reading biblical stories, I pay attention to the body language that is present or absent in the text: the smells, the touches, the body language expressions, and the actions among the characters. This hermeneutics also pays attention to the everyday-life encounters of people in their houses, places of worship, public squares, and the countryside. In sum, it is a hermeneutics that is in tune with the Hebrew understanding that celebrates the totality of the human being.

A feminist hermeneutics from a Cuban social location looks at the realities faced by men and especially women on the island. These realities have to do with issues of survival, where women are the ones who bear the stress of finding ways to survive and sustain their families. Having an understanding of the struggles faced by Cuban women provides me with a lens to explore the realities of women in ancient Israelite contexts, the difficulties they encounter and the choices they make in the midst of the conflicts they face.

Lastly, a survival hermeneutics is deeply shaped by the context of survival, *resolviendo*, which is still very much present in Cuba. Survival in Cuba has been a way of living that has profoundly influenced Cubans for more than twenty years, and still does. *Resolviendo* becomes a hermeneutical lens through which I read biblical texts. This hermeneutical lens is also enriched by the tools that postcolonial, ideological, and feminist critiques have to offer when reading biblical texts.

In this study I begin by exploring the origin and use of the terms *resolviendo* and *resolver* in Cuba today and then proceed to examine a text from the Hebrew Bible in the light of such concepts. In the first major section, I enter the Cuban reality of survival as a "text" in order to dialogue with other texts. I examine the elements of *resolviendo* in conversation with a number of sources, including novels published by Cuban writers who left the island in the early 1990s. Although the latter are works of fiction, the realities portrayed in them record the struggle for survival that affects people on the island. I draw on such works in search of insights that can unveil this reality of *resolviendo*. These are not the only sources that I use in this regard, but they do constitute an entry point, a backdrop, for my quest in understanding the essence of the term. My aim is to construct a hermeneutical lens of survival and *resolviendo*. In the second major section, then, I bring such a hermeneutical lens to bear on the Bible. I do so as I undertake a journey into the story of Rahab in the book of Joshua. In the final major section, I conclude by summarizing the figure of Rahab as a woman who *resuelve*, in the face of her context, a struggle for survival, and by way of her resourcefulness, as a determined survivor.

Resolviendo: Ongoing Struggle for Survival in Cuba Today

The term *resolviendo*, which means finding an answer or solution, first acquired its specific Cuban meaning at the beginning of the 1990s.[1] It was then that Cuba began to suffer the economic consequences of the fall of the socialist bloc of countries, from which a great part of its economic resources and assistance had come during the previous four decades. Without subsidies, Cuba and its people had to create new economic opportunities. This was not an easy task. The Cuban government gave this period of economic crisis the name "special period" in an effort to convince the people that the stringent measures put into effect would last only a short time. The government announced a series of restrictions on food, medicines and medical supplies, and gasoline. This "special period," which still continues today, creates enormous difficulties for Cubans, who can no longer buy what they need to survive with the salary they receive from

---

1. I use the terms *resolviendo* and *resolver* to describe the concept coded by Cubans to explain the reality of survival they face. I also use *resolviendo* as the participle that describes the action of the verb *resolver*. Sometimes, I use the verb *resolver* to describe the same action as *resolviendo*. Finally, I employ the conjugated form of the verb in the third person plural *(resuelven)* to point out how people deal with survival and solving *(resolver)* a situation.

Resolver is originally a Latin word that means to release or to let go. Among its several meanings in Spanish one finds: to strongly take some determination; to resume, to sum up; to resolve a difficulty or a doubt. *Resolver* also has other connotations: finding a solution to a problem, carrying out an action, and taking a decision on speaking up or doing something. A parallel term to *resolver* is *bregar* (see Díaz Quiñones).

the socialist government. In effect, Cuban salaries are sufficient to supply food and other necessities for only half of each month. It is in this context that the words *resolver* and *resolviendo* began to have a special meaning for Cubans. *Resolver* in many ways became synonymous with struggling to survive, or making do.

In Cuba, *resolver* has a more particular meaning. It refers to whatever one has to do in order to obtain the basic things needed to survive. *Resolver* is not about getting what one needs for the long term, but rather to enable, by whatever means one has, one's family to meet its daily needs. Since the government does not provide the food, medicines, or clothing that the people need, and since the people have no money to buy such goods, *resolver* covers a range of activities, including bartering, planting vegetables in one's garden, or keeping chickens and even pigs in one's backyard.

Resolver also refers to taking "illegally" from the government whatever one is able to use directly for selling or bartering. Since the government owns all businesses, and since nearly everyone in Cuba works for the government (the exceptions are the few who work for the churches), people simply take whatever they can from their workplaces. *Resolviendo* has become the main task of most Cubans in order to be able to go on with their lives, to face the situation at hand. Every day Cubans wake up knowing that, besides doing what is required of them at their jobs, they will also have the additional stress of *resolver*, of obtaining what they and their families need in order to make it through the day. *Resolver* is not an individual or isolated task but a communal experience that involves all persons in the struggle for survival.

An interesting aspect of *resolviendo* that I have discovered is that for Cubans the very word itself, its invention and use, becomes a way of *resolver*, for the word covers and legitimizes the struggle for survival. At the same time, having a word to identify the action also legitimates the painful dilemma of dealing with these types of uncomfortable situations, where atypical behaviors and actions that may not be considered moral are required in order to preserve life. Thus, to survive that struggle of breaking laws and moral codes, the word *resolviendo* is in itself a way of *resolver* or coming to terms with this issue.[2]

---

2. I am aware that when talking about *resolviendo* ethical questions may arise. I think that *resolviendo* and ethics are not separate matters. We cannot ask what role ethics plays in *resolviendo*. They are one and the same thing. By this I mean that *resolviendo* is itself an ethics, an uncommon and atypical ethics of survival that shakes

Resolver starts when people find themselves in extremely difficult situations and have to find ways of making it through the day. To find solutions, people have to change the ways in which they have dealt with everyday life. *Resolver* requires one to change the patterns in one's life, to shift one's values, and to make accommodations. I have watched this process in Cuba, in my own life, and in the lives of my family and friends. We have put aside certain values in order to hold on to the highest value—life. *Resolver* becomes a way of facing life, of understanding life, its value and its requirements for survival. It is how one thinks about life: one has to *resolver* in order to live, and one lives in order to *resolver*. *Resolver* makes one be constantly on the lookout for opportunities to obtain the bare necessities of life, like food, medicine, and clothing. If one is not able to *resolver*, one's life is in jeopardy. There are two key features of *resolviendo* that inform my reading of the Rahab story: preserving life at any cost and prostitution or "selling the body" for survival.

Preserving Life at Any Cost

The ultimate goal of *resolviendo* is to survive and preserve life at any cost. I find Karl Jaspers to the point here: "The objective of my *conscious struggle* against an opponent I can see is to expand my living space. It may be waged economically, by peaceful means, or by force of war, by surprising achievements, by trickery and harmful measures—in effect, an equally cruel fight goes on everywhere if the stakes are the expense of material existence, and ultimately life or death" (1970, 205). When life is at stake, it does not matter how we handle the struggle, means, and goals. *Resolviendo* is about people getting what they need in order to survive, regardless of how peacefully or fiercely that struggle may take place, and regardless of whether it happens by trickery or other unconventional ways.

In the following fragment from the novel *Posesas de la Habana* by Elena Dovalpage, Elsa, one of the characters, describes her neighbor's job: "Pancho Rivera works as a security guard at Carlos Tercero Mall and every now and then he sells chocolate candies and soda cans that he steals from

---

the foundation of what traditional ethical understandings may be for the sake of fighting to preserve life as the central common good for humanity. Among untraditional and morally questioned ways of survival one can also find situations of just war, killing another human being as a way of preserving innocent lives, or stealing from those who are more fortunate to allow the less fortunate and the poorest to survive.

the stores. Well, I don't criticize him. In the end one has to defend oneself" (2004, 13). Stealing is Pancho's way of *resolver*. When there are no other choices available, stealing is simply an unconventional way of preserving one's life. Being able to sell what he steals from the stores gives Pancho the money he needs to survive. Stealing is wrong, but when people face a limited situation, preserving life is the highest good, even if it entails deception, stealing, and other normally unethical behaviors.

Prostitution or "Selling the Body" for Survival

Besides leaving professional jobs to work at menial labor or making crafts to sell to tourists, prostitution or "selling the body" is another phenomenon that has appeared in Cuba as part of the "special period." The work of Ivone Gebara is particularly valuable in considering how people survive poverty and oppression, because it addresses that reality precisely from the place of poor people in Latin America.[3] Selling one's body, *jineterismo*,[4] is something done by both women and men, but admittedly mostly by women. However, since this phenomenon occurs more among women than men, the feminist contribution of Gebara on the realities of women in Latin America offers insights into issues of survival on the part of women and *jineteras* in Cuba today.

One of the categories developed by Gebara is *lo cotidiano*.[5] Gebara explores the poverty that daily affects women's lives. This social phenomenon oppresses women, keeps them from living fully, from having the basic things (i.e., shelter and food) that they and their loved ones need in order to survive every day, and brings them to the edge of despair and death. One of the consequences of poverty is having to turn to "selling sex" in order to survive. Gebara insists on the expression *selling sex* instead of using any form of the word *prostitution* to make clear that the women are

---

3. Although the locus for Gebara's work is in the context of Latin America, particularly in Brazil, I think that it provides an important theoretical framework for looking at issues of women's sex trades in other societies.

4. *Jineteras* (hustlers; the word literally means "jockeys"). *Jineteras* is used for female prostitutes, while *jineteros* is used for male prostitutes. The action of prostitution is called *jinetear*, while *jineterismo* is the noun used to describe such action. For a detailed study on prostitution in Cuba, see Trumbull 2004.

5. The expression *lo cotidiano* means everyday life. This term is also used by *Mujerista* theologian Isasi-Díaz (1996, 2004).

not giving up their values but that they are using their bodies to get what they need in order to survive another day. In this way they are able to get what society should have provided for them in the first place.

Many of the *jineteras* in Cuba are professional people like Claudia, a character in *El hombre, la hembra y el hambre*, a novel by Daína Chaviano. With a university background in the history of art, this is the way that she thinks about prostitution before becoming a *jinetera*:

> But I don't want to become another Sissi who even had to change her name. She says it is for protection, a common custom among ones of the same profession, a mask like the one used by the geishas, those Japanese whores and wives who sold their bodies after being women of culture for many years. That is what Cuban women have become: the geishas of the Western hemisphere. What was the point of having treatises about art, discussions about the philosophical schools in Pericles' times, lectures about the Hegelian origins of Marxism, disquisitions about neoclassicism, tours of Old Havana to study the buildings that we have passed so many times without realizing that they were the best examples of Caribbean baroque—to end up in bed with a guy in exchange for food? (1998, 42–43)

Claudia reflects on the agony of becoming a *jinetera*, the frustration of being a highly educated woman and yet not able to support herself. Deeply aware as she is of her daily life, her intellectual analysis of the reality of Cuban women and their choices for survival points out to her the reality that affects her own existence as well as the world to which she and other women belong. As Gebara states, women are subjects of their own struggles, capable of relating not only to their own situations but also to other human beings and the world. Women are immersed *in* and *with* the world that surrounds them.

The Story of Rahab

Given these hermeneutical reflections, I now turn to a biblical text. The story of Rahab (Josh 2:1–24) has been traditionally interpreted as the account of a foreign woman and low-status prostitute who changes the course of her life when she converts to Yahweh, the God of Moses. In return for her faithful act of saving the spies sent by Joshua to search the land of Canaan, Rahab, along with her family, is saved when her city of Jericho is destroyed. This is also a conquest tale, which parallels the story of

Moses and the spies in Numbers 13 (Frymer-Kensky 1997, 58). The book of Joshua tells how, forty years later, a new generation was determined to conquer the land, this time guided by Joshua.

The passage, of course, has layers of complexities. One such is Rahab's status as a female prostitute. Was she really a prostitute, a *zônâ*, or was she perhaps an independent woman with some wealth who was labeled pejoratively as a prostitute by her society? Another is Rahab's intention to embrace the God of Joshua. Was her intention genuine or does her theological discourse in verses 9–23 reveal her conversion simply as a tactic that would allow her to survive, *resolver,* along with her family? Was Rahab's act of hiding the spies motivated by a sense of religious commitment to the God of Moses and Joshua or by a primal desire to survive?

To understand Rahab, it is imperative to examine her social status and the nuances of her personality. Three important aspects of Rahab's personality define who she is and the ways in which she acts and reacts in the story: she is a woman, a foreigner, and a prostitute. Social status defined the level of agency on the part of women. In and of itself being a woman in ancient Israel limited her actions and aspirations. Being a foreigner and a prostitute limited even more her access to power. Rahab is a Canaanite, a foreign (i.e., non-Israelite) woman living in the Canaanite land of Jericho, soon to be destroyed by the Israelite army of Joshua. She becomes a foreigner (to the Canaanites) once her family is spared from death and she joins the Israelites. Rahab is not only foreign among the Israelites; she is also foreign in her own land of Jericho.

She lives by the city wall of Jericho, which metaphorically locates her as an outsider in her own community, among her own people. At the same time, she remains an insider, because, even though on the social periphery, she still belongs to the town of Jericho. This situation creates a tension within Rahab: on the one hand, she may wish to stay faithful to her country and people; on the other hand, she needs to save herself and her family from the upcoming destruction. Her location as both insider and outsider gives her a particular autonomy to move freely in her own land—to be at the center of her community participating in whatever takes place there, and yet at the same time remain by the wall of the city, at the periphery of society. Thus Rahab moves between two communities and two worlds, both of which the narrative implies she knows very well.

There is no account of what happens to Rahab and her family once they escape the destruction of Jericho (Josh 6). However, in some Jewish interpretations she marries Joshua (b. Meg. 14b) and becomes the mother of priests and prophets, such as Jeremiah and Ezekiel (Ruth Rab. 2:1; and cf. Num. Rab. 8:9; Frymer-Kensky 1997, 67). Lastly, Rahab is mentioned in the Matthean genealogy of Jesus as one of his ancestors, which reinforces the presence of marginalized people as part of his ancestry (Tamar, Rahab, Ruth, the wife of David).

Knowing Rahab's status is of help in understanding her actions. In Josh 2:4 Rahab acts for the first time, hiding the spies and lying about their whereabouts. When the king of Jericho learns that the spies are in the land (more precisely, he is told that they are at Rahab's place), he sends messengers there and asks her to deliver the men, but she lies to them, pretending that she does not know where they have gone. Rahab's actions—what she says and does—are profoundly shaped by a sense of survival. That she hides the spies and lies to the king's men unveils the very purpose of her actions. That she received the Israelite spies in her house suggests that she knew Jericho was undergoing a military occupation and that the destruction of the city was imminent. Having inside information of what was going to happen to her town gave her an advantage over others in Jericho. Still, a question of loyalty arises. How can she betray her own people and side with the enemy? One way to answer this question is to remember who Rahab is. She is an outsider in her own town, a prostitute, or an independent woman living by the city wall, belonging to Jericho, yet living at the periphery of her own community. She had no strong ties to her people, and, feeling excluded from society, she recognized the possibility of survival for herself and her family. Thus she lied about the spies' location and hid them on the roof of her house.

Subsequently, in a lengthy speech Rahab acknowledges to the spies the mighty deeds of the God of Moses and recognizes Yahweh as the only God in the heavens and on earth. In this confession the narrator presents a picture of a Rahab who converts to the God of Joshua. It is more likely that the narrator deliberately portrays a view that is acceptable: a woman and a prostitute who is a Canaanite convert to the God of Israel and who "knows" all the deeds that this God has done. We do not and cannot know whether her intentions of embracing Yahweh's religion are genuine. The point is not whether she really means it but the fact that she does it. She tells the spies what they want to hear, maybe gives them sexual favors, and in return obtains salvation for herself and her family. Embracing the God of Israel is her way of *resolver*, of doing what she needs to do at that point. Just as the town of Jericho is seized and colonized by the Israelites under Joshua's command, so Rahab is also colonized by the Israelites. Once she and her family are saved and her town destroyed, she goes to live with the Israelites. Changing location from her Canaanite land to the Israelite land raises issues about the dynamics between the colonizer and the colonized.⁶

From Rahab's speech one sees that she does not have total control over the ways things will turn out. She is very persuasive in presenting her theological and well-articulated discourse to the spies. Still, the spies have to respond to her speech and accept the deal she is proposing to them, to be spared from death and destruction in the name of God. The spies accept Rahab's proposal and promise to fulfill the oath that she has given to them on condition that she does not disclose details about their mission in the land.

Rahab's house is located by the city wall. This is a strategic location: the wall was important in that it was connected to the city gate. Not only is Rahab described as a prostitute (*zônâ*), her house is also described as the house of a woman prostitute (*bêt-'iššâ zônâ*). The Hebrew indicates that the spies entered (*bô'*) the house of a prostitute whose name was Rahab. This background shows that Rahab is both a prostitute and an independent woman, for her house is not the house of her father. As a matter of fact, later in the passage Rahab brings her family to her house (presumably from their own house) to be protected from the destruction of Jericho. Whether her house is an establishment, a brothel, or an inn is not mentioned in the text. It may be that Rahab's house is labeled as the house of a prostitute because she is indeed a prostitute, or it may be that the house received such a pejorative designation because she lived by herself and, even more likely, because she was an independent woman. The house of Rahab is the key space in which most of the action of this narrative happens.

First, we have the spies going to, entering, and dwelling there. I have already suggested that the actions of the spies—coming into the house and dwelling there—evoke sexual overtones, similar to the actions of coming and lying down with someone as sexual intercourse takes place (BDB, 98).⁷ Whether sexual intercourse took place we do not know. However, it is worth mentioning that the house of Rahab can be seen both literally as a

---

6. Rahab, like her land, is colonized by the Israelites. Just as her town is conquered and destroyed, so Rahab is conquered and taken to a different land. For more on postcolonial biblical interpretation of this story, see Rowlett 2000; Dube 2003.

7. For the verb "to come," BDB (98) refers to texts (Judg 15:1; 16:1; Gen 6:4; 16:2; 30:3; 38:8–9; 39:14; Deut 22:13; 2 Sam 12:24; 16:21; 20:3, among others) where the

place for the spies to dwell and rest and figuratively as a space to lie down and engage in sexual intercourse.

Second, the king's messengers come to the house asking for information about the spies. Rahab sends them in the wrong direction, since the spies at that point are still in the house. This time she has hidden them on the roof. After the king's messengers leave, she goes to the roof and talks to the spies.

The upper part of Rahab's house is the area where she hides the spies and also where negotiations between her and the spies take place. With the men relaxed and covered by the stalks of flax, ready to fall asleep and protected from any danger, this is the place that Rahab chooses to communicate her challenging message to them. The roof of her house provides a safe environment for the negotiations to take place. It appears that Rahab here creates an atmosphere of trust and safety for the spies that will allow her to address the pressing issue of saving their lives at the cost of saving her own and her family's. Rahab's use of this space helps her in her plan to survive and *resolver*, to find a solution for her conflict and save herself and her family. The negotiation between the spies and Rahab is successful, and Rahab lets the spies out of her house using a crimson rope that descends from the window.

Once out, the spies run to hide in the mountains, as Rahab had told them to do. The mountains are the last space mentioned in the narrative before they go back to Joshua's camp in Shittim. The mountains are a space Rahab uses to her advantage. By sending the spies there she secures their safety and also the completion of her negotiation with them. The mountains are the safe place where the spies can wait in security until the king's messengers stop their search and they can return to Shittim, having completed their mission.

Rahab and *Resolver*: The Struggle for Life

Rahab is one of those female characters of the Hebrew Bible who manages to work her way out of a limited situation by playing by the rules of her society. Being a woman, a foreigner, and a prostitute puts her in a difficult

---

verb means "entering a woman's tent or apartment (with implication *coire cum femina* [coitus with a woman])."

position in her society. In spite of her lack of power, she uses what she has at her disposal to survive in the midst of a difficult conflict.

Another important aspect of Rahab's story lies in the ways she uses her body as she interacts with others, like the spies. Although the text labels Rahab a prostitute, one does not know whether she engages in sexual activity with the spies. The Hebrew verbs used in the text, which can refer to physical actions of coming or entering a place as well as to sexual activity, give strong sexual nuances to the passage. Thus for the reader it will always be possible to see Rahab as someone who engages in sexual activity with the spies or as someone who may have simply welcomed them. At any rate, the text does leave room to appreciate the sexual overtones that are present in the story. In my opinion, these sexual overtones are present not only because of the types of Hebrew verbs used in the text but also because of the ways in which the text mingles these verbs with Rahab's words and actions. In other words, the entire interaction of Rahab with the spies is couched in sensuality and seduction. I see seduction not only in the use of these verbs but also in Rahab's persuasive words to the spies. Her well-articulated theological speech to the spies is convincing and leads them to believe what she says.

Rahab's wisdom and knowledge of her own location geographically as well as socially contribute to see how she *resuelve,* survives. Her location as someone who lives at the city wall and her identity as someone who is both an outsider and insider help her in her struggle. Rahab knows the worlds inside and outside the city very well. Thus she knows the best way to protect the spies when they are in her house at the city wall. She also gives them advice about the best place to hide outside the city in the mountains. As one who crosses the border and who has the freedom to go back and forth inside and outside two different worlds, Rahab possesses unique power.

Another important aspect of Rahab's power is that she knows the particularities of life and reality inside and outside the city. Thus she controls how she will handle the situation she faces. Her decisions to protect, hide, and advise the spies is based on what she knows about her risky situation. Furthermore, knowing the details of the reality on both sides of the city wall allows Rahab to choose specific ways of acting. Relying on what she sees around her and what she knows, she decides what actions to take and carries them out. At the end of the story, both the spies and Rahab get what they want. The spies search the land and report to Joshua. Rahab obtains security and salvation for herself and her family through deceit, trickery, cleverness, and seduction. All these elements allow me to see her as a survivor, someone who is determined to do whatever it takes to survive. It is in this way that she *resuelve*.

Conclusion

Being a Latina biblical scholar means embracing all that I am as a Cuban feminist living at this particular time in history in the United States (geographical and academic location). Embracing all that I am means embracing my Cuban identity: an identity that is corporal, feminist, and deeply shaped by a sense of survival, family survival. This location, not defined by the mass of water that separates the United States and Cuba, is what I call a socio-emotional and existential location.

This hermeneutic constitutes a way of engaging with Hebrew Bible texts, but it is not the only one. This hermeneutic also allows me to engage in a critical discourse within Latino/a biblical scholarship here in the States, a plurality of discourses that ponder the same question this volume considers and where there is space for other ways of reading texts to take place.

In reading the Rahab story from a lens of *resolviendo*, insights of a woman who crosses the boundaries of ideology, city walls, and gender emerge. From her unique ways of surviving and striving as a foreigner to protect her family, I appreciate a reading that allows for women's power to be born from within the same oppressive system where they find themselves. Rahab's struggle to survive pushes her to cross boundaries and to find hope for her and her people in new places, in other lands. Like Rahab, being a Cuban feminist scholar of the Hebrew Bible living in the United States continues to challenge issues of identity. It is my hope that beyond the two countries that shape my life there will be a liminal space where life continues to flourish and new biblical discourses emerge.

Works Cited

Chaviano, Daína. 1998. *El hombre, la hembra y el hambre*. Barcelona: Planeta.

Díaz Quiñones, Arcadio. 2000. *El arte de bregar: Ensayos*. San Juan, Puerto Rico: Callejón.

Dovalpage, Teresa. 2004. *Posesas de la Habana: Novela*. Los Angeles: Pureplay.

Dube, Musa W. 2003. Rahab Says Hello to Judith: A Decolonizing Feminist Reading. Pages 54–72 in *Toward a New Heaven and a New Earth: Essays in Honor of Elisabeth Schüssler Fiorenza*. Edited by Fernando F. Segovia. Maryknoll, N.Y.: Orbis.

Frymer-Kensky, Tikva Simone. 1997. Reading Rahab. Pages 57–67 in *Tehillah le-Moshe: Biblical and Judaic Studies in Honor of Moshe Greenberg*. Edited by Mordechai Cogan, Barry L. Eichler, and Jeffrey H. Tigay. Winona Lake, Ind.: Eisenbrauns.

Gebara, Ivone. 2002. *Out of the Depths: Women's Experience of Evil and Salvation*. Minneapolis: Fortress.

Isasi-Díaz, Ada María. 1996. *Mujerista Theology: A Theology for the Twenty-First Century*. Maryknoll, N.Y.: Orbis.

———. 2004. *La Lucha Continues: Mujerista Theology*. Maryknoll, N.Y.: Orbis.

Jaspers, Karl. 1970. *Philosophy*. Vol. 2. Translated by E. B. Ashton. Chicago: University of Chicago Press.

Rowlett, Lori L. 2000. Disney's Pocahontas and Joshua's Rahab in Postcolonial Perspective. Pages 68–75 in *Culture, Entertainment, and the Bible*. Edited by George Aichele. JSOTSup 309. Sheffield: Sheffield Academic Press.

Trumbull, Charles. 2004. Prostitution and Sex Tourism in Cuba. *Cuba in Transition* 11:356–71.

Reading from No Place:
Toward a Hybrid and Ambivalent
Study of Scriptures

Jacqueline M. Hidalgo

One mild December evening, while I was still pursuing a Master of Arts degree, I sat with my elder brother Jorge and my father (also Jorge) around my father's kitchen table. His kitchen table sits in the same home my parents owned when I was born, a home located in a suburb of San José, Costa Rica. On this particular evening, I was recovering from surgery, sipping water weakly through a straw, when my brother decided it was time to confront my father about a pressing family matter. My brother pointed out that he was now a father who had been married and divorced himself, but my father denied this recognition of kindred experience. He said, "What do you know of me? You're not Costa Rican. You're not United Statesan.[1] You don't know who you are. At least I know I belong here." At this point, my father used his hands to gesture from his heart toward the ground. He added, "You're not anything, you don't belong anywhere, and you know nothing."[2] Silence fell, before my brother stormed off to smoke outside.

I share this story in order to approach the question of this volume. Whether he knew it or not, my father was pointing to something quite cru-

---

1. Note that my father refused to say "American." Throughout my life, he has maintained that "American" is a referent to the entire hemisphere, whereas the United States of America is but one country in that hemisphere.

2. I am paraphrasing my father in this passage. I have reconstructed this moment through conversation with my elder brother, Jorge G. Hidalgo II. I would like to thank him for speaking with me about this essay. I would also like to thank some significant conversation partners whose ideas and wisdom significantly shaped this essay: Valerie Bailey Fischer, Devyn Spence Benson, Neomi DeAnda, LeRhonda S. Manigault-Bryant, Sourena Parham, and Mérida Rúa.

cial about U.S. Latin@ identities: neither Latin American nor United Statesan, but caught in some world between. My various identities, let alone my U.S. Latina identity,[3] cannot be distilled through one story; but, as I struggled with this essay, this one moment kept returning to my mind as a way of capturing many of the paradoxes of and tensions around Latin@ identities that lay behind the questions I ask and the methods I employ as a scholar.[4] That moment has become something of a touchstone for my brother and myself, though our senses of our Latin@ identities are not the same. Yet it was a moment where both of us started to accept the space we inhabited at the margins of and in between others' identities.

A few months before this incident, I had read an essay by Fernando Segovia that became a resource for me as I rethought this moment, my own identity, and my academic goals. In the essay, Segovia describes his interpretive locus as that of diaspora and exile, a locus where "We are in the world, indeed in two worlds, but we are not of the world, indeed of no world. Such is the point of departure for my theology of the diaspora" (1996, 203). Hence he partially locates himself within that world that is neither world and aptly identifies a central rubric of Latin@ theological visioning as "two places and no place on which to stand" (26). Segovia further describes that, in the "going back and forth" between two worlds, an exile necessarily "ends up constructing a 'home' of his or her own, a world of otherness" (213).

My brother and I came to appreciate that "no place" of otherness as the place we live, as our ambivalent home. Over time, I came to recognize writing and reading from "no place" as such a locus for my work, so that

---

3. In this essay, I generally refer to myself with a panethnic label that is itself multivalent, multidimensional, and highly contested. For more extensive insight into the complexities of that label, see, e.g., Oboler 1995.

4. My Latina identity, itself a nonstatic construct, is certainly not the only social identity that matters to my work as a scholar. Additionally, this story focuses on one aspect of my Latina social identity, and it takes for granted many of the marks of privilege in this situation. In Costa Rica we have a middle-class home in which to live, we have food and potable water to imbibe together, and I am privileged enough by economic factors and national documents to be able to travel between Costa Rica and the United States. Our ability, even in argument, to meditate on our racial, ethnic, and national identities and (un)belonging demonstrates something of the social and economic privileges that mark our family. At the same time, I am not, in this essay, focusing upon many of the challenges vis-à-vis dominant U.S. culture that have shaped my identity and identification as a U.S. Latina.

my current research focuses on utopia, a term that includes "no place" as one of its meanings. At the same time, reading from no place also stands in a rigid and ambivalent embrace with a plurality of others. Reading from a no place of otherness seeks to hold onto the discomfort and ambiguity of that existence. What Gloria Anzaldúa once described as cultivating "a tolerance for contradictions [and] ambiguity" (1987, 79) has come to mark my practices of reading.[5] Ambivalence and ambiguity here are not the same as taking no stand, holding no position, and having no meanings; rather, cultivating ambivalence and respecting ambiguity means holding onto the tensions and plurality of options that can be perceived from those particular (no) places caught between varying worlds.

In this essay, I want to trace something of the personal and scholarly journey that led to the particular work I do in studying scriptures. As someone who recognizes myself as located in that no place that is not just a between place but a particular place, however fluidly conceived, when I say I read from a no place of otherness, I do not mean no place in particular; in fact it is a quite particular no place. As a scholar, I have become especially interested in how others also navigate experiences of (no)placement. My embrace of my particular Latina identity as one locus of my scholarly work has demanded an ambiguous and ambivalent critical lens, one rooted in an ongoing negotiation of an identity of fraught historical mixtures and freighted relationships. How do boundaries of identity and (un)belonging get drawn? Why do these boundaries get drawn, what is at stake in their drawing, and how are texts deployed in order to mark and cross borders?

These questions have necessitated the employment of interdisciplinary methods that better respond to my own sense of mixed identity.[6] Hence

---

5. In light of the importance of Anzaldúa's perspective for my work, I also note that this essay is not written in a style that follows the pattern of a normative, linear argument.

6. While this essay is in some ways about method, I do not want to focus on the question of "method" because of the history of what Yvonne Sherwood and Stephen Moore have called "methodolatry" in biblical studies. Methodolatry developed, according to Moore, because biblical studies scholars so often desired to separate the academic and the sermonic: "Methodology is what is meant to keep our discourse on the Bible from being subjective, personal, private, pietistic, pastoral, devotional or homiletical. Methodology, in short, is what maintains the partition between sermon and scholarship" (2010, 370). For Moore, this methodolatry creates a false dichotomy that presumes homily as the flip side of "objective" scholarship, but methodolatry

my scholarly work ranges between biblical studies, Latina/o studies, and the study of religion and the United States more broadly.[7] The personal episode with which I opened reveals something about the ways in which my questions about power, mixture, and social identities are formed and structure my interdisciplinary and transtemporal interests in scriptures.

Whenever I ask questions about the relationship of scriptures, power, and identity, especially the drawing of the boundaries of identity, I cannot help but think of the end of Revelation.[8] Revelation has long been perceived as a key text among imperial and settler colonial communities; for example, Columbus likened himself to the prophet John of the Apocalypse (Leicester 1892, 152). At the same time, Revelation has also been a focal site of resistance and survival for imperially dominated communities (Blount 2005). Given that Revelation is such an important identity locative text, Revelation's penultimate verses—and, therefore, the near-final verses of most standard Christian Bibles—are striking in that they stridently call for the text's scripturalization,[9] while also threatening exile to those who do not scripturalize the text appropriately: "I witness to all who hear the words of the prophecy of this book: if someone adds to them, God will add onto that person the plagues that have been inscribed in this book. If someone takes away from the words of the book of this prophecy, God will

---

also addresses the problems of a particular European scholarly culture (371). See also Moore and Sherwood 2011, esp. 39–40.

7. My identity informs but does not necessarily determine my work, or vice versa. José Ignacio Cabezón suggests that though personal background can greatly impact how one studies religion, and vice versa, that does not mean that one needs to have a certain background in order to study specific issues or to read in particular ways. Though I focus on my U.S. Latina identity in this essay, my multiple identities all shape what I do and how I do it, but they do not strictly determine my work, because my work also reshapes and reforms my identity. I affirm with Cabezón that, "even though who I am influences what I do (and how I do it), it in no way necessitates in any simple, linear fashion what or how I do what I do as a scholar" (2003, 46). Additionally, I also affirm with him that "who we are is in large measure the result of what we do" (55).

8. While the author is identified as John of Patmos, I do not know who this ultimate author is. Thus I will often speak of "Revelation" as a subject. However, I recognize the text does not do anything on its own; we make the text mean in certain ways.

9. I am using the terms *scripturalize* and *scripturalization* in order to point to the array of practices that surrounds the treatment of a text as Scripture: from writing, to canon, to interpretation and performance in contemporary communities. For more discussion of these terms, see Wimbush 2012.

take away that person's part in the tree of life and the holy city, which have been inscribed in this book" (my trans.).

Although earlier passages certainly promise rewards to those who keep the words of the prophecy, Revelation here promises to withhold the rewards and to enact the punishments that have been specifically written within the text. Moreover, whether you are admitted into the inscribed "holy city" depends on how you deal with Revelation's written text. Special treatment of the text grants you membership in a certain community, but that membership stands on a knife's edge of scripturalization, of treating this text with extra special attention. How can anyone read or hear any text without adding or subtracting? In the end, how assured is anyone of her/his membership in a community whose scriptures present these choices? Who ultimately determines how to properly relate to the text and thus who is granted community membership?

Both my father's and Revelation's words require a certain contextualization amid the rhetorics of empire, though I cannot promise that such contextualization will make them any more pleasant to hear.[10] Most likely crafted and performed in the late first century by communities that lived under but felt marginalized in relationship to the Roman Empire, the identity (per)formative role of Revelation takes on a specific intensity. While Revelation is a text that challenges most readers with its violent imagery (plagues, destruction, and the horrific ravaging of Babylon, for example), such violent imagery is generally directed at oppressive powers in the world, which most scholars identify as Rome. At the same time, Revelation generally makes stark rhetorical maneuvers, positing clear-cut good and evil, inside and outside. Yet Revelation appears to draw these clear lines while being a hybrid text, a mash-up of letters, prophecies, astrological literature, ancient myths, Jewish, Roman, and other ancient Mediterranean texts.

---

10. In pairing these stories (my own and Rev 22), I do not presume a simplistic equivalence or that my context is somehow parallel to Revelation's, allowing me to make better sense of it. In fact, the only relationship that Revelation and my father's kitchen table have is through me, the relationship I create by placing them in conversation. Yet my study of Scripture in general and Revelation in particular has, over the years, come to shape how I now understand this personal story, and vice versa. I assent with Jean-Pierre Ruiz's argument that a hermeneutics of "correlation and correspondence" can romanticize biblical texts and the worlds of those who read, rather than put both worlds in a more critical conversation. On the limits of correlation, see Ruiz 2011, 7–8.

As with my father's words, these final verses in Revelation frustrate me with their apparent call to restrict who can call what place home and on what terms. Who can be admitted to (or even who has the proper paperwork to enter) the ultimate utopian no place, the new Jerusalem? Yet their restrictions may not be straightforward. Revelation cannot always be read as having one, neat, singular message. Not only do biblical texts have a plurality of readers and plurality of readings, but varying and divergent voices contend within biblical texts (Ruiz 2011, 7). The story I told you of my father is but one moment in much fuller life of my family in which we have all said harsh and contradictory words to each other. How can I resist resolving the potential ambiguities at stake in Revelation's ending curse and my father's distinction between being Costa Rican and United Statesan? The interplay of my family's story and my reading of Revelation lays bare something of why I engage in an interdisciplinary study of "scriptures," which I conceive as something more and other than "Bible."

Who Is a Latina Critic?
Of Hybridity and the Necessity of Interdisciplinarity

Before returning to Revelation, first I want to address directly the larger question of the volume: my placement as a Latina critic. As a scholar, my *Latinidad* has informed my critical lens because I have come to presume a locus of Latin@-inflected hybridity as a reader. The texts I read are also hybrid products, and a certain hybridity obtains in that interaction between me as a reader and the reading of those texts. Privileging an assumption of mixture in myself, in other readers and readings, and in the texts themselves pushes me to read beyond biblical and disciplinary borders.

Positioning myself as a specifically Latin@ critic also opens up particular questions. In addressing the problematic that is "Latin(o/a)ness," Segovia argues that no critical Latin@ identity is self-evident. As with all identities, a Latin@ critic's identity is constructed: "always situated and ideological—variegated and shifting, pointed and political" (2009, 199). My U.S. Latina identity is meaningful in particular situations, and it is itself a particular construction, not only because I am my own individual, but also because my country of birth, Costa Rica, is only a small proportion of the larger U.S. Latin@ population, a rather ad hoc conglomeration of many different peoples. Being of Costa Rican descent places me in the minority and at the margins of larger U.S. Latin@ communities, such as Mexican Americans, Puerto Ricans, and Cuban Americans. The Costa

Rican diaspora as part of the larger U.S. Latin@ population is rarely discussed or studied, creating yet another (no) place to which I belong.

How I am a U.S. Latina is highly contingent upon the particular moment-by-moment situation of expression, and specificities of my *Latinidad* adhere to my place as an academic.[11] Even my brother and I, though comparatively experientially proximate, maintain and perform quite different U.S. Latin@ identities.[12] Nevertheless, to choose such an identity as a locus means that I am concerned with identity at large as well as the makings and maneuverings of marginalized identities. Most especially, of course, I am concerned with the complexities of webs of power in the relationships between people(s), though some questions matter to me more than others.

Both my family history and the study of scriptures (and Revelation more particularly, as I discuss below) have made me sensitive to questions of home, empire, and power. My father's challenge to my brother's identity was specifically about how to exist between our father's Costa Rican context and our U.S. one. Segovia suggests that "Latino/a biblical criticism and teaching" should foreground the ongoing relationship to and participation of "Latinos" in the United States since its inception, while recognizing U.S. Latin@ ties to Latin America. This recognition presumes that Latin@s have negotiated Spanish and U.S. imperialism and that Latin@s are a population often marked by a "conflicted relationship to the United States" because of systemic socioeconomic and political inequalities within the United States as well as the hemisphere at large (Segovia 2009, 212–13). To take this relationship seriously is to foreground an ambivalent relationship to imperialism and inequality as dynamics of concern.

Nothing so neat as "Costa Rican" separable from the "United States" exists for my family, nor can we neatly disentangle our varying racial and ethnic backgrounds. In *Culture and Imperialism*, Edward Said argued that "'identity' does not necessarily imply ontologically given and eternally determined stability, or uniqueness, or irreducible character, or privileged

---

11. For an example of a work that elucidates how different aspects of a Latin@ identity can come out in different social contexts among Latin@s themselves, see, e.g., Aparicio 2007, 39–48.

12. We are different people, but we also have differences of education, appearance, and gender that have significantly shaped our *Latinidad*. Moreover, my brother lived in Costa Rica for part of his childhood, whereas I was born in Costa Rica but have spent most of my life in the United States.

status as something total and complete in and of itself" (1994, 315). No "identity," whether "racial/ethnic," national, or otherwise, is stable. Though my father's rhetorical division between Costa Rica and the United States suggests otherwise, often identity is not merely a juggling of two neatly divided poles. One individual's identity can feel more like a Venn diagram, were a Venn diagram's circles three-dimensional spheres in motion.[13]

Homi Bhabha employs the term *hybridity* in an attempt to name the complexity of all identities. His essay "Of Mimicry and Man" (1994, 85–92) emphasizes the varying, interactive projects of imperial power and colonized response that create hybrid subjects among all those involved in imperial and colonial encounters. As Erin Runions contends, Bhabha engages in a complex rereading and destabilization of Self and Other in order to illuminate the mixture that transpires in the uneven exchange between colonial and colonized cultures (2001, 80–81). Because colonial cultural representation are "very vicariously addressed to—*through*—an Other," claims of "essentialist" cultural purity are impossible for any side of the colonial exchange (Bhabha 1994, 58). Moreover, in our era of globalization, both nativists and (im)migrants can feel displaced and anxious about hybrid(ized) identities (Chavoya 2004, 172). Although Bhabha's approach to hybridity has its limits, I assent with Eric Barreto's position that "the notion of hybridity opens a valuable, complex, in-between space" for understanding the world beyond binaries and "the gradation evident in colonial contexts between resistance and accommodation" (2010, 53).

In reading scriptures, I am especially attentive to how those who live varying experiences of hybridity manage the sometimes conflicting paths of juggling identities and contexts. I write as a product of converging, conflicted, mixed histories.[14] Both the violence and the complexity that mark the historical context of the Americas inform my interdisciplinary

---

13. My idea here partially comes from Carmen Nanko-Fernández's emphasis on identity beyond the hyphen. She describes how transformed our identities are in a digital age, when "boundaries are porous" and we must read ourselves as "situatedness in motion" (2010, 35).

14. To reference one's hybridity does require careful recognition of the historical violence and privilege that created and attends hybridity in certain contexts. Among U.S. Latin@ theologians, *mestizaje* and *mulatez* have been popular terms for capturing something of this violent complexity. Yet Néstor Medina (2009) reveals how *mestizaje* especially develops out of a complex colonial Latin American hierarchy into a nationalist ideology that often silences, delimits, and erases African, Asian, and indigenous components of American identities, while also treating Asian, Amerindian, and Afri-

and transdisciplinary turn toward postcolonial theory as well as work that examines diasporic life.[15] At the same time, I turn to postcolonial theory and Bhabha's imagination of hybridity because I want to move away from what R. S. Sugirtharajah has identified as a very Enlightenment-grounded way of thinking, even among liberationist writers, when power is understood in dichotomies such as "rich/poor, oppressed/oppressor, etc." (2001, 241). Recognizing my own hybrid context, my own no place that lies between different worlds, also necessitates that I let go of any neat dichotomies.

How Does a Latina Critic Mean?
Interdisciplinary Study and the Ambiguity of Meaning

While my essay has so far focused on the "Latin@" portion of my identity, I am also a student of Scriptures as phenomena, and I am particularly interested in Scriptures as projects of communal identification. In his theorizing of scriptures, Vincent Wimbush argues for a switch to a "consistent focus upon how societies and cultures continue to be formed and de-formed and re-formed and—on account of the power invested in them—how *texts* in particular are created and pressed into service to effect such things" (2008, 13). To consider scriptures in this way is to consider questions that surround my own hybrid context as a reader, but also I am

---

can cultures as though they were simple cultures that existed in the past instead of recognizing their own ongoing complexity and survival in the Americas today.

15. With "postcolonial" I am referring to a theoretical frame that foregrounds the role of settler colonialisms, imperialisms, and colonized negotiations. Postcolonial theory thus provides a theoretical frame for examining complex dynamics in previous imperial programs (such as those of ancient Rome or early modern Spain) as well as ongoing experiences of colonialism and imperial visions (such as life in the contemporary U.S. Southwest). Roland Boer uses "postcolonial" in this sense because "colonialism is by no means a thing of past, and since we can easily identify earlier forms of colonialism (the Romans for one), 'postcolonial' also refers to a critical way of dealing with those earlier and still contemporary forms of colonialism" (Boer 2008, xi). Additionally, I have my own ambivalences toward postcolonial theory because, as Moore has asserted, "critical approaches that concentrate exclusively on the 'outward' appurtenances of colonialism and its counter-effects ... [while important] cannot account adequately for the immensely complex relations of collusion and resistance, desire and disavowal, dependence and independence that can characterize the exchanges between colonizer and colonized during colonial occupation *and* after official decolonization" (2010, 322).

also curious about how and why many readers turn to these texts, creating and playing certain power games with relationship to these texts, especially when using scriptures in order to form and make sense of identities.

A recognition of Revelation's place as not just a stand-alone text but a scriptural text that lives only in an ongoing exchange with readers and auditors is deeply connected to my own interest in and questions about the very category of "scriptures" that stands behind the work of biblical scholarship. W. C. Smith argued that "scripture" is not a quality inherent to a "text, so much as an interactive relation between that text and a community of persons" (1993, ix). Thus scriptures are defined by the specific kinds of relationships they have with human readers, especially those reading as a community (18). Revelation's final call for its own scripturalization may also be understood as transpiring within a communal practice of scripturalization. In order to grapple with the ambiguity of meaning in Revelation as a scriptural and homing text, I have to push past my first reading of my father's and Revelation's words and think about other contexts with which to make sense of them. How might multiple meanings be buried within each text's harsh restrictions on identity? What might thinking about the logic of scripturalization tell us about rhetorically drawing communal boundaries?

Many contemporary scholars have observed that Revelation was likely a ritual text, read aloud and performed within communities; hence more than just "text" has always been at stake in Revelation.[16] At the same time, our contemporary situation in which Revelation's text is easily accessible outside communal contexts significantly complicates and reshapes how we perceive Revelation's scriptural work.[17] In Brian Blount's examination of Revelation in African American traditions, he moves beyond the borders of the biblical text into not just the worlds outside Revelation's own creation but the worlds present in ours. Blount's study takes up "how

---

16. See especially the approaches taken up below by scholars such as Adela Yarbro Collins, Jean-Pierre Ruiz, David L. Barr, Paulo Augusto de Souza Nogueira, Elisabeth Schüssler Fiorenza, and David A. Sánchez, who all suggest that Revelation is not merely a text being read, but a text that is being performed (liturgically and otherwise) in the communities who read it. Such a recognition that Revelation is a performed text is also consonant with Velma Love's contention that "scriptures" are a "performance genre" (2006, 28). See also Graham 1987.

17. I would like to thank Denise Buell for drawing my attention to this idea in reaction to an earlier draft.

contemporary cultures invest themselves, their agendas, their interests, and their presuppositions into their reading process" (2005, 9–10). Likewise, despite my focus upon myself in this study, generally my work is not invested only in my reading; rather, I aspire to examine how other U.S. Latin@s engage and relate to these texts, which pushes beyond the borders of biblical studies.

Such work in the study of scriptures is consonant with Latin@ theological commitment to *teología de y en conjunto*.[18] Such conjoined theology necessitates interdisciplinarity, because we are in conversation with and concerned with the questions and thinking of scholars in different disciplines. At the same time, such work not only challenges the academic borders of disciplines but the very borders of the academy, forcing us to engage scriptural readings from contexts outside the academy while recognizing that meaning and reading are themselves fluid practices (Ruiz 2011, 8–9). As Thomas Tweed describes it, "meaning is constructed (not given), multiple (not univocal), contested (not shared), and fluid (not static). And, most important, meaning is inscribed by readers, listeners, participants, or viewers" (2002, 65). To focus on scriptures, rather than just trying to exegete biblical texts alone, is to take an interest in what happens in the interaction between readers and texts as a way of thinking about how meaning is created and negotiated.[19]

Yet to center the role of scriptures in meaning making is also to open oneself up to the ambiguity and ambivalence inherent to all meaning making and power tripping. Revelation's final verses call for its own scripturalization in order to lay claim to a place in ongoing meaning making. Significantly, such a call comes at the end of a text that has envisioned a whole other world of belonging for those who commit themselves to Revelation as scripture.

Because the conversation in my family's kitchen transpired in the midst of an argument, it also was about a kind of ambiguous meaning making that transpires in a quick, heated exchange. My brother asserted that he knew something of my father's position because of their shared identities as fathers and ex-husbands. When my father questioned my brother's

---

18. For a fuller discussion of this practice, see DeAnda and Medina 2009, 185.

19. Such work is also consonant with what Tat-siong Benny Liew describes as reading the Bible with and as "theory." Liew explains that by *theory* he means "attempts to understand conditions and consequences of making meaning, making sense, or making reality" (10).

ethnic identity, he also questioned his ability to know with certainty. He suggested that the power inherent in his comparatively stable identity ("At least I know I belong here") granted him a certain kind of knowledge as well. Yet my brother and I accept that belonging is always questionable, and thus we willingly sacrifice some claims to certain knowledge.

While my brother and I may take my father's words in a distinct direction, I also want to query the seemingly obvious power dynamics between my father and my brother at that kitchen table. While my father does hold a certain kind of power by virtue of being our father, his pursuit of this rhetorical construction of his power/ knowledge actually has to do with complexities particular to that conversation. Profoundly present in her absence is my mother, a U.S. citizen, residing in Kansas, a place where my father also spent some of his life. My father himself has an ambivalent relationship to the United States. He has lived there, been educated there, and two of his children live there, but he also experienced racism while living in the United States and the perils of living in the United States as a non-citizen. At the same time, in Costa Rica, his life was frequently impacted by the turmoil of U.S. interventions in Central America throughout the twentieth century, though certainly that experience does not carry the same cost as the impact to those who survived civil wars in Guatemala, El Salvador, and Nicaragua.

My father's frustrations with U.S. hemispheric dominance might explain something of his dichotomous rhetoric, but his experiences also belie the challenges of ambiguity and ambivalence. Although he did not discuss it in the moment I recounted earlier, my father does consider himself a hybrid subject, because of the years he lived in the United States. On another occasion, at that same kitchen table, he spoke to me of how his own hybridity—though that was not the term he used—had made him feel like something of a foreigner in his own land. Ambivalently, he was both proud of this experience and pained by it.

The pain rests in part because other Costa Ricans have made him feel like an outsider in his own supposed homeland. When my father told my brother, "You're not Costa Rican. You're not United Statesan. You don't know who you are," he negated my brother's identity, because he could not fit into the boundaries of two different identities as my father was defining them. Yet my father had experienced those exact same accusations of not belonging from others. That he would choose to push back at my brother for having an unstable identity is because my father knows how much such a push can hurt.

Something of this same transference may be at stake in Revelation's closing curse, and perhaps many such calls for closing the borders of community and foreclosing certain kinds of conversations. While we will probably never know what specific historical person or people stood behind Revelation's textual origins, we may suspect that the author and his audience, as Jews and "Christians"[20] in Asia Minor, generally experienced some form of political, linguistic, cultural, economic, and religious adversity in relationship to the Roman imperial order that dominated Asia Minor in the first century. Moreover, Revelation characterizes its author as a political exile in 1:9. "John" shares with his correspondents "the oppression and the empire and the endurance," but he writes from Patmos, where he is "because of the word of God and the testimony of Jesus" (my trans.). The threat of exile at the end of Revelation may have some grounding in the lived experiences of those who wrote and read the text.

Revelation confronts us with the horrific violence of imperial domination, violence that is both physical and emotional, and we can recognize the ongoing necessity of resistance to earthly powers that suppress and dominate peoples in a plurality of ways.[21] Revelation can thus be perceived as one way in which a marginalized community may struggle to uphold religious and cultural pride while awaiting the fall of those who have dominated them. Therefore, Revelation presents an image of what Margaret Aymer terms "alter-empire," an empire of God that runs above

---

20. Though I am using the term *Christian* here in speaking of Revelation's context, no such clear-cut identity category existed, and I recognize that the lines between Jews and Christians were not easily drawn. Throughout most of the essay, I try to use both Jewish and Christian terms to suggest the ongoing interconnectedness and fluidity of the boundary between those identities in the late first century. Indeed, Revelation may have been challenging other members, perhaps specifically Pauline members, of the Jesus movement as the "synagogue of Satan." The author of Revelation does appear to embrace the term *Jewish* for describing himself and his communities, and Revelation may be laying claim to being authentically Jewish as opposed to other members of the Jesus movement. See Frankfurter 2001. In this particular essay, I am not charting early Christian maneuvers around logics of identity, and especially the relationship of Christian identity to race/ethnicity, with deliberate focus. For a pair of excellent example of works that focus upon the slippages of race/ethnicity in early Christian identification practices, see Buell 2005 and Barreto 2010.

21. Pablo Richard has likewise emphasized the importance of contextualizing the violence of Revelation's rhetoric as the cathartic imagination of a severely oppressed group (1998, 4).

and against a satanic empire, understood in Revelation's historical context as the Roman Empire. As Aymer describes it, Revelation does not entirely challenge imperial rhetoric; rather it challenges Rome by adapting imperial rhetoric and making God's empire an alternative empire to Rome (2005, 145). The god of Revelation's visions is one that takes up the mantle of Roman imperial power in heaven even as it promises Rome's destruction on earth.[22] The employment of an alter-imperial imaginary that draws so heavily on Roman imperial visions can be understood as a tool of resistance. For instance, David Sánchez's work on Revelation 12 and the Virgin of Guadalupe examines how the mimicry of dominant myths, frequently taken up in public performance, often entails mythic subversions when undertaken by dominated groups (2008).

Such subversion can serve multivalent strategies, but such subversion is also not something isolated from or in "pure" opposition to Roman power. Revelation's subversive speech is heavily coded and prone to plural, uncertain, and contradictory meanings. Although Revelation transforms Roman myths, Revelation also transforms Jewish texts in the process. The ending curse can be understood to have a relationship with previous commands to scripturalization in Deut 4:2: "You must neither add anything to what I command you nor take away anything from it, but keep the commandments of the LORD your God with which I am charging you" (NRSV), and something of Revelation's rhetorical flair in the end seems to pull from Deut 29:19–30:8 (Royalty 2004, 291–92).[23]

Intriguingly, the ending curse seems directed not at Rome, but rather at other Jews and Christians. Because of rhetoric from the early part of Revelation, especially rhetoric against the "synagogue of Satan" (Rev 2:9; 3:9) and the figure of a rival "Christian" prophet, code-named Jezebel (2:20), Revelation may be excoriating other Jews and Christians who accommodate themselves to the Roman imperial order. Perhaps Revelation reconfigures Deuteronomy in order to transform words that had been used against Revelation's own communities, not unlike my father's transformation of rhetoric used against him when challenging my brother. In the late first century, many Jewish and "Christian" interpreters may also have experienced a sense of exile in relationship to other Jewish

---

22. For several examples of this discussion, see Carter 2009, 46–47; Moore 1996, 134–38.

23. As Royalty also acknowledges, Deuteronomy itself is revising and rewriting earlier legal traditions (292 n. 38).

communities who disagreed with "Christian" readings of Jesus and scriptures. As with the slippage between my father's identity and his lament at my brother, is Revelation's concluding threat at least partially an echo of how this early community may have been ostracized by other Jewish and Christian groups because of their use of scriptures? Does the end of Revelation perhaps reflect some of the complexities within marginalized communal negotiations? As Royalty suggests, Revelation's own "use of scripture can be read as ideological," and thus "circumscribing the reading of scripture and the *readers* of the Apocalypse was one way to attack" (288). Who can read Revelation and on what terms is part of what we wrestle with because of Revelation's ending.

Scriptures as community projects often depend upon what I term a limiting pliability, a phrase that draws upon Denise Buell's work on the dynamic of fixity and fluidity in early Christian "ethnic reasoning" and ethnoracial discourse. For Buell, ethnicity/race dynamically interplays between "fixity and fluidity" as rhetorics that exist together, not in contrast with each other (2005, 8–9). Revelation's closing employs the scriptural logics of limiting pliability in that the curse is a rhetorical maneuver that ambiguously and ambivalently draws upon center(ing) texts for both limitations and openness. On the one hand, the curse supplies a limiting/fixity, a mandate of clear textual limits and communal borders that separates insiders from outsiders. On the other hand, the image of the new Jerusalem itself offers a certain pliability/fluidity, that meanings are pliable and that communal boundaries are porous: the gates are open and members of all nations may enter (21:24–25).

If we can approach scriptures as sites of contradictory and ambiguous rhetorical maneuvering, it may help us all to handle better the "surplus of meaning" at stake in particular texts. As Elisabeth Schüssler Fiorenza puts it, this approach "enables us to understand the bible as a site of struggle over meaning and biblical interpretation and debate and argument rather than as transcript of the unchanging, inerrant Word of G*d" (2007, 265).[24] In this way, scriptures have themselves served as loci around which individuals and peoples have thought, played, and struggled. Thus Wimbush asserts that the study of scriptures should entail "the study of textures, of

---

24. Schüssler Fiorenza then suggests that the future of biblical studies demands a transformation of this vision toward collaboration and away from metaphors of "battle, combat, and competition." Such a move toward collaboration may also be consonant with *teología de y en conjunto*.

gestures and power relations" (2008, 6). Scriptures can then be conceived of as sites of struggle, and a study of scriptures does not just engage a text's meaning; rather, to study scriptures is also to attend to the power dynamics that encircle community relationships to scriptures.

What Does It Mean to Be a Latina Critic? (Un)Welcoming Homes and the Ambivalence of Reading Scriptures

My discussion of the importance of interpretive location and the treatments of scriptures as sites of struggle does not mean that texts can mean whatever I would like them to mean. Scriptures are tools of power, and as such their meaning very much depends upon who is using them and how.[25] Scriptures easily reinscribe imperial, heteronormative, and patriarchal authority, not unlike the kitchen table where I sat as the silent subject. In thinking of scriptures as communal identificatory projects that deal in a limiting pliability, I see scriptures and reading scriptures to be, at least partially, about projects of homing.

Yet to use the term *home* is to take up an ambivalent discourse. The story of my own home, which is a home of a comparatively happy and loving family, points to the ways that homes are not always safe spaces of absolute belonging.[26] Both my story about my father and the end of Revelation speak to me of the complex ambiguities and ambivalences that attend a certain promise of home, my literal home in Costa Rica and the home of scriptures and the new Jerusalem in Revelation. How is one ever assured of one's place in those homes? Is assurance of that place what really matters?

"Home" enjoys a range of complex positive and negative connotations and debate in postcolonial theory. Said advocates the experience of being unhomed (1994, 326–36), and Bhabha writes of the impossibility of homing in the contemporary moment, with unhomeliness signaling the blurred boundaries between "home and world ... private and public"

---

25. Here I echo Liew's observation that "apocalyptic can and is likely to be both utopian and dystopian or transformative and accommodative at the same time." Moreover, "the meaning of apocalyptic is relational to or contingent upon its particular use" (2008, 136).

26. The work of Irit Rogoff also points to whether "belonging" is even a useful question to ask anymore (2000).

(1994, 9). Additionally, homes do not necessarily connote comfort, safety, or belonging; Anzaldúa recast "homophobia" as the fear a lesbian Chicana has of returning to an unwelcoming home that denies her space (1987, 19–20). Other scholars have observed the privileged tone of such meditations on being unhomed, because those postcolonial scholars who write fondly of exile (including myself) generally have actual houses as well as legal recognition in the countries in which they work. Both are significant homing privileges that distinguish scholars from many of the people with whom we are concerned.[27]

Some scholars interested in the lives of those who live in exile and/or diaspora turn to the metaphor of "homelessness," and such a terminology speaks to a struggle with home that is more clearly a matter of life and death than the story I have shared with you about my life. Imperial logics can also lead to economic, enslaving, and political compulsions that drive people into exilic or diasporic life for various reasons—some by choice, some by unpreferred choice, and some by no choice of their own but rather the will of others. A sense of being unhomed or homeless and a life-or-death necessity to manage the tension of such an experience may be considered major aspects of daily life for many people in our globalized world.

Perhaps the limiting pliability of scriptures is a tool for "diasporic hermeneutics" that can be deployed then "to address the state of 'homelessness' … to find a home for those people who have been made homeless" (Sugirtharajah 2002, 191) Yet diaspora can also be seen as "a critique of discourse of fixed origins, while taking account of a homing desire which is not the same thing as desire for a 'homeland'" (Brah 2003, 614–15). In Cristina García-Alfonso's work on *resolviendo* in the Hebrew Bible, she considers strategies for "making do" both in Cuba and the Bible when people live in situations of duress (2010). Diasporic peoples may use scriptures as homing mechanisms as a form of *resolviendo* or "making" do in order to survive. Scriptures among those who traverse through the no place can be about homing, without necessarily fixating on origins and authority on the same terms that imperial homing may do. Thus to treat scriptures as "homing" mechanisms necessitates an ambivalent and ambiguous read of home and diasporic (un)belonging.

---

27. For a striking biblical studies critique of postcolonial romanticization of itinerant ways of being, see Boer 2008, 80–107.

My father's kitchen table in the story I shared is an ambivalent space, a place where my brother was welcomed and loved by my father, but it is also a place of struggle and contention where neither my brother nor my father felt fully at home. I also sat silently at that table, though I now exercise a certain power by being the one who writes of this exchange years later. As ambivalent as I feel about home, so too am I ambivalent about what scriptures are and what they (can) do. Ultimately, my interdisciplinary questions, methods, and commitments also mean my scholarly identity is only ambivalently and partially situated in "biblical studies," which perhaps is not surprising, given my own ambivalence toward identifications in general. In so doing, I seek to hold onto the ambiguity of meaning that obtains between a hybrid student reading hybrid texts, but such hybridity and ambiguity lead to a certain ambivalence that is fraught with its own challenges of privilege and power.

That final curse in Revelation draws us into the ambivalence of alter-imperial rhetoric. The ambivalence of belonging nowhere, as much as it can be a product of differential exclusions and inclusions, as nice as it can be to belong some place even if it is just an affirmation of belonging "no place," can also easily lead to replicative domination. How long did it take for my brother and me to try to listen openly to what my father was saying in that conversation? In Revelation the ambivalence of alter-imperial rhetoric threatens punishment, especially the punishment of exile outside God's holy no place, the new Jerusalem. Perhaps Revelation summons divine and scriptural authority in order to subvert and redirect the judgments passed on its communities. At the same time, this final curse encapsulates the ambivalent limits of alter-imperial rhetoric and scriptural authorization. While the book may end by a curse upon those who add or subtract, the history of Revelation's reception suggests that ongoing communal life has been one of performing and interpreting, adding to and subtracting from the text. Even the written text itself, as Juan Hernández shows, was a site for faithful addition and subtraction (2006).

Revelation's own role as a communally performed text implies that its place as scripture is more about its ongoing practice in community than any authority adhering to a fixed text. In chapter 10, John is oddly commanded not to write something down, suggesting perhaps that important revelations still exist outside the text. Chapter 10's miniscroll may remind us that not all divine words have been written in a text that can be read. Perhaps this final curse in chapter 22, from a figure who has played so transformatively with different myths and scriptures, is also a reminder that the important additions and subtractions transpire outside the formal text.

Concluding Comment

No identity can be circumscribed by one text or one reading. In working on this project, I find that my readings of my father and Revelation have changed over time. They are not always the same, and not always confined to one way of grasping the meaning of that text or moment. I can ambivalently embrace reading Revelation and that moment in my father's kitchen table, and for all the limits, dangers, and privileges of ambivalence, as a U.S. Latina critic, I still seek to read from that no place caught between worlds.

Works Cited

Anzaldúa, Gloria. 1987. *Borderlands/La Frontera: The New Mestiza*. San Francisco: Aunt Lute.

Aparicio, Frances R. 2007. (Re)constructing Latinidad: The Challenge of Latina/o Studies. Pages 39–48 in *A Companion to Latina/o Studies*. Edited by Juan Flores and Renato Rosaldo. Malden, Mass.: Blackwell.

Aymer, Margaret P. 2005. Empire, Alter-Empire, and the Twenty-First Century. *Union Seminary Quarterly Review* 59, nos. 3–4:140–46.

Barreto, Eric D. 2010. *Ethnic Negotiations: The Function of Race and Ethnicity in Acts 16*. WUNT 2/294. Tübingen: Mohr Siebeck.

Bhabha, Homi K. 1994. *The Location of Culture*. London: Routledge.

Blount, Brian K. 2005. *Can I Get a Witness? Reading Revelation through African American Culture*. Louisville: Westminster John Knox.

Boer, Roland. 2008. *Last Stop before Antarctica: The Bible and Postcolonialism in Australia*. 2nd ed. SemeiaSt 64. Atlanta: Society of Biblical Literature.

Brah, Avtar. 2003. Diaspora, Border, and Transnational Identities. Pages 613–34 in *Feminist Postcolonial Theory: A Reader*. Edited by Reina Lewis and Sara Mills. New York: Routledge.

Buell, Denise Kimber. 2005. *Why This New Race: Ethnic Reasoning in Early Christianity*. New York: Columbia University Press.

Cabezón, José Ignacio. 2003. Identity and the Work of the Scholar of Religion. Pages 43–59 in *Identity and the Politics of Scholarship in the*

Study of Religion. Edited by José Ignacio Cabezón and Sheila Greeve Davaney. New York: Routledge.

Carter, Warren G. 2009. Accommodating "Jezebel" and Withdrawing John: Negotiating Empire in Revelation Then and Now. *Interpretation* 33:32–47.

Chavoya, C. Ondine. 2004. Customized Hybrids: The Art of Rubén Ortiz Torres and Lowriding in Southern California. *CR: The New Centennial Review* 4, no. 2:141–84.

Columbus, Christopher. 1892. Letter to Juana de la Torres. Pages 151–76 in *Writings of Columbus: Descriptive of the Discovery and Occupation of the New World*. Edited by Paul Leicester Ford. New York: Webster.

De Anda, Neomi, and Néstor Medina. 2009. *Convivencias*: What Have We Learned? Toward a Latino/a Ecumenical Theology. Pages 185–96 in *Building Bridges, Doing Justice: Constructing a Latino/a Ecumenical Theology*. Edited by Orlando O. Espín. Maryknoll, N.Y.: Orbis.

García-Alfonso, Cristina. 2010. *Resolviendo: Narratives of Survival in the Hebrew Bible and Cuba Today*. New York: Lang.

Graham, William A. 1987. *Beyond the Written Word: Oral Aspects of Scripture in the History of Religion*. New York: Cambridge University Press.

Hernández, Juan, Jr. 2006. *Scribal Habits and Theological Influences in the Apocalypse*. WUNT 2/218. Tübingen: Mohr Siebeck.

Liew, Tat-siong Benny. 2008. *What Is Asian American Biblical Hermeneutics? Reading the New Testament*. Honolulu: University of Hawai'i Press.

Love, Velma. 2006. Odu Outcomes: Yoruba Scriptures in African American Constructions of Self and World. Ph.D. diss. Claremont Graduate University.

Medina, Néstor. 2009. *Mestizaje: (Re)Mapping Race, Culture, and Faith in Latina/o Catholicism*. Studies in Latino/a Catholicism. Maryknoll, N.Y.: Orbis.

Moore. Stephen D. 1996. *God's Gym: Divine Male Bodies of the Bible*. New York: Routledge.

———. 2010. *The Bible in Theory: Critical and Postcritical Essays*. Society of Biblical Literature Resources for Biblical Study 57. Atlanta: Society of Biblical Literature.

Moore, Stephen D., and Yvonne Sherwood. 2011. *The Invention of the Biblical Scholar: A Critical Manifesto*. Minneapolis: Fortress.

Oboler, Suzanne. 1995. *Ethnic Labels, Latino Lives: Identity and the Politics of (Re)Presentation*. Minneapolis: University of Minnesota Press.

Richard, Pablo. 1998. *Apocalypse: A People's Commentary on the Book of Revelation.* Maryknoll, N.Y.: Orbis.

Rogoff, Irit. 2000. *Terra Infirma: Geography's Visual Culture.* New York: Routledge.

Ruiz, Jean-Pierre. 2011. *Readings from the Edges: The Bible and People on the Move.* Maryknoll, N.Y.: Orbis.

Runions, Erin. 2001. *Changing Subjects: Gender, Nation, and Future in Micah.* London: Sheffield Academic Press.

Royalty, Robert M., Jr. 2004. Don't Touch This Book! Revelation 22:18–19 and the Rhetoric of Reading (in) the Apocalypse of John. *BibInt* 12:282–300.

Said, Edward W. 1994. *Culture and Imperialism.* New York: Vintage.

Sánchez, David A. 2008. *From Patmos to the Barrio: Subverting Imperial Myth.* Minneapolis: Fortress.

Schüssler Fiorenza, Elisabeth. 2007. *The Power of the Word: Scripture and the Rhetoric of Empire.* Minneapolis: Fortress.

Segovia, Fernando F. 1992. Two Places and No Place on Which to Stand: Mixture and Otherness in Hispanic American Theology. *Listening* 27:26–40.

———. 1996. In the World but Not of It: Exile as Locus for a Theology of the Diaspora. Pages 195–217 in *Hispanic/Latino Theology: Challenge and Promise.* Edited by Ada María Isasi-Díaz and Fernando F. Segovia. Minneapolis: Fortress.

———. 2009. Toward Latino/a American Biblical Criticism: Latin(o/a)ness as Problematic. Pages 193–223 in *They Were All Together in One Place? Toward Minority Biblical Criticism.* Edited by Randall C. Bailey, Tat-Siong Benny Liew, and Fernando F. Segovia. SemeiaSt 57. Atlanta: Society of Biblical Literature.

Smith, Wilfred Cantwell. 1993. *What Is Scripture? A Comparative Approach.* Minneapolis: Fortress.

Sugirtharajah, R. S. 2001. *The Bible and the Third World: Precolonial, Colonial, and Postcolonial Encounters.* Cambridge: Cambridge University Press.

———. 2002. *Postcolonial Criticism and Biblical Interpretation.* New York: Oxford University Press.

Tweed, Thomas A. 2002. Between the Living and the Dead: Fieldwork, History, and the Interpreter's Position. Pages 63–74 in *Personal Knowledge and Beyond: Reshaping the Ethnography of Religion.* Edited by

James V. Spickard, J. Shawn Landres, and Meredith B. McGuire. New York: New York University Press.

Wimbush, Vincent L. 2008. Introduction: TEXTureS, Gestures, Power: Orientation to Radical Excavation. Pages 1–20 in *Theorizing Scriptures: New Critical Orientations to a Cultural Phenomenon*. Edited by Vincent L. Wimbush. New Brunswick: Rutgers University Press.

———. 2012. *White Men's Magic: Scripturalization as Slavery*. New York: Oxford University Press.

Toward Latino/a Biblical Studies: Foregrounding Identities and Transforming Communities

Francisco Lozada Jr.

What does it mean to do Latino/a biblical studies? In this essay I shall attempt to address this question not by examining a history of the scholarship in the field, but by critically examining the meaning and implication of the three designations in question—Latino/a, biblical, and studies. It is not my intention here to merely define these terms. Rather, this is meant to be a discussion about how these three interlocking components interact to form the basis for how I see myself doing Latino/a biblical studies.

Latino/a biblical studies, like many other approaches based on ideological and/or contextual frameworks, is not uniform or universal in its strategy or orientation. It is quite diverse and particular in its approaches, aims, and principles. For instance, two principles that underlie my own particular understanding of Latino/a biblical studies are: (1) the foregrounding of Latino/a identities, and (2) the transformation of the Latino/a community from one of marginality in the political sphere to a community that has gained some representation in various mainstream institutions, including religious communities. These principles are expressed in the interpretive processes of engaging the text and evaluating those Latino/a readings of the text that are employed in the field.

The first principle concerns the foregrounding of the Latino/a identity or identities. This foregrounding may be expressed in various ways, but the underlying principle focuses on the dynamic relationship between the reader's personal and community identity(ies), the community or communities' histories, the sources emanating from the community, and other social factors that combine to help the reader engage the text from a Latino/a context. In this way, the Latino/a identity(ies), contexts, and conditions become prime factors of what it means to do Latino/a biblical studies.

The second principle involves the transformation of the Latino/a community from a marginal social group to one that has achieved significant representation in the religious, social, and political systems. This does not mean that the Latino/a community has been assimilated into these systems, nor does it mean that the community has simply become distinct from other communities in the systems. Rather, this principle suggests that Latino/a biblical studies must contribute in some way toward assisting Latino/as and others to gain access to a variety of systems and aim to establish significant representation in these systems. This transformation affects not only the Latino/a community, but other dominant ethnic/racial groups as well.

Having identified the principles that underlie my approach to this work, the remainder of this essay consists of three main sections. The first section examines the expression *Latino/a*: the complexity behind the nomenclature and issues regarding who can do Latino/a biblical studies. The second section explores the expression *biblical*: what it signifies and what a Latino/a approach to the text looks like. Finally, the third section examines the term *studies* by exploring what it suggests within the field of Latino/a biblical studies. I hope, via this examination, not only to present my framework for doing the work of Latino/a biblical studies, but, perhaps more importantly, to begin a discussion of the field in general and of the essential questions of Latino/a biblical studies in particular. My goal is not to provide a definitive answer regarding Latino/a biblical studies' methodology, but to give readers some tools to evaluate the field and perhaps scaffolding for proposing or developing a perspective of their own.

Latino/a as Concept

The concept (or adjective) *Latino/a* is an issue of contention inside and outside the Latino/a communities. What does the term signify? Is it an expression that points to the ethnic/racial and national identity of a group of people in the United States whose ancestry is most recently traced back to Latin America, the Caribbean, and the U.S. Southwest? Is it a term that points to racial hereditary background to Spain, Africa, and/or indigenous communities spread throughout the Americas? Is it a term that captures the ethnic/racial identity of people whose native tongue was once or still is Spanish or one of the many indigenous dialects? Or does it signify a group with a shared history of colonialism at the hands of Spain, Roman Catholicism, and, most recently, Protestantism?

The term *Latino/a* is simply a slippery term with no hard boundaries to define it. The task of delineating the concept *Latino/a* is very challenging, as it means different things to different peoples and groups. For instance, not all Latino/as point to a national identity in the traditional sense (e.g., Chicanos). Nor do all Latino/as share the same ethnic/racial background (e.g., black Latinos, indigenous Latinos, white Latinos). Neither do all Latino/as speak Spanish, and not all Latino/as see their identity anchored in a paradigm of pan-nationalism. However, what all Latino/a groups do seem to have in common is the perception by "non-Latino/as" that they are "Others" in the United States. Even so, conceptually, the term *Latino/a* remains difficult to fix, as it is constantly changing based on the cultural and political landscape of those who identify as Latino/as in the United States. Indeed, depending on the generation, the national ethnic/racial identity, and/or the geographical location of any given group of Latino/as in the United States, the term is either well received, rejected, or, at times, used interchangeably, signaling other significations. Thus the term *Latino/a* remains fluid within the Latino/a communities throughout the United States, although some scholars are keen to fix the identity along hereditary lines (or via what is termed *essentialism*). One avenue we may use to begin to grasp the background or signification of the term *Latino/a* is to explore the various Latino/a groups' collective histories in the United States and their engagement with the larger political society.

Another way of identifying the collective, although not as ubiquitous as it once was, is the term *Hispanics* or *Hispanic Americans*. This term is less used currently because its history is quite conflicted. For some, this term identifies Spain rather than Latin America as their most recent ancestral home. For these individuals, *Hispanic* accurately speaks to their experience in the United States. For others, the term is anathema and signifies internalized colonialism, particularly because the U.S. government employed it for the purposes of the U.S. Census in 1969.[1] Conversely, the term *Latino/a* is perceived by some people as an emic designation—one that emanates from within the group—and that contains political significance and agency. For these individuals, the term *Hispanic* not only

---

1. For a useful introduction to the interrelationship between the U.S. Census and Latino/a identity, see Rodríguez 2000.

signifies the relationship to Spain but also evokes the notions of assimilation, neutrality, and group invisibility in the political arena. However, an either/or construct attached to either of these terms seems flawed, as many people use both terms interchangeably, and with different persuasive motives.

Historically, the terms *Latino/as* and *Hispanic* were not viable distinctions used within the groups under discussion. Instead, members of differing Latino/a groups identified themselves via their geographical and national origin (i.e., Cuban, Puerto Rican, Mexican, Dominicano, Colombiano, etc.). The tradition of using one's ethnic particularities to identify subgroup membership generally remained private, while in the public arena one of the nomenclatures referring to the broader collective, Latino/a or Hispanic, were more commonly used. One major exception to this rule is that specific subgroups can create their own labels for political and/or economic purposes.

For instance, in the 1960s, to reflect their unity during the labor and political battles that took place in the Southwest and West (e.g., the United Farm Workers under César Chávez and Dolores Huerta; *Raza Unida* in Texas), many Mexican Americans referred to themselves as Chicano/as, a term that they still use today to signify their continued unity. This inclination to nationalize identity based on a nation paradigm of race and/or ethnicity also is reflected among the population of Puerto Ricans living in New York City. These Latino/as identify themselves as Nuyoricans, a designation that is partially the result of battles for equal rights waged by the New York chapter of the Young Lords political party. Similarly, after their migrations to the United States as political refugees and exiles beginning in the 1960s, Cubans began to nationalize their identity by using a hyphen, Cuban-Americans, as a way to politically and economically position themselves as a minoritized or ethnic/racial group among other Latino/as or Hispanics in the United States. These names are also commonly used among Latino/as intellectuals and activists, including many (not all) Latino/a biblical interpreters who are influenced by Latino/a cultural studies. In the years to come, it will be interesting to discover how and if cultural national identity is reflected among the newer or more recent Latin American migrant communities. It will also be quite interesting to see if these nation-based understandings of ethnicity/race filter into Latino/a biblical studies.

However, even though there continue to be political, economic, and social challenges within ethnic or racial subgroups, this naming duality (i.e., Latino/a or Hispanic) does not always continue with second- and third-generation Latino/as, who may no longer look toward or dream of their parents' homeland, but instead resonate more with the experiences of other Latino/as in the United States. This seems especially pertinent for those who are living or teaching in multiple Latino/a ethnic/racial communities and who see the United States as home. For these individuals, the notion of the collective "Other" outweighs the notion of national or geographic identities. This image of Latino/a as "Other" is portrayed across modes of discourse, including film, literature, and television profiles; and scriptural, theological, sermonic, and political discourses. Interestingly, this "Othering," especially when it involves anti-immigrant or nativist discourses, reconnects second- and third-generation Latino/as with their parents' or grandparents' migrant past or colonial history, such as Mexican Americans in the Southwest or Dominicans in the Northeast. Indeed, the incorporation of this "Othering" has served to consolidate and perhaps solidify the racial/ethnic consciousness and organization of Latino/as in the current era.

What does all this have to do with biblical studies? Simply put, this complex web of social, historical, and political factors involved in the construction of Latino/a identity is the basis of a Latino/a reading of the biblical text. In other words, each reader/interpreter brings her or his own unique identity set to the text, and this provides the worldview through which the meaning and relevancy of the narrative is determined. This is an essential component of the approach. The foregrounding of Latino/a identity, specifically, is what differentiates this approach from, say, Latin American, African American, Asian American, Native American, or other contextual readings that are based on very different political and historical realities.[2] Of course, it is also very dissimilar from those readings of the text that do not consider identity at all as well as those that claim to be solely informed by the principle of objectivity during the reading experience.

The inclusion of the reader's identity into the dynamics of interpretation allows not only for the particularity of each Latino/a ethnic/racial group to emerge but also for the particularity of each reader within these groups. In this way, it destabilizes any potential master narrative that

---

2. For an understanding of some similarities among minoritized biblical studies, see Segovia 2009.

might mistakenly assume that a Puerto Rican, Mexican American, Cuban American, Dominican, Salvadoran, Guatemalan, or Bolivian (to name a few) reading is representative of the views of the entire Latino/a community in the United States It also negates the idea that "ethnic" identity or "race" are the only modalities that define Latino/as. Indeed, there are other, competing modalities at work such as class, gender, sexual orientation, and religious or political affiliation that also speak to the particularity of the reader or community. Most importantly, by foregrounding the Latino/a experience, this approach destabilizes not only the myth that the United States is a homogeneous, monolingual, or monocultural country, but also the field of biblical studies and the paradigms of privileged cultures. Said another way, it challenges the notion that the production of knowledge emanates from one particular economic and socio-educational exclusive community.

As noted, the inclusion of Latino/a identity in the reading experience of texts may also touch upon many issues affecting Latino/as, such as colonial and neocolonial realities and the current cultural representations of Latino/as. For instance, at the colonial level, this approach engages the factors that bring Latino/as together—such as their colonial histories (1492–1898)—by examining the implementation of imperial political, religious, and economic policies. Such policies have led to the subjugation of the indigenous peoples, the hybridization of communities, the exploitation of the working class, the colonial acquisition of land, the dislocation of many Latino/as in the United States, and the colonial cultural, political, and religious ideologies implemented by Christian theology in particular (e.g., Manifest Destiny and the Monroe Doctrine). At the neocolonial level (1898–1990), the approach focuses on the influences of Latino/a particularity and collective identity. This includes topics such as migration laws, guest-worker programs, economic and foreign policies, all of which are part of what it means to be Latino/a in the United States At the cultural level (past and present), foregrounding the Latino/a experience allows one to be aware of how it is constructed through the Internet, television, print media, and other forms of global and geopolitical communication. It is at this level that a closer examination of the foregrounding of the Latino/a identity presents the most challenging—but necessary—course of study, because it must also include the issues of black Latino/as and people of mixed Latino/a backgrounds as well as issues such as masculinity, sexism, language, education, class, and religion, among others. In sum, the construct of "Latino/a" is a nomenclature that strongly defines what it means to do Latino/a biblical studies, yet it is always between some notion of fixity and fluidity and so must be located and studied both historically and politically.

There is one final question to be considered here. Does someone need to be Latino/a to do Latino/a biblical studies? That is, can someone be, say, Anglo-American, African American, or Asian and still do Latino/a biblical studies? The answer to this question depends on whether one sees "Latino/a" from an essentialist or a constructionist point of view. In other words, does one need to be biologically connected to or a descendant of a parent who is Latino/a (an essentialist perspective), or can someone who is not Latino/a but committed to Latino/a issues of social justice and a liberating representation also be a legitimate practitioner of Latino/a biblical studies (a constructionist perspective)? Some Latino/a critics would argue that it is desirable to have a combination of the two perspectives, thus moving the question away from an either/or scenario.

One might ask whether such a question is even relevant. The question is important, because there is concern among essentialists that non-Latino/as will use the growing popularity of the field (and population) to attempt to speak for a community that they may only understand from an etic perspective. Thus essentialists feel that there is a hazard that these scholars may misrepresent the experience of the broader Latino/a community. This was and continues to be an issue with other contextual hermeneutics communities as well—namely, who can speak for the "subaltern"? Another related issue is that non-Latino/a scholars often do not have a direct investment in the community, and so presumably are not subject to the same dynamics and conditions as "actual" community members. Because of this, essentialists contend that it is best that people who do not have ethnic ties to the community not practice Latino/a biblical studies.

Conversely, those who lean toward the constructionist perspective, that one does not have to be "Latino/a" to do Latino/a biblical studies, believe that the Latino/a community needs all the allies it can muster to contribute to and provide a positive representation of the Latino/a community. From this latter perspective, all practitioners who are sincere in the work are welcome. I position myself and my work closer, but cautiously so, to the constructionist position. This is because what is of greatest significance to me is that the Latino/a experience and dynamic be at the core of the work and that the work provide a positive representation of Latino/a identity and the Latino/a community. I believe that these elements are crucial to the field, regardless of the scholar's background. Still,

I remain conflicted, because foregrounding and the challenge of representation, even when one is doing it with the best intentions, can be problematic. For instance, a Latino/a scholar can foreground Latino/a identity in a universal, objective, and positivistic fashion or construct a Latino/a representational identity in a very myopic or stereotypical fashion. For this reason, all Latino/a readings of the text must undergo a critique.

In sum, the question of whether to use an essentialist perspective, a constructionist perspective, or both remains a key issue in the field, one strongly debated. These types of questions—who is a Latino/a, what constitutes Latino/a identity, and what constitutes Latino/a biblical studies in general—are ongoing in the field. This tension between fixing Latino/a identity (essentialist) and seeing Latino/a identity as fluid (constructionist) demonstrates that the field is still emerging and that understanding its contours and shape is a task that will continue for the foreseeable future.

Biblical as Concept

The second concept under discussion is *biblical*. Unlike the term *Latino/a*, the concept *biblical* is not as ambiguous within the field. Here it refers to the canonical writings of the Bible. For the majority of Latino/as scholars in the field, the object of examination is the Christian Bible, that is, the Hebrew Bible and New Testament. Unlike Latino/a scholars in other fields, who may focus primarily on the question of identity within their respective disciplines (e.g., ethnography, history, literature), in this field the Christian Bible has been and remains the focus of study. In addition, to my knowledge, research has also focused strictly on the "canonical" texts that play a major role in the faith of the Latino/a community.

The Latino/a interpreter's stance toward the process of interpreting biblical text varies. Most interpreters work under the assumption that the text is "sacred." However, this does not preclude the interpreter from engaging the text critically, nor from challenging the idea that the word of God is synonymous with the words of the text. Nor does it, for the most part, inhibit the interpreter's understanding of the world/context "behind" the text. Indeed, for many Latino/a interpreters, the text is examined (or read) in a way that includes the condition of the interpreter or his/her community, thus reifying the notion that the text is speaking to the conditions of the community. Much of this theological assumption is strongly influenced by liberation hermeneutics, which, generally speaking, holds that God is on the side of the oppressed/marginalized and that this support is made visible (revealed) through the stories of marginalization and liberation in the biblical text. This stance toward the text is, therefore, one in which the word of God is present in the text as well as in the interpreter's/community's respective experience. The text is therefore "sacred" in making sense of their reality and marginality.

Much of this theological assumption is also supported by strategies that correlate the experience of the interpreter/community with the experience of those marginalized in the stories. It is this theological aspect that is accentuated in the process of interpretation rather than the contextuality of the text. In other words, the experience of marginality in the text is analogous to the experience of the interpreter and her or his community in the present. Certain methodological approaches are used to support this strategy, such as historical criticism or the social- or literary-critical approaches. It is interesting to note that, at moments, the critical social and critical literary approaches may also be seen as allegorical approaches to reading. Thus interpretations using these approaches are often presented without any engagement or assessment of how the approach is used or applied. Unfortunately, this lack of examination may in turn lead to the mistaken assumption that one's interpretation is liberative for the community and others who are marginalized.

Other Latino/a interpreters have created a different framework for understanding the "sacredness" of the text. For these scholars, the text is considered "sacred" in the sense that it plays a vital role in the construction of Christian identity within the Christian tradition and therefore is a living and lived text. However, from this perspective the text undergoes an examination of its contextuality relative to its production and reception. In addition, the interpreter is also contextualized, usually by way of foregrounding his or her identity. Given that the text is viewed as an active participant in the construction and representation of a marginal identity, it is approached pointedly and suspiciously, and thus must undergo an examination that allows for its ideological dimensions to be scrutinized. Methods such as minoritized biblical approaches, ideological criticism in its many forms, feminist criticism, or imperial studies allow for this perspective, which also identifies the text as "sacred" not in the sense that the reality of the world behind the text corresponds to the reality of Latino/as, but rather that the text participates in the construction and representation of Latino/a Christian identity as well as the identity of others. Still, these types of construction must be evaluated for their ramifications for the community and toward other minoritized communities.

This focus on the Christian Bible leads to different engagements with the text framed around different reading strategies. The two framings that I discuss and that I alluded to above are examples of the use of correlation and ideological readings as ways to engage the text. The first correlates the stories of marginality with the historical or social changing conditions of the reader or with his or her community, while the second confronts any ideological conceptions or perceived worldview of the text that may shed light on the human condition in general or the Latino/a identity in particular. Another strategy engages the text as a dialogue partner, thus using the reading experience as a launching pad to explore other issues within the text and/or within the Latino/a community. The goal is to glean new insights into certain issues and themes from the text that based on the reader's identity. The next part of this discussion examines these three reading strategies, beginning with the one that I feel best represents my overall understanding of Latino/a biblical studies.

The Text as Correlation

This particular tactic correlates the historical experience of marginality of the characters (historical figures for many) in the narratives of the text with similar and concurrent experiences of marginality among Latino/as.[3] The biblical text, therefore, is seen as a mirror of sorts between the world behind the text and the world in front of the text (reader). Thus the text is an avenue that joins the current Latino/a experience and reality to the reality within the biblical text. In other words, the biblical text is engaged from a Latino/a perspective with the hope of an encounter that relates to or is analogous to the Latino/a experience. Sometimes this process takes the form of a strong dichotomous approach such as context/text, where the context of the reader is first presented ("My social location is …"), followed by an analysis of the text, so that the former will make a contribution toward understanding the latter. At other times, this process takes the form of a "cross-textual" experience, where the reader's Latino/a identity and the narrative are both seen as texts and examined accordingly. The Latino/a reader therefore works under the assumption that his or her context contributes to the interpretation of the text. He or she also

---

3. For a demonstrative and recent volume employing elements of this strategy, see Carroll 2008.

understands himself or herself as a Latino/a biblical scholar as well as a Latino/a Christian theologian.

The biblical text therefore is viewed most often as an ally in the quest for a transformative experience of some nature within the Latino/a community. Correlating the experiences of Latino/as members of a marginal group (ethnic/racial marginality, that is) with the experience of those marginalized in the text calls on readers to resonate with the biblical story even more. The theological assumption is that this resonance indicates that God is on the side of Latino/as.

The Text as Dialogical Partner

This particular tactic involves using the text as a way to speak about a particular issue that pertains primarily to the identity of the interpreter as well as to the issues of a text.[4] In other words, the text is used as a sounding board to explore issues that pertain to the realities of the Latino/a interpreter and how these realities open the door to exploring the identity of a text. Current issues such as immigration, language, and hybridity, for example, are used to explore other issues such as migration, language, and hybridity in the biblical text. The methodological approaches employed may vary, but literary approaches are the most widely used. The text as a dialogical partner is in many ways also a conversation partner. There is very little confrontation related to the text. Instead, many scholars employ the text to agree, disagree, or problematize an issue in the narrative or in the general experience of Latino/as. Since the process of interpretation involves the construction of the Latino/a Christian identity, the text is engaged in a way that makes sense of or produces an image of an identity that assists in this particular construction.

The Text as Ideological

This particular tactic involves the employment of the text as a point of departure to explore issues related to Latino/a identity.[5] In other words, it is not just the text that undergoes explorative analysis of its composition but also aspects of the reader and her or his community. Therefore

---

4. For an illustrative essay that draws from this reading strategy, see García-Treto 2009.

5. A representative and recent volume that draws from this strategy is Ruiz 2011.

personal factors such as gender, ethnicity, race, and language become the focus of analysis as well. This look at the text as ideology involves employing the dialogue in Latino/a studies to expose any issues, silences, or absences reflected in the history of the engagement with the text. In other words, the biblical text is explored to foster both a better understanding of the text itself and, more importantly, a better understanding of the particular aspect of the reader (or his or her community) that the reader wishes to discuss. The aim overall is that engagement or tactic with the text will bring a new point of view to the text. It functions to make other readers see differently how the text might be reinterpreted.

The biblical text, therefore, is viewed as an ideological-discourse partner for a transformative experience of helping other readers understand the identity formations that emerge within the Latino/a community, which perhaps may not be so obvious. As such, for some Latino/a critics of the biblical text, the text is seen as ideological. Whereas the first strategy (correlation approach) mentioned above might be framed as "speaking complicatedly with" the biblical text, and the second strategy (dialogical approach) seen as "speaking interactively with" the biblical text, the third strategy (ideological approach) is viewed along the lines of "speaking back to" the text. The text is an "Other," yet it also participates, although not exclusively, through its history of interpretations that constructs the "Other" as marginal. The text is viewed as a medium to be examined in various ways with the intent to understand the power dynamics at play in the narratives. In turn, such analyses are used to help Latino/a scholars of the Bible better understand the power or political dynamics in the world of Latino/as.

As already alluded to, these three approaches do not have clear boundaries. Each blends into the other, yet for this study's purposes, there are demarcations that provide heuristic understandings of how some Latino/as engage the biblical text. The different strategies or tactics of Latino/a biblical studies continue to include more varied points of reference to inform its readings, including cultural and environmental studies. Even the expansion of questions like "What is biblical?" to questions like "What is scripture?" contribute to the forum for discussion that would include other religious texts and readings from a Latino/a perspective.

Studies as Concept

The third concept that we will examine here is *studies*. What does this term signify in the context of Latino/a biblical studies? To answer this question,

I will engage in an analysis of the four dominant paradigms of biblical criticism. Specifically, the remainder of this discussion will address historical criticism, cultural criticism, literary criticism, and ideological criticism and how each is involved in or related to Latino/a biblical studies.

Historical Criticism

There is no question that historical criticism still has a strong foothold in the field of biblical interpretation. Its presuppositions are that meaning exists in the world behind the text as something to be extracted or excavated and that the interpreter of the text is a neutral party, who, at her or his best, is able to maintain objectivity, promote positivism, and support universality. For Latino/a biblical studies specifically, historical criticism still plays a major role. Its role may not be direct, yet it continues to inform the work of many scholars—even though the principles and assumptions that uphold the paradigm are challenged at times. This means that no longer are the principles of objectivity, positivism, or universality believed to be inherent in historical reconstructions of the text. Instead, scholars have become aware that, although some historical distance from the text is desirable, the assumption that using the historical-critical method implies complete objectivity is no longer viable. In other words, no perspective or interpretation is completed in a vacuum. Given this, some scholars wonder whether the approach—developed during the European Enlightenment—remains relevant or useful as a tool for Latino/a biblical studies. Many also wonder if the field of Latino/a biblical studies requires specific analytical tools that are developed exclusively for and within the Latino/a experience. The discussion of these issues remains debated in the field.

Cultural Criticism

Similar to historical criticism, certain tools from this particular paradigm are employed in Latino/a biblical studies. The text is viewed as a means to both the social world of the text and the social codes/language within the text. Although the underlying principles of this approach are similar to those of the historical approach, there is a difference in their use and application in Latino/a biblical studies. The body of literature based on this perspective is still small, but it continues to play a minor role in the reading strategies of some Latino/a biblical interpreters. I suspect that the issues of poverty, class, and family that shape the discourse of Latino/as in the present will give way to a fuller employment of this approach in the near future—including broadening the contours to include discussions of sexuality, economics, and geopolitics within and in front of the text.

Literary Criticism

Again, similar to historical criticism, the tools from this paradigm are used frequently in Latino/a biblical studies. From this perspective, the text is viewed as a medium between the reader and the narrative of the text. I would argue that the principles of neutrality, objectivity, positivism, and universality are more available in literary criticism than they are in historical criticism, particularly in the text-dominant approaches of literary criticism (e.g., narrative criticism). This is less so in the reader-dominant approaches (e.g., reader-response readings). Interestingly, it is this latter, reader-dominant, approach that opened a door for Latino/as to explore how their social location influenced the story world of the biblical text. Like the historical approach, it continues to be used as one tool, among many others, that provides understanding of the narrative text for the Latino/a community. However, literary criticism is simply a tool to see not just the narrative as text but also the engaged reader or community as a text that also must be scrutinized.

Ideological Criticism

The last paradigm that I wish to discuss is ideological criticism. Moving away from the assumptions of neutrality, objectivity, positivism, and universality found in historical criticism and literary criticism, ideological criticism is an approach that not only engages the text as an historical or rhetorical document but also identifies the text as an ideological document. From this perspective, the text is a repository of information, but it is always positioned or constructed information and always influenced by the role of the interpreter and his or her positionality. Ideological criticism provides a wider platform from which one can engage both the biblical text and the reader's Latino/a identity as constructions. In this way it provides an avenue for Latino/a biblical criticism to explore other tools and strategies for interpreting a text, such as "reading with" or "reading against" the ideological worldview of the text.

Ideological criticism also embraces postcolonial approaches. It is the foregrounding of the legacy of colonial, neocolonial, and postcolonial history that informs my engagement of the question of Latino/a identity as well as the biblical tradition. Regarding Latino/a identity, the approach focuses on understanding how U.S. and European scholarship (European colonial countries) have constructed Latino/a identity and its particularities. It notes that U.S.- and European-based scholars have codified this identity as "Other" and examines how this process of "Othering" occurred, particularly through the history of colonization. This method also applies to Roman Catholicism and Protestantism, since these religious bodies have contributed to the social construction of Latino/as as the "Other" through religious instruction, missionary endeavors, and other colonial activities. In addition, the approach also examines the resistant writing of Latino/as as a way to undo the colonizing characterization and "natural" constructions of Latino/as as colonial subjects. It aims to highlight the value of Latino/a identity and identify Latino/as as moral agents. With regard to biblical tradition, the postcolonial approach is applied to how U.S. and European scholars have constructed a colonial framework of the world behind, in, and in front of the text, through which they study the biblical tradition. At the same time, the postcolonial approach provides alternative readings of the text and reclaims the text's meaning for those affected by colonization and oppression in today's world.

Finally, I see ideological criticism as providing an opening for liberation hermeneutics to enter the discourse. I feel that liberation hermeneutics is the other area that identifies me as a Latino/a biblical critic. For me, this approach, like postcolonial studies or Latino/a cultural studies, is not a method per se but rather an ideological orientation toward the text and the reader or the reading communities. My position of liberation is not simply focused on the economic factors of Latin America. It also intersects with the hope that all marginalized peoples will be liberated from oppression. Liberation hermeneutics—as I see it—also does not aim to reassert the authority of the text or the reader but rather to engage both, with the goal of sifting out what is liberative and what is not from such interaction or readings of texts. Most importantly, it always provides the space for such readings to be challenged by others. Like postcolonialism, my use of liberation hermeneutics allows me to interpret the reading process as resistance reading and the text as problematic in the sense that it is not the only source for morality and theology—context plays a role in the decision-making process. I engage or employ liberation hermeneutics not as a way to see liberation from the biblical text, but rather as one tool, along with Latino/a biblical studies and postcolonialism, toward a liberative hermeneutic.

Conclusion

In this study I have sought to provide a general understanding of what Latino/a biblical studies is all about. By exploring the separate but intertwined concepts of *Latino/a*, *biblical*, and *studies*, I have attempted to discuss some of the issues, objectives, and problematics involved with the field, while simultaneously presenting my framework for engagement in discussing the field and the principles and assumptions I currently employ in applying the approach. To conclude, for myself both the foregrounding of Latino/a identity and the transformation of the Latino/a community are two principles that shape my work within the discourse of Latino/a biblical studies.

Works Cited

Carroll R., M. Daniel. 2008. *Christians at the Border: Immigration, the Church, and the Bible*. Grand Rapids: Baker.

García-Treto, Francisco. 2009. Exile in the Hebrew Bible: A Postcolonial Look from the Cuban Diaspora. Pages 65–78 in *They Were All Together in One Place? Toward Minority Biblical Criticism*. Edited by Randall C. Bailey, Tat-siong Benny Liew, and Fernando F. Segovia. SemeiaSt 57. Atlanta: Society of Biblical Literature.

Rodríguez, Clara E. 2000. *Changing Race: Latinos, the Census, and the History of Ethnicity in the United States*. New York: New York University Press.

Ruiz, Jean-Pierre. 2011. *Readings from the Edges: The Bible and People on the Move*. Maryknoll, N.Y.: Orbis.

Segovia, Fernando F. 2009. Poetics of Minority Biblical Criticism: Identification and Theorization. Pages 279–311 in *They Were All Together in One Place? Toward Minority Biblical Criticism*. Edited by Randall C. Bailey, Tat-siong Benny Liew, and Fernando F. Segovia. SemeiaSt 57. Atlanta: Society of Biblical Literature.

Toward a Latino/a Vision/Optic for Biblical Hermeneutics

Rubén Muñoz-Larrondo

It is impossible to speak in terms of initial explorations in Latino/a hermeneutics, given the number of authors who have been at work on this task over the course of the last twenty to thirty years. The following come readily to mind: Justo González, in *Mañana Theology* (1990); Virgilio Elizondo on *mestizaje*, in *Galilean Journey* (1983); Fernando F. Segovia, in *Decolonizing Biblical Studies* (2000); Ada María Isasi-Díaz on *mujerista* theology, in *En la lucha* (1993); and Miguel De La Torre and Edwin David Aponte, in *Handbook of Latino/a Theologies* (2006)—to name but a few. However, the task of fashioning and refining a detailed vision or optic continues.

At the same time, to define a single vision for Latino/a hermeneutics is impractical for a number of reasons. The following two I view as central. First, the demographics involving the Latino/a population show an ever-increasing number, over fifty million as of July 2011, situating them as the most numerous minority group in the country.[1] The majority possess strong religious values and a pronounced spiritual attitude regarding everyday life. Such growth reflects both the enormous diversity of and sharp need for Christian spiritual traditions and practices among Latino/as (Aponte and De La Torre 2006, 123–284; García-Treto 1999). Second, the issue of integration into the mainstream of religious-spiritual life, whether in the Anglo-American church or in other Latino/a churches, is nonexistent. With regard to the former, this is so initially due to the language barrier, although such rejection continues even after learning the language. With regard to the latter, Latino/as—whether new or long-time

---

1. See http://www.pewhispanic.org/2013/02/15/hispanic-population-trends/ph_13-01-23_ss_hispanics2/. The projection for 2050 calls for over a hundred million.

immigrants, educated or not, fluent in English or not—do not dissociate themselves from the religious-spiritual practices of their countries of origin. Generally, they continue to worship among those of the same national origins, to the point that Latino/as are sometimes accused of segregationism. It is typical to see Latino/a churches with a majority of Peruvians, Dominicans, Cubans, Mexicans, and so forth.

This attitude of not wanting to be absorbed or assimilated creates a twofold crisis of identity. On the one hand, Latino/as find themselves in the awkward situation of being perceived by their fellow citizens back home as "contaminated" by the mere fact of living in the United States. On the other hand, they encounter apathy on the part of Americans and other immigrants, including other Latino/as in their new country, when they try to implement religious-spiritual practices from their own countries of origin. This complex situation produces a sense of uncertainty regarding identity. This increases as individuals feel that they belong neither to their places of origin (birth, ancestry, education) nor to their present location. These psychological effects of the diaspora increase as they participate in the daily life of their home countries through such means as the Internet, newspapers, television, sports, reality shows, soap operas, and so on. The result is a sense of in-betweenness, of living between the spaces of a borderland. Not from there, not from here. This hybridity is more intense for those who have been educated in the North/West.[2]

As a Protestant evangelical minister who was educated in the United States and who has worked as a pastor and teacher in the country for more than twenty years, I have experienced this reality of diaspora in our communities. This is a diaspora that is marked by a Christian hybrid identity and that stands in need of a hermeneutical vision that will contribute to a process of liberation from the established patterns, imposed and/or accepted, of our traditional structures, in order to avoid domestication by or passivity under such established institutions. It is such a vision that I should like to pursue in what follows. First, I will lay out a theoretical framework for such an optic. Second, I will show its application in criticism by analyzing, from a postcolonial perspective, the episode involving Paul's submission to the authorities in Jerusalem (Acts 21–22).

---

2. Latin Americans and Caribbeans still view with suspicion any U.S. intervention in their countries of origin, at any level—politics, economics, military (e.g., guerilla wars), and so on, including religion, especially if Protestant in orientation.

Theoretical Framework for Latino/a Hermeneutics

The theoretical framework envisioned for Latino/a hermeneutics involves five criteria: (1) tuning our Christian identity beyond nationalistic overtones; (2) accepting an inclusive message of hope and liberation from faith to faith—yours and mine; (3) seeking balance and prudence between paradigms based on the biblical texts and complete acceptance of practices grounded in popular beliefs; (4) revising the structures of power in our own traditions; and (5) bringing back the Bible from theoretical and philosophical speculations to a complete vernacular form of communication with our communities of faith.

A Christian Identity beyond Nationalistic Overtones

We must refer to ourselves first and foremost as Christian believers—Protestants, Catholics, Pentecostals, and so forth—before appealing to any regional, ethnic, or territorial designation. In our Latino/a communities of faith, the experiment of a "melting pot" does not work. We remain South Americans, Central Americans, Caribbeans. We continue to identify ourselves as Puerto Ricans, Dominicans, Mexicans, Guatemalans, Cuban, Chileans, and so on. This first hermeneutical criterion calls for us not to let boundaries on a piece of paper represent our identity, a point for which Acts 17:26 is most relevant: "From one he [God] has made the people so that they dwell in the entire face of the earth."

Let me illustrate this point with a basic question that new immigrants invariably encounter in the United States. I have often wondered what would be the response of a Christian of the Latino/a diaspora if asked how he or she would prefer to be identified, whether in terms of religious beliefs or national provenance. Let the question be posed as follows: What do you think represents yourself best? Is it religious affiliation (e.g., Christian, Jewish, Muslim, atheist; if Christian: Protestant, Catholic, nondenominational, etc.) or national status (citizen)? I have an inkling that, if this question were to be asked of a native U.S. citizen, the response would be: first, as a citizen of the United States; then, as a follower of a religion—Christianity, Judaism, Islam, and so on. The answer, I suspect, would be the same among Christian Latino/as in the diaspora: first, as citizens of their respective countries; then, as followers of a religion or church.

I would argue that the first criterion for this vision should be a self-identification that moves beyond such nationalistic overtones and presents ourselves as Christians—Protestants, Catholics, nondenominational, and so on—with a sense of hope, mission, and character.³ This criterion is meant not to erase our various territorial identities but to foreground our belief that we are citizens of the kin-dom of God (Isasi-Díaz 1996, 326 n. 1), be it in terms of a nonworldly eschatological understanding or of a social-temporal worldly representation (Phil 3:20).⁴ I do not deny the value of human diversity, with its relevance as a marker of sociological and even theological identity, but I would insist that such identification should not serve as the primary marker.

As believers, I would argue, we should seek the optic of a scriptural Savior and biblical practices that bring about the transformation of our communities into a "sanctified people." This reality should manifest itself in a twofold process of material renewal, moving away from economic exploitation, and spiritual renewal, moving "out of darkness into his marvelous light" (1 Pet 2:9).⁵ This temporal designation as believers and members of the people of God would also serve as a caution not to isolate ourselves from a global perspective and from other diaspora communities in search of and in need of identity.⁶

A Message of Hope and Liberation from Faith to Faith: Yours and Mine

Our reading of the Bible must be one of hope, salvation, and liberation as *a way of life*. This message must lie at the intersection of two worlds: the inescapable, violent teaching and preaching of the "Lamb who was slain"—the core of the gospel (grace, ransom, and substitutionary salvation); and the wrath of "the Lamb who is seated at the throne for judgment"—the good news involving the hope of eschatological reversal, when

---

3. I think the apostle Paul would answer: first, as a Jew, a Pharisee and son of a Pharisee; then, as a Roman citizen (see Acts 22–23; Phil 3:5).

4. I prefer the term *politeuma* (citizenship, homeland) rather than *basileion hierateuma* (kingdom of priests; see 1 Pet 2:9), given the imperialistic overtones of superiority associated with the latter.

5. Again, I translate the expression *ethnos hagion* (1 Pet 2:9) as "holy group of people or foreigners" rather than as "holy nation," given the expansionistic connotations of the latter term.

6. My comment has in mind the number of Latin Americans who live in different places of the world without the benefits of a community. For example, many Latin Americans are doing community for the kin-dom of God in such new locations as the Arab Emirates, definitely without home and roots.

Death and Hades will be destroyed (Rev 5–6, 20).[7] This second hermeneutical criterion calls for preaching and teaching about a perceived difficult God, one who deserves worship and adoration but also one who demands "fear and glory" (14:7).

Our community of faith must not wait patiently for an eschatological reality; it must seek instead, with a vibrant faith, the sharing of goods and blessings with the *desposeídos* (dispossessed), the powerless and marginal (see Matt 25).[8] It must strive for both faith and mission with the understanding that salvation must be communitarian and not individualistic or personal ("our common salvation," Jude 3).[9] It must seek out those who are *desarraigados* (uprooted) in every corner of the world. This community of faith must be one that is devoted not to the lack of responsibility signified by individualism and personal salvation but rather to a responsibility marked by a *luchar por la fe dada a los santos*, a "struggling for the faith given to the saints."

This must be a community of faith that seeks as well a spirituality that is "from faith to faith" (Rom 1:11–12), avoiding thereby regionalism, superiority in denominationalism, sectarianism, or exclusivism in origins. Its interpretation of the Bible must be ecclesiastical-communitarian in effort and purpose. This second criterion seeks to obey the counsel of Paul in Romans, given to base communities as part of the body of Christ, to accept the diversity of gifts and to encourage sharing "spiritual gifts" among one another (Rom 1:11).[10] It should follow Paul's admonition to be mutually

---

7. Here I am indebted to various scholars: Fernando Segovia and his construction of a paradoxical God who "counts the hairs" and is "silent and [in] hiding" at the same time (1996, 215–17); to Daniel Patte for the phrase "from faith to faith: yours and mine," which was engraved in my memory from a seminar on Romans; and to George R. Knight for the concept of a "violent lamb" (2008). The common popular phrase *predicando un poco de cielo e infierno* (preaching a little of heaven and hell) perhaps reflects this paradoxical situation.

8. There is no need to romanticize the margins or the poor. However, all efforts in this regard must be undertaken according to a pastoral plan of transformation-conversion.

9. The verb *epagōnizesthai* (to struggle on behalf of, to contend, to make strenuous effort, to fight hard) appears only here in the Bible, where it stresses the point of "our common salvation," *peri tēs koinēs hēmōn sōtērias*.

10. The verb *metadidōmi* (to give part of, to transfer something to another, to impart, to share), used only five times in the New Testament and seven times in the Septuagint, illustrates the idea of sharing food—not hoarding, holding back, or hiding

encouraged[11] "from faith to faith: yours and mine" (Rom 1:12; 12:3–21). This is contrary to what has become popular in some emerging church movements (McKnight 2007), where a personal-individualistic relationship is sought, what might be characterized as a "nice feeling attitude in worship and life." The process of salvation—physical and spiritual—must not be personal and individualistic.[12] Salvation, rather, must be participatory in community, *en conjunto*.

A Balance between Biblical Paradigms and Popular Beliefs

For us as Christian believers, biblical, canonical orthodoxy must take precedence over any popular praxis or belief that grants supremacy to feeling and fellowship, in contrast to "It is written" or "Thus says the LORD" (*Así dice Jehová*). Consequently, any syncretism with popular religion that is marked by "feel-good relational alternative worship services" must be avoided. This third hermeneutical criterion calls for a twofold plan of action: on the one hand, acknowledging the reality of U.S. Latino/as, with its variety of popular religious beliefs and practices, an "anthropological perspective" that, as Harold Recinos argues, definitely serves to "enhance[s] the value of theology" (2006, 219–21); on the other hand, making sure that such a reality is never allowed to compromise an "It is written" or a "Thus says the LORD." Likewise, at no point should popular practices—global missiology, "alternative traditions" and "alternative conversations," particular forms of worship—be allowed to foster a sense

---

the grain. See, e.g., Job 31:17: "Have I eaten my bit of bread on my own without sharing it with the orphan?" (my trans.); Prov 11:26: "He that hide up corn, shall be cursed among the people: but a blessing upon the head of them that sell" (my trans.).

11. The term *allēlōn* (of one another) reflects the need for corporate transformation and assumption of the spiritual and ecclesiastical body of Christ on earth. Romans 12:5, "In the same way, all of us, though there are so many of us, make up one body in Christ, and as different parts we are all joined to one another," reflects the individuality of members in regard to one another.

12. The well-known phrases of Moses, responding to Pharaoh, in Exod 10:9 ("We will go with our young and our old, we will go with our sons and daughters") and Joshua in Josh 24:15 ("me and my house will serve the LORD") as well as the narratorial comments of Acts 16:15 ("Lydia and her household were baptized") and 16:33 ("the Philippians' jailer and those of him—his family") all reflect the corporate dimension of salvation and liberation. Interestingly, the final liberation of resurrection is also a communal experience.

of superiority or even yield parallel "expressions of sacred space" (De La Torre and Aponte 2006, 211).

This third criterion calls, therefore, for an experience of liberation as a salvific movement of transformation, one that allows for expressions of popular religiosity but does so without assuming syncretistic practices and expressions that might contradict the authority of the Bible. This stance might come across as imperialistic, but I would argue, in the light of my Protestant upbringing, that there are issues that are simply nonnegotiable and that what is needed instead is a good balance. Readings from my place? Definitely! Yes to social and cultural readings. Indeed, these must be mandatory axioms, but with the caution that such interculturalism in no way devalues or compromises the validity of the basic principles of the Scriptures. No Latino/a hermeneutical vision should allow itself to be compromised to the point that it becomes a popular religion where anything goes. History demonstrates that the origins of Christianity have never been considered logical or popular.[13]

This tension envisions a complete paradox: a seemingly nonexisting God of justice and a God who is a giver of peace and hope to those who are in the world but not part of it (John 17). Therefore, no Latino/a hermeneutic would be complete and satisfactory, if it were not shared with other similar religious-spiritual representations. This optic should thus seek dialogue with the hermeneutics of other minority formations that share a similar need for representation, clarification, and differentiation.

Here I anticipate the next criterion. The community of faith, as depository of the Christian Scriptures, the sacred texts of antiquity, cannot interpret these in isolation from the visible and corporate body of Christ. This criterion requires a confessional and ecclesiastical reading of the texts as well as authoritative responsibility in interpretation. Communal reading does not grant the right to have independent views, dissociated from the general sense of the Bible. Here I agree in principle with Orlando Espín, "I

---

13. This is demonstrated in such issues as the following: the preferential option for the poor over the rich; the saving meaning of the cross; loving the enemy and rewarding the meek. These have always been considered countercultural, even absurd and abnormal, by the standard of the world. On this, see, e.g., 1 Cor 2:2–14, "My speech and my proclamation were not with plausible words of wisdom, … so that your faith might rest not on human wisdom but on the power of God … none of the rulers of this age understood this … for they are foolishness to them, and they are unable to understand them."

realize that many within Protestant congregations feel uncomfortable with the label popular religion when it is applied to what they simply consider an authentic analysis or interpretation of the Christian message and/or of specific biblical texts" (2006, 6–7). It is true that forced orthodoxy or orthopraxis cannot guarantee the validity of an interpretation, regardless of who stands behind it. However, though "Christianity is a lifestyle before it is a body of doctrines" (10), this lifestyle must be a real "sense of the faithful," based on "sound doctrine."[14] I agree with Espín that sometimes "hegemonic groups in societies and churches" (I would say *all churches*) continue to exercise the power of "doctrinal differences," yielding "in true radical importance to other differences (class, gender, race, culture and so forth) … [and] have been hidden from most ordinary Christians" (15).

This criterion must serve as a warning to any interpretation that does not demonstrate the character of the history of salvation in the message of the Bible. This optic should seek neither a literalism that kills the common goal of hope and salvation nor a spiritualism that is sickly and escapist (*espiritualismo enfermizo y escapista*). In addition, communities of faith and popular expressions must have some relationship to the wholeness of the body, and hence must not be isolated from ecclesiastical representation, which leads to the next criterion.

Revising the Structures of Power in Our Traditions

Our reading of the Bible must seek voluntary submission on the part of individuals and communities to the body of the church and its various ecclesiastical representations. Such submission, however, must be not in terms of domination from the center but rather as subordinates who freely express their opinions and dissent from within.[15] Throughout history, the people of God have functioned as an organized rather than a loose community, with some type of clearly established structure in place.

For such a reading, I find the distinction made by Ellen Davis to explain the process of the "faithful transmission of the text" helpful. Adopting the terminology of Michael Fishbane, she explains this process as a "complex interaction between the two aspects of tradition: *traditio*, the process of

---

14. As expressed in 2 Tim 1:13, "Hold to the standard of sound teaching that you have heard from me, in the faith and love that are in Christ Jesus."

15. An example would be, as I shall show later on, the case of the voluntary submission of Paul to the structures of power, the Jewish and Christian Sanhedrin, in Acts 22.

creating, changing, and passing on; and *traditum*, the literary deposit that is received as authoritative, interpreted (i.e., changes), and passed on, still authoritative in its altered form" (2003b, 168–69). This distinction can be applied to the function of the structures of power and the importance of tradition in the process of interpretation. This fourth hermeneutical criterion posits that the tradition of the Christian church, especially in terms of its Judeo-Christian heritage, cannot be ignored. No interpretation is done in a vacuum; all our presuppositions are permeated by our social location. Consequently, a legitimate hermeneutic will take into account the readings of ancient sacred texts as well as the readers of those texts (Segovia 2000, 140).

I further find Davis's vision of "critical traditioning" to be helpful in explaining the process of interpretation, with its view of the latter as a "tradition that earns its authority through long rumination on the past" (2003b, 169). "A living tradition," she states, "is a potentially courageous form of a shared consciousness, because tradition, in contrast to an ideology, preserves (in some form) our mistakes and atrocities as well as our insights and moral victories." She adds, "So the price that must be paid by those who are (from a biblical perspective) privileged to live within a tradition is accepting a high degree of inherent tension" (2003b, 169). Therefore, I see the church as the people of God seeking *voluntary submission without domination* to the tradition of the Christian church and the representations of its body, while resisting any institutionalized effort at domination.

This tension of belonging to and being independent of the body at the same time reflects Jesus' words of John 15:5, "because apart from me you can do nothing." We must not devalue one at the expense of the other. However, clarification is needed. Thus Latino/a biblical hermeneutics must not empower the tradition of institutionalization, whether in interpretive or historical fashion. Although we live in a postmodern world, in which we want to believe that the metanarratives of the centers of power "have lost their power to convince" (González 1996, 346), neo-empires continue their control and oppression of others. What I mean is that there are ecclesiastical centers of powers that still exert their rule over interpretation in our traditions. At the same time, I cannot imagine a hermeneutic of liberation that is dissociated from the tradition of interpretation of the people of God. A hermeneutic that is completely isolated, without any roots in tradition, is merely an ideology.[16] One cannot ignore the hundreds of years and

---

16. Perhaps, this is similar to what Efrain Agosto concludes with regard to Pente-

the myriad of interpretations.[17] The paradox continues;[18] it is impossible to live disconnected and without representing the body of the church.[19]

In this context, I would propose voluntary submission to and conversation with the totality of the church, the people of God, but without domination from the center, without a hold over interpretation in our traditions. In other words, one cannot ignore the role in interpretation on the part of institutionalized leadership, as represented, for example, by such bodies as a general synod, dioceses, the magisterium, the general conference of a church, or an association of independent churches. At the same time, the church, the people of God, should not accept passive subordination to or cooptation from these centers. The "subaltern" must have a firm, respected voice—a literature of dissent, a voice of resistance, even to the point of dissociating themselves from such institutionalized centers if they do not represent the cry of the people.

The institution is a necessary component of the body, but without institutionalism. When the latter occurs, it becomes corrupt in a drive for supremacy and control. In order to maintain balance and establish justice, it must have an opposition, a voice that defends the voiceless as a conversational partner. As Francisco Lozada rightly states, "We need to ask how one's reading strategy of the biblical tradition, or of any tradition, for that matter, contributes to the authorization or de-authorization of that tradition" (2006, 113).[20] This criterion puts forward the ideal of "submitting

---

costal biblical scholars on the understanding of *sola scriptura*, "It was never meant to exclude the role of tradition, reason, and experience in the unfolding story of what is scripture what it teaches" (2009, 84). See also Solivan 1989, 72.

17. I reaffirm the study and appropriateness of the Old Testament/Hebrew Bible. Ellen Davis states that "Christian biblical interpretation is dangerous when it is pursued in ignorance or disregard of the long history of Jewish interpretation" (2003a, 23).

18. Richard Bauckham reminds us that "Jean-Francois Lyotard also later recognized that his own story of obsolescence of all metanarratives in postmodernity was paradoxically itself a kind of metanarrative" (2003, 45).

19. The recent trends in declining membership in mainline Protestantism (Episcopalians, Presbyterians, Methodist, etc.) and the recent reintegration of the Anglican Church to Roman Catholicism are proof of this phenomenon (see Woodward 1993).

20. Lozada, using strong language, speaks against the structures of power. He states, a "way to unsettle or to de-emphasize the biblical tradition is to be quite conscious of one's reading strategy. ... I believe that a 'reading with others' strategy is what is needed in order to de-emphasize and unsettle the authority of the biblical tradition. In other words, in order to avoid committing hermeneutical apartheid by focusing on

yourselves one to another in the fear of God" (Eph 5:21), knowing that, historically, the prophets, John the Baptist, Jesus, the apostles, and Paul all respected the traditions and order but also fought against the institutionalism of their day. Furthermore, all submitted to and confronted the authorities, most of them at the price of death.[21]

From the Theoretical and Scholarly to the Practical and the Vernacular

As Latino/a scholars, we should avoid scholarly terminology and hierarchical structures in addressing the base communities, for such language and attitude prove incomprehensible to the reality of the church. This fifth hermeneutical criterion calls on scholars to speak in the vernacular, in the *idioma* or language of the church. This means adopting the everyday language of the people, the language of individuals like Hermana Charito and Don Pancho and countless others, who sustain the work and life of the church with their faithful contributions and missionary zeal.

Our communities of worship, teaching, and ministry must seek after an experiential transformation of humanity. It is time for scholars, therefore, to communicate at the level of the churches and base communities, in a language that our sisters and brothers are able to understand, and, in so doing, put aside the accepted jargon of the educated elite when addressing them. Theologizing as voices from the margins may be seen as a critical intellectual exercise, but it can also fail to bring transformation to the body of Christ. In an effort to be heard and recognized by our counterparts as legitimate conversational partners in academia or to gain financial or professional status, we—as scholars, teachers, priests, pastors, as people of power—may interpret and theologize for them. In so doing, however, we must take care not to do a disservice to our call to be shepherds to the congregations. As Marcella María Althaus-Reid states, "Theology becomes a product to sell, but not allowing new producers to come on the scene," all

---

one community alone, and thus constructing a new 'magisterium of authority' ... it is important that our own histories and experiences are read along with those of *other* marginalized communities" (2006, 134–35). He adds, "I am not calling for an expansion of the tradition, but rather for an overturning of the tradition by allowing a new, more inclusive line of tradition" (136).

21. For an example of voluntary submission to the authorities, yet full of mimicry and ambivalent mockery and resistance, see my analysis (2012) of the Lukan Paul in front of the Christian Sanhedrin (Acts 22).

done for the sake of "perpetuat[ing] its preservation" (2000, 47). A vernacular hermeneutic should express the daily language of the believers, with all of our *idiosincrasias* (idiosyncrasies).

Further, our communities have the tendency to remain ethnically Latino/a, but unfortunately some are using in worship the language of the land, especially with respect to the second and third generations. Should this practice continue and increase, we will transform ourselves into monolingual silence, losing our identity. We will mute ourselves and successive generations. This criterion specifies that we—as teachers, preachers, and pastors—do not represent our communities *si no nos expresamos en nuestro propio idioma*, if we fail to express ourselves in our own language.[22]

As we rejoice in the growth of Christianity in Africa, Asia, Latin America, as well as the United States by way of the Latino/a population, we sadly experience the decline of a dying church in the North Atlantic. We need to be cautious that we do not domesticate or convert ourselves into a "mimicry of European Theology" (Althaus-Reid 2000, 56). A Latino/a vernacular hermeneutic calls, therefore, for publication at two levels. We must speak to the intellectual Other, who is increasingly becoming our interlocutor, since this is necessary for us to participate in academic circles. We must also speak to our communities at the level of their daily lives and struggles, because they are what we are and represent. We cannot speak to them without having a full vernacular hermeneutics.[23]

---

22. In the area of biblical studies, especially in volumes employing the historical-critical method, it was common to find full untranslated paragraphs in German, because a knowledge of German was a prerequisite for critics. By way of contrast, in publications in English over the last thirty years, most noticeably since the 1990s, few words and notes appear in *castellano*. Some of these have a descriptive character, ranging from the funny (picturesque and laughable, as in *estamos chambao*) to the fancy (elegant and academic). For an interesting article on the need to abandon Eurocentric curriculum and forms of expressions for our communities, see Dube 2007.

23. Gustavo Gutiérrez's remarks are to the point here, "We definitely will not have an authentic theology of liberation until the oppressed themselves can freely and creatively express themselves in society and among the People of God" (quoted by Cadena 2003, 167).

Concluding Comments on the Theoretical Framework

I have set forth above a tentative theoretical framework for a Latino/a hermeneutical vision or optic. Its five major components may be summarized as follows: (1) self-identification, first and foremost, as Christian believers; (2) a message of hope and liberation, with the community, and especially the dispossessed, in mind; (3) the appeal to popular tradition in the light of a canonical use of the sacred Scriptures; (4) voluntary submission to the body of the church, involving a twofold commitment to the history of interpretation and to free expression and dissent; and (5) attention to the community and its social location as vernacular interpreters living in the diaspora, with transformation in mind.

A Latino/a Reading of Paul in Acts 21–23

By way of example, I now proceed to analyze, in the light of the hermeneutical optic outlined above, the representation of Paul's identity in the Acts of the Apostles, with a focus on chapters 21–23, his appearance before both the Christian Jewish Sanhedrin (which is what I call the Christian council of elders) and the Jewish Sanhedrin, which I see as an act of voluntary submission to authority on his part.[24]

The Lukan Paul

Paul has a hybrid identity: on the one hand, he is a Jew, born in the Diaspora, educated and trained as a Pharisee in Jerusalem, with close ties to the religious and political institutions; on the other hand, he is a Roman citizen by birth. In general, this Paul differs from the Paul of the Epistles. At the beginning of Acts, his identity is shaped by his voluntary submission to the Jewish authorities—as a zealous Pharisee persecuting the followers of the Way. Later in the narrative, he continues as a passive and submissive apostle of the Jewish Christian institution. Therefore, any traditional reading of Paul based on the Epistles—antinomian, anticircumcision, bearing an exclusive message to the Gentiles—lacks any foundation in Acts.

---

24. A version of this section is also found in my now-published dissertation "A Postcolonial Reading of the Acts of the Apostles" (2012).

Although such identity does not seem to be a problem for this "chosen instrument" to the Jews and the Gentiles, others are troubled by his mission. From both directions, from his own group (the Jerusalem Jewish Christians and Jewish institutions) as well as from Rome (officials with whom he comes in contact), there are those who see him as an "agitator" and a "troublemaker," with a conflictive hybrid identity. In what follows I expand on such views.

The Jewish, Pharisee Paul

Acts presents Paul as a member of the social elite: highly educated, trained in the philosophy and rhetoric of the Greco-Roman world. Discussing the social education and location of Paul, Jerome Neyrey writes: "He is a typical male of considerable social status; he regularly appears in public space; he frequently performs traditional elite male tasks such as arguing, debating and speaking boldly in public. Luke would have us think of him as a person at home in places reserved for elites" (2003, 162; see also 1996, 275–76). This view stands in contradiction to how most scholars see Luke—a defender of the oppressed, the poor, women, and the disinherited in general.

Paul's elite status is clear throughout. He is educated under Rabbi Gamaliel (Acts 5) and has a special affinity for association with the higher social caste in both the Jewish and the Roman systems. Before his call, he has direct communication with the high priesthood, which authorizes him and sends him out as their representative (9:1–2; 22:5). Afterward, he may be found in the company of Roman proconsuls, like Sergius Paulus (13:7–12) and Gallio (18:12–15); and he speaks before Roman governors, such as Felix (23:23–24:27) and Festus (25:1–26:32), who invite him for ethical and philosophical discussion. He also associates easily with leading citizens of the Greek cities, as in Malta with Publius, a "leading man of the island" (28:7), and in Thessalonica with "not a few of the leading women" (17:4), who join him. Further, he is able to organize churches in the Diaspora and among Gentiles, even convincing them to send financial support through him to the establishment in Jerusalem. This cosmopolitan and extrovert portrait of Paul clashes to some extent with that of the self-effacing Jesus, his Lord and Savior.

Paul and the Jews

Paul shows no animosity toward any Jews, or toward the community, its boundaries, and its marks of identification. When Acts uses the term *Ioudaioi* or "Jews" with respect to Paul's opponents, it does so not in general terms, "the Jews," but with reference to a specific contingent or location, along the lines of "the Jews who" or "the Jews of." The text makes clear that Paul's identity and markers of identity are not an issue. He is a Jewish man, acknowledged as such by both centers of power. The attorney for the Sanhedrin, Tertullus, identifies him as a "ringleader of the sect of the Nazarenes" (24:5). Paul represents himself as a Jew (21:9; 22:3) and as a member of the "strictest sects of our religion and [one who] lived as a Pharisee" (21:39; 22:3; 26:5; 28:19–20).

Acts contains 79 occurrences of the term *Ioudaioi*, more than any other book in the New Testament, including the Gospel of John. Again, this identifier is used, and must be read, as part of an expression that conveys reaction to the apostles (acceptance or rejection) or reveals provenance. The following examples are clear in this regard. With respect to attitude, there is the reference to "disobedient/unbelieving Jews" in Iconium (14:2). With respect to location, one finds allusions to the Jews of Thessalonica (17:13), the Jews of Beroea (17:11), the Jews of Asia (21:27; 24:19), the Jews from Antioch and Iconium (14:19), and the Jews of Jerusalem (21:11; 25:7), in contrast to the Jews who accepted the proclamation of the apostles during Pentecost and the "thousands of believers among the Jews." Thus, in the course of the early chapters, which involve Peter and the rest of the apostles in Jerusalem, no prejudice is attached to the designation "Jews"; indeed, many accept the message of the apostles. It is only with his presence and work in the Diaspora that Paul has to defend his citizenship and religion. All instances of the term *Ioudaoi(os)* show it to be positive, therefore, except in the context of the encounters with Paul, where it acquires a negative connotation. However, Luke does not include the term *Ioudaismos* of Gal 1:13–14, or the famous inclusive declaration (baptismal formula), "There is neither Jew nor Greek" (Gal 3:28; Col 3:1; see Rom 10:12; 1 Cor 10:32; 12:13), so familiar in the Pauline corpus.

Two conclusions are thus in order. First, Jewish Christians in general do not suffer any kind of discrimination or rejection by their own people. Second, Luke tries to portray Paul as always submissive and obedient to the customs of the tradition, as a faithful Jew. Avoiding any problem related to circumcision and being loyal to the customs, Paul submits to the general opinion of the Jews of Lystra regarding the hybrid ancestry of Timothy, his disciple of Jewish-Lystran-Greek ancestry. One reads in Acts 16 that he has Timothy circumcised "because they knew that his father was a Greek." Later, in Jerusalem, Paul submits voluntarily to the wishes of the Christian council, performing the rite of purification in the temple, which brings about his arrest and the end of his career as an apostle.

Paul and Other Groups

Cyprians

Acts always introduces the Cyprian believers as a different group than those from Jerusalem (11:19). Paul is brought by brethren from Caesarea to the "house of Mnason of Cyprus" in Jerusalem (21:17). There seems to be a distancing here from the organized church in Jerusalem. It is also a Cyprian, Barnabas, who convinces the Jerusalem church to accept the former persecutor, Saul/Paul. Again, it is Barnabas who went to Tarsus "until he found him" in order to fulfill the Antiochian mission. In addition, Cyprus is important, because it is the place from where Barnabas and Saul begin the first of only two organized commission journeys:[25] "Set apart for me Barnabas and Saul for the work to which I have called them" (13:3). There are also the brothers from Cyprus living in Antioch, who decided, against orders from Jerusalem, to proclaim the word "among the Hellenists/Greeks" (11:19–20). In so doing, they created a hybrid and ambivalent identity for a new group of believers, moving from fixity to fluidity—the followers of the Way, who from this moment on receive a new signifier, "Christians." After an entire year of confrontation and discipleship, there is a shift of identity and leadership from the church in Jerusa-

---

25. I speak in terms of commission rather than the common missiological and colonial term of "Paul's missionary journeys." I see Paul as having been commissioned but twice by the church to visit other communities with a specific message. The rest of the travels, or itinerant preaching (though visitation for reinforcing the churches), take place without a definite plan or pattern. Sometimes, such travels are attributed to the Holy Spirit. At other times, they are occasioned by the denial of permission to remain in a city or by moving from place to place as a result of persecution, not by any sense of an elaborated and prayerful "missionary journey." Furthermore, the organized missionary journey of Paul to Rome is never accomplished.

lem to Antioch, where prophets (11:27) and teachers (13:1) are moving to what seems another seat of the Christian movement.

Jerusalem

Later, when Paul visits Jerusalem (ch. 21), the ambivalent dialogue of "they" versus "we" becomes a subject of discussion for Paul in front of "all the elders" in Jerusalem (21:17–26). It is ironic that the hybrid Paul, before the trial in front of the Jewish Council or Sanhedrin, must first testify in front of what seems like a Christian Sanhedrin, where he is judged—or at least evaluated—and sentenced, by way of "What is then to be done?" The criteria set by the Jerusalem Christian council seem to indicate that somebody has to pay for and repair the damage wrought by the accusations against this itinerant preacher and that this should be done in front of the thousands of Jerusalem believers or "all who are zealous for the law." At this point, the reader wonders if the Jerusalem Christian council is part of the "they" or of the "we." Luke introduces here again the enigmatic figure of James, together with "all the elders," though in Acts James is not identified as the brother of the Lord (Gal 1–2) but as the one who seems to be in charge of the church of Jerusalem (Acts 12, 15).[26]

The odd and ambivalent position of standing in two places, which obliges the council to speak in terms of "they" (the impersonal plural) rather than "we" (the first person plural), creates conflict with regard to the identity of these groups. The narrator describes the process like this: "When they heard it, ... they said to him: 'You see, brother, how many thousands of believers are among the Jews [with the reappearance of the conflictive hybrid term *Ioudaioi*] and 'they' are zealous for the law'" (21:20). It is interesting to note that the reference is to people outside this group. It is not clear whether Luke really wants to portray the Jerusalem Christian council as "zealous" for the law or whether this is intended to be an ironic and ambivalent designation.

The expression "zealous for the law" should not be confused with the political uprising by the Zealots (the same term) of the year 66 CE against the Romans (Dunn 1996, 285). The issue here is that the political-religious stand of the Zealots—described by James Dunn as "maintain[ing] Isra-

---

26. Acts 1:14 includes in the list of those present in the upper room, "Mary the mother of Jesus, as well as his brothers," but without describing them by name.

el's set-apartness to God, [in order] to avoid or prevent anything which smacked of idolatry or which would adulterate or compromise Israel's special relationship with God as his peculiar people" (286)—shares the same characteristics as that of the Jerusalem church and its leaders, including James, the brother of Jesus, and the elders, who are "zealous" for rightful adherence to the customs and Moses. Paul describes himself as zealous for God rather than zealous for the law. Dunn cites Philo and the Mishnah in this regard (286). First, Philo in *Special Laws* 2.253 describes similar circumstances: "There are thousands who are zealots for the laws, strictest guardians of the ancestral customs, merciless to those who do not anything to subvert them." In addition, the Mishnah (Sanh. 9:6) warns and threatens, "If a man ... made an Aramean woman his paramour, the zealots may fall upon him. If a priest served (at the altar) in a state of uncleanness his brethren the priests did not bring him to the court, but the young men among the priests took him outside the Temple court and split open his brain with clubs." Most likely, these are traditions that reflect the general practice in these circumstances. It is not, therefore, surprising to read that the mob literally wants to kill Paul.

Paul yielded to the exigencies of the Christian elite. In this regard Joseph Fitzmyer argues, "This was not a compromise that Paul makes of his own beliefs or teachings ... Paul performs the Jewish ritual acts in an effort to keep peace in the Jerusalem church, because he knows that those rites do not undercut his basic allegiance to the risen Christ" (1998, 692). I think that Fitzmyer makes light of such adherence to the Christian elite as the center. I do not see Paul making a "compromise" as a way of negating Jewish values, for to affirm this would imply that Paul is lying to the Christians elders. Besides, as I have already argued above, Acts never portrays Paul as denying any dimension of his Jewishness. To my mind, there is no conflict or problem for him regarding his Jewishness, since he still follows all these rites in a voluntary manner, without the pressure of any institution (18:18).

The compromise to which Paul submits, perhaps as a result of the jealousy of the Jerusalem party (which includes James), fails completely. Whatever had been the motivation and intentions of the leadership, a fragile combination of sacredness, preservation of purity laws, and commercialism were required of Paul in order to show allegiance to their authority and supremacy—performing sacrifices and vows, paying for offerings and purifications. Paul had already presented to the Jerusalem church the generous offerings of the Asian churches, but now additional conditions involving the temple and its activities were placed upon him. What is ironic in the narrative is that it is not the Jerusalemites or the "thousands among the people" who denounce Paul, but rather another group of Jews from Asia, who lie completely outside the reality of the Jerusalem church. This makes it necessary to establish if these accusations or presumptions against Paul were made in complete isolation from the normal routine of the church initially led by Peter and the apostles (chs. 4–5).

Appealing to the postcolonial category of mimicry, one may read Luke as accusing the Christian church in two respects: on the one hand, for not being really zealous for the law, a characteristic that the Lukan Paul has never invalidated; on the other, for not recognizing that the admittance of non-Jews (or Gentiles) into the Christian movement is at the same time a denial of the law. The text can be also read as Luke pointing the finger at the Jerusalem church for not being "zealous enough" in their fulfillment of the law and the inclusion of the Gentiles in the eschatological salvation movement. Read this way, Paul becomes a critic of resistance.

In contrast, the reader continues to wonder whether the accusation against Paul is real and accurate, since there is no denial of it. The elite of the Jewish Christian church cite the ambivalent group, identified as "they," saying: "You teach all the Jews living among the Gentiles to forsake Moses, and you tell them not to circumcise their children or observe the customs" (21:21). The imposition brought on the submissive Lukan Paul is not refuted. The accused one simply hears the sentence: "What then is to be done? We will tell you." The power of the Christian Sanhedrin is unquestioned, even by the narrator. The judgment is handed down so that "all will know" that the Jerusalem church portrays itself as still upholding the law and the customs, at least in the sight of others: even when a response is not accepted, the traditions must be kept and the accused must submit to the authorities.

In this regard I see Luke as making light of the Christian Sanhedrin: first, because of the accommodationist attempts attributed to them, as a way to keep everyone happy; second, given the unparalleled ambivalence regarding the identities of the three groups. The narrator makes no effort to clarify who these three groups are: (1) The elite of the Jerusalem Jewish Christian group identified as "we," perhaps a faction of the leadership of the Christian Sanhedrin. (2) The thousands of Jerusalem Christians referred to in the phrase "they will hear" (21:20, 22), probably the same Christian group that includes representatives of the civil religious authorities ("many priests," 6:7) and the Pharisees mentioned in previous chapters (15:5). It is difficult to believe that the general population of Jerusalem, let alone the civil and religious authorities as a group, would be preoccupied with the development of the Way among the Gentiles. Therefore, the term "they" cannot refer to them. It must be read as another segment within the inside group of the Jewish Christians. Perhaps, this "they" should be associated with those who previously went from "us," "though with no instructions," disturbing and unsettling "your" minds (15:24). (3) Finally, Paul and the rest of his delegation.

The accusation incorporates another group of passive and absent believing "Jews" who live "among the Gentiles" (21:21). These are Jewish people of the Diaspora. The accusation is not that Paul is teaching Gentiles not to circumcise their children or to forsake Moses. Though Gentiles are being converted to the Christian Way, the Lukan Paul does not reflect the same antagonism found in the Epistles. Furthermore, the council's decision also includes, regarding the "Gentiles/peoples/nations who have become believers" (21:25), a restatement of the previous decisions not to trouble them (15:19–20) by imposing further burdens other than the four essentials.

Thus the structures of power within the Christian group are clearly established: the elite of the group, as *another center*, are the ones who impose rules on everyone, to the point that they seem to make of Paul an observer and keeper of the law. This is ironic, since Acts always portrays Paul as not being against any custom but rather as a careful observer. The sentence has a dual meaning: it orders Paul to participate in a rite of purification, which the submissive and obedient apostle follows strictly; and it rectifies a previous judgment (Acts 15) to the rest of the passive and absent group of Gentiles, "We have sent a letter with our judgment." There is no doubt how to follow procedure for the conversion of the Gentiles.

The ratification of the previous judgment does not leave the reader puzzled about whether Paul participated in the decisions of the Jerusalem Council on behalf of the conversion of Gentiles, as some have suggested. The basic problem in Acts 21 is not the Gentiles who are converting but the "Jewish people living among the Gentiles." Paul satisfies the sentence of the elite by fulfilling the vow and participating in the rite of purification in the temple, which in turn provokes his arrest and incarceration, due to an accusation by a new antagonist group, the Jews from Asia. The accusations of this new group are contrary to those of the Christian Sanhedrin: they claim that Paul is "teaching everyone, everywhere against our people, our law, and this place [temple]" (21:28), including the profanation of the temple by bringing Gentiles to it. The reader again wonders if this arrest was a setup, a kind of conspiracy theory against the preacher to the Gentiles.

After this point, the Christian Sanhedrin and the thousands of Jerusalem believers are absent from the narrative. There are no prayer-intercession groups as there were earlier (see chs. 3–4). There is no defense of Paul to the Gentiles. The sinister silence of the Jerusalem church works as a rapprochement with the powerful Christian Jerusalem group, who did not even have to leave the city during previous persecutions (8:1), because they seemed to enjoy a good relationship with the city authorities. The situation continues calm for the thousands of believers and this power group. This is inferred from the response of the Jewish leaders in Rome, who state that they have not received any letters from Judea, although they "know that everywhere, with regard to this sect, it is spoken against" (28:22).

Paul's Hybridity

Luke presents the complex situation of hybridity among the believers since Acts 6, with the inclusion and division of the widows of the Hellenists and the Hebrews, an awkward designation, as well as the grumbling of the Hellenists to the Hebrews. Acts 11, then, introduces the term *Christianoi* as a designation, in distinction to those from Cyprus, who decide to contravene the ruling by speaking outside the regular groups of Jews. It seems that there is a subgroup within the group. Now, in Acts 21, Paul arrives in Jerusalem to celebrate Pentecost and visits the elders in order to report on the progress of his labors. This visit, however, gives way to what seems to be another council of the church, involving "all the presbyters." The aorist form of the verb, *paregenonto* ("they also came," 21:18), seems to indicate that the presbyters also came to this special meeting.

At his arrival, Paul has to face what is an already organized institution within the community, comprising "James and *all* the presbyters-elders" (21:18). A suspicious reader will distinguish this group from that of Mnason and the "brothers," who welcome them warmly. The Cypriot Mnason is identified as "an early disciple," as if a separation should now be made between those who have long been disciples and those who have only recently come to believe. Perhaps the constituency of the Jerusalem group has changed since the early days, and perhaps these new members are not as "zealous" compared to the "many thousands," which included some believers from among the priests and Pharisees (6:7; 15:5). This Cyprian group, probably Jews of the Diaspora, offer a place for lodging. It is interesting that Paul himself is a diasporic Jew and that he gets a better reception from this group.

I see Acts as casting a suspicious look at the rest of the Jerusalem Jewish Christian group—a group of disciples who remain completely silent after the arrest of Paul in Jerusalem. This scenario of suspicion regarding the leadership is reminiscent of the situation during the early persecution in Jerusalem (Acts 8), where everyone suffered persecution except "the rest," identified as the Jewish Christian leaders who continue immune to any sufferings and perhaps also in good terms with the authorities. One reads, "All except the apostles were scattered" (8:1–2). Thus the silence after Paul's arrest makes these circumstances very suspicious and suggests a cover-up from the Jewish Christian elite or the Jewish Christian Sanhedrin. This stage leads the Jerusalem group to question Paul's identity. It is true that Jews from Asia present the accusation to the Jewish authorities; however, their attitude is no different from that of the zealots among the Jerusalem disciples (Dunn 1996, 289).

In addition, there is no church vigil of prayer or intercession for this arrested member of the community, as there had been for Peter earlier (4:12). It seems that the Jerusalem church does not exist at all. Are these new characters, the Asian Jews, just the perfect alibi for the leadership to continue their supremacy and eliminate Paul? Perhaps, if Luke had not indicated that the accusers were Asian Jews, the chances of internal conflict among the Jewish Christians, Paul included, would have been significant.

The great mockery of Luke is to present Paul as fulfilling the customs and as made *almost* or *"not quite"* "holy to the LORD" (Num 6:5–21)—perhaps expressing the relationship of trying to mimic but not being good enough? Acts 21:27 explains that the arrest occurred almost at the end of the seven days of purification. The narrative interrupts the celebration of the vow and the festival, in celebration of the reception of the blessing of God, the firstfruits (Num 28:26), and the "renewing of the God's covenant."[27] Paul is accused of profaning and desecrating or defiling this "holy place." Paul submits himself to the jealousy of the Jerusalem Jewish Christians, but when he is almost perfect/holy (according to the fulfillment of the rite)—similar to the postcolonial category of hybrid mock-

---

27. Fitzmyer shows that "in the pre-Christian period at least some Judean Jews were celebrating the Feast of Weeks … as the renewal of the Sinai covenant (*Jub.* 1:1; 6:17–19; 14:20; in 22:1–16)" (1998, 233–34). Later, he adds that "he arrives in Jerusalem (21:17) in time for the feast of Pentecost" (686).

ery, "almost the same, but not quite"—the temple doors are shut for this teacher of apostasies. Neither the Jewish Christians nor the Jews accept him, although he is behaving like and carrying out the same rituals as the rest of them.[28] Most likely, the Asian Jews were completing the similar ritual of purification. The center does not accept competition or mimicry.

In relation to the first Lukan Pentecost, Fitzmyer writes, "when Peter 'stood up with the Eleven' (2:14) and confronted the Jews, the 'twelve apostles' confronted the 'twelve tribes of Israel' (Luke 22:29; cf. Acts 2:36, 'the whole house of Israel') and functioned as their judges" (1998, 234). Now, in this second Pentecost, the hybrid-mimic Paul cannot be accepted by any of the groups; he is without any alliance and left to suffer alone. The narrative shows the typological shutdown of the temple with the interruption of the vows and the festival. This interrupted Pentecost, which commemorated and celebrated the renewing of the Sinaitic experience of liberation and the receiving of the law, is in contrast to the previous Pentecost narrated at the beginning. The ambassador and representative, the one who initially was sent by those authorities of the same temple, is expelled.

In this interrupted Pentecost narrative, there is no shofar imitating the voice of God from the heavens giving the blessing. The only voice is Paul's proclamation in Aramaic, which mentions Ananias, who, in this repetition of the explanation of the calling episode (Acts 9), is described as "a man according to the law well spoken of by all the Jews living there" (22:12). The description of Ananias's character acquires other functions in this particular retelling of Paul's calling episode, all of which are later excluded completely in the third narration in chapter 26, where Ananias is no longer even needed for the story. The purpose seems to be a contrast with the Jews of Jerusalem and Asia, who are no longer "men according to the law."

These men who are not acting according to the law are mentioned twice with the expression *epebalon autois tais cheirais* (laid hands upon him), a technical term describing the arrest of the authorities of the temple (4:1–3; 5:17–18). The temple functionaries, as part of the *ochlos* (crowd), have the authority to arrest him publicly. Here, I believe, Luke parallels the Mishnah passage cited earlier to clarify why Paul was expelled and beaten outside the temple. The profane and unclean must

---

28. Either this vow corresponds to the Nazirite ritual, as I believe it does, or to the purification of seven days coming from foreign lands.

be banished outside the perimeter of sanctity. I would argue that Luke mocks the division between those who are common (*koinon*) and those who are pure, reflected in the *thanatos* of Herod, which proscribes the entrance of Gentiles into the inner places of the temple on pain of death.[29] Luke explains that this misunderstanding is a mistake: Paul did not bring Gentiles into the temple. However, the emphasis shows that perhaps ethnic and religious purity are contrasted with the destroyed barrier for those who belong to the Way (10:15; 11:9). The terms k*atharizomai* and *koinon* (clean and common distinctions) are contrasted and compared to *akathartos*—unclean and profane, which seem to be issues of the past. Again, there is submission of the subaltern to the authorities; yet they do not acquiesce completely. There is a hidden script and agenda in the narrative: distinctions of clean and common are not part of the new group's underlying ethos.

Conclusion

Luke presents the hybrid Paul not as a rebel against the customs of the ancestors but as a submissive disciple, perhaps along the lines of the postcolonial category of mimicry—accepting the assigned role, obedient to the structures of leadership, even inside the church in order later to declare his independence. This would indicate that the Jerusalem church elite, which represent the institutionalism of the nascent tradition, are not really convinced by his teaching. Yet the powerful elite accept the monetary gifts and enable the continuous commitment of raising money for the poor of Judah (ch. 15; 24:17). It is in these matters that I see the hybrid and ambivalent complex situation of Paul: checking into his teaching and seeing him as competition in regard to numbers of believers and public recognition by the center, what I call the Christian Sanhedrin or council of elders. The author makes this confusion escalate, not only within the circle of James and the elders, but also reaching out to the hyperbolic "whole city," "the temple," which is publicly shut down for the disciple, thus impeding everyone else's access in the preparations for the Pentecost feast. The chapter ends when the mob, full of adrenaline, beats the profane one who tacitly has desecrated the temple.

---

29. The inscription reads, "No one of another nation may enter within the fence and enclosure round the Temple. Whoever is caught shall have himself to blame that his death ensues" (Fitzmyer 1998, 698).

This is definitely an ambivalent and difficult example of voluntary submission to the ecclesiastical authorities, which ends up with the imprisonment of the one who announces different nuances in the process of inculturation of the same message in the expansion of the people of God. Conversely, the challenge remains to look for new elements in refining a Latino/a hermeneutics.

Works Cited

Agosto, Efrain. 2009. *Sola Scriptura* and Latino/a Protestant Hermeneutics: An Exploration. Pages 69–87 in *Building Bridges, Doing Justice: Constructing a Latino/a Ecumenical Theology*. Edited by Orlando O. Espín. Maryknoll, N.Y.: Orbis.

Aponte, Edwin David, and Miguel A. De La Torre, eds. 2006. *Handbook of Latina/o Theologies*. St. Louis: Chalice.

Althaus-Reid, Marcella María. 2000. Gustavo Gutiérrez Goes to Disneyland: Theme Park Theologies and the Diaspora of the Discourse of the Popular Theologian in Liberation Theology. Pages 36–58 in *Interpreting beyond Borders*. Edited by Fernando F. Segovia. Bible and Postcolonialism 3. Sheffield: Sheffield Academic Press.

Bauckham, Richard. 2003. Reading Scripture as a Coherent Story. Pages 38–53 in *The Art of Reading Scripture*. Edited by Ellen F. Davis and Richard B. Hays. Grand Rapids: Eerdmans.

Cadena, Gilbert R. 2003. The Social Location of Liberation Theology: From Latin America to the United States. Pages 167–82 in *Hispanic/Latino Theology: Challenge and Promise*. Edited by Ada María Isasi-Díaz and Fernando F. Segovia. Minneapolis: Fortress.

Childs, Brevard S. 2008. *The Church's Guide for Reading Paul: The Canonical Shaping of the Pauline Corpus*. Grand Rapids: Eerdmans.

Davis, Ellen F. 2003a. Teaching the Bible Confessionally in the Church. Pages 9–26 in *The Art of Reading Scripture*. Edited by Ellen F. Davis and Richard B. Hays. Grand Rapids: Eerdmans.

———. 2003b. Critical Traditioning: Seeking an Inner Biblical Hermeneutic. Pages 163–82 in *The Art of Reading Scripture*. Edited by Ellen F. Davis and Richard B. Hays. Grand Rapids: Eerdmans.

De La Torre, Miguel, and Edwin David Aponte. 2006. Alternative Traditions. Pages 206–11 in Aponte and De La Torre 2006.

Dube, Musa W. 2007. Curriculum Transformation: Dreaming of Decolonization in Theological Studies. Pages 121–38 in *Border Crossings:*

Cross-Cultural Hermeneutics. Edited by D. N. Premnath. Maryknoll, N.Y.: Orbis.

Dunn, James D. G. 1996. *The Acts of the Apostles*. Valley Forge, Pa.: Trinity Press International.

Duval, Scott, and Daniel Hays. 2005. *Grasping God's Word: A Hands-On Approach to Reading, Interpreting, and Applying the Bible*. Grand Rapids: Zondervan.

Elizondo, Virgilio. 1983. *Galilean Journey: The Mexican American Promise*. Maryknoll, N.Y.: Orbis.

Espín, Orlando O. 2006. Traditioning: Culture, Daily Life and Popular Religion, and Their Impact on Christian Tradition. Pages 1–22 in *Futuring Our Past: Explorations in the Theology of Tradition*. Edited by Orlando O. Espín and Gary Macy. Maryknoll, N.Y.: Orbis.

Fitzmyer, Joseph A. 1998. *The Acts of the Apostles: A New Translation with Introduction and Commentary*. AB 31. New York: Doubleday.

Garcia-Treto, Francisco. 1999. Reading the Hyphens: An Emerging Biblical Hermeneutics for Latino/a/Hispanic U.S. Protestants. Pages 160–76 in *Protestantes/Protestants: Hispanic Christianity within Mainline Traditions*. Edited by David Maldonado Jr. Nashville: Abingdon.

González, Justo L. 1990. *Mañana: Christian Theology from a Hispanic Perspective*. Nashville: Abingdon.

———. 1996. Metamodern Aliens in Postmodern Jerusalem. Pages 340–50 in *Hispanic/Latino Theology: Challenge and Promise*. Edited by Ada María Isasi-Díaz and Fernando F. Segovia. Minneapolis: Fortress.

Hirsch, Eric Donald, Jr. 1967. *Validity in Interpretation*. New Haven: Yale University Press.

Isasi-Díaz, Ada María. 1993. *En la lucha—In the Struggle: A Hispanic Women's Liberation Theology*. Minneapolis: Fortress.

———. 1996. *Un poquito de justicia*—A Little Bit of Justice: A *Mujerista* Account of Justice. Pages 325–39 in *Hispanic/Latino Theology: Challenge and Promise*. Edited by Ada María Isasi-Díaz and Fernando F. Segovia. Minneapolis: Fortress.

Isasi-Díaz, Ada María, and Fernando F. Segovia, eds. 1996. *Hispanic/Latino Theology: Challenge and Promise*. Minneapolis: Fortress.

Knight, George R. 2008. *The Apocalyptic Vision and the Neutering of Adventism*. Hagerstown, Md.: Review and Herald.

Lozada, Francisco Jr. 2006. Reinventing the Biblical Tradition: An Exploration of Social Location Hermeneutics. Pages 113–40 in *Futuring Our

Past: Explorations in the Theology of Tradition. Edited by Orlando O. Espín and Gary Macy. Maryknoll, N.Y.: Orbis.

McKnight, Scot. 2007. Five Streams of the Emerging Church: Key Elements of the Most Controversial and Misunderstood Movement in the Church Today. *Christianity Today* 51, no. 2:34–39. Online: http://www.christianitytoday.com/ct/2007/february/11.35.htm.

Muñoz-Larrondo, Rubén. 2012. *A Postcolonial Reading of the Acts of the Apostles.* Studies in Biblical Literature 147. New York: Lang.

Neyrey, Jerome H. 1996. Luke's Social Location of Paul: Cultural Anthropology and the Status of Paul in Acts. Pages 251–79 in *History, Literature, and Society in the Book of Acts.* Edited by Ben Witherington III. Cambridge: Cambridge University Press.

———. 2003. The Social Location of Paul: Education as the Key. Pages 126–64 in *Fabrics of Discourse: Essays in Honor of Vernon K. Robbins.* Edited by David B. Gowler, L. Gregory Bloomquist, and Duane F. Watson. Harrisburg, Pa.: Trinity Press International.

Recinos, Harold J. 2006. Pastoral Anthropology in Latino/Cultural Settings. Pages 219–26 in Aponte and De La Torre 2006.

Riebe-Estrella, Gary. 2006. Tradition as Conversation. Pages 141–56 in *Futuring Our Past: Explorations in the Theology of Tradition.* Edited by Orlando O. Espín and Gary Macy. Maryknoll, N.Y.: Orbis.

Segovia, Fernando F. 1991. A New Manifest Destiny: The Emerging Theological Voice of Hispanics Americans. *Religious Studies Review* 17:101–9.

———. 1994. Toward a Hermeneutics of the Diaspora: A Hermeneutics of Otherness and Engagement. Pages 57–74 in *Social Location and Biblical Interpretation in the United States.* Vol. 1 of *Reading from This Place.* Edited by Fernando F. Segovia and Mary Ann Tolbert. Minneapolis: Fortress.

———. 1996. In the World but Not of It: Exile as Locus for a Theology of the Diaspora. Pages 195–217 in *Hispanic/Latino Theology: Challenge and Promise.* Edited by Ada María Isasi-Díaz and Fernando F. Segovia. Minneapolis: Fortress.

———. 2000. *Decolonizing Biblical Studies: A View from the Margins.* Maryknoll, N.Y.: Orbis.

Segovia, Fernando F., and Mary Ann Tolbert, eds. 1994. *Social Location and Biblical Interpretation in the United States.* Vol. 1 of *Reading from This Place.* Minneapolis: Fortress.

Soliván, Samuel. 1998. *The Spirit, Pathos and Liberation: Toward an Hispanic Pentecostal Theology.* Sheffield: Sheffield Academic Press.

Vanhoozer, Kevin J. 1998. *Is There a Meaning in This Text? The Bible, the Reader, and the Morality of Literary Knowledge.* Grand Rapids: Baker.

Woodward, Kenneth, L. 1993. Dead End for the Mainline? Religion: The Mightiest Protestants Are Running out of Money, Members and Meaning. *Newsweek* (Aug. 9):46–48.

A Latina Biblical Critic and Intellectual:
At the Intersection of Ethnicity, Gender, Hermeneutics, and Faith

Ahida Calderón Pilarski

This essay emerged as a subsequent study on the question addressed to the inaugural panel of the Latino/a and Latin American Biblical Hermeneutics program unit at the 2008 annual meeting of the Society of Biblical Literature (SBL).[1] This question lies behind my title: What does it mean to be (in my case) a *Latina* biblical critic? This question is perhaps one of the most challenging—and necessary—identity questions that all biblical scholars (substituting, as appropriate, their own ethnic self-designation in place of *Latina*) should ask about themselves at some point in their professional careers. My brief response to the question at the time was that to be a Latina biblical critic is to take, through a process of conscientization,[2] a well-informed and well-engaged stance in the inquiry process. This particular stance, I argued, should be informed by at least four distinct but intersecting perspectives: ethnicity, gender, hermeneutics, and faith. A

---

1. Interestingly, this section was inaugurated 128 years after the founding of the society in 1880. This event follows the gradual trend of incorporating distinct cultural traditions and theological discourses within the SBL. The African American Biblical Hermeneutics section started in 1987 (although it acquired this title only in 1999), the Asian and Asian American Hermeneutics group in 2000. Phyllis Bird indirectly introduces this important information as she describes the process of historically accounting for the incorporation of women's voices in the SBL (2005, 79–80).

2. Here I refer to Paulo Freire's well-developed idea of *conscientização* as the possibility for all human beings to enter the historical process as responsible subjects in search of self-affirmation of their humanity. Fernando Segovia also refers to conscientization, defining it as a process that leads to the espousing of Latino/a causes and concerns (2009, 206).

standpoint so informed situates me within the larger community of Latina intellectuals,[3] and it is from this locus that I speak as a biblical critic.

In speaking of a stance, I refer to a sustainable hermeneutical platform that can allow a Latina/o biblical critic (or any biblical critic conscious of his or her ethnic heritage) to incorporate a critical and constructive vision into the analysis of the biblical text as well as into the analysis of the different coordinates left by Latina and Latino communities (or other ethnic groups) in their historical continuum. The aim of taking this stance is to adequately appropriate and craft a transforming ethnic heritage and discourse that claims for every Latina and Latino (and ultimately for every person) the same human dignity that has been afforded to normative groups in academia, the church, and society.

Given the space limits involved, in this study I elaborate further on the first two perspectives and address the latter two more briefly, in connection to the future role of Latina intellectuals. So I divide it in three sections: (1) ethnicity, (2) gender, and (3) the role of Latina intellectuals (hermeneutics and faith).

Ethnicity

For Hispanic/Latino persons in the United States, the concept of ethnicity is connected to the complexity of choosing the appropriate nomenclature to refer to one's own identity and that of one's communities. I use myself as an example in trying to answer the first part of the question at stake in this study—What does it mean to be a Latina? I was born in a South American country and have lived for almost half of my life in the United States of America; so am I Hispanic or Latina? In order to answer this question adequately, I will refer to the work of Fernando Segovia. Based on contemporary Latino/a studies, he illustrates the complexity of the nomenclature issue by way of a theoretical spectrum. Segovia distinguishes three positions in this spectrum: the objectivist-inflationary pole, the central range, and the constructivist-deflationary pole (2009, 209–14).

Language and culture are the distinctive features determining who is Latino/a according to the first position, the objectivist-inflationary pole. At this pole, explains Segovia, one claims that "Latinos are citizens from the Spanish-speaking world [Latin America and Spain] living in the United

---

3. I will develop this notion in the final section of this paper.

States; Hispanics are citizens from the Spanish-speaking world living elsewhere [than in a Spanish-speaking country]. All Latinos are Hispanics, therefore; not all Hispanics, however, are Latinos" (210). Those who locate themselves at this pole present an objectivist and universalist definition. They argue that, through a process of clash and fusion, Latinos will eventually inhabit a life-beyond-the-hyphen.

The second position, the central range, is more restrictive, connecting the distinction in nomenclature to the social-cultural origins and context of the communities. According to this position, "a Hispanic is defined as born or raised and educated in Latin America [this position excludes Spain] and a Latino as born or raised and educated in the United States. … A Hispanic may, in the course of time, become a Latino, especially if arrival in the U.S. takes place at a young age" (212). Therefore, observes Segovia, for the central range position, being a Latino/a can be defined by birth or upbringing and education, and also by immigration and consciousness.

The third position, the constructivist-deflationary pole, offers no formal distinction for the nomenclature. Instead it refers to Latinos "as Latin Americans who have either migrated into or have been incorporated by the United States, who constitute a 'community' within the American community, and who construct such a community in different ways, as a result of varying historical experiences and shifting identity factors" (213).

Segovia concludes that Latino/a criticism should tilt toward the last pole, which considers the material and cultural context(s) of the Latino/a communities. He proposes that a definition of *Latino/a* should incorporate three additional elements, which are worth citing word for word:

> First, its [i.e., Latino/a culture's] roots in Latin America—not simply as the diasporic presence of "Hispanic civilization" in the United States, but rather as the bearer of a legacy of dominion by and struggle against Spain. Second, its historical presence in the United States—the result of expansionary policy westward and southward, through war and annexation, and of population movement northward, in the light of political and economic insertion. Third, its conflicted relationship to the United States—the driving relation of inequality at work not only in the hemisphere as a whole but also within the country itself, yielding domination and marginalization at home. … In the end, although I would still prefer the expression "U.S. Hispanic Americans," I would argue that the term "Latino/a" captures well all such dimensions of the country. (213–14)

This introductory subsection offers just a glimpse into the complexity of defining the appropriate nomenclature for the Latino/a communities in the United States. Integrating Segovia's observations regarding the constructivist-deflationary pole, I do consider myself a Latina. Now, looking from a larger analytical framework, connected to this intricacy is also the ambiguity posed by the reference to ethnic identity itself. This reference presents two challenging but necessary questions for all ethnic groups today: (1) What is meant by *ethnic*? and (2) What is meant by *identity*?

Meaning of Ethnicity

The definition of *ethnicity* based on its etymology ("'ethnic' derives via Latin from the Greek *ethnikos*, the adjectival form of *ethnos*, a nation or race" [Petersen et al. 1980, 1])[4] can no longer suffice to explain the nature of the dynamics behind this term today. The understanding of ethnicity has developed significantly in the last decades. For instance, a definition used by the Center for the Study of American Pluralism at the University of Chicago in 1977 stated that in American society ethnicity could be "understood as religious, racial, national, linguistic, and geographic diversity" (Tracy 1977, 91). Today, however, the possibility of clearly defining the distinctive characteristics of most of these categories (as they apply to individuals and communities) has been challenged by people's constant changes through ethnic fusions and fissions (Horowitz 1975). Strikingly, *ethnicity* is a term that became widely used only in the 1970s, and now it is central to the public discourse.

Steve Fenton explains that as a general rule "there cannot be a theory of ethnicity, nor can 'ethnicity' be regarded as a theory. Rather, there can be a theory of modernity, of the modern social world, as the material and cultural context for the expression of ethnic identities" (2003, 2). This distinction is crucial to all discourses that deal with people's ethnic identities, because it prevents any attempt to construct theoretical definitions that, if exclusive (i.e., based on the experience of one particular group within one particular context), run the risk of presenting only the view of theoretical mainstreams as the normative ones. For instance, although the term *ethnicity* has been used mainly to refer to ethnic minorities—and the bib-

---

4. For a discussion on the etymologies and usage histories of the English words derived from the Greek *ethnos* and *ethnikos*, see Fenton 2003, 14–16.

lical field is not an exception in this pattern—there can be no reference to an ethnic minority without acknowledging the existence of an ethnic majority. Fenton speaks about Britain as an example of a society that has developed an awareness of itself as multiethnic and adds that the ethnic majority was actually "scarcely conscious of itself as 'ethnic' at all" (11). Ethnicity is a relevant aspect in all human societies. So the question of ethnicity certainly pertains to all biblical scholars.

Fenton clarifies that the best way to think about ethnicity today is as "an intellectual construct of the observers," and, more specifically, as having to do with "descent and culture." So, in order to speak about "ethnic groups," one needs to understand the dynamics within "descent and culture communities" (2–3).[5] As a result, the notion of culture and cultural differences in relation to ethnicity is an area that will require further research. I include only an important observation made by Homi Bhabha: "The question of cultural difference faces us with a disposition of knowledge or a distribution of practices that exist beside each other, *abseits* designating a form of social contradiction or antagonism that has to be negotiated rather than sublated" (1994, 162). For this reason, observers of ethnic groups must be cautious when developing intellectual constructs. Scholars should remain aware of who is doing the construction and for what purposes. Fenton points to three particular challenging structures of observation that a critic, when trying to define her or his ethnic identity, should be attentive to: (1) the idea of an ethnic group as not constructed by "us" but "for us by others" ("a colonial structure"); (2) the building of a group identity as based on the work of an elite within it; and (3) groups as formed "as a consequence of *state* actions, power and administrative fiat" (2003, 10; see also ch. 4).

Meaning of Identity

Closely connected to this development in the understanding of ethnicity is the notion of identity. Already in 1989, Stuart Hall—one of the most prominent scholars in discussions of race and nation in the last century and director of the Centre for Contemporary Cultural Studies (1972–1979) at the University of Birmingham—stated that the modern concept

---

5. For a more detailed description of the technical terms signaled here with quotation marks, see Fenton 2003, ch. 8.

of identity, as a stable and fixed point, was no longer tenable. Hall proposes a reconceptualization of it as "a *process of identification*. ... It is something that happens over time, that is never absolutely stable, that is subject to the play of history and the play of difference" (14). Furthermore, he argues that ethnicity is actually "what we all require in order to think the relationship between identity and difference" (17). Two relevant elements regarding the understanding of identity here, says Hall, are that identity happens within discourse and that it is two-sided. On the one hand, identity is a narrative of the self (individual or collective), and people/groups impose structures on those narratives; on the other hand, this narrative is always in relation to difference (16).[6]

One begins this relationship by acknowledging and reevaluating one's hidden histories, creating in this way the sense of a continuum in the process of conscientization, and also by reevaluating in those same histories one's traditions and heritages of cultural expressions. This is how the ethnic element emerges as a person or critic develops his or her identity. "[T]he past," Hall states, "is not only a position from which to speak, but it is also an absolutely necessary resource in what one has to say" (18). This relationship to history is a complex one, because it requires looking at one's past not to pluck it up out of that past and possess it (or codify it), but to appropriate it critically so as to identify not only its positive influence on the person but also any negative influence it may have by way of ideologies of oppression. Through such an appropriation one can create the space needed to interact with difference. Ethnicity, Hall adds, "has not lost hold of the place and the ground from which we can speak, yet it is no longer contained within that place as an essence" (20). Ethnicity continues to be constructed in history, to be part of one's narrative, and to be part of one's discourse. This notion seems to support Segovia's suggestion that Latino/a criticism tilt toward the constructivist-deflationary pole in the understanding of Latino/a communities, because this view takes into consideration the diverse material and cultural context(s) throughout their historical continuum.

---

6. In the study of biblical narratives, this insight will have to be considered seriously in future research.

Concluding Comment

In sum, ethnicity provides a complex category for considering the changing material and cultural context(s) of the Latino/a communities in the United States. Ethnicity also, as a perspective, should provide a theoretical framework of analysis that enables Latino/a criticism to account for the positive aspects of its cultural/ethnical heritage as well as for that legacy of dominion by and struggle against Spain in the past, and for the different forms of domination, marginalization, and discrimination that persist in the United States.[7] Understanding a community's ethnicity requires a constant process of identification that acknowledges and reevaluates the histories of traditions and the heritages of cultural expressions, and appropriates them—critically—in current narratives and discourses, creating in this way a transforming ethnic heritage and discourse that upholds the primary value of human dignity for every person.

Gender

To reveal one's identity as a Latina critic, one must consider gender at many levels. For example, a 2007 study by the Pew Hispanic Center, "Hispanic Women in the United States, 2007" (Gonzales 2008, 1),[8] reported that of the 30.1 million Hispanic adults in the United States—of a total Hispanic population of more than 45 million in 2008—48 percent were women (14.4 million). The analysis of the data also revealed significant disparities between Hispanic and non-Hispanic women in terms of education, employment, and poverty levels. Latina women were discriminated against by other groups to a greater degree than Latino men or non-Latina women. Moreover, even within their own communities Latina women were oppressed by some men expressing their *machismo*,[9] or sexism (an idea rooted in a patriarchal ideology).

---

7. For cases in which there is considerable evidence of discrimination against Latino/as based on their race/ethnicity in the United States, see Rodriguez 2000, 20–23.

8. This study is based on data from "U.S. Hispanic Population Surpasses 45 Million—Now 15 Percent Total," U.S. Census Bureau Press release (May 2008).

9. American anthropologists define *machismo* as "The cult of virility, the chief characteristics of which are exaggerated aggressiveness and intransigence in male-

Latina women, like African American women and women from other racial/ethnic minorities, stand at the intersection of two systems of oppression: race/ethnicity and gender. Patricia Hill Collins refers to this conjunction as "a matrix of domination characterized by intersecting oppressions" (2000, 23). From a constructive angle, the oppression created by this matrix can provoke Latina women (1) to identify the common problematic issues for their communities so as to address them (and not just one of them), and (2) to create a space of shared experiences and responses that elucidate the unique wisdom of their community and thereby empower them to identify, resist, challenge, and change systems of oppression.

Walsh's distinction between sex and gender reflects the long journey, social and academic, of a key epistemological paradigm shift (1997, 7).[10] A Latina critic should notice and value the role that feminist inquiry, as an epistemological element, has played in this paradigm shift to avoid having a reductive gender perspective, that is, one that reflects only scholarship in the field of gender studies. To this end, in this section I elaborate on two areas that are significant to the development of this perspective: (1) the connection between feminist inquiry and gender studies in religion, and (2) feminist biblical hermeneutics.

Feminist Inquiry and Gender Studies in Religion

At the core of feminist inquiry is a paradigm shift that relocates the experience of women "as both subject matter of and creators of knowledge" (Nielsen 1990, 19). It is in the incorporation of this paradigm shift in different academic trends and areas that the discipline known today as gender studies came to exist. Given the scope of this paper, I will focus briefly only on the fields of theological and biblical studies.

Elisabeth Schüssler Fiorenza, tracing back the journey of feminist inquiry in theology, distinguishes the following areas: feminist studies, feminist studies in religion, wo/men[11] studies, gender studies, and gender

---

to-male interpersonal relationships and arrogance and sexual aggression in male-to-female relations" (Stevens and Pescatello 1973, 90).

10. For a review on the sex-gender discussion, see also Gould and Kern-Daniels 1977 and Ruether 1988.

11. Schüssler Fiorenza intentionally uses the term "Wo/men" (instead of the generic term "men") in an inclusive way to lift into consciousness, she says, "the linguistic violence of so-called generic male-centered language" (2009, 25 n. 8).

studies in religion. All but the last were more influential in the 1970s and 1980s, with gender studies in religion becoming more prominent in the 1990s. She clarifies that, although these trends are connected, the "history of feminist theology and studies in religion should not be construed in progressive developmental terms" (1998, 33).

Next are some elements worth considering in the incorporation of feminist inquiry in these academic disciplines until the consolidation of gender studies as a field. Scholars in feminist studies have concentrated on investigating how throughout the centuries women have been excluded from the academy and institutionalized religion. By pursuing this methodological perspective, they have offered a different model of intellectual discourse, which enabled students and faculty to develop discourses of critique, empowerment, and possibility. Scholars of religion began to realize that feminist studies in religion would have to "rearticulate again and again its categories and lenses of interpretation in particular historical situations and social contexts" (1998, 40).

The next discipline to be developed was wo/men studies.[12] This began as a wo/men's movement and developed in two different ways: "On the one hand it has come to mean the study of wo/men as objects of inquiry. … On the other hand, wo/men's studies can also be understood as placing wo/men at the center of its attention, both as subjects of scholarship and research and as critical agents in academic institutions" (1998, 33–34). The former emphasis, now more theorized, became the basis of a new discipline—gender studies.

Schüssler Fiorenza observes that the discipline of gender studies reached a stage of stagnation when it adopted a modified structuralism. This discipline limited its critical scope to describing and accounting for "the functioning of society without making any explicit value judgments and without paying attention to the implicit power imbalance implied in gender constructions" (1998, 35). Even as this discipline moved to the field of religion, it not only detached itself from the wo/men's movements for political change, but it tried to become a scientific discourse oriented mostly toward a male audience as "a serious intellectual malestream discipline" (1998, 34). So, although gender studies focuses its research on gender and has contributed to the development and articulation of femi-

---

12. The first recognized program for women studies in the United States was in San Diego State College (May 21, 1970).

nist discourse(s), feminist inquiry—as an epistemological enterprise—continues to be developed in other fields.

Feminist Biblical Hermeneutics

Turning now to the field of biblical studies, I will focus on the history of feminist biblical hermeneutics (hereafter FBH) discourse(s).[13] I have argued elsewhere (Pilarski 2011) that as FBH discourses have emerged in the United States, those who have developed them have again recognized the importance of focusing on people's concrete realities as part of the process of biblical interpretation. This renewed focus occurs in what I identify as the third wave in the development of the FBH discourse. Although the first two waves chronologically coincided with efforts in the fields mentioned above, many feminist biblical scholars focused their work on specific biblical passages and books. The first wave begins in the nineteenth century, and its practical discourse is mainly expressed as a political movement; in the second wave, beginning around the 1960s (in the wake of a major political event—the civil rights movement), the discourse finally enters academia; and in the third wave, since the 1990s, FBH discourse incorporates the cultural component, and, as a result, the influx of work (and voices) from ethnic minorities in the field has been crucial.

The third wave reflects the feminist inquiry in combination with other perspectives brought by contextual and ideological critical approaches. FBH discourse has gradually realized that women, and by and large all human beings, embody many particularities besides gender—like race, ethnicity, culture, class, sexual orientation, age, type of physical ability, and so forth. In other words, it is important to analyze gender, but not in isolation. Sociopolitical and economic ideologies, as well as others, can influence and affect the understanding of gender. This situation clearly reflects what sociologist Collins calls intersectionality. In FBH discourse, out of this realization, came another paradigm construction in biblical studies, which Schüssler Fiorenza refers to as the emancipatory-radical democratic paradigm (2009, 78–81), to which an ethical-political-emancipatory dimension is central.

---

13. Hereafter I will use the singular "FBH discourse" to refer to the activity of generating FBH discourse in all its diversity and to all instances thereof.

This paradigm calls for a hermeneutic-scientific process that can both (1) delve into the ways in which the Bible "[exercises] influence and power in cultural, social, and religious life" (Schüssler Fiorenza 2009, 81) and (2) seek to achieve personal, social, and religious transformation for justice and well-being for all. So it is a process that must involve two tasks: on the one hand, a critical analysis of the Bible that is able to identify the negative influence of ideologies in the text in order to disable those interpretations that perpetuate cycles of oppression; and, on the other hand, enabling a hermeneutical conversation between this text and the present communities of faith, for whom its message of justice and well-being continues to be central.

Concluding Comment

In sum, a gender perspective provides the analytical space for biblical critics (and others) to identify critical dynamics that determine social practice. The journey of feminist inquiry, as an epistemological enterprise, in the fields of gender studies, theological studies, and biblical studies has certainly advanced feminist discourse, which, although it must focus preferentially (not exclusively) on social practices that affect women (positively and negatively), has not lost focus on the connection of these practices with the larger society. Feminist inquiry continues to be at work in other disciplines so that the well-being of all can be achieved. As Collins observes, "On both the individual and the group level, a dialogical relationship suggests that changes in thinking may be accompanied by changed actions and that altered experiences may in turn stimulate a changed consciousness" (2000, 30). As communities are able to change (expand) their thinking in regard to gender, their members may alter their behavior. We hope that these behaviors will, at the same time, produce changes in thinking about the larger network of society, locally and globally.

The Role of Latina Intellectuals: Hermeneutics and Faith

As important as the ethnic and gender perspectives are, the hermeneutical perspective and the faith perspective are equally important for understanding the aim of a Latina biblical critic. The former deals with the concepts behind our role as critics in relationship to the biblical text; the latter is a dimension of life that has been central for both Latino individuals and Latino communities in the United States. In this section I elaborate briefly on these two perspectives, including some remarks on the future role of Latina intellectuals and of Latina biblical critics in particular.

Hermeneutical Perspective

Biblical critics should be able to adequately account for their aim in approaching the Bible. An overview of the development in the understanding of hermeneutics and its connection to theories of text interpretation (since the Bible is a text, or a collection of texts) can be helpful tools for this enterprise. Three significant epistemological breakthroughs (or paradigm shifts) have occurred in the last three centuries. These paradigm shifts have influenced both the way we know (epistemology) and the way we interpret the world around us (hermeneutics). These three shifts are the epistemological, the ontological, and the linguistic.[14]

As I explain in my study of FBH discourse, "the modern and postmodern history of hermeneutics reveals a transitional integration of essential aspects in the interpretive process (of texts in particular) from understanding of the contextual realities of the text(s) [epistemological turn] to that of the author(s) [ontological turn] to that of the communities of readers [linguistic turn]" (2001, 18). In this same article I also explain how these paradigm shifts have influenced the development of biblical methods (diachronic and synchronic). Most scholars today agree that the hermeneutical process involved in biblical interpretation includes giving an account of both the horizon of production and the horizon of reception. This acknowledgment requires the consideration of three distinctive worlds (the world behind the text, the world of the text, and the world in front of the text), and biblical scholars and critics are responsible for adequately addressing each world in this circle of communication.

It is worth noting that "paradigm shifts in history occasioned by epistemological breakthroughs have not brought new realities into existence; rather, these realities (already in existence) have come to light. These shifts have yielded new ways to articulate new discourses that can help us understand and explain our world more adequately" (19). So, although it may seem that the voice/discourse of Latino/a and Latin American biblical scholars (and their communities at large) have joined the bibli-

---

14. These three paradigm shifts have also been significant for the development of feminist inquiry (see Pilarski 2011, 17–19).

cal hermeneutical journey recently, the fact is that our relationship to the Bible (either positive or negative) started already a few centuries ago when Christianity arrived in the Americas. This idea helps us transition then to the next topic—faith.

Perspective of Faith

Understanding language as discourse (the linguistic turn)—that is, recognizing the dialectic between event and meaning in a discourse—is at the core of biblical interpretation today. For many Latino/a and Latin American communities, the Bible is considered a witness to the faith experiences of communities in the past. The dialectic of a discourse enables scholars to recognize that many faith communities believe the Bible has a dual identity. It is both an ancient and a contemporary word, and, as Phyllis Bird observes, it demands that people "honor the claims of both" as they develop their theology (2005, 69). Yet acknowledging a faith dimension in the experience of people in the Bible does not prevent a person today from approaching it critically, using adequate forms and principles of interpretation, to assess the validity of the diverse claims raised in the text.

Schüssler Fiorenza differentiates four paradigm constructions in biblical studies and argues that biblical scholars should be introduced to these paradigms as part of their professional training. These paradigms are: (1) the religious-theological-scriptural paradigm, (2) the critical-scientific-modern paradigm, (3) the cultural-hermeneutic-postmodern paradigm, and (4) the emancipatory-radical democratic paradigm (2009, 51–84). This kind of approach to the education of a biblical scholar will prepare a person to use the different methods available to analyze the Bible. It will also provide a critical platform to understand that, before deploying these methods in the text, one has the responsibility to carefully investigate "the epistemological presuppositions of these methods, their theoretical epistemological frameworks, and the institutional discursive practices operative in them" (2009, 56).

Regarding the faith dimension, I believe that not enough attention has been paid to the first paradigm construction in biblical studies. This is due perhaps to the influence of modernity in the structuring of the university curriculum, which in the Middle Ages caused a split between biblical and theological studies, which persists today in most institutions. Biblical scholars and theologians need to be able to address together the theological perspectives[15] that are raised in the biblical text(s) and that can no longer be ignored because these texts continue to have meaning for many communities of faith, including the Latino/a communities, today.

Future Role of Latina Intellectuals and Latina Biblical Critics

Segovia speaks about the need to endow the concept of Latin(o/a)ness with a twofold semantic dimension: (1) a sense of identity and locus, and (2) a sense of praxis and agenda (2009, 200–201). The perspectives I develop in this article may help Latino/a critics to engage in this twofold enterprise. At one level is the active engagement with one's own reality or locus, locating oneself as an active subject in our own history and that of the communities in which we live. The first two perspectives, especially for Latina critics, provide insights into the development of a consciousness in regard to this first semantic dimension. At the other level, a Latino/a biblical critic has also the responsibility to engage in the same manner (active engagement) in the critical analysis of the Bible. The latter two perspectives may facilitate the sort of engagement that can help elucidate a concrete praxis and agenda to empower our communities. This second task entails, therefore, a critical and constructive analysis of the biblical material in search of hermeneutical mediations that can adequately address the practical implications of the text(s) for diverse cultural/ethnical communities.

Now, Latina intellectuals have a significant role in verifying that praxis and agenda do empower Latina women in this process of interpretation. My concept of *intellectuals* is based on the work of sociologist Patricia Hill Collins, who, in developing a black feminism, challenges the current understanding of the word:

> Not all Black women intellectuals are educated. Not all Black women intellectuals work in academia. Furthermore, not all highly educated Black women, especially those who are employed in U.S. colleges and universities, are *automatically* intellectuals. … One is neither born an intellectual nor does one become one by earning a degree. Rather, doing intellectual work … requires a process of self-conscious struggle on behalf of Black women, regardless of the actual social location where that work occurs. (2000, 15)

---

15. Here I use Jeanrond's understanding of "theological perspective": "these [biblical] texts raise in their different ways the question of God" (1993, 88).

Based on this definition, the work of Latina intellectuals already began centuries ago. Here, however, I want to refer specifically to the work of two important Latin American scholars who have advanced the theological discourse regarding Latinas in the United States and have addressed in their own works the twofold semantics behind the concept of Latin(o/a)ness—locus and praxis. They are Ada María Isasi-Díaz (2005) and María Pilar Aquino (2002). Both have realized that the theology they are developing starts with the actual life conditions of Latina women. Both have also demonstrated a need to develop a Latina feminist biblical hermeneutics discourse.

Isasi-Díaz defines the *locus theologicus* of a Latino community in its *mestizaje* (mixture of white people and native people) and *mulatez* (mixture of black people and white people). *Mestizaje* and *mulatez* socially situate the Latino community and allow it to delineate "the finite alternatives we have for thinking, conceiving, expressing our theology." These particularities, says Isasi-Díaz, contribute to a new understanding of pluralism and "a new way of valuing and embracing diversity and difference" (2005, 65). From this locus *mujerista* theology looks at the everyday-life (*lo cotidiano*) and shared (not common) experiences of Latina women, and uses it as its theological source. Theology here is understood as a liberative praxis, which "means that we accept the fact that we cannot separate thinking from action" (73).

Aquino, on the other hand, although she does not use the term *locus*, refers to the term *Nepantla* as an "in-between state."[16] To enter this location is "to engage in new explorations about God and ourselves from the creative 'border' locations" (2002, 149). It is in the daily-life plural experiences of excluded Latina women that Aquino sees the starting point of theological critical reflection. Methodologically, it is in the concrete contexts where Latinas live that one can find the primary indicators for their quality of life (measured mainly by their access to goods, knowledge, and social inclusion). The vision of Latina feminist theology is to create "a new model of society and civilization free of systemic injustice and violence due to patriarchal domination. It seeks to affirm new paradigms of social relationships that are capable to fully sustain human dignity and the integrity of creation" (139).

---

16. *Nepantla* is a Nahuatl word used by Gloria Anzaldúa in her book *Borderlands/La Frontera: The New Mestiza* (2007). It refers to "the space between two bodies of water, the space between two worlds" (237).

Both of these theological projects assert that it is important to look at the concrete situations of Latina women's lives and that their participation is essential to the theological discourse. These are two key elements for constructing a discourse of empowerment for Latina women. Isasi-Díaz says that "popular religion is the most important identifying characteristic of Latinas, the main carrier of our culture" (2005, 74), and Aquino claims that for Latina feminist theology "the faith experience of women and men in popular religion ... [is] its principle of coherence" (2002, 152). If popular religion is so important to Latina identity, and if faith experience is the principle of that religion's coherence, then clearly to be a Latina intellectual one must be a Latina woman.

This is true for other reasons as well, four of which may be adapted from Collins's argument that black women intellectuals must be black women. First, the shared experiences of Latina women provide a unique angle of vision concerning Latina womanhood unavailable to other groups. As actual members of an oppressed group, Latina women are more likely to have "critical insights into the condition of [their] oppression than ... those who live outside those structures" (2000, 35). Second, Latina "intellectuals both inside and outside the academy are less likely to walk away from [Latina] struggles when the obstacles seem overwhelming or when the rewards for staying diminish" (35). Third, it is essential to empowerment that Latina women craft their own agenda. Without empowering people from the affected communities, it will be difficult to challenge intersecting oppressions. Collins argues, "Because self-definition is key to individual and group empowerment, ceding the power of self-definition to other groups, no matter how well-meaning or supportive ... they may be, in essence replicates existing power hierarchies. ... As Audrey Lorde points out, 'It is axiomatic that if we do not define ourselves for ourselves, we will be defined by others—for their use and to our detriment'" (36). Fourth, Latina intellectuals are central in the production of Latina thought because they "alone can foster the group autonomy that fosters effective coalitions with other groups" (36–37).

To assert that Latina intellectuals must be Latina women is not to exclude the work of allies. Coalition building and collaborative scholarship are also necessary. However, the intracommunity dialogue that can empower Latina women has to come first (and from within)—before and during any coalition building happens—if we hope for this discourse to be effective for the survival and empowerment of these communities.

Conclusion

To be a Latina biblical critic, then, is to take, through a process of conscientization, a well-informed and well-engaged stance in the process of inquiry. This particular stance should be informed by at least four distinct but intersecting perspectives: ethnicity, gender, hermeneutics, and faith. This intersection, as a standpoint, situates me together with the larger community of Latina intellectuals, and it is from this locus that I speak as a biblical critic.

Works Cited

Anzaldúa, Gloria. 2007. *Borderlands/La Frontera: The New Mestiza*. 3rd ed. San Francisco: Aunt Lute Books

Aquino, María Pilar. 2002. Latina Feminist Theology: Central Features. Pages 133–60 in *A Reader in Latina Feminist Theology: Religion and Justice*. Edited by María Pilar Aquino, Daisy L. Machado, and Jeanette Rodríguez. Austin: University of Texas Press.

Bhabha, Homi K. 1994. *The Location of Culture*. London: Routledge.

Bird, Phyllis A. 2005. Old Testament Theology and the God of the Fathers: Reflections on Biblical Theology from a North American Feminist Perspective. Pages 69–107 in *Biblische Theologie: Beiträge des Symposiums "Das Alte Testament und die Kultur der Moderne" anlässlich des 100. Geburtstags Gerhard von Rads (1901–1971) Heidelberg, 18.–21. Oktober 2001*. Edited by Paul D. Hanson, Bernd Janowski, and Michael Welker. Münster: Lit.

Collins, Patricia Hill. 2000. *Black Feminist Thought: Knowledge, Consciousness, and the Politics of Empowerment*. 2nd ed. New York: Routledge.

Fenton, Steve. 2003. *Ethnicity*. Cambridge: Polity.

Freire, Paulo. 1986. *Pedagogy of the Oppressed*. Translated by Myra Bergman Ramos. 1970. Repr., New York: Continuum.

Gonzales, Felisa. 2008. Hispanic Women in the United States, 2007. Online: http://www.pewhispanic.org/2008/05/08/hispanic-women-in-the-united-states-2007.

Gould, Meredith, and Rochelle Kern-Daniels. 1977. Toward a Sociological Theory of Gender and Sex. *American Sociologist* 12:182–89.

Hall, Stuart. 1989. Ethnicity, Identity and Difference. *Radical America* 23:9–20.

Horowitz, Donald L. 1975. Ethnic Identity. Pages 111–40 in *Ethnicity: Theory and Practice*. Edited by Nathan Glazer and Daniel P. Moynihan. Cambridge: Harvard University Press.

Isasi-Díaz, Ada María. 2005. *Mujerista Theology: A Theology for the Twenty-First Century*. Maryknoll, N.Y.: Orbis.

Jeanrond, Werner G. 1993. After Hermeneutics: The Relationship between Theology and Biblical Studies. Pages 85–102 in *The Open Text: New Directions for Biblical Studies?* Edited by Francis Watson. London: SCM.

Nielsen, Joyce McCarl. 1990. *Feminist Research Methods: Exemplary Readings in the Social Sciences*. San Francisco: Westview.

Petersen, William, Michael Novak, and Philip Gleason. 1980. *Concepts of Ethnicity*. Cambridge: Belknap.

Pilarski, Ahida E. 2011. The Past and Future of Feminist Biblical Hermeneutics. *BTB* 41:16–23.

Rodriguez, Clara E. 2000. *Changing Race: Latinos, the Census, and the History of Ethnicity in the United States*. New York: New York University Press.

Ruether, Rosemary Radford. 1988. Sexism as Ideology and Social System: Can Christianity Be Liberated from Patriarchy? Pages 148–64 in *With Both Eyes Open: Seeing beyond Gender*. Edited by Patricia Altenbernd Johnson and Janet Kalven. New York: Pilgrim.

Schüssler Fiorenza, Elisabeth. 1998. *Sharing Her Word: Feminist Biblical Interpretation in Context*. Edinburgh: T&T Clark.

———. 2009. *Democratizing Biblical Studies: Toward an Emancipatory Educational Space*. Louisville: Westminster John Knox.

Segovia, Fernando. 2009. Toward Latino/a American Biblical Criticism: Latin(o/a)ness as Problematic. Pages 193–223 in *They Were All Together in One Place? Toward Minority Biblical Criticism*. Edited by Randall C. Bailey, Tat-siong Benny Liew, and Fernando F. Segovia. SemeiaSt 57. Atlanta: Society of Biblical Literature.

Stevens, Evelyn P., and Ann Pescatello. 1973. *Marianismo: The Other Face of Machismo in Latin America*. Pittsburgh: University of Pittsburgh Press.

Tracy, David. 1977. Ethnic Pluralism and Systematic Theology: Reflections. Pages 91–99 in *Ethnicity*. Edited by Andrew M. Greeley and Gregory Baum. New York: Seabury.

Walsh, Mary Roth. 1997. *Women, Men and Gender: Ongoing Debates*. New Haven: Yale University Press.

Interpretive World Making: Formulating a Space for a Critical Latino/a Cultural and Biblical Discourse

David Arturo Sánchez

> From the outset I want to state that I see the problem to be investigated in these pages not as one of "data" but as one of epistemology, that is, as how scholars make meaning out of the "data."... [Biblical] discourses collude with the production and maintenance of systems of knowledge that either foster exploitation and oppression or contribute to a vision and praxis of emancipation and liberation.
> — Elisabeth Schüssler Fiorenza 2001, 3–4

As I reflect on framing a question concerning the problematics, objectives, and strategies of Latino/a biblical hermeneutics, my thoughts drift immediately to the consideration of the need for such a conversation at all. How have we come to this place where the reality is that such a unique hermeneutical barrio exists? It brings to mind my questioning of the academy that I/we negotiate where departments of Latin American studies, Chicano/a studies, African American studies, Asian American studies, women's studies, and so on, subsist. Do not all of these departments in some way contribute to the larger umbrella fields and discourses of historical, political, social, religious, ethnic, and cultural studies? Should not contributors to essentially the same disciplines be housed in the same environment so that intellectual cross-pollination can take place? What do we signal to educational consumers and ourselves with such disciplinary categorizations and physical separations?

This is a question that, in my estimation, must be addressed because each of the above-named fields has had to carve—or has been exiled to—a unique proprietary space within the larger academic environment. Even more problematic is that there exists an unarticulated but widely recognized hierarchy among the disciplines themselves—especially in relation to the "traditional" Western disciplines listed above—that deflects critical scrutiny and goes largely unacknowledged. The same can be said for recent trends in the field of biblical studies. Multiple ethnic, cultural, gendered, theological, and sexually oriented interpretive categories continue to demonstrate their enduring presence and vitality in the field. Yet, like the academy itself, each of these unique and critical areas suffers from their inherent ghettoization in relation to dominant modalities of biblical interpretation (i.e., the higher biblical criticisms).

What is going on here? At this point I refer back to the quote of Elisabeth Schüssler Fiorenza that began this essay: "I see the problem to be investigated in these pages not as one of 'data' but as one of epistemology, that is, as how scholars make meaning out of the 'data'" (2001, 3–4). One can infer from this quotation, then, that the key to power is knowledge, and not just any knowledge, but rather that knowledge deemed consistent with dominant interpretive strategies. To this observation I add a corresponding problem, that certain meaning-making modalities are privileged within the academy, including the discipline of biblical studies. The problem is not one of data, but of data analysis and the capacity of the dominant (academic) culture to attach value to the various fields and methodologies of intellectual inquiry.

On the other side of the power equation, each of these (sub)disciplines and hermeneutical postures has formulated its own critical space by arguing that traditional (i.e., dominant) knowledge systems are inadequate for representing, articulating, and defining our/their multifaceted existences and experiences in a postmodern world. Transhistorical and transcultural metanarratives have undergone rigorous scrutiny to the point of rendering them challenged or obsolete in some enlightened circles. Accordingly, these new disciplines and methodological approaches are, at their ideological core, counter-knowledge systems or intellectual resistance movements contra "dominant cultural hermeneutic spin[s] that in so many respects assumes modern European [and] North American Christian culture as the natural modern reification and rightful interpreter of ancient biblical communities and traditions" (Wimbush 2000, 13).

I see the development of a unique space for an emerging and enduring Latino/a biblical hermeneutic, therefore, as the derivative of two opposing forces: the process of othering on the part of dominant Western interpretation and the process of exiting from such dominance on the part of the othered.

The first force is that of traditional hegemonic Western spins on the Bible that have posited so-called objective metanarratives as idyllic, thereby categorizing all non-Western interpretive schemas as illegitimate or other. On the issue of these embedded Western presumptions, R. S. Sugirtharajah contends that

> in order to qualify for inclusion, the hermeneutical output of the Third World [and other peripheral] interpreters must conform to the rules or criteria developed within the Western academic paradigm. The practice of referring to European or Western interpretations as the interpretation and routinely designating other regional discourses as Asian, African or Chinese is a sign of neocolonialism. (2001, 61)

Sugirtharajah's observation on these regional discourses and practices is readily adaptable and transferable to a specifically Latino/a biblical discourse. The postcolonial, liberationist, and resistance readings of many Latino/a scholars fall well outside of accepted Western academic paradigms, which has resulted in their collective relegation to the fringe margins of the Western academy and its discourses. In this critical space they/we exist as intellectual mimics in a quasi-scholarly state of, "almost the same, but not quite" (Bhabha 1994, 86), scholarly enough to merit subdiscipline status, yet readily identifiable for purposes of isolation, oversight, scrutiny, and domination.

The second driving force behind the development of a particularly Latino/a biblical hermeneutic is what African American "scriptural" scholar Vincent Wimbush has labeled "exiting," "flight," or "de-formation," which he explains as an "escape from [and] de-formation of dominance, whether in the form of old sociopolitical regimes in general, religious tradition, traditional social (class and gender) orientations, arrangements and associations, and certainly enslavement and imprisonment" (2000, 25). What Wimbush here refers to is the first of three steps he has identified as a moment or phase in African American world-making dynamics in relationship to sacred text(s). It is a process of constructing a new world (African America) when your former world (Africa) has been violently removed. It is also a rejection of the "new" world (European America) that has been imposed on you while simultaneously employing the dominant's scripture (i.e., Bible) to promote your own emancipatory agenda.

(Interpretive) World Exiting, Forming, and Reforming

Wimbush's process of world making constitutes a first model for understanding the ideological and cultural impetuses behind the emergence of a specifically Latino/a biblical hermeneutics. The paradox of adopting the "master's" scripture for one's own strategic purposes is a phenomenon that requires some critical parsing. How do we begin to think about the appropriation and subversion of Christian Scripture by peoples of African ancestry? Is this phenomenon culture-specific, or does it have the potential to function as a transcultural survival tactic? Any attempt to answer these questions must come to terms with why the exiled peoples of Africa read themselves into the Christian Scriptures as analogous biblical actors.

Here Wimbush suggests that in the Bible these diaspora peoples found "a rich storehouse of languages and rhetorics, including stories of heroic individuals and groups, songs, vision, poetry, exhortative and excoriatory/denunciatory speeches—all of which have reflected and continue to reflect some parallel phases in African American formation and strivings" (27). As a result, he goes on, "the Bible was less the source of, the impetus behind, the explanation for, the movements [of human striving and formation], than a record or mirror of such" (27). How could people of African ancestry not read themselves into these biblical narratives? How could any people "experiencing the lags of the human cycle—persistent hurt and trauma" (28)—not do the same once exposed to Christian Scripture from their existential reality?

Wimbush also notes that the phenomenon of flight is "a nearly universally shared human sentiment" for "those for whom trauma continues to be most palpable and persistent" (25). Applying these observations, I therefore infer that the creation and perpetuation of a specifically Latino/a biblical hermeneutic is also a process of Latino/a cultural and ideological flight (in relation to the dominant culture and their reading of Bible) for the purpose of cultural and ideological world making. Does not the creation of a specifically Latino/a biblical hermeneutic represent a critical exiting from and "de-formation" of the dominant culture's hermeneutic spin(s) of Bible and their "objective" and universalized world-imposing process? Is not the development of a particularly Latino/a biblical hermeneutic section at the national meeting of the Society of Biblical Literature and the devotion of an entire Semeia journal publication symbolic of such exiting in the hopes of creating a collective intellectual space for critical de-formation?

If so, then, do Latino/a biblical scholars also exhibit the other two characteristics identified by Wimbush in his world-making schema?

According to his model, the second marker in world making is formation or settlement and building on a site of marronage. Marronage refers to exit or escape, especially in reference to "the dramatic history of black runaways, especially runaway slaves, often called maroons" (3 n. 12). According to Wimbush, formation "builds upon the first phase [de-formation] insofar as the turn towards settlement and building presumes escape from domination, at least a degree of freedom from danger, and a different and relatively safe site of enunciation and different space" (25–26).

The development of a Latino/a biblical hermeneutic seems quite consistent with the first two points of the model. The processes of de-formation and formation are distinctly palpable in the creation of a socially located interpretive space for Latino/s biblical scholarship. The formation that occurs after de-formation is a natural result of the process, lest one continue (not by choice) to exist as continuously unformed or marooned. To remain in the state of perpetual marronage is to remain completely vulnerable and "on the run" from the dominant world and without a place. Therefore, the process of formation is a privileged place that requires tactics of world forming on the site of marronage. The maroon and/or site of marronage are, under ideal circumstances, always aspiring to or in transition toward formation. The category of a Latino/a biblical interpretive space is, therefore, demonstrative of both de-formation and formation in relation to dominant interpretive modalities. It represents the offensive tactic of critically de-forming dominant biblical paradigms and discourses and the defensive tactic of creating a "safe" place from which to advocate a specifically Latino/a reading of Christian Scripture.

The third movement in Wimbush's world-making schema is re-form[ul]ation. In re-form[ul]ation, the processes of "self-making, self-naming, and negotiating with the outside world" (23) are key. Re-form[ul]ation is a maturation of the formation movement. The continued process of self-making enters a new level of creativity in that the emerging cultural entity has coalesced into an identifiable "subject" through reformation and is now eligible for (self) renaming. This is a dramatic moment in world making in that the naming process is now in the hands of the autonomous subject. The name by which the group is to be identified is no longer an external (internalized) label but rather a label conceptualized by the group itself. On occasion, this self-generated label can be a play on the former external label imposed by the dominants. However, in the hands of the world-making group, the label is resignified to represent the new self-understanding and value system of the group.[1] The renaming process is therefore representative of "sharply cut articulations of identity" (26).

Another component of the third movement is that "it reflects sharp criticism of American and African American mainstream society, including its religious culture," while also promoting a "challenge to return to and privilege traditional African and African American traditions and sensibilities" (26). Again, I view this development as part of the maturation process of the formation stage in that the world-making group is now in the position to reengage the dominant society from a culturally evolved and critical position. Contrary to the deconstructive criticism of the deformation stage, the critical position of the re-form[ul]ation stage produces the potential for a critical reengagement with dominant society or "negotiation with the outside world" (26) The re-form[ul]ation stage also represents the group's capacity to critically define its own boundaries from within by taking issue with those African Americans who are perceived as being too comfortable with, and uncritical of, the mainstream dominant society.

The complexities and textures of the third movement of Wimbush's model are readily discernible in the field of Latino/a biblical hermeneutics. The process of formation or re-form[ul]ation is apparent in the ongoing constructions of a self-definition or "sharply cut articulations of identity"

---

1. A fascinating example of this naming resignification has occurred in my own Chicana/o culture in which the title "Chicana/o" represents, for the more revolutionary minded, a term of ethno-political pride and resistance. However, this was not always the case, as argued by Matt Meier and Feliciano Rivera (1981, 83–84) and summarized by me in an earlier work (Sánchez 2008, 95): "*Chicana/o* originated as a derogatory term employed by Anglo landowners in the southwestern United States in the early twentieth century to refer to Mexican farm workers. The native tongue of many of these workers was not Spanish but the indigenous Nahuatl, in which language the word *mexicanos* was pronounced *mesheekanos*. Landowners, therefore, began referring to their Mexican employees as *sheekanos*. Matt S. Meier and Feliciano Rivera, somewhat differently, contend that *Chicana/o* was originally derived from the word *Mexicano*, which through elision was transformed to *Xicano*, the letter X in Nahuatl being pronounced as *s/sh*, which resulted in the current spelling, *Chicana/o*. Meier and Rivera also note that the term was used pejoratively by upper-class Mexicans to refer to Mexicans from the lower classes. In any case, the term was originally used as a derogatory label for working-class, indigenous Mexicans in both the United States in Mexico."

among Latino/a biblical scholars. The creation of organizations, groups, and programs in which many Latino/a biblicists participate include entities such as the Hispanic Theological Initiative, the Academy of Catholic Hispanic Theologians of the United States (ACHTUS), La Comunidad of the American Academy of Religion and the Society of Biblical Literature, the Latino/a Biblical Hermeneutics unit within the Society of Biblical Literature, and the Hispanic Summer Program—just to name a few recent examples. Each of these entities represents cooperative attempts by Latino/a scholars to collectively reformulate our identity from without and within the larger academic guild of biblical studies in particular, and religious and theological studies in general.

The process of Latino/a self-naming has been a bit more complex. On occasion we coalesce around the terms Hispanic (grudgingly, in my case), Latino/a, or, in some instances, under more specific titles usually defined by our specific ethno-cultural-political allegiances (e.g., Chicano/a, Boricua) or nation of origin (e.g., Mexican, Puerto Rican, Cuban). On other occasions, we appropriate titles imposed on us by the dominant culture only to resignify them in our favor (see n. 1 above). Whatever the strategy, the process of self-naming is a definitive moment in the progression toward a Latino/a disciplinary project of world making. It is definitive moment, because the naming is done internally and is therefore an act of empowerment, self-definition, and self-representation in contrast to the "objectified" process of being labeled by an external dominant source.

Since my first exposure to Wimbush's schema over a decade ago, I have been haunted by his invitation to read Christian Scripture through the "dark" optic of an African America while simultaneously asking such questions as the following:

> How might putting African Americans at the center of the study of Bible affect the study of Bible? What impact might it have on the politics of the conceptualization and the structuring of academic guild study of the Bible? How might the academic guild of biblical scholarship in North America and beyond be influenced? What then would be the profile, the carriage, the orientation of the biblical scholar? ... What might be the implications and ramifications of construing the study of Bible — its impetus, methods, orientations, approaches, politics, goals, communications, and so forth—on bases other than European cultural presumptions and power, interests and templates? (2)

I have also been intrigued by the potential for adapting the model for a specifically Latino/a reception history of sacred text(s). Is it possible that a Latino/a reception and interpretation of Bible—a process that began with the Iberian peninsula's colonization of the Americas—is analogous to the reception and interpretive histories of our African American cohorts? To begin to answer this question, it is important to recognize Wimbush's observation that the model did not so much classify and divide peoples in the world-making process along ethnic, cultural, and/or national lines. Rather, the model was composed for "those for whom trauma continues to be most palpable and persistent" (25) and who hold the Bible or another sacred text(s) in common. Even with our complex and divergent histories, the shared reality of acute cultural trauma is a profound point of cultural contact and a powerful point of departure for deeper probings into the phenomenon of textual interpretation in the creation of other friendlier worlds.

The Minority Identity Model

A second model for understanding the ideological and cultural impetuses behind the development of a specifically Latino/a biblical hermeneutic comes from the social sciences, specifically the field of psychology. The model is also quite congruent with Wimbush's model of world making and offers an insightful expansion on its three movements of de-formation, formation, and re-form[ul]ation. The model is the production of Donald Atkinson, George Morten, and Derald Sue, and is called the Minority Identity Development (MID) Model. According to their own assessment,

> The model defines five stages of development that oppressed people may experience as they struggle to understand themselves in terms of their own minority culture and the oppressive relationship between the two cultures. Although five distinct stages are presented in the model, the MID is more accurately conceptualized as a continuous process in which one stage blends with another and boundaries between the stages are not clear. (1998, 34)

The model is illustrative, from a psychological perspective, of how minorities negotiate the dominant culture while simultaneously attempting to construct and understand their evolving notion of "self" in relation to that dominant culture. My interjection into the model will be placing it in critical conversation with Wimbush's model and factoring in the role the Bible plays in shaping the "oppressive" relationship and the creation of an autonomous Latino/a self. The model and its five stages (34–40) may be summarized as follows:

Stage 1: Conformity. In this stage the minority attitudes toward self are depreciating. Attitude toward members of the same minority is also depreciating. Attitude toward members of a different minority is discriminatory. Attitude toward the dominant group is appreciating.

Stage 2: Dissonance. Attitudes toward self are in conflict between depreciating and appreciating. Attitude toward members of the same minority is also in conflict between group-depreciating and group-appreciating. Attitude toward members of a different minority is in conflict between dominant-held views of minority hierarchy and feelings of shared experience as minorities. Attitude toward the dominant group is in conflict between group appreciating and group depreciating.

Stage 3: Resistance and Immersion. Attitudes toward self are appreciating. Attitude toward members of the same minority is group appreciating. Attitude toward members of a different minority is in conflict between feelings of empathy for other minority experiences and feelings of cultural centrism. Attitude toward the dominant group is depreciating.

Stage 4: Introspection. Attitudes toward self focus on concern with basis of self-appreciation. Attitude toward members of the same minority focuses on concern with nature of unequivocal appreciation. Attitude toward members of different minority focuses on concern with ethnocentric basis for judging others. Attitude toward the dominant group focuses on the concern with the basis for group depreciation.

Stage 5: Synergetic Articulation and Awareness. Attitudes toward self are appreciating. Attitude toward members of same minority is group appreciating. Attitude toward members of different minority is group appreciating. Attitude toward the dominant group is selective appreciation.

A close assessment of the five stages of the Atkinson-Morten-Sue model demonstrates a close affinity to, albeit with some expansion of, the world-making model proposed by Wimbush. I proceed stage by stage.

I contend that the first stage, conformity, is a preexiting or predeformation stage as proposed by Wimbush. In this stage, "minorities view themselves as deficient in the 'desirable' characteristics held up by the dominant society" (36). There is also an "unequivocal preference for dominant cultural values over those of their own culture" (36). Again, it is a pre-deformation stage in that the minorities seek to assimilate or acculturate to the dominant culture rather than to "exit" it.

The second stage, dissonance, is demonstrative of an emerging cultural ambivalence on the part of the minority group in relationship to the dominant group. In this context, I use the term cultural ambivalence to reflect its use in psychoanalysis (Ashcroft et al. 2000, 12–13):

> A term first developed in psychoanalysis to describe a continual fluctuation between wanting one thing and wanting its opposite. It also refers to a simultaneous attraction toward and repulsion from an object, person or action. ... [I]t describes the complex mix of attraction and repulsion that characterizes the relationship between colonizer and colonized. The relationship is ambivalent because the colonized subject is never simply and completely opposed to the colonizer. Rather than assuming that some colonized subjects are "complicit" and some "resistant," ambivalence suggests that complicity and resistance exists in a fluctuating relation within the colonial subject.

In the dissonance stage the "blending" of stages is readily apparent as defined by Atkinson, Morten, and Sue. It is in this stage that the denial system of the conformity stage is challenged—the denial of those characteristics that identify individuals as minorities that are repressed from consciousness. Therefore, feelings of ambivalence begin to manifest themselves, because of an emerging awareness of minority cultural strengths and a growing suspicion of the dominant group and their worldviews. These are the initial cues that lead to what Wimbush terms deformation. It is in the dissonance stage that (minority) individuals begin to shift cultural allegiances away from (i.e., exit) the dominant culture. It is in this stage that we witness the initial stages of the deformation of dominance.

In the third stage, resistance, the balance of the ambivalent relationship between minority and dominant cultures takes a decided shift in preference of the minority culture. Here "the minority individual completely endorses minority-held views and rejects the dominant society and culture" (38). In this stage there is a continued appreciating attitude toward other minority groups and a complete rejection of minority stratification systems, as composed and imposed by the dominant culture. In this stage Wimbush's notion of deformation comes to full fruition. The resistance stage represents complete marronage from the (safe) dominant group-appreciating state once held by the minority group or individual. It is a transitory period that combines attributes of both deformation and formation. It is an exiting that will eventually allow the minority group to form and reform[ul]ate itself on its own terms apart from the gaze of the dominants.

In the fourth stage, introspection, a process of reverse ambivalence takes place in relation to the ambivalence encountered in the dissonance stage. In the dissonance stage the cultural ambivalence led to a greater appreciation of the minority culture with the simultaneous devaluation of the dominant culture. In the introspection stage the balance begins to shift in the opposite direction from an extreme appreciation of the minority culture and depreciating posture of the dominant culture to a quasi-ambivalent phase where allegiance to the minority group and its rigid negative positions toward the dominant group are challenged. It is a phase where concerns are raised regarding "the unequivocal nature of group appreciation" as pertains to the minority culture and the recognition of "the utility of many dominant cultural elements" (39). This stage is analogous to Wimbush's re-form[ul]ation phase, which also demonstrates the beginnings of a reverse cultural ambivalence in that it actuates "heightened collective criticism, sharply cut articulations of identity, and efforts at self-making, self-naming, re-formulation, and re-orientation among African Americans, *as well as negotiation with the outside world*" (Wimbush 2000, 26, emphasis mine).

In the final stage, synergetic articulation and awareness, the introspective work of stage 4 has been resolved and leads to a "sense of self-fulfillment with regard to [minority] cultural identity." This stage also examines the "[c]ultural values of other minorities and those of the dominant group ... and accept[s] or reject[s them] on the basis of experience gained in the earlier stages of identity development" (Atkinson et al. 1998, 39). This stage is representative of a cognitive maturation of the processes begun in the introspection stage. The reverse cultural ambivalence balances out at the moment where minority group attitudes return to an appreciative state, however now nuanced by the critical self-reflection that occurred through introspection. The process of revaluing selective components of the dominant culture also comes to full fruition. In relation to Wimbush's re-from[ul]ation movement, the synergetic articulation and awareness stage reflects the potentiality of the re-form[ul]ation work. Here the processes of collective criticism, sharply cut articulations of identity, self-making, self-naming, reformation, reorientation, and negotiation with the outside world are constructed with the benefit of the experience achieved by undergoing the previous culturally critical, ambivalent, and accepting stages (i.e., de-formation and formation).

Implications for Adopting the World-Making and Minority Identity Development Models for Assessing the Construction of Latino/a Interpretive Worlds

Western cultural practices were invoked to arrive at or impose a particular meaning. This, in a way, inaugurated one of the critical questions for modern hermeneutics, the link between interpretation and power, and the related and equally important question, the interface between indigenous and imported knowledge (Sugirtharajah 2001, 73).

One of the most painful legacies of cultural domination is the colonization of the peripheral or othered mind. Indeed, as Frantz Fanon puts it, "Colonialism is not satisfied merely with holding a people in its grips and emptying the native's brain of all form and content. By a kind of perverted logic, it turns to the past of the oppressed people, and distorts, disfigures and destroys it" (2004, 169). Once that history is destroyed, the only history in which to frame peripheral or othered existence is through the mythological history of the dominant. It is a dehumanizing process in that it perpetuates, as Enrique Dussel (1995, 67–68) argues, a

> myth of origin that is hidden in the emancipatory "concept" of modernity, and that continues to underlie philosophical reflection and many other theoretical positions in European and North American thought, [and] has to do above all with the connection of Eurocentrism with the concomitant "fallacy of developmentalism." The fallacy of developmentalism consists in thinking that the path of Europe's modern development must be followed unilaterally by every other culture.

One of the options a dominated people has is to internalize the "fallacy of developmentalism," thus emptying themselves of any claims to cultural autonomy or worth. It is this allegiance that is best demonstrated by the conformity stage of the Atkinson-Morten-Sue model, where attitudes toward self, members of the same minority, and members of other minorities are acutely depreciating. It is also in this stage that attitudes toward the dominant group are appreciating. It is a loathsome and self-deprecating state of being and should not be confused with the subliminal weapons of the weak or arts of resistance articulated in the work of James Scott (1987, 1992). In his provocative essays, Scott describes the appearance and performance of cultural deference as a tactic or public strategy of minority peoples to deflect the critical gaze of the dominant classes. This is not the case with "cultural conformity," which is hereby recognized as a total self-emptying and loss of self, while simultaneously idealizing the dominant culture (people who demonstrate this phenomenon in African American and Mexican American or Chicano/a cultures are sometimes referred to as Uncle Toms or Tio Tacos). It is a state of marronage in relationship to one's own culture.

In my estimation, the implications for adopting the world making and minority identity models is to take seriously the question of Paolo Freire, who wrote in his Pedagogy of the Oppressed: "How can the oppressed, as divided, unauthentic beings, participate in developing the pedagogy of their liberation?" (2003, 48). If we are to take these two models seriously, the logical answer to that question is that we must first go through that painful and unstable project of cultural marronage (in relationship to the dominant culture). From the perspective of biblical hermeneutics, we must flee from those interpretations constructed by the dominant interpretive classes that reify dominant worldviews. We must run from the cover of conformity toward the painful yet emancipatory site of marronage in hopes of constructing (i.e., formation and re-form[ul]ation) other worlds.

Therefore, the models suggest to me that we must be a dynamic people in relationship to texts and domination lest we become static again, finding a comfortable interpretive home where we can be domesticated, scrutinized, and dominated once again. Hence the models are dynamic processes with blending of stages being the rule rather than the exception. Formulation thus always builds on the site of critical de-formation, while simultaneously aspiring to move into the more reflective and complex stages of formation or re-form[ul]ation. The same dynamism is applicable to the five stages of the Minority Identity Development Model. Thus, as Wimbush states, "Flight is evident as primary movement or phase in the larger cycle of return" (2000, 25). However, the return to cultural contact with the dominant group is marked by an evolved understanding of self, because the return marks the confidence of being a self-made, self-named, reformulated, and new subjective self.

Those of us in the academy who identify as Latino/a interpreters of Bible will no doubt recognize the rhythms of conformity, deforming, forming, and reforming that lead to new synergetic professional (i.e., academic) identities. We have exited the dominant interpretive paradigms to talk among ourselves for a while, to revision ourselves and the field in which we participate. We are now formed, reformed, and ready to reengage.

Works Cited

Ashcroft, Bill, Gareth Griffiths, and Helen Tiffin. 2000. Post-Colonial Studies: The Key Concepts. New York: Routledge.

Atkinson, Donald R., George Morten, and Derald W. Sue. 1998. Counseling American Minorities. Boston: McGraw-Hill.

Bhabha, Homi K. 1994. The Location of Culture. London: Routledge.

Dussel, Enrique. 1995. Eurocentrism and Modernity (Introduction to the Frankfurt Lectures). Pages 65–76 in The Postmodernism Debate in Latin America. Edited by Michael Aronna, John Beverley, and José Oviedo. Durham, N.C.: Duke University Press.

Fanon, Frantz. 2004. The Wretched of the Earth. Translated by Richard Philcox. New York: Grove.

Freire, Paolo. 2003. Pedagogy of the Oppressed. Translated by Myra Bergman Ramos. 1970. Repr., New York: Continuum.

Meier, Matt S., and Feliciano Rivera. 1981. Dictionary of Mexican American History. Westport, Conn.: Greenwood.

Sánchez, David A. 2008. From Patmos to the Barrio: Subverting Imperial Myths. Minneapolis: Fortress.

Schüssler Fiorenza, Elisabeth. 2001. Jesus and the Politics of Interpretation. New York: Continuum.

Scott, James C. 1987. Weapons of the Weak: Everyday Forms of Peasant Resistance. New Haven: Yale University Press.

———. 1992. Domination and the Arts of Resistance: Hidden Transcripts. New Haven: Yale University Press.

Sugirtharajah, R. S. 2001. The Bible and the Third World: Precolonial, Colonial and Postcolonial. Cambridge: Cambridge University Press.

Wimbush, Vincent L. 2000. Reading Darkness, Reading Scriptures. Pages 1–43 in African Americans and the Bible: Sacred Texts and Social Textures. Edited by Vincent L. Wimbush. New York: Continuum.

How Did You Get to Be a Latino Biblical Scholar? Scholarly Identity and Biblical Scholarship

Timothy J. Sandoval

The short answer to the question "How did you get to be a Latino biblical scholar?" is simple: I am a person of Mexican descent living in the United States with the last name Sandoval, *and* I earned a PhD in Hebrew Bible. A genuine answer is, however, significantly more complex. It has to do, at least, with what it means in the early twenty-first century to be Latino(a) in the United States (can one really be "Latino" anywhere else?), what it means to be a biblical scholar and to do biblical scholarship, and, of course, exactly what being a "Latino(a) biblical scholar" and doing "Latino(a) biblical scholarship" might possibly signify. In short, the answer to the question "How did you get to be a Latino biblical scholar?" has to do with identity and how identity takes shape and forms individuals and different sorts of communities.

"Identity" remains a hot topic in much academic discourse. Critiques of so-called essentialist—or what Janet Halley has called "coherentist"—understandings of identity, in which "group membership brings with it a uniformly shared range (or even a core) of authentic experience and attitudes," abound (2000, 41). I am quite sympathetic to this line of criticism of identity discourses. There is no stable or unchanging set of criteria upon which our identities—"racial," ethnic, or otherwise—are situated. There is no natural or authentic core to being Latina/o, Puerto Rican, gay, working class, African American, or whatever that can merely be discovered or uncovered within us to reveal our true and unchanging essence. Rather, our identities—including our "racial"/ethnic, class, sexual, gender, and even professional identities—are constructed and constantly hewed out dialogically in our ongoing and shifting social existence.[1]

---

1. It is in queer theory where much of the constructivist critique of identities,

Yet important questions about this powerful critique of essentialist discourses of identity are also widely heard. It is troubling to some that the critique of identity as "constructed"—understood as "merely" constructed or illusory—has arisen precisely at that historical moment in the United States (post-1960s) when women, African Americans, Latino/as, sexual minorities, Asian Americans, and others had begun to achieve success in demands for equality of citizenship and rights. I am sympathetic to this concern as well. Indeed, simply because an identity is socially constructed does not make it any less real. "Race," of course, has long been a discredited biological concept, a notion now understood as socially constructed. Yet very few would deny that processes of "racialization," or what Kwame Anthony Appiah calls "racial ascription" (1996, 80), do not continue. Despite the falsity of the biological concept of race, there still exist blacks and whites and Asians and, of course, African Americans and Asian Americans and European Americans as well as Hispanic Americans or Latino/as, who are sometimes raced as Hispanics and sometimes as whites, blacks, or Native Americans.

Nonetheless, a critique of coherentist ideas about identity that seems to deny the reality of race, ethnicity, or other socially significant differences can appear as decidedly unprogressive, as undergirding the notion that claims for equality and fair treatment of marginalized social bodies, or "group rights," are unjustified. Although this unprogressive danger attends the critique of essentialist identity discourses, as Appiah (1996, 2005) and others have suggested, we should not cease to pursue right understanding of identities and how they are given "for the sake of human liberation" (1996, 104–5). This is not to say that human liberation ought not to be a paramount value. Rather, it is to believe that better understanding can and ought to serve the pursuit of justice. For instance, Appiah himself contends that "if we are to move beyond racism" and all its injustices and evil effects, "we shall have, in the end, to move beyond current racial identities" (1996, 32).[2]

---

particularly sexual identities, has developed. For a brief introduction to queer theory that is convenient for biblical scholars and that touches on the constructivist critique of essentialist notions of identity, see Schneider 2000.

2. It is precisely this sort of claim regarding the desirability of transcending racial identities that has generated significant controversy regarding Appiah's work. See the largely affirming yet critical response to Appiah by David Wilkins (1996, 3–29) and the more critical review of Appiah's basic position by Molefi Kete Asante. For impor-

The title of my essay is adapted from the title of Kevin Johnson's book, *How Did You Get to Be Mexican? A White/Brown Man's Search for Identity*. Johnson's autobiographical work traces his struggles of understanding and creating his identity as a Mexican American. The son of an "Anglo" father and an "assimilationist" Mexican American mother who did not want her children to speak Spanish, Johnson's story of an ethnically hybrid childhood and youth, as well as his efforts in traversing an often hyper-identity-conscious academic world to arrive finally at a law professorship, parallels my own story. This narrative, from "biracial" or bicultural beginnings in California (incidentally also my home state) to Latino legal scholar at the University of California at Davis (incidentally also my alma mater), provides the background for and is the stuff from which Johnson's musings on identity flow. For my own reflections on Latino/a biblical scholarship and becoming a Latino biblical scholar, I follow his method of presenting some autobiographical framing, a practice pioneered by feminist thinkers but also common in much of Latino/a theological and biblical studies.[3]

Autobiographical Framing

"Mexican" Maybe, but Not Yet Latino

I grew up in a diverse working- and middle-class section of the San Francisco Bay Area in the 1970s and early 1980s. It was an era, and an

---

tant, more Marxist-oriented rejoinders to a "postmodern" critique of essentialism, see Barbara Epstein (1996) and, more polemically, Terry Eagleton (1996, 97–104). In my view Appiah's position is subtle and supple enough to address the criticisms and concerns of all these authors in a way in which demands for justice retain their integrity.

3. See, for instance, the autobiographical remarks of Miguel De La Torre and Edwin Aponte (2001, 2–8), Francisco García-Treto (2009), and Jean-Pierre Ruiz (2009). Throughout this essay I refer to "Latino/a theological and biblical scholarship," or some similar turn of phrase. I do this because, although Latina/o biblical studies need not necessarily be linked strongly with the theological academy and certainly fruitfully draws on other disciplines (including ethnic studies, Latino/a studies, critical race theory, ancient Near Eastern and Greco-Roman studies, etc.), in my view Latina/o theology remains its primary locus of discourse. See Fernando Segovia (2009), who notes the paucity of critically trained Latino/a biblical scholars and the fact that Latina/o theologians often write on biblical texts. Segovia also notes Latino/a biblical scholarship's relationship to both the theological academy and to Latino/a studies (2009, 221).

area, little affected by identity politics, questions of multiculturalism, and political correctness. As a result, in that time and place, questions of "racial" or ethnic identity did not emerge for me in urgent ways, at least not consciously so. Few had much sustained interest in my Mexican heritage and the rich stories of migration and struggle of my father's family, including my father's family. *No one* outside my mother's family was ever concerned with my Norwegian heritage and their equally rich stories of migration and struggle. Thankfully, I was never the victim of vitriolic and sustained prejudice and racism, as so many Latino/as, African Americans, Asian Americans, and others have been and continue to be. Nonetheless, upon reflection it is clear that there were issues of "racial"/ethnic identity to be negotiated. These issues perhaps ought not to be strictly identified as "racialization" of me as nonwhite, as is the case for many people of Latin American or Caribbean heritage, but more as the ascription to me of a Mexican or Latina/o ethnic identity.

As early as grade school I remember having to negotiate this ascription, if not racialization, as a Mexican. I recall, for instance, being taken aback on the playground at racist jokes directed toward Mexicans, for I knew that to some extent I, and certainly my father, was Mexican. Now, as an adult, I am even more taken aback by the recollection that my schoolyard pals would tag these jokes with words like, "No offense, Tim." These fifth graders were wrapped up in the process of ascribing to me a Mexican identity and then disparaging it. How did this come about? My Norwegian heritage left me fairly tall and no darker than many of my Italian American (and other) classmates, and hence my physical characteristics would not have led immediately to an ascription of Mexican ethnic identity. Would fifth graders have known that Sandoval was a Mexican last name? Perhaps they saw me at a Little League baseball game with my father, who did "look Mexican." He *was* easily racialized as Mexican. Or perhaps their parents had pointed out that my father, or our family, was Mexican. Whatever the case, the process of ethnic identity ascription was underway.

These sorts of schoolyard experiences helped to make clear to me early on in life that being Mexican was not regarded by many around me as a social advantage and perhaps might even prove a handicap. My father's experiences of discrimination in California schools and picking fruit and working in the state's agricultural industry during his youth and young adulthood—most of which took place in the pre-Chicano movement era and none of which he ever talked much about—I am convinced made clear *to him* that there was primarily disadvantage to being Mexican in the

United States. It was obvious, though not explicitly stated, that he wanted his children to be "Americans," not "Mexicans." Probably I picked up on this project of what might be called assimilation in subtle ways, not only from my father but from other family members as well, especially my uncle. Both brothers had married non-Mexican American women, did not really make efforts to promote "Mexicanness," and, except in moments of patriarchal privilege and *enojo*, did not speak Spanish to their children or encourage us much to learn the language. That I learned well there was little advantage to being Mexican is also clear from the fact that I further recall responding on more than one occasion to the "No offense Tim," uttered by joking schoolyard friends, with the words, "That's OK, we're Spanish, not Mexican." From whence precisely I inherited that idea of European exceptionalism I have no idea.

Yet to label my father "assimilationist," as Johnson (1999, 63) refers to his Mexican American mother, and to say that I learned early on that there was little advantage to being "Mexican," even only "half Mexican," in the United States is not to say that my father and my father's family rejected all things Mexican. Nothing could be further from the truth. Certainly, they did "deny" or distance themselves (and their families) from aspects of their heritage. Nonetheless, my father could lead us from the Bay Area to Mexico on family road trips only slightly less boisterous and filled with family drama than those depicted by Sandra Cisneros in her novel *Caramelo*. English was spoken at home primarily because my mother did not speak Spanish, not because my father—whose English was perfect except for the occasional, misplaced accent—intentionally avoided Spanish.[4] Indeed, we would find dad watching Spanish TV, and he would converse in Spanish with whom it was necessary. During holiday gatherings at my aunt's home in a largely Mexican barrio in San Jose, it was often Spanish that was heard between him and his siblings, while all of us enjoyed my aunt's tamales and enchiladas and the music flowing from my cousins' accordion, guitars, and drums. If it is correct to label my father assimilationist, it is primarily so from something like an essentialist or coherentist theoretical standpoint. From another perspective, one more constructivist and focused upon notions of hybridity rather than "racial"/ethnic essences, he was quintessentially "Mexican American."

---

4. It is not uncommon for mixed families to adopt the language of the dominant culture. See the studies cited by Ruiz 2009, 90.

As the years passed, the process of ascribing to me a Mexican "racial"/ethnic identity, and of course my ascription and racialization of others, continued in subtle and not so subtle ways. Although I had done very well in all subjects in junior high school, I remember in my first semester in a majority white but nonetheless quite diverse high school that I was assigned without any sort of placement exam to a basic English class that was probably 75 percent black and brown, downstairs in one of the large rooms adjoining the cafeteria. That the class was 75 percent nonwhite by itself means nothing. However, it begins to acquire meaning when one notes that, by contrast, most of my white friends with whom I completed junior high were upstairs in smaller classrooms off one of the main school hallways in "college prep" or "AP" (Advanced Placement) English courses. At that time, I did not think much about it all, except to believe that high school classes seemed to be disorganized and "not very good." In retrospect, I believe it likely that I was placed in that class based on the school's (probably nonformalized) racialized expectations that minority students (discerned as such via our names?) would not or could not achieve to the same level as nonminority students.

Although, as I said, my high school was largely working- and middle-class white, many of my classmates were like me. A lot of us (perhaps more than 20 percent of the school) with last names like García, Gómez, Rodríguez, and Uribe were of mixed descent (mostly of Mexican and European heritage) and/or second- and third-generation Latino/as. However, in that time and place we were not yet Latino/as, and I imagine that some of my high school colleagues of Mexican descent may have never become Latino/as. Although everyone knew about and could reference our Mexican or "Latin" heritage, we did not consider ourselves a distinct ethnic group, nor, as far as I know, did others strongly or clearly distinguish us in a public way (except for the kind of "placement" incident I mentioned above). We did not speak Spanish much, if at all; at least no one was doing so around school. We were not blacks and we were not Samoans or Filipinos, all of whom were more clearly socially distinguished, and whose physical features more often facilitated their racialization or ascription into a particular "racial"/ethnic identity. Importantly too, we were not *cholos*, the first-generation or 1.5-generation Mexican immigrants, who were more or less relegated to the temporary trailers near the gym, where the ESL classes were held. These were the "real" Mexicans whose baggy pants, buttoned up flannel shirts, distinctive hairstyles, and cadence of speech underscored that their difference was of greater social significance than ours.

Upon graduation from high school, I was accepted to the University of California at Santa Barbara. However, for a variety of reasons ranging from financial to motivational, I did not attend. Eventually, after an unsuccessful attempt at a local community college, I caught my academic stride at another school. After three semesters there, I applied to, and was accepted by, the University of California at Davis. Coming from a high school where, as far as I know, not many more than a dozen or so students from my graduating class immediately attended a four-year university, my understanding of the world of college was not terribly sophisticated. Hence when my university application asked me about my "racial"/ethnic heritage, I happily "checked the box"—although I do not remember exactly how it was labeled: "Mexican," "Hispanic," "Latino," or some combination of terms.

Not Becoming Hispanic

It was only some time later, in an African American studies course at Davis in the late 1980s, that I learned about the different boxes and what ends they served in the world of higher education in the United States. They were designed to promote, register, and construct an institution's ethnic, racial, and gender diversity. Like Johnson (1999, 31), who checked the box on his way to Harvard Law School (and I imagine many others in many other academic contexts), this new knowledge triggered a kind of personal crisis for me, a double crisis really. On the one hand, I wondered to myself (as perhaps many minority students have) if I had been admitted to this prestigious university solely or largely because I had checked the box. Did I belong here? Was I actually smart enough to be studying at the University of California? On the other hand, I wondered too if it had been right for me to "check the box." Was it legitimate to do so? Was I really a Mexican American? Or was I unintentionally involved in a kind of ethnic identity fraud? After all, I was not as brown as most of the Chicano student leaders and only knew a bit of Spanish, and, of course, in any case I was only "half" Mexican.

My new knowledge about the boxes and the internal questioning that it provoked—which I kept to myself for fear of being uncovered as a fraud—also produced a couple of side effects. First, it served to motivate my studies. I was determined to achieve high grades and academic honors as a way to verify to myself that I actually did belong in the university, that I was intellectually as good as anyone else at UC Davis, white or black,

Asian or Latino/a. I was determined to prove to myself that I was smart enough to be there "on my own" and not due to the university's attempts to diversify and register diversification. Second, along with the stress that accompanies the drive to overachieve,[5] the new knowledge about the boxes also produced in me a reluctance to self-identify as Mexican American, Hispanic, Latino, or Chicano.

I do not recall to what extent constructivist approaches that highlight the unstable, shifting, and socially constructed aspects of identity were highlighted at Davis in those days. If they were, they did not have as much impact on me as more essentialist or coherentist narratives of identity, for I was fundamentally unsure if I was truly or authentically a Latino. Hence, at the end of my undergraduate career, as I applied to graduate schools and theological seminaries, I resolved not to "check the box." On the one hand, I did not want to appear as a kind of ethnic free rider. On the other hand, I also did not want to receive what I imagined might be a kind of "preferential consideration" for being a Latino and then to be plagued by thoughts that I had been admitted to a graduate program, even partially, out of an institution's concern for diversity rather than merely on the basis of my academic potential. That institutions, whether by policy or not, had long considered other factors beside academic potential for admitting *nonminority* students, and the fact that universities (and other public institutions) have good reasons to actively promote diversity, did not yet factor in my deliberations.[6]

"Hey, You, Latino Biblical Scholar!"

Of course, if identity is something that is socially constructed, as I suggested at the outset, individuals alone do not decide upon or elect their identities. Although individual agency does play a significant role in fash-

---

5. See the remark of Appiah: "It is at least arguable that in our society the cost to competent, well-behaved, individual Blacks and Hispanics of being constantly treated as if they have to measure up—the cost in stress, in anger, in lost opportunities is pretty high" (1996, 101). Appiah's talk of "well-behaved" blacks and Hispanics seems odd, and even troubling, if there is the suggestion that regularly blacks and Hispanics prove themselves ill behaved. He appears, however, to be thinking about behavior in relation to something like bourgeois norms, as he states in n. 98, "many of these people are not middle-class."

6. On these matters see the persuasive arguments of Gutmann 1996; see also Wilkins 1996.

ioning an identity (see below), what we are given to work with remains in some sense out of our hands. To borrow a concept from Louis Althusser's much-discussed account of the formations of ideologies, we are, in significant ways, "interpellated" into identities.

In Althusser's famous example, the ideological recruitment of subjects, their being hailed or interpellated, "can be imagined along the lines of the most commonplace everyday police (or other) hailing: 'Hey, you there!'" (2008, 48). Janet Halley (2000, 43), who also alludes to Althusser's work in her discussion of identity, points to the key passage in Althusser's essay on ideology where he notes further:

> Assuming that the theoretical scene I have imagined takes place in the street, the hailed individual will turn around. By this mere one-hundred-and eighty-degree physical conversion, he becomes a *subject*. Why? Because he has recognized that the hail was "really" addressed to him, and that "it was *really him* who was hailed" (and not someone else). (Althusser 2008, 48)

Analogously with the formation of identities, it is as if a larger social voice calls out, for example, "Hey, you, Latina/o!" or "Hey, you, Hispanic!" or "Hey, you, Latino/a biblical scholar!" Upon responding, "Who, me?" we are, at least partially, shaped into Latino/as, or Hispanics, or Latina/o biblical scholars.

The various processes of racialization and ethnic ascription I have noted above can be construed as aspects of my being "hailed" as a Latino. Yet the process of "identity interpellation," of being hailed as a Latino (biblical scholar) in the theological academy, initially manifested itself to me in an obvious way somewhere in the middle of my M.Div. studies.

I had requested a transcript from the seminary's registrar in order to apply for a ministry-related job; I do not recall exactly what sort of position. In any case I paid my few dollars, and the registrar happily handed over an unofficial transcript. Upon examining it, I noticed that there was an *H* printed next to my name. Knowing full well what the letter designated, I nonetheless inquired of the registrar what it meant. I was told it identified me as "Hispanic." I responded that I was surprised to hear that since I deliberately had not self-identified as Hispanic on my application or on any other seminary-related document. I indicated as well that I was not entirely sure if the seminary administration should be identifying students' ethnicities instead of leaving that to the students themselves.

Only later would it become clear to me that it was not worth the energy, or even really possible, to control much how social forces and institutions would or would not seek to interpellate me into a Latino or Mexican American or Chicano identity. Despite an ongoing anxiety about the (in)authenticity of my Mexican Americanness, I thus eventually resolved to let institutions that might have an interest in my ethnic identity discern for themselves what counts for being (authentically, or authentically enough) Latino/a.

Although again I refused to "check the box" when applying to Ph.D. programs, during my doctoral studies there was once more a certain interest in my ambiguous ethnicity. Although my interest in reconnecting with the Mexican side of my background was growing, my emerging scholarly focus was not on Latina/o biblical hermeneutics. I was, however, told by some that I would have better success on the job market if I would "play up" my Latino identity. Indeed, I am certain that my interest in further exploring my "Mexican heritage" did open up employment opportunities, including my first position, where I was from the outset expected to nurture ties that our seminary was seeking to strengthen with a Latina/o church.

I was happy and excited to take on this role, just as I have been happy since receiving the Ph.D. to engage in projects sponsored by the Hispanic Theological Initiative, to teach in the Hispanic Summer Program and in the Advanced Latin@ Theological Education program, and even write an article for a book on Latino/a biblical hermeneutics and scholarship. Although my publication trajectory could not (and cannot) easily or unproblematically be characterized as Latino/a biblical hermeneutics, as this is often understood (see below), in a sense each of the service activities I have named, to which I was invited to participate and sometimes for which I was paid, ought to be considered further moments in my being hailed as a Latino/a biblical scholar.

If this is so, my biological Mexican heritage and the last name of Sandoval along with the hybrid Mexican American/mainstream upbringing I experienced were perhaps important but not sufficient causes in my becoming, at least in part, a Latino biblical scholar. The hailing of the theological academy in the United States—from being designated an *H* in seminary to being invited to teach a Bible course in the Hispanic Summer Program—were also required. These interpellations were necessary, not merely because I am only "half Mexican" but because of other factors. Both social processes and related personal decisions had led to the/my minimizing of my Mexican heritage.

On the one hand, I learned well from my father and his experiences, as well as other events throughout my own childhood and youth, that being Mexican in the United States was likely not to prove a simple social advantage. This devaluation of my Mexican heritage remains with me as a kind of slow-healing wound, and the disappointment and anger with my father for not more actively embracing his heritage and passing it on to me lingers. Johnson's words about his mother echo in certain respects my sentiments vis-à-vis my father: "She tried to deny her heritage. ... She shielded her sons from Spanish and the disadvantages that it brought her generation; but she could not escape. Her denial of her ancestry is a sad but revealing indication of a more general phenomenon among Latinos in the United States" (1999, 63). He continues: "I love my mother, but I grow angry with her at times. Why did she try so hard to assimilate and rob me of the Mexican American culture that she shed?"

On the other hand, my interpellation as a Latino biblical scholar was also required because of my wrestling on a more intellectual level with questions of identity and the identity politics of the academy. With essentialist notions of identity in the forefront of my thinking, I was uncertain of my ethnic authenticity and, consequently, ambivalent about self-identifying as a Latino or Mexican American. More specifically, the interpellations into Latino/a biblical studies were also required because, as I said, I had/have not consciously constructed my scholarly identity as a Latino biblical scholar, at least not explicitly in terms of the discourse upon which much Latin(a)o theological and biblical scholarship had/has been constructed.

Identity and Latina/o Theological and Biblical Studies

In an article titled "*Oye, ¿Y Ahora Qué? / Say, Now What?*" Benjamín Valentín contends that Latina/o theological studies has been preoccupied with discussions of "identity, symbolic culture, and subjectivity," and has been enchanted by "a general discursive paradigm of culture and identity recognition" (2003, 112). For Valentín, this situation has "served to engender certain debilitating oversights" (112) in matters that Latino/a theologians might address.

Valentín recognizes that a denigration of Latino/a cultures and identities (like those experienced by my father and significantly less vitriolically by me) as well as a lack of recognition of Latina/o theology in mainstream theological circles have warranted a strong focus on culture and identity in Latino/a theological studies. As Charles Taylor has stated,

"Due recognition is not just a courtesy we owe people. It is a vital human need" (1994, 26). Demanding and achieving recognition, celebrating and analyzing Latino/a identity, culture, and subjectivity, are thus some of the—and perhaps the most—significant achievements of Latino/a scholars in the theological academy. To the extent that cultural denigration continues, Latina/o theology's demands for recognition and its focus on identity and culture continue to be warranted.

Nonetheless, for Valentín, who is concerned about identifying a scholarly tendency rather than making exhaustive claims about every contribution to Latino/a theology, "when we practice to depict identity," such a discursive orientation can weave a "tangled web" (2003, 110). For Valentín, the dangers of depicting identity consist in paying too little attention to "the multifaceted matrices that impinge upon the realization of a broader emancipatory political project and energy" (112). He calls for "Hispanic/Latino(a) theologians" to address injustices "that are traceable not only to the denigration of their culture and identities, but also to socioeconomic exploitation and inequity" (113). In short, Valentín suggests that "class" categories of analysis find a fuller place in Latina/o theological studies.

I am largely in agreement with Valentín, both in terms of his evaluation of Latino/a theological discourse as having been largely focused on questions of culture and identity and in terms of his call for a broadening of the concerns of that discourse.[7]

Of course, even before and certainly since Valentín published his essay, Latino/a theological and biblical scholarship has addressed the trends that he succinctly diagnosed (De La Torre and Espinosa 2006). Although this is happily the case, it was in fact precisely the significant concern with culture and identity in Latino/a theological studies that Valentín describes that led me in part not to identify myself as a "Latino biblical scholar."

Latina/o theological discourse and biblical scholarship certainly have not discussed identity simply or only in essentialist terms. Nonetheless,

---

7. Besides attending more fully to socioeconomic issues that Valentín highlights and how these class dimensions interface with the construction of a Latina/o ethnic or cultural identity, other matters that Valentín does not highlight (but of which he is certainly aware) can also be mentioned. For instance, the many and diverse contributions of Latina scholars around gender issues and the less often broached questions of sexuality can also find a fuller place on the agenda of any theological discourse—not merely Latina/o theological scholarship—concerned with broad and integrative notions of justice.

for a person of mixed heritage like myself in the midst of negotiating identity issues, its focus on identity, history, and culture has often carried such coherentist undercurrents. Indeed, as Tat-siong Benny Liew notes, "memory, history, and the 'past' may be effectively used to establish tradition and identity" but "this very efficiency often ends up—or even depends on—masking the essentializing implications of such a construction" (2008, 9). If I was not sure I was authentically a Latino, I was not going to attempt to pen a work on Latino/a biblical hermeneutics or offer interpretations of biblical texts "through Hispanic eyes"—the reading orientations in biblical studies that have incarnated the concern with identity and culture in Latina/o theological studies more generally.[8] Again, as Liew contends, "Racial/ethnic identity is not something that one can figure out, tidy up, authenticate, and then adopt as one's springboard for intellectual and interpretive endeavors" (6). It is a bit more complicated than that. Valentín's work is valuable because, among other reasons, in sketching trends in Latina/o theological scholarship he is able to recognize that our ethnic Latina/o identities are not essential or essentially stable, but are always "embedded in a larger web of shifting social, political, and economic relations" (2003, 113). I am interested in what this space, this larger web, might possibly mean for Latina/o biblical scholarship.

A Too Tight Script

Althusser's model of ideological interpellation that I alluded to above has been widely criticized for envisioning subjects that are utterly incapable of resisting interpellating forces. Althusser's ideological subject is hailed and can do no other but conform to the interpellating voice. As Halley has put it, Althusser's "depiction of the 'subject'" is one that is "abject" and "completely powerless to resist or reshape the 'hail' issued by ideology" (2000, 43–44).

Yet this image of the "abject" subject passively shaped by the ideological hail obviously does not correspond in its entirety to the manner in which I have intimated my identity as a Latino (biblical scholar) has been created,

---

8. See, for instance, the well-known work of Justo González (1996) and Fernando Segovia (1995a, 1995b) as examples of Latino/a/Hispanic hermeneutic programs. Although both are careful to recognize something like a text's autonomy, both emphasize a reader-oriented hermeneutic that depends largely on Hispanic or Latino/a identity and experience.

or the manner in which identities in general seem to be constructed. Individuals often understand themselves as contributing in important ways to the construction of their identities. For instance, as Mary Waters has noted (1990), often people understand themselves to have chosen an ethnic identity. In some sense, then, we can resist the interpellating forces that seek to mold our identities and shape our own identities, as perhaps I in part have done in not taking on explicitly the mantle of Latina/o biblical scholarship toward which I have been hailed—although this fact may merely mean that I have been more fundamentally interpellated by mainstream biblical studies, or have other explanations. Whatever the particulars of my case, interpellating forces can nonetheless sometimes be experienced as almost irresistible. Indeed, certain identities hewed out in the midst of shifting social situations may be more sharply interpellated than others. Appiah, for instance, writes, "racial identification is simply harder to resist than ethnic identification" (1996, 80).

Appiah has explained and explored this tension in identity formation in helpful ways (1994, 1996, 2005). His musings on the individual and the question of compulsion in identity discourses may also prove important in considering certain prospects of Latina/o biblical hermeneutics.

Like Valentín and Taylor, Appiah too recognizes the vital importance of the politics of recognition, the requirement that the cultures and identities of particular individuals and groups be acknowledged and respected and the imperative of demanding such recognition when it is missing or distorted. This is a vital piece of any integrative and adequate notion of justice. Appiah does not use the Althusserian language of being hailed or interpellated into an identity, but he does speak of various social "scripts" that "go with" particular identities (1996, 97): "There will be proper ways of being black and gay, there will be expectations to be met, demands will be made" (1994, 162; 1996, 99). Just so there will be proper ways to be Latina/o, or even a Latina/o biblical scholar.

Appiah, however, is also very concerned about individual liberty, although he by no means understands individuals in some hyperlibertarian, reductionist fashion as isolated beings emerging apart from particular social contexts and relations (2005). Rather, the social is prior logically, materially, and psychologically to the individual. Appiah, who self identifies as a gay man and who is, like me, a person of mixed heritage (Ghanaian and English), is nonetheless concerned that individual lives might be "too tightly scripted" by discursive identity formations. He continues (in a passage also cited by Halley 2000):

It is at this point that someone who takes autonomy seriously will ask whether we have not replaced one kind of tyranny with another. If I had to choose between the world of the closet and the world of gay liberation, or between the world of *Uncle Tom's Cabin* and Black Power, I would, of course, choose in each case the latter. But I would like not to have to choose. I would like other options. …

It is a familiar thought that the bureaucratic categories of identity must come up short before the vagaries of actual people's lives. But it is equally important to bear in mind that a politics of identity can be counted on to transform the identities on whose behalf it ostensibly labors. Between the politics of recognition and the politics of compulsion, there is no bright line. (1994, 162–63; cf. also 1996, 99)

As Halley explains, "*if* advocacy constructs identity, *if* it generates a script which identity bearers must heed, *if* that script restricts group members, then identity politics compels its beneficiaries. Identity politics suddenly is no longer mere or simple resistance: it begins to look like power" (2000, 42). Power can be exercised by making people become people "they would not otherwise be" and not merely making them do things "they would not otherwise do" (42). Moreover, although the Althusserian hail "always comes from above, from a high center of power," Halley contends that such interpellation, "with all its invisible subjections, can come from below, from within resistant social movements" as well (44). To the extent that Latina/o biblical scholarship seeks to resist the dominant construction of the field of biblical studies, with its concerns for genetic and historical explanations, in favor of other sorts of studies—for instance, works that draw on a range of intellectual discourses such as postcolonial theory or which highlight reader-oriented hermeneutics that depend on the identities and experiences of Latino/as/Hispanics and hence often attend more fully to synchronic readings of biblical texts than does much of biblical scholarship—it is a discourse of resistance.[9]

Understanding the existence of an intimate link between identity construction and power, even the power of a discourse of resistance, can call attention to the ways in which Latina/o biblical scholarship, with its concern for culture and identity recognition, are tied to concrete matters such as hiring and promotions, access to publishing mechanisms, and a range of other sorts of resources. This is not to say that this relationship

---

9. For Latino/a scholarship as a discourse of resistance, see Segovia 2009.

between power and identity is necessarily a bad thing or somehow unique to Latino/a (or other forms of minority) scholarship, but it is somehow miraculously absent from some innocent "mainstream" scholarship. Nor is it to suggest there has been no resistance to Latina/o scholarship in the theological academy, so that the construction of the field can be reduced to a mere power grab. Indeed, as Fernando Segovia rightly notes, "dominant critics" largely continue to "control the centers of learning and professional organizations" (2009, 194). It is only to acknowledge that Latina/o theological and biblical scholarship has much at stake in reproducing itself and in (compelling) the ongoing construction of Latino/a scholars and scholarship.

Some Legroom, Please

Besides highlighting the issues of power that is a piece of identity politics, Appiah's concern with the individual—who again is not some Hobbsian caricature of an independent and isolated being—is important for considering the prospects of Latina/o biblical scholarship and hermeneutics in another way. If Latino/a theological and biblical scholarship has tended to be constructed and constrained by a focus on culture, identity, or reader-oriented hermeneutics, as Valentín has argued, if this is the dominant script to which Latina/o scholars are in some sense hailed, then it is possible that some, like me, will feel that this script is a bit too tight and attempt to resist it and seek a bit more legroom for our scholarly identities. On coherentist assumptions in such a situation, either one becomes something like a genuine Latina/o biblical scholar who adopts the given script and reproduces the field largely as it is given, or one turns to other scripts and other aspects of biblical scholarship and thereby runs the risk of appearing disloyal to Latino/a scholarship or merely inauthentically Latino/a.[10]

Echoing Appiah, however, choosing between these scripts is not the only option I would like to have. The tension may be particularly acute for a person of mixed heritage like me and/or for some second- and third-generation Latina/os. Unlike many Latino/a scholars whose origins are

---

10. Halley notes that "coherentist assumptions about identity politics make it possible to have an extremely rich discourse of loyalty among group members" but that "without stable assumptions about who belongs to the group and what their interests are, and about who can speak for the group, disloyalty loses much of its sting" (2000, 45).

from outside the United States, for second- or third-generation Mexican Americans or Puerto Ricans or Guatemalans born in the United States, or Latina/os of dual descent, our connections with Latin America and Latin American culture are often largely symbolic.[11] As Edwin David Aponte's brief account of life as "Puerto Rican Yankee" attests, the roots and influences of many Latino/as can be traced (only) in complicated ways throughout the United States and Latin America or the Caribbean (De La Torre and Aponte 2001, 2–5).

Like Aponte, as one who has been born and raised in the United States, I am deeply impacted by North American culture. For me in particular the value that U.S. culture places on individuality, choice, and freedom from the constraints of traditions and social conformity is significant. Although there are certainly plenty of spaces for criticizing aspects of this ideology, especially as regards economic and social arrangements, I, like Appiah, am not persuaded that it is bad through and through. For example, the more typically North American notions can create a space for critiquing the often overtly patriarchal, heterosexist, and other socially rigid aspects of the Mexican American culture (which, of course, are also present in varying degrees in "mainstream" U.S. culture) to which I am heir, just as more "Mexican" aspects of that Mexican American culture (its more communal orientation, its emphasis on social solidarity, etc.) can point toward shortcomings in especially uncritical forms of the North American ideology.

Indeed, even if I wanted to completely escape the libertarian-individualist orientations of my North American context, this would likely not be possible in any full way. As Charles Taylor has argued, our identities are always dialogically constituted (1994). If Appiah, who follows Taylor in this regard, is correct that African American identity is "centrally shaped by American society and institutions" and cannot be regarded "as constructed solely within African-American communities" (1996, 95), so too is it hardly possible for a Latino/a identity like mine, of one born and raised in the United States, to escape the profound influence of that same North American society.

Rather, it is the "American" and the "Mexican in America" (as well as the Norwegian in America) that form what Appiah calls the "toolkit" (96) out of which I fashion a self, an identity. And the "I" is important

---

11. See David Gutiérrez's discussion regarding the symbolic ties to Mexico and Mexican culture of second- and third-generation descendants of Mexican immigrants (1999, 555).

here. If identities are in some sense socially constructed, the self is by no means erased. It is rather from the given social materials that an individual can strive to actively shape an identity, to choose, in Mary Waters's terms (1990), an ethnicity. Similarly, for Latina/os who are biblical scholars trained in North America or Europe and/or in North American and European methods and modes of scholarship, it will obviously be impossible (and for some perhaps not desirable) to persistently and significantly resist that training. With good reasons, individual Latino/a scholars may often thoroughly and legitimately challenge the field's assumptions and procedures, while others may critically and equally legitimately embrace them.

The theologian Michelle González in her essay on "Rethinking Latina Feminist Theologian" (2006) also recognizes the fluid and ambiguous nature of our ethnic identities, their social givenness, the role of the individual agent in fashioning an identity, and how choosing an identity is a political act. She quotes appreciatively Iris Marion Young's insights on gender construction and identity: "No individual woman's identity, then, will escape the markings of gender, but how gender marks her life is her own" (197). For González, Young's statement "removes the paradox of identity as choice and as imposed and … resonates with the experiences of Latino/a communities" (197). González, however, does not subscribe completely to a constructivist view of identity formation. She is anxious to preserve something of the "cultural and historical unity of Latino/as" (197). Hence she finds Jorge Garcia's Wittgensteinian notion of "family resemblances as adequate to represent the relationship between and diversity of Latino/a people" (197). These cultural and historical family resemblances appear to make up for her what in Appiah's idiom was the "toolkit" out of which individuals create selves.

There is a bit of a tension in González's scenario between the socially constructed aspects and the "organic unity" of Latina/o identity, which she herself recognizes. The tension suggests that she wants to acknowledge slightly stronger or more permanent boundaries around Latina/o culture, history, and identity than would I (or Appiah), even while recognizing the significant diversity of particular Latino/a identities—Mexican, Cuban, and so on.[12] Nonetheless, it is from within this theoretical perspective that

---

12. González's concern with Latino/a "cultural and historical unity" suggests that Liew's remark regarding "memory, history, and the 'past'" as "effectively used to establish tradition and identity" but as "masking the essentializing implications of such a construction" (2008, 9) is again apt.

González offers a further suggestion relevant to considering the prospects of Latina/o biblical studies, one that is also related to questions of power and identity, especially Appiah's hope for a bit of individual freedom from the scripts or interpellating disciplining of our identities. González contends that Latina theologians ought to more regularly address

> more traditional theological categories. It is essential for voices deemed minority to write on traditional theological *loci* in order to enter into dialogue and challenge dominant theological constructions through this shared discourse. If not, our theological contributions are reduced to side projects that do not impact mainstream theological discourse. (2006, 192)

Later she further queries whether there are ways "in which we separate ourselves from the broader academy" and wonders about how "our categorization as 'minority voices' affects our theological contributions" (197).

González's concern is something like a worry that Latina/o scholars will be too tightly scripted, not merely ethnically but in terms of Latina/o scholarship. Her worry, however, is a kind of flip side of the one I (with the help of Appiah) outlined above. It is not an anxiety that the individual Latino/a scholar will be too tightly constrained but that the work of too tightly scripted Latino/a scholars and theology will (continue to) be marginalized (further) in the academy.[13] I share this concern. As academic (theological) institutions rightly remain devoted to addressing diversity issues, I wonder whether Latino/a scholars will be too strongly interpellated into narrow roles of doing Latina/o scholarship, addressing only Latino/a issues, or offering readings of biblical texts only through Latina/o eyes, or constructing Hispanic hermeneutic orientations.

Such relatively tight scripting need not be so—and, of course, is not always so. By loosening the script, by insisting on a bit more "identity legroom," as Latino/as and as Latina/o biblical scholars, individuals can preserve more autonomy to construct their own scholarly selves. They can also resist any tendency in the academy to minimize the contributions of Latino/a scholars by regarding us as those who are not capable of, or not interested in, doing anything else within the theological and biblical disciplines and hence unable to impact our broader fields in broader

---

13. See Segovia, who also alludes to the problem of "institutional tokenism and branding" (2009, 199).

ways.[14] The dialogical structure of an identity called "Latino/a biblical scholar" can permit any individual to construct a scholarly self in which, at different moments, the "biblicist" and "Latino/a" aspects of the identity equations are differently weighted, sometimes more biblical and sometimes more Latina/o.

Latina/o Scholars and Scholarship

When we consider what constitutes Latino/a biblical scholars(hip), it may be helpful to distinguish more clearly between Latina/o biblical scholars whose scholarship can cover a range of topics in biblical studies and Latino/a biblical scholarship. Segovia makes a similar distinction in his efforts to map what Latino/a biblical scholars(hip) are (is). For Segovia "provenance and conscientization" (2009, 203) are the key factors that constitute a Latino/a biblical scholar. Yet neither one's origins in nor commitment to a Latino/a community alone suffices to be a Latino/a biblical scholar. One must in some sense be both "flesh and blood" (provenance) Latino/a *and* take up the "spirit and truth" (conscientization) of Latina/o biblical criticism, the "critical parameters" of which he likewise sketches (2009, 220–22).

Segovia acknowledges the constructed and shifting aspects of identities. Yet, on the view I am developing here, his program remains a bit too tightly scripted, although the proposal itself of (what I assume is) provisional closure around Latino/a biblical scholarship is both legitimate and helpful. By contrast, with an approach that promotes some significant legroom for our identities, the "big tent" of Latina/o biblical scholars might legitimately cover first-generation immigrants, second- and third-generation Latino/as, but also the more ambiguous cases of mixed-race persons and others who are interpellated or hailed into Latino/a biblical studies and not merely those born of "flesh and blood."[15] (With González's "family

---

14. That such a caricature of Latina/o biblical scholars is patently untrue can be seen by a brief perusal of the range of scholarly work of contributors to this volume, some of whom have published technical and historical studies of the highest caliber. To mention just a couple of examples with which I am familiar, see Avalos 1995 and Botta 2009.

15. Segovia's emphasis on provenance, or "flesh and blood," begs the question of whether certain ambiguous ethnic identities qualify as Latino/a. For instance, would someone born and raised in Latin America to North American parents, who subse-

resemblance" metaphor this would include those who are not "naturally born" Latino/as but adopted into the family.)

This hailing as a Latino/a biblical scholar, however, will come with a looser script, a script that would not define Latino/aness in sharp essentialist terms, as essentially a matter of blood or culture, ethnicity or "race," nor identify a Latino/a biblical scholar exclusively or primarily in terms of whether and how much of a particular sort of scholarship one produces. Indeed, other matters (that Segovia too recognizes) also might legitimately come into play when considering what counts in making a Latino/a biblical scholar. Commitment to Latina/o theological students, offering theological education to Latin(a)o communities of faith, as well as dedication and service to the broader Latino/a community, Latin America, and its immigrants—among others—can also help make up a Latino/a biblical scholar.

The big-tent approach to Latino/a biblical scholarship, which resists defining Latina/o identity too narrowly on essentialist assumptions and scripting Latino/a biblical scholarship too sharply, will of course not demand that the exploration, analysis, and celebration of Latino/a culture, identity, and hermeneutics in Latino/a biblical studies stop. Indeed, it ought to continue, even as the discussion of what might legitimately count as Latino/a biblical scholarship ought to move forward. It is, however, the freedom of the Latino/a scholar to choose to range widely in scholarly writing that I want to promote, for it not only honors the individual who may wish to more or less conform to particular scripts of what it means to be a Latina/o biblical scholar, in regard to both academic publishing and other forms of scholarly activity and service (see above), it also promotes vitality for Latino/a biblical scholars and scholarship by resisting the marginalization of Latino/a theological studies that González worries about.

There is, however, a large bit of hazy middle ground when schematizing in this way the question of precisely who and what counts as (a) Latina/o biblical scholar(ship). For instance, I recently published (with Dorothy BEA Akoto) "A Note on Qohelet 10,10b," proposing a small emendation of one word in the biblical text. Based on all that I have said, one might suggest that this note was (in large part) authored by a Latino biblical scholar. Yet, except for expressing some sort of genetic relationship with its prin-

---

quently migrates to North America, count? What about the adopted white child of Latin American immigrants? On Segovia's view, the answer is apparently no.

cipal author, it is difficult to imagine how the article might meaningfully be regarded as a work of Latino/a biblical scholarship or hermeneutics. It is perhaps possible that my seeing a solution to this textual problem was a result of the Latino eyes I bring to the text, but it seems more likely a function of knowing a bit about Classical Hebrew and text criticism of the Bible. On the other hand, the present study, which explicitly thematizes Latina/o identity and biblical scholarship and hermeneutics, is unproblematically regarded as a piece of Latino/a biblical scholarship, though one would not necessarily have to identify as Latino/a to discuss notions of Latino/a identity and trends in Latino/a biblical studies.

If it is difficult to imagine designating in a meaningful way "A Note on Qohelet 10:10b" as a work of Latina/o biblical scholarship/hermeneutics, then on first glance an article like "The Strength of Women and Truth: The Tale of the Three Bodyguards and Ezra's Prayer in First Esdras" (Sandoval 2007) or "Satirical Elements in Tobit and Hellenistic Jewish Identity" (Sandoval, forthcoming) likewise sound as if they have little to do with Latina/o biblical scholarship/hermeneutics. However, in these instances one might make a case for designating them as such. On the one hand, they are authored by someone who might at least provisionally be designated a Latino biblical scholar, even if this alone might be insufficient to warrant the description of them as works of Latino/a biblical scholarship. On the other hand, as the titles begin to intimate and as the articles themselves sketch more clearly, the analysis of the ancient Jewish texts revolves around issues that are regularly the concern of much of Latino/a scholarship, namely diaspora existence and (ethnic/religious/national) identity.[16]

It is indeed precisely (though not only) because so many Hellenistic Jewish texts (the so-called Apocrypha and Pseudepigrapha) appear to grapple with questions of identity and diaspora experience that I, as a biblical scholar who also grapples with what it means to be a Mexican American, am drawn to these texts. The questions and debates about what counts for being a Jew while living often for generations outside the Jewish homeland and without much knowledge of Hebrew are of course not the only issues that might be foregrounded in studies of these texts. Yet they are issues that I am concerned with both as a biblical scholar and as one

---

16. On the various modes by which one might reckon Hellenistic Jewish identity, see Cohen 1999. For work on Diaspora hermeneutics in the theological academy from a Latino/a/Hispanic perspective, see Segovia 1995a, 1995b; Rivera-Rodriguez 2007; Cuéllar 2008.

hailed into a Latino identity. However, my studies of these works do not directly allude to my Latino identity or refer explicitly to much Latina/o biblical scholarship.[17]

That my articles on 1 Esdras and Tobit do not much or explicitly allude to specifically Latino/a biblical scholarship or directly identify my Mexican American experience as motivating forces for my readings or as shaping my analysis of these texts might have various explanations. It surely is related to the struggles of hammering out an identity as a Latino biblical scholar that I have highlighted throughout this essay. On "coherentist assumptions about identity," it might appear as a case of ethnic disloyalty (Halley 2000, 43), a downplaying of the "Mexican" in "Mexican American," an assimilation or choosing to identify with the script of mainstream biblical scholarship rather than Latino/a biblical scholarship, which often invokes a strong identity-based hermeneutic. More positively, it might also be regarded as an effort to demonstrate that Latino/a scholars need not be prejudicially relegated to doing only a certain kind of (Latino/a) biblical scholarship; or it may point to the dialogic structure of my professional identity as a biblical scholar who is also Latino and the different weight those two aspects of my identity can have in different moments and in different professional spaces. I would not want to eliminate as completely wrong any of these possible responses nor valorize only one as entirely correct. Perhaps related to all of them, however, is a fundamental question of hermeneutics.

Hermeneutic Options

It has long been commonplace to recognize that readers of any significant text (e.g., the Bible rather than, say, the phone book) interpret that text or achieve an understanding of it in light of their experiences and context, and that significant contextual differences can lead to significant differences of interpretation. The dramatic disparity, for instance, between the biblical interpretations of American slaves and the understanding of the Bible's message promoted by the master class have been well documented

---

17. See Liew's more explicit efforts to construct an Asian American biblical scholarship not directly via "a narrative of identity or authenticity but through repeated references to existing (biblical) scholarship by Asian American scholars" (2008, 15). I discuss this aspect of Liew's work briefly below.

by, among others, Allen Dwight Callahan in *The Talking Book: African Americans and the Bible* (2006).

Since Martin Heidegger developed the notion of our "being thrown" into the world and the inevitability of "preunderstanding" in interpretation, most, except for the most conservative hermeneutists or reactionary political forces, have accepted the idea that we all are inescapably imbedded in our contexts and our interpretations relate to this context. Certainly, after Heidegger there still remain voices in biblical studies that insist upon a reading process that is, as Francisco Lozada Jr. has put it, "objective, universalistic, and positivistic" (2006, 114) in the hope of somehow, someday arriving at a unanimously agreed upon single and original meaning of a text. Nonetheless, few critical biblical scholars would still slavishly insist that this is a genuine possibility.

A good number more would, however, likely maintain that biblical scholars ought primarily to pursue historically oriented questions and concerns. As Paul Ricoeur recognized:

> The general tendency of literary and biblical criticism since the mid-nineteenth century has been to link the contents of literary works, and in general of cultural documents, to the social conditions of the community in which these works were produced or to which they were directed. To explain a text was essentially to consider it as the expression of certain socio-cultural needs and as a response to certain perplexities localized in time and space. (1981, 183–84)

Ricoeur notes as well that Heidegger's notion of "preunderstanding" has sometimes been (wrongly) thought to be "indistinguishable from a simple projection of the prejudices of the reader into his reading" (190). Indeed, what Lozada and others call "social location hermeneutics" have sometimes tended to suggest, or have been thought to imply, that any sort of "objective" encounter with a text is hardly possible or not terribly desirable. For instance, the diaspora and cultural hermeneutic programs of Justo González (1996), Segovia (1995a, 1995b), and Cuéllar (2008), strongly oriented toward the reader's role in interpretation as they are, might be understood to suggest as much.

This emphasis on the reader's role in social location hermeneutics is an easily understandable position for scholars who possess a strong interest in Hispanic or Latino/a identity and culture. It is, as I said above, the incarnation in biblical studies of those broad tendencies in Latino/a theological studies that Valentín sketches. Furthermore, as Lozada notes, this sort of hermeneutic perspective that privileges a reader's particular context and perspectives has proven "quite valuable and essential to the field of contemporary biblical hermeneutics," for "it has raised the consciousness of the interpreter's identity as well as that of many 'minority' groups who struggle to change current negative viewpoints or representation of their group" (2006, 114). Within the field of biblical studies—which at least until the last few decades of the twentieth century was nearly completely dominated (and still somewhat is) by historical and genetic concerns and devoted to generating readings of biblical texts that valorized these concerns by universalizing them and thereby masking the male, European, and North American character of the discipline—it is a necessary, and historically an easily explainable, hermeneutic response.

However, in keeping with Appiah's hope for a bit of freedom for individuals within certain identity formations, adopting a strong identity- and reader-based hermeneutic ought not to be the only script available to Latino/a biblical scholars. Ricoeur's efforts to construct a text-oriented hermeneutic by which some "objective" criteria for recognizing validity of interpretation might be construed is an example of another option. It takes seriously the Heideggarian insight of "preunderstanding" as well as the ideological critiques that social location hermeneutics has directed toward mainstream biblical studies and biblical texts; it, however, does not foreground the reader's role to the extent that much social location hermeneutics at times appears to. My scholarly questions and readings of the literature of the ancient Jewish Diaspora, for instance, are clearly if subtly informed by my Latino identity and especially the struggles of its formation. These readings, however, do not explicitly privilege that identity. Rather, in Ricoeurian fashion they seek to be grounded in arguments about the structure of the texts developed with a variety of (not just historical) tools available to biblical scholars. Indeed, whatever the contours of my Latino identity, as I noted, it relates dialogically to my professional training and identity as a scholar familiar with a range of hermeneutic perspectives and trained in a range of critical methods.

This is not to argue that a single, valid reading of any significant cultural text is possible, nor to assert that the reader's role is not significant in interpretation. Neither Ricoeur nor I would make such claims. Nor is it to suggest that interpreters working out of a reader-oriented social location hermeneutic (Latina/o or otherwise) do not pay close attention to the texts and their structure or rhetoric. Rather, a Ricoeurian hermeneutic suggests only that arguments about the structure of the text, and not the subjectivity or identity of the reader, ought to be the principal criteria for developing and evaluating any reading. Although some might argue that Ricoeur's program is another version of the masking and universalizing tendencies of other hermeneutic projects, I believe that by and large his understanding of Heidegger's notion of "preunderstanding," the recognition of the inevitability of multiple readings, as well as the need for ideological critique adequately meet these objections.[18]

From something like Ricoeur's hermeneutic perspective one might even contend that my analysis of wealth and poverty rhetoric in Proverbs (2006), which in Ricoeurian fashion is very much oriented to the "architecture" of the book, qualifies as a work of Latino/a biblical scholarship. It is likely in some way related to and motivated by my Latino identity that was aware of, and would like to see addressed, the widespread poverty in Latin America and disproportionally among Latino/as, Latin American immigrants, and other racial and ethnic minorities in the United States. If so, however, the impact of my Latino identity (and the struggles to understand that identity) on this work is less significant than it is for the studies of 1 Esdras, Tobit, and especially this article.

Indeed, if one were to imagine a continuum of works that might be considered Latino/a biblical scholarship, there would be on the one end the works of Segovia and Cuéllar that I have mentioned, which are clearly marked as the work of Latino scholars undertaken with an obvious Latino/diaspora hermeneutic orientation. Next on this continuum would be my articles on 1 Esdras and Tobit, written by one who arguably could be described as a Latino scholar and that analyze topics often of concern for Latino/a theological and biblical studies. Although motivated in a significant way (but not only) by a Latino identity, the hermeneutic of these articles is more Ricoeurian and text-oriented, and perhaps more akin to what is the norm in "mainstream" biblical scholarship; perhaps with such a hermeneutic orientation they too are simultaneously insisting that Latino/a scholars(hip) not be unduly marginalized from the larger discipline. On the far end of the continuum would be the kind of critical note on Qoh 10:10b that I spoke of above. Although arguably the work of a Latino scholar who may be interested in insisting that Latino/a biblical scholars(hip) not be marginalized from the larger discipline, this technical

---

18. In addition, such a hermeneutic, I believe, is able to address many aspects of the "critical parameters" for Latina/o biblical studies that Segovia sketches (2009, 220–22).

work can hardly be called Latino/a scholarship except in its genetic relation to a Latino author.

Depending on who is deciding and on what grounds, the first kind of scholarship discussed above would always seem to be regarded as Latino/a biblical studies, but the last only in a certain limited or special sense. (Although my work on Proverbs [2006] might also count, its inclusion would likely be debated.)[19] I think, however, one might legitimately include the second or middle type of scholarship as Latino/a biblical scholarship as well, although it is related to a more constructivist notion of Latino/a biblical scholarship than some may wish to adopt and points to a significant hermeneutic difference with that first category of scholarship that epitomizes how Latina/o biblical studies has been constituted. It is, however, precisely the legitimacy and desirability of this sort of hermeneutic distinction and the readings that emerge from such a distinction that Latino/a biblical scholars should be debating among themselves and with biblical scholars of all stripes.

Although the above provisional or tentative schema is meant only to provoke a bit broader discussion of what counts as Latino/a biblical scholarship or a legitimate Latina/o hermeneutic, certain objections might be raised.

Liew, for instance, is wary of founding or narrating Asian American biblical hermeneutics on essentialist discourses of "identity or authenticity" that focus too much on the "'who' and/or 'what'" of scholarship. Rather, "in addition" he seeks to "narrate Asian American biblical hermeneutics into legitimacy" via "repeated references to existing (biblical) scholarship by Asian American scholars" (2008, 15). The "in addition" here is important, since this program of referencing, although helpful in establishing a scholarly tradition of discourse, really only pushes back the question of the "who" and/or "what" to the moment of referencing.

A further, perhaps more obvious objection would be to suggest that the kind of scholarly legroom I am calling for adopts too easily, or accepts too earnestly, dominant Eurocentric norms. Liew recognizes this tension when he notes that Asian American biblical hermeneutics seeks "to avoid becoming exotic on one hand and conforming to Eurocentrism on the

---

19. For instance, by Segovia 2009. Interestingly, because it does not foreground significantly his own Latino identity or a Latino/a perspective, Segovia—ironically for one who so keenly understands how even unstated identities impact interpretation—does not consider some of his earliest work to qualify as Latino/a biblical scholarship.

other" (2008, 15). González's concern that Latina theologians and theology address more traditional theological loci to avoid marginalization reflects the same preoccupation.

This tension in Latina/o biblical scholarship is one that I can live with. It has often proven to generate remarkably creative and insightful scholarship. To live with the tension, however, means that there will be ongoing conversation and different proposals about what Latina/o biblical hermeneutics and scholarship is or ought to be and who and what is included, like the suggestions that Segovia, for example, has offered (2009). As Liew notes, "Identity … is often invented by chance or happenstance and becomes recognizable only in hindsight" (2008, 8). Living with the tension thus also means taking responsibility for the way we provisionally mark closure in the shifting field of Latina/o biblical scholarship and for the political effects of this provisional closure.

Autobiographical Framing

Arriving at "Medio-Chicano"

I have now begun self-identifying as "medio-Chicano," a designation first applied to me by my Guatemalan wife a few years ago. Initially, it was merely a pithy, shorthand way to express that I was a person of mixed "race" or mixed descent, someone born to a Mexican American family on my father's side and a family descended from Norwegian immigrants on my mother's side. It was a way to help interlocutors, mostly in the academy, but elsewhere too, understand "what I am"—Latino or not. However, even though "Chicano" is not a term as widely heard as it once was, more and more it serves me as a strategic identification about who I say I am, again often, but not only, for the interpellating academy.

The "Chicano" portion of the designation "medio-Chicano" of course recalls the activist movement among Mexican Americans that began in the 1960s and that, as Gregory Rodriguez explains, dominated the "academic and journalist interpretation of the Mexican American experience" through "the 1970s until the early 1990s" (2007, 221). On the one hand, for me, the "Chicano" in "medio-Chicano" thus serves to register the fact that I resonate with the movement's efforts at constructing a meaningful Latina/o, specifically Mexican American, identity that is concerned with justice for, and the well-being of, Latino/a/Mexican American individuals and communities. On the other hand, the "medio" in the designation serves to register a resistance to the Chicano movement's essentialist notions of race and coherentist identity politics and its creation of a romantic notion of peoplehood.

I would rather want to acknowledge the validity and political usefulness of a provisional closure of an isolatable Mexican American identity like that of *Chicanismo*, which also recognizes its boundaries to be fluid, permeable, and ultimately not able to encompass the history and experience of all Mexican Americans or interpellate equally all Mexican Americans into any such identity. The designation "medio-Chicano" thus also signals an understanding of multiple Mexican American and Latino/a identities, where individuals will, at least in part, be able to resist, in Appiah's terms, any particular script provided them, while again acknowledging a real and recurring political need for constructing more stable and recognizable, if ultimately provisional, Mexican American/Latino/a identities. Similarly, when speaking of my scholarly identity, "medio-Chicano" serves to point to the legroom or hermeneutic and scholarly flexibility I hope to preserve for myself as a biblical scholar in North America.

Concluding Ambiguities

About a decade ago, while chatting with a colleague and a couple of Latino students, I was groping for language to explain "who I was" ethnically speaking. I explained that my mother was of Scandinavian descent and my father's family was Mexican. Upon hearing this, one of the students immediately responded, "Oh, so you are Mexican American." Straightaway my colleague, who does not identify as Latino, remarked (about me), "More American than Mexican." This may certainly be true, but the point is this colleague no doubt had particular, essentialist ideas about what constituted an authentic Latina/o or Mexican American identity. Being only "half Mexican," not speaking very good Spanish, and not being as brown as the students with whom we were conversing indicated to him that I did not quite measure up. Interestingly, however, I gained the impression from the students that the "half Mexican blood" pulsing through my veins was sufficient to link us in a common Latino/a identity—a different conclusion drawn from a related essentialist discourse.

This is simply to say that different people will have different ideas about what it means to be Latino/a and that these notions will be governed by the way the available terms of different discourses of identity are put together. It is also to say that the question, "How did you get to be Latino biblical scholar?" is open to a variety of responses. The account of how I understand myself to (have) be(come) a Latino biblical scholar may not be satisfying to all. Indeed, one might hear the question "How did you get to be a Latino biblical scholar?" then read my narrative and respond hesitantly, "You are, really?" or perhaps incredulously, "You're really not!"

Works Cited

Althusser, Louis. 2008. Ideology and Ideological State Apparatuses (Notes towards an Investigation). Pages 1–60 in *On Ideology*. London: Verso.

Appiah, Kwame Anthony. 1994. Identity, Authenticity, Survival: Multicultural Societies and Social Reproduction. Pages 149–63 in *Multiculturalism: Examining the Politics of Recognition*. Edited by Charles Taylor and Amy Gutmann. Princeton: Princeton University Press.

———. 1996. Race, Culture, Identity: Misunderstood Connections. Pages 30–105 in *Color Conscious: The Political Morality of Race*, by Kwame Anthony Appiah and Amy Gutmann. Princeton: Princeton University Press.

———. 2005. *The Ethics of Identity*. Princeton: Princeton University Press.

Asante, Molefi Kete. A Quick Reading of Rhetorical Jingoism: Anthony Appiah and His Fallacies. Online: http://www.asante.net/articles/11/a-quick-reading-of-rhetorical-jingoism-anthony-appiah-and-his-fallacies/.

Avalos, Hector. 1995. *Illness and Health Care in the Ancient Near East: The Role of the Temple in Greece, Mesopotamia, and Israel*. HSM 54. Atlanta: Scholars Press.

Botta, Alejandro. 2009. *The Aramaic and Egyptian Legal Traditions at Elephantine: An Egyptological Approach*. New York: T&T Clark.

Callahan, Allen Dwight. 2006. *The Talking Book: African Americans and the Bible*. New Haven: Yale University Press.

Cisneros, Sandra. 2003. *Caramelo*. New York: Vintage.

Cohen, Shaye J. D. 1999. *The Beginnings of Jewishness: Boundaries, Varieties, Uncertainties*. Berkeley: University of California Press.

Cuéllar, Gregory Lee. 2008. *Voices of Marginality: Exile and Return in Second Isaiah 40–55 and the Mexican Immigrant Experience*. New York: Lang.

De La Torre, Miguel A., and Edwin David Aponte. 2001. *Introducing Latino/a Theologies*. Maryknoll, N.Y.: Orbis.

De La Torre, Miguel A., and Gastón Espinosa, eds. 2006. *Rethinking Latino(a) Religion and Identity*. Cleveland: Pilgrim.

Eagleton, Terry. 1996. *The Illusions of Postmodernism*. Oxford: Blackwell.

Epstein, Barbara. 1996. Why Poststructuralism Is a Dead End for Progressive Thought. *Socialist Review* 95, no. 2:83–120.

García-Treto, Francisco O. 2009. Exile in the Hebrew Bible: A Postcolonial Look from the Cuban Diaspora. Pages 47–64 in *They Were All Together in One Place? Toward Minority Biblical Criticism*. Edited by Randall C. Bailey, Tat-siong Benny Liew, and Fernando F. Segovia. SemeiaSt 57. Atlanta: Society of Biblical Literature.

González, Justo L. 1996. *Santa Biblia: The Bible through Hispanic Eyes*. Nashville: Abingdon.

González, Michelle A. 2006. Rethinking Latina Feminist Theologian. Pages 176–99 in *Rethinking Latino(a) Religion and Identity*. Edited by Miguel A. De La Torre and Gastón Espinosa. Cleveland: Pilgrim.

Gutiérrez, David G. 1999. Fostering Identities: Mexico's Relation with its Diaspora. *Journal of American History* 86:545–67.

Gutmann, Amy. 1996. Responding to Racial Injustice. Pages 106–78 in *Color Conscious: The Political Morality of Race*, by Kwame Anthony Appiah and Amy Gutmann. Princeton: Princeton University Press.

Halley, Janet E. 2000. "Like Race" Arguments. Pages 40–74 in *What's Left of Theory? New Work on the Politics of Literary Theory*. Edited by Judith Butler, John Guillory, and Kendall Thomas. New York: Routledge.

Johnson, Kevin R. 1999. *How Did You Get to Be Mexican? A White/Brown Man's Search for Identity*. Philadelphia: Temple University Press.

Liew, Tat-siong Benny. 2008. *What Is Asian American Biblical Hermeneutics? Reading the New Testament*. Honolulu: University of Hawaiʻi Press.

Lozada, Francisco, Jr. 2006. Reinventing the Biblical Tradition: An Exploration of Social Location Hermeneutics. Pages 113–40 in *Futuring Our Past: Explorations in the Theology of Tradition*. Edited by Orlando O. Espín and Gary Macy. Maryknoll, N.Y.: Orbis.

Ricoeur, Paul. 1981. *Hermeneutics and the Human Sciences*. Edited and translated by John B. Thompson. Cambridge: Cambridge University Press.

Rivera-Rodriguez, Luis R. 2007. Toward a Diaspora Hermeneutics. Pages 169–89 in *Character Ethics and the Old Testament: Moral Dimensions of Scripture*. Edited by M. Daniel Carroll R. and Jacqueline E. Lapsley. Louisville: Westminster John Knox.

Rodriguez, Gregory. 2007. *Mongrels, Bastards, Orphans, and Vagabonds: Mexican Immigration and the Future of Race in America*. New York: Pantheon.

Ruiz, Jean-Pierre. 2009. "They Could Not Speak the Language of Judah": Rereading Nehemiah 13 between Brooklyn and Jerusalem. Pages 65–78 in *They Were All Together in One Place? Toward Minority Biblical Criticism*. Edited by Randall C. Bailey, Tat-siong Benny Liew, and Fernando F. Segovia. SemeiaSt 57. Atlanta: Society of Biblical Literature.

Sandoval, Timothy J. 2006. *The Discourse of Wealth and Poverty in the Book of Proverbs*. Biblical Interpretation Series 77. Leiden: Brill.

———. 2007. The Strength of Women and Truth: The Tale of the Three Bodyguards and Ezra's Prayer in First Esdras. *JJS* 58:211–27.

———. Forthcoming. Satirical Elements in the Book of Tobit and Hellenistic Jewish Identity.

Sandoval, Timothy J., and Dorothy BEA Akoto. 2010. A Note on Qohelet 10,10b. *ZAW* 122:90–95.

Schneider, Laurel C. 2000. Queer Theory. Pages 206–12 in *Handbook of Postmodern Biblical Interpretation*. Edited by A. K. M. Adam. St. Louis: Chalice.

Segovia, Fernando F. 1995a. Toward a Hermeneutics of the Diaspora: A Hermeneutics of Otherness and Engagement. Pages 57–73 in *Social Location and Biblical Interpretation in the United States*. Vol. 1 of *Reading from This Place*. Edited by Fernando F. Segovia and Mary Ann Tolbert. Minneapolis: Fortress.

———. 1995b. Toward Intercultural Criticism: A Reading Strategy from the Diaspora. Pages 303–30 in *Social Location and Biblical Interpretation in the United States*. Vol. 1 of *Reading from This Place*. Edited by Fernando F. Segovia and Mary Ann Tolbert. Minneapolis: Fortress.

———. 2009. Toward Latino/a American Biblical Criticism: Latin(o/a) ness as Problematic. Pages 193–223 in *They Were All Together in One Place? Toward Minority Biblical Criticism*. Edited by Randall C. Bailey, Tat-siong Benny Liew, and Fernando F. Segovia. SemeiaSt 57. Atlanta: Society of Biblical Literature.

Taylor, Charles. 1994. The Politics of Recognition. Pages 25–73 in *Multiculturalism: Examining the Politics of Recognition*. Edited by Charles Taylor and Amy Gutmann. Princeton: Princeton University Press.

Valentín, Benjamín. 2002. *Mapping Public Theology: Beyond Culture, Identity, and Difference*. Harrisburg, Pa.: Trinity Press International.

———. 2003. *Oye, ¿Y Ahora Qué?* / Say, Now What? Prospective Lines of Development for U.S. Hispanic/Latino/a Theology. Pages 101–18 in *New Horizons in Hispanic/Latino(a) Theology*. Edited by Benjamín Valentín. Cleveland: Pilgrim.

Waters, Mary C. 1990. *Ethnic Options: Choosing Identities in America*. Berkeley: University of California Press.

Wilkins, David B. 1996. Introduction: Race in Context. Pages 3–29 in *Color Conscious: The Political Morality of Race*. Edited by K. Anthony Appiah and Amy Gutmann. Princeton: Princeton University Press.

El Sur También Existe:
A Proposal for Dialogue between Latin American and Latino/a Hermeneutics

Osvaldo D. Vena

With its hard hope
The South also exists.
....
With its veteran faith
The South also exists.
....
Let the whole world know
That the South also exists.
Excerpt from *The South Also Exists* by Mario Benedetti

This famous poem by Uruguayan poet Mario Benedetti is a call to recognize that there is a geopolitical southern hemispheric reality that the North tends to ignore and that needs to be brought to its attention. Much to the chagrin of the North, says Benedetti, the South also exists. I would like to use this image in order to throw some light on the goal of this project, which is to bring together in dialogue Latino/a and Latin American biblical scholars who face the challenge of interpreting the Bible from their particular placements and optics in society and culture. In this study I will raise two theoretical questions. First, to what extent has the Latino/a perspective been influenced by its geopolitical position in the North? Second, how can a hermeneutics from the margins of the empire, from the South, contribute to a refining of the Latino/a way of interpreting the Bible from inside the empire, from the North?

In answering these questions I will be guided in some ways by Raúl Fornet-Betancourt's idea of intercultural philosophy. In *Hacia una filosofía intercultural latinoamericana*, he advocates liberating the philosophical *logos* from any fundamental structure of rationality dictated by the

Western tradition, thus allowing the possibility of a philosophical discourse that is genuinely intercultural rather than monocultural (1994, 33). He also proposes that this philosophical discourse should be interdisciplinary, that is, it should allow for a dialogue, a consultation, among the rationalities of the various disciplines (30). I understand this project to encourage us to do precisely that. Even though we all have been influenced by Iberian culture (Spain and Portugal), our dialogue is still intercultural, for we not only represent different nuances of that original culture but also are placed in different contemporary cultural settings, which give rise to a variety of social locations. I would further contend that one of the variables that affect these social locations is whether we are located in the South or in the North.

As a way of developing these questions I am going to make three basic inquiries that, in my opinion, need to inform any reading process: (1) *Who* am I as a reader/interpreter? (2) *How* do I read, that is, what kinds of influences mediate the reading process and where do they come from? How many of them have been incorporated into a conscious methodology? (3) *Why* do I read the way I do, that is, what is the ultimate purpose or motivation in reading the text in this way?

Context and Social Location: Who Am I as a Reader?

I am very much aware of the polyphony of voices present both in my own cultural upbringing and in my present cultural context. That is why defining my present context for doing biblical exegesis is not easy. A series of realities play an important role, yet none of these realities claims absolute control over my life. I will start with the most obvious, my life as a South American in the United States of America, and then proceed to my life as a professor in a seminary.

Sudamericano Living in the United States

The Challenge of Living between the Adopted Culture and the
Native Culture

Even though I was born and raised in Argentina (hence *sudamericano*[1]), I have lived in the United States for a total of thirty years. Naturally, I

---

1. I take *sudamericano* to be a subset of the term *latinoamericano* (Latin American).

preserve some of my Argentine traditions, ways of thinking, feeling, sensing the world, but these are all intertwined with my adopted culture, the United States. These two cultures coexist, sometimes harmoniously, sometimes at war with each other. Yet, between the cracks of this split, there is good news. This split, this "in-betweenness," to use Fernando Segovia's expression, is pregnant with life. It is painful, but it is also very creative. It is also always in danger of succumbing to the pressures of either the adopted culture or one's own native culture, both of which are contingent and limiting. These are two worlds at war with each other and always competing for supremacy. When one allows one of these two worlds to win out, then the creative state of being split ceases to exist and one concedes to one side or the other. When one concedes to one's own culture, then one cannot function anymore in the adopted culture. When people allow this to happen, they retreat into a ghetto type of life, always in the margins, ignored, lacking real agency. On the other hand, when one concedes to the other side, to the dominant culture, one loses the primary identity given by one's culture and becomes part of the "melting pot" that some think is the United States. All cultural individuality is melted into this giant pot of "being American."[2]

A View from the South

The challenge for me has been how to be a *sudamericano* living in the United States. Notice that I do not say *Latino*, for that is not a name I gave myself. The term *sudamericano* positions me in that part of the Americas that has the South as its primary identity. Fornet-Betancourt talks about the need to historicize the problem of hermeneutics, that is, the theory of understanding, repositioning it in light of contemporary historical processes, especially those that can be detected in the broader frame of the conflict North-South (1994, 19). He argues that the perspective of the South on the world and history needs to be incorporated into the way of reason. This rationality has to be seen not as a foreign element but as a constitutive one, a valid one. This all means that my vision of the world and of history, my way of knowing, informed as it is by my being from

---

2. "American" is being used here in the popular and mistaken understanding of the term as referring to a country, when in reality it refers to a continent.

South America, needs to be highlighted any time I interact with the U.S. dominant culture as well as with the minority cultures represented in it.

As someone from that part of the world, I have been formed socially, politically, emotionally, and spiritually in ways that are similar but also very different to many Latinos living today in the United States. All of this affects my rationality, the way I think, the way I interpret reality. Reality is not only informed but also formed by my being a South American, more specifically an Argentine. This is not, as it were, lenses I wear occasionally, but my eyes, permanently stuck in the sockets of my consciousness. I interact with the culture I live in, but I never quite adopt it, since according to Fornet-Betancourt in the intercultural dialogue any given culture is never a final destination, but a journey (1994, 28).

I used to believe that these formative years were tools for understanding and decoding the new culture in which I was living, but that once this goal was accomplished, once I arrived at the final destination (to use Fornet-Betancourt's metaphor), they had to be discarded. Today, I think differently. These are not just tools. They are who I am, and I cannot discard who I am lest I become a nonentity, a robotlike individual, a two-dimensional person in a three-dimensional world, a cartoon figure that bends to the slightest touch. My culture gives me the depth[3] that allows me to interact with other individuals in society and to journey into intercultural dialogue. Unless I foreground my culture as the basis for any social interaction, I have no depth, no backbone, and no real "form."

As a South American, I bring to the table: a specific history of colonization (Spain) and neocolonization (United States); a specific culture, the mixture of *criollo* and immigrant; and a specific geopolitical orientation: the South (*el Sur*).Therefore, anytime I engage in any kind of interaction, verbal or nonverbal, there is a part of me that speaks and moves with the voice and gestures of the *gaucho* and the *indio* from the pampas, from where I am. There is a part of me that speaks and moves like the humble worker of the city I was born, a son of immigrants like my father, who rides his bicycle to work every day under the intense heat of the siesta, because he does not own, or will ever own, a car. Like the woman who comes from the grocery shop perspiring heavily under her summer dress; or the child who plays with a homemade toy; or the beggar who sits in the downtown

---

3. Fornet-Betancourt says that each culture has a *tronco* (core, trunk) that is proper to it. This core is the first reference I have in any intercultural exchange, because it is a concrete universe of life and thought (1994, 35).

area waiting for a *limosna*; or the public employee who takes a break from his job to eat steak, salad, and a glass of cheap wine in a neighborhood restaurant; or the man who takes the bus to go to work in one of the barrios of Buenos Aires and gets robbed on his way home. I speak and move a little bit like all of them, my body language and speech having been deeply influenced by my cultural experiences and formation.[4]

Reality being a kind of "text,"[5] I approach it with the nuances described above. The biblical text is part of that macroreality, itself a text among thousands of other written, oral, and nonverbal texts. It is necessary, then, that I approach it the same way I approach reality in general, namely, acknowledging who I am, where I come from, what is the primary culture that has given me the epistemological lenses I use to decode the world. This can be a tricky endeavor, for when it comes to the interpretation of written texts in general, and the Bible in particular, the tendency is to equate these lenses with, and limit them to, the training gained in European-oriented institutions—schools, universities, and seminaries. However, the culture that has given me the tools to understand reality is larger than these. It contains also the wisdom of the noneducated people, the smells and sounds of my country, music, costumes, the feelings provoked by relationships, the experiences of happiness and sadness, failures and successes—all of which constitute the map of my psyche, who I am. To think that these are not relevant in the exegetical task has been the delusion of the historical methods, which privileged objective reason and the scientific method over subjectivity, intuition, creativity, and imagination. These are as important in the interpretive task as the methods gained in academic circles. All of them, together, bring something important into the work of reading and teaching the Bible. Therefore, I approach the biblical text similarly to the

---

4. This can be clearly seen by the comment an African American student of mine, Edward Stivers, once made. As I was walking by in the main building of the seminary where I teach, he exclaimed from behind: "Dr. Vena, you walk as if you were born in the *hood!*" What this student noticed was the marginal language of my body movements, something that only another marginal body could detect. Mainline bodies do not see this. They only perceive a different posture but cannot really interpret it.

5. My understanding of reality as text is very similar to that of Marcella Althaus-Reid: "text is not only a written discourse, but … the arts, architecture and social structures of our society work as texts which can be interpreted. The churches and their traditions are like texts in themselves. … Another important text to interpret is the historical one, especially from the perspective of marginalized people" (2004, 17).

way I approach life in the United States: cross-culturally, interculturally, specifically in the way I have described it above.

Resisting the Melting Pot Mentality

I have always tried to resist the melting pot mentality present in some biblical circles, namely, that when it comes to exegesis everyone is supposed to use the same methodology. This was true of my seminary training in the United States, when the historical-critical method functioned as the norm for all interpretation. It was true of my doctoral training in Argentina, where to divert from the semiotic method almost cost me my degree. It is also true sometimes of the present postmodern tendency among postcolonial interpreters. When it comes to methodology, it is very easy to manifest colonial and totalitarian tendencies![6] What I am proposing instead is a dialogue between methodologies, something similar to what Fornet-Betancourt proposes as an intercultural dialogue between philosophies. He says that it is necessary to depose any feeling of any possible philosophical superiority and to recognize that our own tradition—I would say here "exegetical method"—is as finite as any other. It can, therefore, be complemented, enriched, corrected, amplified, and discerned by other traditions (1994, 38). That is why it is so important that I name the social location from where I do the hermeneutical task.

In this study I am saying, then, that apart from—and perhaps more than—Latino,[7] I am South American and that this social location brings to the task of biblical interpretation some specific lenses that are often missed by mainline interpreters who tend to group all Spanish-speaking scholars as Hispanic or Latino/as.

Struggling to be recognized as a South American thinker has drawn criticism not only from the mainline culture but also from people in the

---

6. Fernando Segovia has said that "as a model within cultural studies, postcolonial studies has no choice but to see itself and represent itself as *unus inter pares*, otherwise it could easily turn into an imperial discourse of its own" (1998, 64).

7. I believe this nomenclature is not the choice of people from the other two parts of the Americas but the imposition of the dominant culture, the same as with the term *Hispanic*. In its desire to control and to dominate, the main culture has institutionalized these terms, promoting them to the level of axioms. If one were to ask a person from Puerto Rico how she would prefer to be called, she would say "Boricua" or "Puerto Rican," not "Latina." The same goes for any other country in Central and South America. See Segovia 1995, 62–64.

Latino camp,[8] who think I am betraying their cause by aligning myself with philosophies that are more akin to the European way of thinking, or that I am being different for the sake of just being different. The reality is much more complex than that. The truth is that I tried to think as a "Latino" and it just did not work, simply because in many ways I am not one. I can identify with the Latinos as companions in the struggle for self-identity, and this I certainly do. However, I cannot be forced to act or to think as one. We share cultural characteristics;[9] we share the language, some traditions; we share a common struggle for justice; but we differ in one fundamental thing: proximity to the center of power, namely, the United States. While Latinos in the United States live in the belly of the empire, we in the South are much farther away from the immediate influence of the U.S. culture[10] and its stereotyping of others.[11] Since our everyday life is not so intricately united with that of the United States, we have more time, and less social pressure, to decide how we want to respond to the neocolonial influence of the North. For example, Latin American biblical criticism and theology

---

8. During the question-and-answer period following the delivery of a paper at the 1998 AAR/SBL annual meeting in Orlando, Florida, a Latino Bible colleague mentioned that, whereas he had always identified himself with an specific group of people, namely the Latinos in the United States, I seemed to not be able to do the same.

9. For example, when Harold Recinos speaks of the barrio (1992, 21–37), the visual image that first comes to my mind is a barrio in Buenos Aires, not in New York. Then, adjusting the imagery a bit, I can think of a villa in the outskirts of Buenos Aries as the closest parallel to Recinos's description. Still, the ghettolike nature of these "barrios" is not present in the *villas de emergencia* of my country, true shantytowns comparable to the Brazilian *favelas*. There are ghettolike neighborhoods in Buenos Aires (Jewish, Korean, and others), but they do not present the same social problems as the "barrios" of New York or Los Angeles. Therefore, I have to make a conscious effort to change these images and to replace them with the idea of "barrio" that is meant in his writing.

10. For example, the English influence in the language of Argentina is less prevalent than, say, in Mexico or Puerto Rico. We tend to adopt the language of technology and commerce ("e-mail" for *correo electrónico*; "marketing" for *mercado*) but reject the language of everyday life, such as "puchar" (to push) for *empujar*, "parkear" (to park) for *estacionar*, or "trimear" (to trim) for *podar*.

11. Benedetti's poem, "El sur también existe," points at the need to highlight that there is a region of the Americas that is ignored by the center to such an extent that it amounts many times to nonexistence. The same cannot be said of the Latino/a presence in the United States, especially now that they represent about 14 percent of the total population of the United States (http://www.strictlyspanish.com/white_paper4.htm).

have been less affected by U.S. thinking than Latino theology has.[12] Our distance from the center gives us pause to react to it, not being influenced daily by its demands.

Besides, we have access to other *cosmovisiones* with which we dialogue and with which we form a common front against imperial ideology and theology: Amerindian and Afro American cultures with their particular religions; immigrants from Asia and Africa, who have not been influenced by the U.S. culture (therefore different from what we normally call Asian American, or African American); immigrants from Eastern European countries and Russia; Jews, Palestinians, Arabs, and so forth. All of this makes us behave, many times, as a center with a cultural autonomy that is not present in the groups that make up the Latinos in the United States. South America represents a sort of center in the periphery that relates to the peripheries in the center represented by the United States differently than the way they relate to one another. When South Americans come to live in the United States, their sense of center is lost and its peripheral characteristic takes over, as they are placed on a par with other minorities. Subjected to the stereotyping policies of the empire, the cultures represented by South America are now flattened in the melting pot that classifies them as Hispanics or Latino/as, and so they lose their particular cultural characteristics. The same happens, I would contend, with our way of doing biblical interpretation: it becomes assimilated to Latino/a hermeneutics.

A SEMINARY PROFESSOR, ACCOUNTABLE TO THE ACADEMIC COMMUNITY AND THE CHURCH AT LARGE

Reading Communities

When trying to define one's social location, the idea of a community behind the reader is crucial. The isolated reader does not exist. We all belong to some sort of community. The important thing is to define what community we belong to. Given the fact that I just defined myself as South American more than Latino, naming an academic and/or religious reading community in the United States that would contain me can be a little

---

12. The tendency of U.S. biblical exegetes to disregard semiotic analysis and structuralism and to embrace rather narrative criticism, reader-response, and deconstruction is also seen in Latino/a exegesis, where the kind of textual analysis proposed and practiced by Severino Croatto and many others is practically nonexistent.

tricky. First, let me define what I understand by "reading community."[13] It is a group of people who read the biblical text united by shared goals and a shared understanding of reality based on a similar epistemology or worldview (*cosmovisión*), out of which emerges a similar praxis—in other words, a group of people who share the same or a similar identity. In the United States, that community has been composed of two different groups: (1) the academic community, which in my case is made up of students, scholars, and staff; and (2) the church. These are basically the two main locations for my reading. They are my reading communities. I interpret the Bible with and for them. I write books and articles for, and informed by, them.

Seminary

The seminary, as part of the academic community, has internalized the latter's requirement of scholarly publications in order to merit tenure. As the saying "publish or perish" goes, you do not exist in the academic world unless you are published! The institutions one represents do not get much recognition unless their faculty members are published authors. As a direct consequence of this, thousands of books and essays have flooded the market, creating a surplus of biblical and theological resources, much of which is repetitious and stereotyped, for the same author is supposed to publish his or her ideas in slightly different ways, in different formats, through different media, and for different audiences.

At the same time, curriculum revisions, prompted by mandated policies of institutional assessment on the part of the Association of Theological Schools as well as marketing strategies, have transformed these places of biblical and theological reflection into institutions that follow the laws of the market, competing with one another to attract the best students, the best professors, and the best grants. On the other hand, personalized, on-site teaching, which used to be the primary function of professors and instructors, has taken a secondary role, slowly being replaced by online education and smart classrooms. Theological reflection is thus being replaced by theological information. Used as I was to being part of a South American theological community where what drove the publication of

---

13. This idea is based on, though not identical to, Stanley Fish's notion of interpretive communities, as developed in his book *Is There a Text in This Class? The Authority of Interpretive Communities* (1980).

books and articles, at least in principle, was the needs of the academic and ecclesial communities, and not necessarily the survival of the institutions or the professional success of their members, it has been difficult, to put it mildly, to find a locus from where to read the text.[14] The dislocation that I have experienced in general between research and its impact on praxis has been the major obstacle to my involvement in this community. In my opinion, the academic community does not read the text in the way I will describe later, but it simply subjects it to analysis, deconstruction, and application. As the reader will soon realize, this is not what I mean by "reading."

Church

My experience of the church community has also been marked by disappointment. In general, I have noticed either a marked literalism in the interpretation of Scripture or a liberal, moralistic application of the biblical text to the problems of the day. The idea that the text may be subjected to more than a "face-value" reading or an existential, spiritual reading is practically nonexistent. Sermons upon sermons betray either the fear on the part of preachers to communicate what I am sure they received in their seminary education, or the belief that these methods may harm more than help the church, or simply the lack of adequate preparation due to the many other responsibilities that a minister is supposed to undertake—preaching and teaching being second to finances and church growth concerns. Reading the text in community is relegated to Bible studies or groups of discussion, and many times the materials used do not reflect the latest trends in biblical research; or, if they do, they are studied for the curiosity of knowing something new and exciting, not necessarily to influence the ministry of the church. The ecclesial community continues to play, with some exceptions, its traditional role as an institution that supports the status quo.

The reason for describing in some detail my reading communities is that I believe that it is only in community that one can tackle the task of

---

14. The present project, launched within the Latino/a and Latin American Biblical Interpretation program unit of SBL, and the previous unit on the Bible in Africa, Asia, and Latin America Consultation (BAALAC), constitute perhaps exceptions to the rule, for in these forums I have found a commitment to the contextual nature of hermeneutics and a liberating understanding of praxis.

hermeneutics. Regardless of methodology, we should all have the same goal: a praxis of liberation that arises from a proper understanding of the gospel. Without a clear sense of what this praxis is, it is impossible to engage in the interpretive task of reading the Bible. Unfortunately, what we have very often is too many personal agendas, too much desire for power and self-aggrandizement, which impede the attainment of the common goal of liberation, and, in the case of institutions, a frantic drive to self-preservation. Since we lack common goals, and we do not share a common praxis, our reading of the text appears to be dislocated, incoherent, and, what is worse, irrelevant.

Both the seminary and the church in the United States are my reading communities, and they inform my approach to the text. These two communities send mixed and confusing signals as to what their practice of reading is. The academy reads the text mainly for scientific reasons,[15] the church for spiritual reasons, and these two approaches many times oppose and even contradict each other. In a sense these two ways of reading the text are embodied in my own journey as a scholar, for I too first started reading the Bible looking mainly for spiritual guidance, and only later did I learn to read it through the mediation of the historical and literary methods. When this happened, I felt my theological and religious horizons being stretched and broadened in ways that would include other Christian traditions and religions. This, in turn, helped me to appreciate my own tradition and to reformulate its main affirmations. Concepts such as ecclesiology, evangelism, eschatology, and salvation had to be reevaluated and given new interpretations and practical applications. Here is where J. Severino Croatto, my former mentor and teacher, played an invaluable role. It was his hermeneutics, craftily fleshed out in his books and articles,[16] that provided me with the necessary tools to tackle the job of interpreting the Bible in this new reality I was living now. Of all the insights Severino furnished me with, none has shaped my teaching more than the concept of rereading. This brings us to the second point of my essay.

---

15. Speaking of Western exegesis, Pablo Richard says: "Exegesis normally takes place in closed academies, where the search for power and prestige has been informed by the spirit of competition and the economy of the marketplace" (1995, 275).

16. For a complete bibliography of Croatto's works, see Hansen 2000, 611–38.

Hermeneutics: How Do I Read the Text?

Part of being a South American biblical scholar includes a methodology for reading the text that I received and that I still practice and teach to my students. This method of reading is common to almost all Latin American Bible scholars, made popular by the late J. Severino Croatto in his book *Biblical Hermeneutics* (1987), one of the most influential books in Latin American biblical interpretation, which has shaped a generation of interpreters and continues to do so. Below I will highlight some of the salient aspects of Croatto's hermeneutics. At the same time, I will attempt to make a critique of Latino/a hermeneutics with an eye toward supplementing it with Croatto's theory of reading. Therefore, let me first briefly analyze how I understand Hispanic and Latino/a hermeneutics.

Hispanic and Latino/a Hermeneutics

Even though approaching the biblical text from different perspectives, which depend on the particular cultural setting or the gender of the interpreter, has become almost axiomatic among Hispanic and Latino/a Bible scholars,[17] still, to my knowledge, none of them has proposed a method for reading the biblical text as straightforward and clarifying as that of Croatto. They all agree that the text should be read on its own terms and that, in order to do this, one has to use the tools made available by historical and related methodologies.[18] They also agree on the importance of the reader's context. Reading the biblical text is more a dialogue between text and reader than a scientific, unilateral search for the objective meaning of the text on the part of the reader.[19] Yet no one tells how this could be done. Even though the text is given an important role in the dialogue, the principal focus seems to be on the reader and the reader's social location. One sees this clearly in the approach to biblical interpretation advocated

---

17. Hispanic scholars in the United States have been able to go beyond the historical-critical method and are using increasingly the contribution of postmodern and postcolonial theory in their treatment of the text. See Fernández 2000; Jiménez 1995.

18. One of the most used methods among Hispanic scholars involves the social sciences, especially cultural anthropology. Another is postcolonial theory. Both approaches do not emphasize as much the text as the context of either the biblical audience or the reader (Segovia 1998).

19. See, e.g., González 1996, 14; Jiménez 1997, 70–71; Ruiz 1999, 115–16; Segovia 1995a, 68.

by Ada María Isasi-Díaz and Virgilio Elizondo. According to Fernando Segovia, the former proposes a canon within the canon from the outside, while the latter argues for a canon within the canon from the inside (1994, 168–69). We add to these two a third Hispanic scholar, Justo González, who does not espouse a "canon-within-the-canon" approach but who rather sees the whole Bible as authoritative.

Isasi-Díaz contends that Hispanic women approach the biblical text searching for elements that justify and legitimize their struggle.[20] In this endeavor it is not the biblical text that passes judgment on the praxis of Hispanic women, but rather it is such praxis that passes judgment on the Bible. This is a typical example of a canon-within-the-canon approach, and one that is determined from outside the Bible by a superior canon—a Hispanic, feminist, liberative canon. Thus the Bible remains subordinate to the praxis of Hispanic women (Segovia 1994, 170).

Virgilio Elizondo explores the borderland experience and the reality of the Mexican Americans in the Southwest, which is marked by what he calls *mestizaje* (mixedness), that is, a place of racial and cultural mixing, the product of the Spanish-Indian confrontation and the Anglo-American–Mexican confrontation. This reality is supported by the biblical example of Jesus of Nazareth, who lived and preached in a similar context in Galilee. As a Galilean, Gentiles and Jews alike considered him impure and inferior. As a *mestizo*, then, Jesus embodies God's option for the poor of the world (Segovia 1994, 169). Elizondo then affirms, "It is in their margination from the centers of the various establishments that Mexican-Americans live the Galilean identity today" (1999, 101). *Mestizaje*, then, is seen as a locus from where one does theology and interprets the biblical text, something similar to the "poor" as *locus theologicus* in Latin American liberation theology. This approach represents a canon within the canon from the inside, says Segovia, for Elizondo picks up from the entire Bible the Galilean nature of Jesus of Nazareth as depicted in the Gospels (1994, 168).

Justo González sees the whole Bible as liberating but in a "non-innocent" way. That means that "the liberation of the people of God in the Bible is carried out by the God of liberation and life in spite of the people of God. In other words, God remains fully at work in and through such a non-innocent and concrete history" (Segovia 1994, 171). In order to find this liberation in the pages of the Bible, one has to engage the text in a

---

20. A clear example of this approach is found in her 1995 essay.

dialogue that will respect it in all its foreignness. He says: "I must listen to the text as I would to another, respecting and trying to understand its otherness" (González 1996, 14). Since he is a historian and a theologian, not a biblical scholar, he does not develop a systematic method of reading the text. Rather, even though he uses a variety of exegetical methods, he seems to stress more the relevance of the social location of the community that enters in dialogue with the Bible (Jiménez 1995, 47).

In the examples mentioned above, as also in most of the works of Hispanic exegetes, little is said, for example, about the text, how it was produced, the social location of the first readers, the theological shaping of the individual books in particular and the canon in general.[21] I believe Croatto's hermeneutics provides us with a tool that is missing—or has not been emphasized enough—in Hispanic and Latino hermeneutics. Conversely, and in all fairness, Croatto's theory of reading does not flesh out in detail the reader's social location. His method seems to be more "universal" and therefore capable of being *applied* to many different contexts. It is important then that whoever is using his hermeneutics supply the specific context from which the text is being read. Consequently, the relationship between Hispanic and Latin American hermeneutics should be one of complementarity rather than one of competition.

Latin American Hermeneutics: Croatto's Theory of (Re)Reading

If there is a word that encapsulates Croatto's hermeneutics, that word is *rereading*. Some scholars choose to translate it as "reappropriation," but this expression tends to hide the reading aspect of the process. What does Croatto mean by *rereading*? In the glossary of his book, he defines it as "an interpretative reading of a text 'enlarging' its 'originary meaning'" (1987, 90). We need to unpack this.[22]

---

21. The closest one gets to a theory of reading is in Segovia's description of the otherness of the text. He considers the text as "a literary, rhetorical, and ideological product in its own right: an artistic construction with underlying strategic concerns and goals in the light of its own point of view, its own vision of the world and reality, within a given historical and cultural matrix. As such, a consideration of the text as other should avail itself of any variety of literary and sociocultural methodologies that allow us to bring this multidimensional character of the text to the fore" (1995a, 69).

22. In this section I will depend heavily on Croatto's description of the reading process as outlined in his book (1987, 13–35).

Following traditional structuralist theory, Croatto states that, when a text is produced, three factors contribute to the "closing" of that text's meaning: (1) the *sender*, who selects the signs (words, sentences, codes, literary genres, etc.) to transmit the message; (2) the *receiver*, a concrete interlocutor to whom the message is addressed; and (3) a *context*, a horizon of understanding common to both the sender and the receiver. When a text is read, a distancing takes place in the three factors that had previously contributed to its "closure," producing now an "opening" of its meaning: (1) the original *sender* disappears, for authors "die" in the very act of coding their message; (2) the first *receiver* or interlocutor no longer exists; and (3) the *context*, the horizon of understanding of the original discourse, also disappears.

The result of this new situation is semantic wealth. Since the original author is not present to tell us precisely *the* meaning of his or her written communication, the text is now autonomous, open to new and unprecedented meanings. The appearance of a new receiver removes the text further from its original context and from contact with its author, whose finite horizon is now replaced by a textual infinitude. The account opens up again to a new *polysemy*, one that is not only "potential"[23] but "potentiated," that is, made possible by the network of meanings that constitute a work. This textual openness awaits new addressees, with their own "world," who will produce a plurality of readings, none of which repeats another. The greater the distance, the greater the dimensions acquired by the rereading of a text.

Following Paul Ricoeur's theory of reading, Croatto will say that what makes possible a rereading is the text's *reserva de sentido* (reservoir or surplus of meaning), that is, "the capacity of a text to say more than its author consciously intended" (1987, 90). What generates meaning is not the author's intention, or the text's historical referent, but the text itself, by the very nature of being a text, namely, "as structuration of signifiers and significates that generate meaning" (1987, 27).

---

23. See Brian Blount's idea of "meaning potential" (1995). While Blount seems to say that the meaning potential of a given text is unlocked when it is approached from different cultural settings, Croatto seems to believe that the potential for different meanings is *already implicit in the text* by its very nature of being a text. To this point one has to add the potential of meaning that is present within different contextual realities.

Croatto then goes on to affirm that any reading, of any text,[24] is a production of meaning.[25] The reader does not discover *the* meaning of the text intended by its author, but produces a discourse based on the potentiated text he or she is reading. When one approaches the text utilizing a variety of disciplines such as narrative semiotics, historical-critical methods, psychology, and sociology, a new discourse is produced, a text on a text, thus making clear that a text does not have only one meaning but rather the capacity to produce a plurality of meanings. How does this work? When we interpret a text, we exhaust the reservoir of meaning, the polysemy of the text. We appropriate for ourselves the meaning of the text for that moment and for that context. We make a totalitarian claim on the meaning of the text, which does not leave room for other interpretations. Therefore, every rereading is an appropriation of meaning, and this creates a conflict of interpretations, since each interpreter pretends to exhaust the meaning of a text, leaving nothing to another reading.

Croatto exemplifies this process by using the Suffering Servant motif of Isaiah 53, a text that has been interpreted differently not only in the Septuagint, the New Testament, and the Targum, but also inside the Old Testament proper. This demonstrates that a rereading is not only an *intertextual* phenomenon but also an *intratextual* one. For example, in the Hebrew text of Isa 49:3, the servant is Israel, but in verses 5–6 he is sent *to* Israel. This shows a transfer of meaning to an updated referent in virtue of the needs of the community that is handing down the text. In the Septuagint the collective interpretation predominates. It refers to the persecuted Israel of the Diaspora. In the New Testament the songs are interpreted individually, which helps to read them christologically. Finally, in the Targum of Jonathan (second century C.E.), the collective interpretation of the servant is resumed, as the servant of Isa 49:7 becomes Israel again. "How were so many rereadings of a single text possible unless it was actually open somehow?" Croatto ponders. He then goes on to encourage the reader to reinterpret these texts without being constrained in any way by the existing interpretations of it, since "none of these readings of the Deutero-Isaian text are conditioned by the first reference, a reference that is now lost once

---

24. During the original presentation of this essay, Jorge Pixley, a renowned liberation theology biblical scholar, made the remark that Croatto's theory of reading is helpful for reading any text, not only the Bible.

25. This concept is similar to Segovia's "construction of meaning" yet a bit different (1995b).

and for all. They are conditioned only *by the text itself*, in virtue of its coded literary polysemy" (1987, 28).[26]

One of the most helpful insights in Croatto's hermeneutics, one that is often missed in other hermeneutics, including Hispanic and Latino/a, is that, even though the text is the privileged locus of any rereading, this text has a history; it did not just appear out of the blue. The interpretation of texts presupposes the existence of another process, namely the interpretation of particular events reflected *in* the text. This is especially true in regard to the Bible, where the particular events witnessed by the text are, according to Croatto, "God's wondrous deeds of salvation" (1987, 28). Therefore, a text is born out of an experience that is *interpreted*, and this same text is read later from a concrete experience in life that in turn *interprets* it. A text is, so to speak, sandwiched between two existential moments or historical poles: the moment of its production, which already interprets the event that gave birth to the text; and the moment of its rereading, which recontextualizes and rereads the text for and from a new situation in the life of the community.[27] Thus every new rereading becomes a new "text" that reinterprets the event that gave birth to the text, namely, the contextual situation that prompted its creation in the first place. In this manner, experience or context is always prior to the act of writing or (re)reading.

When the two existential poles of the text coincide—when there is a correspondence of relationships between the originary text and its context and the reread text and its context, which Croatto, following H.-G. Gadamer, calls a "fusion of horizons" (1987, 51)—then we have no longer a case of "intertextuality" but of "intratextuality."[28] The new text constitutes a rereading of the first one, which has become lost in the new web represented by the new text, which is open now to new interpretive possibilities. If this is true of the biblical text, it is also true of the interpretations of the biblical text that are fixed in writing, such as commentaries, Bible studies, monographs, and so forth, all of which betray a particular con-

---

26. "Reference" translates the Spanish *referente*. A better rendition would be "referent."

27. Croatto affirms: "From the hermeneutic viewpoint, text and event or praxis are already mutually conditioned" (1987, 2).

28. Croatto's definition of these two terms is as follows. *Intertextuality* signifies the meaning of one text in the light of others, within the same worldview. *Intratextuality* signifies the meaning of a text in itself, with the text taken as a structured totality (1987, 89).

textual reading of the Bible.[29] They become authoritative and even axiomatic for certain groups of people engaged in a similar praxis of liberation. This is the case of so many readings of the biblical text done from Latin America that utilize reading strategies similar to the one proposed by Croatto. They have become a sort of extracanonical scripture, which claim for themselves an authority that mimics that of the biblical text, because it is born out of a similar process of liberation.

Why is Croatto's hermeneutics important? I believe that his approach provides some helpful and concrete ways of handling the text that enable the reader to engage it with a sense of respect and freedom. Respect, because the reader realizes that there are certain rules that govern the text, that are intrinsic to it, and that need to be acknowledged. Freedom, because the reader is invited to participate in the production of meaning. Not knowing how to treat the text results in anachronistic and ethnocentric readings. Not knowing how to treat my own *context* results in the tyranny of the text over my own life. When the interpreter is aware of his or her own context, which gives him/her a unique perspective, the text renders meanings that were already potentially part of both the text and the interpreter. The hermeneutical potentialities of the text—inherent in its "textual" nature (surplus of meaning)—are matched by the hermeneutical potentialities inherent in the interpreter's "human" nature, that is, his or her social location/s, making the latter as important for the work of interpretation as the former. Both need to be equally acknowledged and emphasized.

It is precisely this kind of theorizing that I do not see as being emphasized enough in Hispanic hermeneutics and that, I am suggesting, needs to be brought into dialogue with it. Croatto's theory of reading as the production of meaning would then have to be balanced by the Hispanic correct emphasis on the reader as one who constructs meaning, and not simply one who extracts it from the text.[30] Without each other these two

---

29. During one of the sessions of the original consultation, the discussion centered on the need to expose the contextual nature of the historical-critical methods and their by-products (books, commentaries, etc.). It was suggested that what we need is not to get rid of the methods altogether but to make sure that they are valued by what they are: contextual expressions, biased tools, not the universal and objective discourse they pretend to be.

30. Segovia asserts: "even when attempting to understand the text as an other to us … we ultimately play a major role in the construction of such otherness" (1995a, 72).

methodologies run the risk of becoming totalitarian in their own claims, for each has a tendency to privilege certain aspects of the reading process, namely, the text (Croatto) or the reader (Segovia and others).

What does it mean, then, when, as a South American, I tell people in the North American academy, both Anglos and Latinos, that *el sur también existe*? How can a South American hermeneutics be brought into dialogue with a North Atlantic but also with a Latino hermeneutics that, in my opinion, has been conditioned methodologically by its proximity to the center?[31] Given that in general Latino hermeneutics has embraced a postmodern outlook, I think that it is important that they recognize the value of a method that is not as intentionally postmodern as theirs but that can be seen still as basically structuralist, that is, *pre*-postmodern. Influenced by Croatto's hermeneutics, but also by all the different methodologies that I have encountered in the U.S. context, including feminist and postcolonial approaches, I position myself in a place somehow between structuralism and poststructuralism, a territory that tries to link these two discrete bodies of knowledge. This hermeneutical in-betweenness has the advantage of being able to accommodate to different situations and audiences and has proven, in my case, to be a creative source for exploring the text's surplus of meaning.

Praxis: What Drives My Reading?

Croatto used to bring his hermeneutical approach to churches by means of workshops and conferences. He taught the laity how to read the Bible and in that sense was able to bridge the two reading communities that I described above, the academy and the church. His feet were rooted in the praxis of the people of God. The dedication of his *Biblical Hermeneutics* is

---

31. Jiménez recognizes that there are similarities between Hispanic and Latin American hermeneutics. He mentions: (a) the interpreter as a new social subject; (b) a reading of Scripture that transcends textual and historical interpretations and addresses issues in people's liberation; and (c) an opposition to oppressive interpretations that are used as instruments of domination. Still, he says, differences abound. One of them is that liberation theology's preference for structuralism has made Latin American theologians more confrontational than Hispanic theologians, who in general tend to emphasize reconciliation more than confrontation (1995, 55–56). I would add that one of the main reasons for this tendency is geopolitical, that is, the fact that Latino/a exegetes write from a location inside the empire, where their need to coexist brings about a certain amount of social and methodological borrowing and conditioning.

proof of this: "Dedicated to all who make their lives a living witness of the word of God, rereading it from the vantage point of their commitment to the dispossessed."

One of the reasons for the different ways in which the academy and the church read the Bible is that the academy uses the text as a window (to discover and analyze the communities behind the text) or as a literary playground (spending countless hours enjoying the pleasure of deconstructing and rearranging the text). Both approaches, however, are reductionistic. They reduce the text either to its prehistory or to its form. The church, on the other hand, uses it as a mirror that reflects the church's contemporary problems. The text is then spiritualized and applied to people's lives. Croatto suggested a third way, that of hermeneutics as the production of meaning. This way of reading the text, or better yet rereading it, is one that allows for the practice of *eisegesis*, where the reader's social location is given an ontological and epistemological value that was lacking in the historical method popularized by the academy or in the devotional readings of the church. The text is also treated with respect, as an "other" that needs to be given its own literary autonomy. Croatto's premise was not so much to actualize the biblical message but to recreate it for a new day. This is what the rereading process I have outlined in this essay is all about and in that sense represents an important contribution to Hispanic and Latino hermeneutics.

I need to say, as a last word, that, in spite of being a South American and Latino scholar, my own rereading of the Bible is done from a praxis of solidarity with the oppressed and marginalized of every culture, race, and religion. I try to do this situated somehow between the academy and the church, trying to bridge these two realities by utilizing a method of reading that can be used, with some modifications, by both.

Conclusion

I have argued in this work that, as a South American scholar living and teaching in the United States, I live a reality that is marked by cultural, methodological, and praxiological in-betweenness. As a concluding remark, I now want to add another layer to that reality, namely, an existential in-betweenness. Using Croatto's ideas developed in this essay, I want to believe that as a "text"[32] I am also sandwiched between two existential

---

32. I borrow this helpful metaphor from Segovia 1995a, 70.

poles: the moment of production, my original social location in South American communities (church, seminary, society at large), which defines who I am; and the moment I live now, my praxis in U.S. society, which recontextualizes me as a person, placing me in new communities (church, seminary, society at large). Thus every new context or social location adds a new layer and in that sense makes me a new "text." Therefore, those who "read" me have to be aware of these two existential poles; otherwise, they will misread me as a Latino, when in reality as a "text" I was produced in South America,[33] but now I am being "read" from my new context in the United States, where I interact intertextually with other "texts" and intratextually with the socializations that left an imprint in my psyche. This process re-creates me as a new "text" that is then read again and again in an unending chain of rereadings.

When it comes to reading the Bible, a similar process takes place. It becomes an intertextual activity (I and the Bible as texts, or the community and its stories and the Bible stories), but also an intratextual activity, as I converse with the layers of interpretations that are piled up inside me, the product of years of being exposed to different hermeneutical theories.[34] So we come to the end of this hermeneutical exercise, which has taken us from a theory of intercultural philosophy to a theory of reading that acknowledges the intercultural dynamics of the reading process expressed both as an intertextual activity, engaging the biblical text and others as texts, and an intratextual activity, the self-reflective awareness of one's own socialization. The purpose has been, all along, to offer these sketchy reflections as

---

33. I mean here my core being, but new layers have and are being added, as I continue to live in the United States. When I go back to my country, a similar rereading of me as a "text" is required of those with whom I interact. The same hermeneutical necessity is placed on me, as I recognize that people's social location has changed during all these years in which I have lived outside my primary culture.

34. My life context, all of it, past and present, enters into a creative dialogue with the text, and produces new meanings. One has to be honest, though, to recognize those cultural and religious influences in one's past and present that have the potential to generate oppressive readings. It is important to be aware of their existence, for they are there, buried in the innermost layers of the psyche, ready to return with a vengeance, if one is not careful. Indeed, in my own experience these influences, especially the ones from my conservative religious upbringing, are the first to come out when I engage in exegetical work, and it is up to me either to resist these "demons" or to let myself be fooled or coerced by them into less liberating readings.

the starting point for a dialogue between Latin American and Hispanic and Latino/a hermeneutics.

WORKS CITED

Althaus-Reid, Marcella. 2004. *From Feminist Theology to Indecent Theology: Readings on Poverty, Sexual Identity and God*. London: SCM.

Blount, Brian K. 1995. *Cultural Interpretation: Reorienting New Testament Criticism*. Minneapolis: Fortress.

Croatto, J. Severino. 1987. *Biblical Hermeneutics: Toward a Theory of Reading as the Production of Meaning*. Translated by Robert R. Barr. Maryknoll, N.Y.: Orbis.

Elizondo, Virgilio. 1999. *Galilean Journey: The Mexican-American Promise*. 1983. Repr., Maryknoll, N.Y.: Orbis.

Fernández, Eduardo C. 2000. *La Cosecha: Harvesting Contemporary United States Hispanic Theology (1972–1998)*. Collegeville, Minn.: Liturgical Press.

Fish, Stanley. 1980. *Is There a Text in This Class? The Authority of Interpretive Communities*. Cambridge: Harvard University Press.

Fornet-Betancourt, Raúl. 1994. *Hacia una filosofía intercultural latinoamericana*. San José, Costa Rica: Editorial Dei.

González, Justo L. 1996. *Santa Biblia: The Bible Through Hispanic Eyes*. Nashville: Abingdon.

Hansen, Guillermo, ed. 2000. *Los caminos inexhauribles de la palabra (Las relecturas creativas en la Biblia y de la Biblia). Homenaje a J. Severino Croatto*. Buenos Aires: Lumen-Isedet.

Isasi-Díaz, Ada María. 1995. By the Rivers of Babylon: Exile as a Way of Life. Pages 149–63 in *Social Location and Interpretation in the United States*. Vol. 1 of *Reading from This Place*. Edited by Fernando F. Segovia and Mary Ann Tolbert. Minneapolis: Fortress.

Jiménez, Pablo A. 1995. In Search of a Hispanic Model of Biblical Interpretation. *JHLT* 3, no. 2:44–64.

———. 1997. The Bible: A Hispanic Perspective. Pages 66–79 in *Teología en Conjunto: A Collaborative Hispanic Protestant Theology*. Edited by José David Rodríguez and Loida I. Martell-Otero. Louisville: Westminster John Knox.

Recinos, Harold J. 1993. *Jesus Weeps: Global Encounters on Our Doorsteps*. Nashville: Abingdon.

Richard, Pablo. 1995. The Hermeneutics of Liberation. A Hermeneutics of the Spirit. Pages 263–80 in *Social Location and Biblical Interpretation in Global Perspective*. Vol. 2 of *Reading from This Place*. Edited by Fernando F. Segovia and Mary Ann Tolbert. Minneapolis: Fortress.

Ruiz, Jean-Pierre. 1999. The Bible and U.S. Hispanic American Theological Discourse. Pages 100–120 in *From the Heart of Our People: Latino/a Explorations in Catholic Systematic Theology*. Edited by Orlando O. Espín and Miguel H. Díaz. Maryknoll, N.Y.: Orbis.

Segovia, Fernando F. 1994. Reading the Bible as Hispanic Americans. Pages 167–73 in vol. 1 of *The New Interpreter's Bible*. Edited by Leander E. Keck. Nashville: Abingdon.

———. 1995a. Toward a Hermeneutic of the Diaspora: A Hermeneutics of Otherness and Engagement. Pages 57–73 in *Social Location and Interpretation in the United States*. Vol. 1 of *Reading from This Place*. Edited by Fernando F. Segovia and Mary Ann Tolbert. Minneapolis: Fortress.

———. 1995b. Cultural Studies and Contemporary Biblical Criticism: Ideological Criticism as Mode of Discourse. Pages 1–17 in *Social Location and Biblical Interpretation in Global Perspective*. Vol. 2 of *Reading from This Place*. Edited by Fernando F. Segovia and Mary Ann Tolbert. Minneapolis: Fortress.

———. 1998. Biblical Criticism and Postcolonial Studies: Toward a Postcolonial Optic. Pages 49–65 in *The Postcolonial Bible*. Edited by R. S. Sugirtharajah. Sheffield: Sheffield Academic Press.

Conclusion

Advancing Latino/a Biblical Criticism:
Visions and Missions for the Future

Fernando F. Segovia

Latino/a biblical criticism has from the beginning raised the question of critical task: the identity and role of the critic. This problematic it has pursued in recurrent fashion through the years, with greater intensity in recent times. Such focalization may be viewed as the result of various intersecting factors, social as well as cultural: the striking rise in population numbers within the country; the widening presence of points of origin from Latin America and the Caribbean; and the growing sophistication in matters of method and theory within the field of studies. With exploding demographics, multiplying backgrounds, and expanding discourses, the question of vision and mission for Latino/a criticism has become ever more pressing, ever more beckoning, and ever more challenging. In taking it up, the present volume stands within a well-established trajectory of inquiry within this critical movement.

In such concentrated preoccupation with method and theory, Latino/a biblical criticism has by no means been unique. To the contrary, it has followed the path of critical approaches in general within the field of studies. Similar developments may be observed throughout: among approaches by other formations of minoritized critics, such as African Americans and Asian Americans; among other angles of inquiry within the paradigm of ideological criticism; and among approaches in other paradigms of interpretation. Indeed, all such reflection stands as a result of an age of introspection in which the field of studies has found itself since the mid-1970s. These forty years have signified a time of swift expansion in repertoire, sustained attention to principles and practices, and expanding interaction in matters of method and theory. To be sure, biblical criticism has not been alone in this regard. It has followed the course of other fields of studies across the academic-scholarly world as a whole, with which it has progressively entered into dialogue as well.

Within such general reflection on method and theory, the problematic of critical task has occupied a central role in Latino/a biblical criticism. In this it has more in common with its counterparts in minoritized criticism, African American and Asian American criticism, than with other critical approaches. No doubt, such a focus constitutes a reflection of and reaction to the dialectical process of minoritization that affects critics from minoritized groups at all levels of being and doing, insofar as identity and role in such formations are always under patrol as well as under challenge by the dominant formation. Indeed, only rarely does one find any sense of contextualization and theorization among the latter ranks, not even with regard to a topic that should form part and parcel of criticism, the identity and role of critics.

Within Latino/a biblical criticism, this intense focus on the critical task as such is well conveyed by the recent series of major proposals regarding the vision and mission of criticism. Taken together, they provide a sharp mapping of the whence, where, and whither—past trajectories, present configurations, envisioned futures—of Latino/a biblical criticism. The result is a sharp sense of diversity among recurrent similarities. The present project is intended as, and constitutes, a further step in such analysis by way of collective endeavor. It brings together a variety of faces and voices from the Latino/a circle of critics—hence members of the minoritized formation of Latino/a Americans in the United States—in the field of studies to address the problematic of what it means to be a Latino/a critic. In issuing such a call, the project further represents an exercise in conscientization, discursive as well as material. It problematizes the critical task from within the axis of relations involving dominant-minority ethnic-racial formations in the field, and thus from within the dialectical process of minoritization.

The results reveal further diversity along persistent similarities. A fundamental similarity should be highlighted from the start. This is the affirmation of the process of minoritization in field and formation alike, which makes its way, in one form or another, through all of the studies. Over and over again, in a solemn incantation of denunciation, one finds a description of Latino/a communities, religious communities, and biblical critics as the object of marginalization, with all the consequences that such relegation to the periphery entails. At the same time, over and over again, in an unflinching recitation of resolve, one also finds a call to resistance, based on the principle of human dignity, with liberation from marginalization in mind—in the field of studies, in the religious-ecclesial realm, and in the social-cultural scene of the nation.

In what follows, I shall examine the present collection of studies in three steps: first, in individual fashion, exposing the dynamics and mechanics at work in each study; second, in collective fashion, approaching the project as a whole in terms of its activation of the rhetorics of minoritized criticism; third, in comparative fashion, looking at major tendencies and directions at work in the collection in the light of such directions and tendencies in the set of major proposals.

Critical Expositions and Reflections

I begin, then, with a detailed analysis of the dynamics and mechanics at work—personal and professional, social and cultural, ecclesial and national—in these reflections on a vision and mission for Latino/a biblical criticism. I do so as an exercise in minoritized criticism in general and Latino/a criticism in particular, paying close attention to the faces and voices of the marginalized by examining various dimensions of each proposal—social-cultural location and agenda, academic-scholarly evaluation and approach, religious-theological ruminations—as appropriate in each case. As such, I have recourse again, as I did in the case of the major proposals, to the rhetorical strategy of interrupting stocktaking (Segovia 2009, 286), with particular emphasis on the tactic of the personal turn.

As minoritized critics, I would argue, we must devote as much time, if not more, to reading ourselves in close and critical fashion as the dominant formation has always done with regard to one another. This does not mean abandoning the goal of critical dialogue with dominant criticism, but it does mean granting more time to the Latino/a minoritized formation as such, given the need to interrupt the process of minoritization at all levels and the resolve to break through the situation of peripheral relegation. This I pursue in alphabetical fashion.

Efrain Agosto—Activating the Pentecostal Impulse

Agosto takes Latino/a criticism as an established and ongoing project, for which he offers reflections on future directions as a "senior" figure within it. The problematic that he raises—not so much as a pressing or controversial issue, but rather as a foundational matter—has to do with context and aim: the religious-theological dimensions of the movement. This problematic he pursues in concrete rather than abstract fashion. What is the relation, he asks, of Latino/a Pentecostal churches, and their way of approaching the Bible, to the exercise of academic criticism? The response is formulated in personal as well as social-cultural terms. From an autobiographical point of view, first of all, Agosto identifies himself as a product of the Pentecostal religious-theological tradition, although no longer a member of it. Then, from an ecclesial point of view, he describes the tradition as emerging out of and surviving in marginalization, both religious and economic. The response is further formulated as a word of tribute to and gratitude for the tradition. Thus it was in his ranks, he explains, that he acquired a profound love for the Bible—reading, teaching, discussing—which ultimately took him to the pursuit of criticism. Further, such love and practices allowed members, such as himself, to be fruitful amid and despite marginalization. The response is thus very much a word of tribute and gratitude to the tradition.

Agosto foregrounds the social-cultural matrix of the Pentecostal Latino/a tradition and its ramifications for criticism. This is a community of poor Latino/as of "the inner city"—the "least of these" of the Gospels—who find themselves in acute disadvantage: on the one hand, barred from access to the "systems and structures" of the dominant society; on the other hand, devoid of resources of their own for the development of professional programs, whether in religious education generally or the training of leaders in particular. At the same time, this is a community that, despite such marginalization, is able to "empower" its members to become strong and effective leaders by way of its own organizational channels. Such a matrix is said to have a twofold impact on a critic emerging from its ranks: first, keen awareness of the crucial role that personal experience plays in interpretation—in line with theoretical developments within the discipline; second, drawing on the Pentecostal experience to establish a dialogue with the text—using such experience as point of entry. In his own case, Agosto observes, such a matrix has led to an ongoing interest in the comparative analysis of community leadership involving the early churches of Paul and the present-day churches of Latino/as.

Agosto similarly highlights the approach to the Bible among Pentecostals and its consequences for criticism. Love for the Bible, profound as it is, is also nuanced, as the Latino/a Pentecostal theological tradition shows, exemplified by such figures as Eldin Villafañe and Samuel Solivan. It certainly includes enormous regard for the "authority, guidance, and literary beauty" of the Bible; it also entails, however, sharp awareness of the "challenges, abuses, and confusion about interpretation" posed by the Bible. Interpretation thus involves a conversation between the biblical text and the Pentecostal experience, in which the Spirit serves as the driving force in a process of transformation, with justice and community in mind. Such a conversation grows out of the periphery, religious-theological as well as social-cultural, and has liberation as its "fundamental agenda." Such liberation extends to the text as well, as the critic sifts through "positive and negative aspects" of the Bible toward the envisioned transformation.

Agosto addresses Latino/a biblical criticism from the outside through the inside. His concern is with the religious-theological dimension of such criticism, specifically in terms of Latino/a Pentecostal communities and interpretive practices. What such background brings to academic criticism is a focus on the role of experience in interpretation, signified by multidimensional oppression and the drive to survive. This focus yields an adoption of liberation as driving objective and a vision of critical dialogue with the Bible with liberation in mind. From such a perspective, then, Agosto outlines from the inside a number of pressing tasks for Latino/a criticism: pursuing a conversation with texts that have a bearing on matters of social importance to Latino/a communities; placing Paul in dialogue with racial-ethnic discourse, especially Latino/a studies; and addressing the issue of a biblical pedagogy for Latino/as that has justice in mind. In all such endeavors, Agosto argues, critics should have a clear agenda in mind: caring, as instructed by Jesus, for "the least of these."

Hector Avalos—Opting against Religionism and for Secularism

The problematic of Latino/a criticism for Avalos has to do with its adoption of a religious-theological agenda, following not only the model of liberation hermeneutics but also the tradition of Western biblical scholarship as a whole. Such a perspective, which he refers to as "religionism," he explains in terms of an attitude toward religion in general and the Bible in particular. It is grounded, first of all, in a high view of religion, affirming it as an "essentially good and valuable phenomenon that should be supported and maintained in human society." It further subscribes to a high view of the Bible, involving an exalted sense of its status and role ("the superiority of the Bible in modern society") and a strategy of selective deployment (bypassing or downplaying "any negative views"). For Avalos, religionism amounts, in effect, to an exercise in apologetics.

Although he himself does not do so, this critique is open to nuancing. For example, the problematic is identified as crucial for "most" Latino/a criticism, and thus not for all. Similarly, it involves the adoption of a particular type of religious-theological perspective, and hence not the entire spectrum. One could argue, therefore, that the critique does not apply to any Latino/a criticism that engages in ideological critique of the Bible and that looks upon religion as a complex and conflicted factor in society and culture. In posing the problematic, Avalos does identify himself as a Latino, more specifically, as a "Mexican American Pentecostal Protestant" in origins. At the same time, however, he rules out altogether any influence of ethnic identity upon his work as a biblical scholar. Such work, he suggests, has been impacted, rather, by two other factors of identity: disability, as a result of a chronic illness, and religion, given his adoption of a "secularist" stance.

Avalos critiques mainstream biblical scholarship for its positive bias toward the biblical texts, despite the claims to neutrality in historical criticism. Two strategies are identified as crucial in this regard: representativism, or foregrounding positive aspects to the detriment of negatives ones; and reinterpretation, or bypassing authorial intent (an historicist principle to which he subscribes) in favor of a different meaning on the part of and for the sake of faith communities. This critique is extended to liberationist hermeneutics as well, for, while challenging mainstream approaches, it ends up imitating its positive orientation and strategies. Such critique is grounded in secularism, which he describes as an "openly atheist" angle of vision whose aim it is to deconstruct such bias and strategies for the purpose of liberating modernity from "the authority of ancient imperialistic and violent texts."

Avalos shows how the biblical texts present a very different picture than the one advanced by religionist approaches in general and liberationist readings in particular. While the texts do show, for example, concern for the poor, a call for love of strangers, and an emphasis on mercy and love, it is imperialism, genocide, and intolerance of other religions that prevail. Further, instead of the prophets as paradigms of liberation, Avalos represents them as follows: opposed to multiculturalism and "any sort of ethnic and religious pluralism"; espousing a reign of peace based on submission or destruction of opponents, not on justice; standing for brutal imperialism, both with regard to other empires and to Yahweh himself, "the ultimate imperialist." It is secularism that brings this out, relativizing the status of the Bible and eschewing any attempt at mitigation.

With regard to Latino/a criticism, Avalos's approach is from the outside and remains outside. It is the outside of a "thorough" secularism that has dispensed with any concept of God and that remains committed to historicism as a way to expose and oppose the agenda of religionism, very much at work in Latino criticism. As a Latino, Avalos argues, he stands with the many Latino/as who hope for liberation of the oppressed. Interestingly, in this regard he does not describe himself as anti-imperialist, for imperialism, he argues, represents an inevitable geopolitical condition. Liberation, rather, is defined as follows: from the Bible, "a thoroughly imperialist text"; from all religious empires, including Christianity; and from the religionist impulse of (most) biblical scholarship, which has served as an agent of the Christian empire. As a Latino critic, consequently, he stands, first, for the rejection of the idea that an ancient text should exercise any authority in the present and, second, for doing away with the authority and privilege bestowed on the Bible at the cost of other ancient texts. As such, his aim is to deconstruct "the religionist and imperialist bibliolatry that lies at the core of [the] profession."

Eric Barreto—Refining the Ethnic Edge in Criticism

For Barreto the problematic of Latino/a criticism lies in the way in which it has appealed to and deployed the concept of ethnic-racial identity in its work. While Latino/a criticism has played a key role in foregrounding issues of identity in the field, it has failed to do so, until recently, in terms of critical dialogue with ethnic-racial studies. Such absence, he argues, has led to a number of problematic stances in its interpretation and appropriation of Christian antiquity, which have, unfortunately, blunted its critical edge. Barreto thus subscribes to the movement with appreciation but also with redirection in mind. He sees his task as a Latino critic as one of steering the project—in line with recent developments in the field as well as within the movement—toward interdisciplinary conversation. His goal in so doing is to regain and sharpen the critical edge it once possessed, drawing on the distinct placement of Latino/as as heirs of two worlds—the United States and Latin America.

Such placement—Latino/as as "living intersections of the cultural, political, imperial, racial, and ethnic forces that have shaped contemporary life"—proves key to his proposal and vision. Barreto posits a dialectical relation at work in the country regarding race and ethnicity. On the one hand, racial-ethnic scholarship across fields has come to view such concepts as constructed, and thus as fluid, shifting, ambiguous. On the other hand, racial-ethnic discourse across society and culture continues to use them as natural, and hence as fixed, unchanging, determinate. Within this discourse, Barreto argues, Latino/as sit uneasily, with much potential for deconstruction and transformation. Theirs is indeed a tenuous position: not only was an official category ("Hispanic") created to account for an expanding demographic presence within the traditional ethnic-racial system of classification, but also this category defies the system, insofar as it represents an ethnic formation with a variety of racial options. Theirs is, therefore, a potentially disruptive position: the designation serves as a sharp signifier of the constructed nature of all such categories, and such ambiguity can be used to undo the reigning discourse on race and ethnicity. Toward this end, moreover, two other dimensions of Latino/a life are mentioned: first, Latino/as embody an enormous variety of experiences, a situation that resists any category; second, Latino/as are the heirs of a different system of ethnic-racial classification in Latin America, an awareness that underlines the constructed nature of all such systems.

For Barreto, Latino/a biblical criticism has made effective use of such privileged placement, but insufficiently so. This he brings across through analysis of the work of two founding figures of the movement, Virgilio Elizondo and Justo González. By using the lens of Latino/a experience, both break through the binomial of race and ethnicity by foregrounding inbetweenness, *mestizaje/mulatez*, in the present and, through the present, in the past. However, by using such a lens without due attention to ethnic-racial theory, both end up reifying the concept of hybridity—affirmation rather than construction, inherent rather than negotiated. Most problematic in this regard is the binomial created in ancient Jewish identity between "ethnically obsessed dogmatic Jews" and "libertine, more ethnically conscious (*mestizo*) Christ-followers." For Barreto, therefore, recourse to ethnic-racial scholarship is of the essence.

Barreto approaches Latino/a criticism from the inside looking out. Theorization grounded in ethnic-racial studies is imperative for Latino/a criticism to assume and wield the critical edge that it should have, in light of the reality and experience of Latino/a life. This edge would involve three fronts. To begin with, the Latino/a critic is to foreground and engage the complexities of ethnic-racial discourse in culture, scholarship, and the Bible. Thus Latino/a criticism should review its understanding of hybridity, revisit its use of this concept in the analysis of antiquity, and pay attention to the intersection of ethnicity-race with the other dimensions of identity. In addition, the Latino/a critic is to undertake a critique of the dominant ethnic-racial discourse in society and culture. This Latino/a criticism should do by questioning the definitions of race and ethnicity and pondering how to hold together the various components of ethnicity as "a dynamic and complex matrix." Lastly, the Latino/a critic is to focus on the consequences of such reevaluation for theology and criticism. Here Latino/a criticism should emphasize the negotiation of ethnicity in the biblical texts and reexamine the notion of Christianity as a movement transcending all difference. In this way Latino/a criticism can contribute directly to the present ongoing rethinking of ethnicity in early Christianity.

Aida Besançon Spenser—Bringing Hope to a Community in Need of Hope

For Besançon Spenser, Latino/a criticism poses no problematic, either materially or discursively, and as such is not analyzed formally or programmatically; it is a movement taken for granted. Its configuration can be discerned from her reading of the Magnificat and the figure of Mary in the Gospel of Luke (1:46–55). Two main components can be identified. First, a Latino/a critic is someone related to the "Latin American" or "Hispanic" community in the United States. Within this relationship, the Latina critic is specifically linked to the situation of Latinas in the community. Second, a Latino/a critic is someone related to the Bible as Scripture, approaching the text in religious-theological fashion, from the perspective of and for the benefit of the Latino/a. Within this relationship, a Latina critic works specifically from the optic and for the betterment of Latinas. Besançon Spencer follows suit in both regards. Her critical option is for the community in general and Latinas in particular—hers is an engaged Latina, hence ethnic and feminist, lens. Her critical approach views the Bible as "authoritative and reliable" and adopts a mimetic reading in which the story of the text conveys the path of history—hers is an explicitly evangelical optic.

Each component merits further exposition. To begin with, the community to which the critic is related is defined in terms of the socialcultural reality of Hispanics as a minority within the country. This is a reality marked by oppression, social as well as cultural, for many: invisibility in everyday life, a lower standard of living, obstacles in education. In this reality Latinas fare worse, both in society at large, where women in general are viewed as having little impact on culture, and in Latino/a

Christian communities, where possibilities for development are minimal. Further, given this sense of a "limited and humbled" community, the critic approaches the biblical texts in search of a message of hope, a message with "social ramifications," for a "people in need." This the Latina critic does with Latinas foremost in mind. Here the message envisioned is twofold: greater acceptance on the part of religious institutions and greater participation on the part of women. Lastly, the model of Latina criticism espoused by Besançon Spenser, in by no means exclusivist fashion, is one governed by a high view of the Bible as the Word of God—the text, as it stands, is revelatory, hence normative and trustworthy. The consequences for her reading of Mary and the Magnificat are evident: Mary's status and role as a woman are foregrounded; further, what the literary character of Mary does and says faithfully reflects what the historical figure of Mary did and said in history.

Thus in Luke 1:46–55, the song of praise uttered by Mary upon her encounter with Elizabeth, Besançon Spenser finds a message of hope for all oppressed and downtrodden, especially women, given the key figure of Mary, as the mother of Jesus, in this regard—hence for Hispanics, and for Latinas in particular. The Magnificat, she argues, represents a "foundational theology" revealed by God to Mary, a lowly and devout woman "steeped in the Old Testament and inspired by God," who breaks into "simple poetry." Its message is one of liberation: God is the savior of the humble (slaves, real or metaphorical; the hungry; the poor) who brings about a reversal of positions in the world, leading to the exaltation of the humble. This is a message present throughout the Old Testament; received and carried out by Jesus, to the point of death as one of the oppressed; and to be appropriated and put into practice, unto death if need be, by all disciples of his, from the earliest followers through the present. Mary, a woman, emerges thereby as a pivotal figure in the history of revelation and for the interpretation of the Bible. For Hispanics, therefore, the Magnificat—and through it the Bible—brings a message of hope with radical social ramifications. It is a hope, however, that is not automatic and irreversible, for it demands ongoing appropriation and praxis on the part of the oppressed themselves.

Besançon Spencer thus comes at Latino/a criticism from both the inside and the outside. From the inside, such criticism finds a point of departure in a view of Hispanics as a minority oppressed and in need of hope, and Latinas as pointedly so. From the outside, such criticism has a point of departure in a view of the Bible—as it stands—as revelation from God. The result is a stance of correspondence along the lines of traditional liberation hermeneutics. On the one hand, the Bible offers, as resumed and revealed by Mary's Magnificat in Luke, a God of liberation and reversal for the downtrodden; on the other hand, such is precisely the message sought by Hispanics, and above all Latinas. Latino/a criticism thus functions as a mediator between the religious-theological realm of the Bible and the social-cultural realm of the community, with liberation in mind—above all for Latinas.

Alejandro Botta—Opting for Liberation from Racial-Economic Oppression

Botta sees Latino/a criticism as a problematic in and of itself. The question is not whether it does exist, for it does, or why it exists, for that too is clear; the question, rather, is whether it should exist at all. The response is dialectical: a trenchant no, from an ideological perspective; a reluctant yes, from a strategic point of view. Botta approaches Latino/a criticism from the optic of an immigrant, "an emigrant worker in the United States." This optic reveals a twofold dimension: on the one hand, he came to the United States as an adult and has been in the country for a relatively short period of time; on the other hand, he has long and profound ties outside the United States—by way of origins, to Argentina and Latin America, and by way of education, to Europe and Israel. Upon arrival, Botta finds himself assigned a new and altogether unknown identity as a "Hispanic" or "Latino." Such classification proves jarring and brings about a twofold reaction: utter rejection, as the product of racializing practices in the country; acceptance under protest, as a racialized framework to be taken on for the sake of liberation.

Both reactions forge a matrix for Latino/a criticism. What Botta finds in the United States is a system of racial classification grounded in the political economy of the country, its economic structures and relations among economic classes. This system needs a class of cheap and unskilled labor, which the dominant "white" class proceeds to label, by way of ideological justification, in racial, "nonwhite" terms. Latino/as are by no means unique in this regard; many other groups have found themselves similarly classified in the past. Consequently, he rejects any racial label, such as Hispanics or Latinos, as an "imposed, forced, and artificial categorization[s]," emerging out of "U.S. racist and discriminatory ideologies of the nineteenth century." Acceptance of such terminology, he argues, will not lead toward transformation of systemic structures and inequalities. What Botta finds in the Latino/a community, both historically and at present, is oppression and discrimination on all sides. Such treatment applies even to skilled workers, such as himself: as a nonwhite minority, he has been duly advised to know and keep his place in the academy. As a result, he accepts the racial label as a way of showing solidarity with the besieged community and with a commitment to work for justice and transformation of the system.

Out of such a dialectic, then, comes his proposal for reading the Bible as a Latino critic. Such reading, Botta explains, is one that he developed during his studies in Argentina in the 1980s and that he inherits from his social-cultural background in his native country. It is historical criticism, not of the traditional variety, but rather what he calls "holistic." It brings to the fore social-cultural factors bypassed in traditional criticism—contextuality, economics, gender. This it does, moreover, both at the level of the texts and at the level of its readers, for it is conscious of how such factors affect the interpretations of texts. It is a type of engaged criticism, certainly, in distinction to the "encaged" criticism of traditional historiography. It is further an approach that he finds in unison with his personal background among the working classes, his enculturation into and analysis of the Latin American scene in terms of social formations and relations, and his disdain of political oppression and corruption—especially when in league with religious authorities and institutions.

Botta constructs Latino/a criticism from both the inside and the outside. From the outside, he brings a transnational lens of oppression and liberation in national and global perspective, forged in the convulsed decades of the 1980s and 1990s in Latin America. From the inside, he exposes a national system of racial-economic oppression affecting Latinos and Latinas. A Latino/a critic, therefore, is someone who reads with a focus on the "dynamic of oppression" and the pivotal role of "the elites/dominant classes in such a dynamic." Such a critic, moreover, is someone who seeks to wrest interpretive authority from elites who bring "bad news to the oppressed." Ultimately, a Latino/a critic is someone who fights any oppression, not just that of the Latino/a community. Indeed, should Latinos become at any point the dominant class, the Latino critic would have to strike against the Latino/a community itself. For the Latino/a critic, Botta concludes, "the metaphorical goddess ... is not white, black, or Hispanic—she is just poor."

Gregory Cuellar—Surfacing the Cultural Archive

Cuellar takes Latino/a biblical criticism for granted. He does not directly address the question of what the modifier *Latino/a* in conjunction with *biblical criticism* signifies, nor is he explicitly intent on joining a discussion on the character and objective of such criticism. Yet both the meaning of the term and the nature of such a critical task are very much present in the study. The problematic for him involves the perception of this criticism within the guild of biblical scholars in the United States. This he describes in terms of marginalization: viewed as a novel phenomenon and classified as an "emerging hermeneutics"—in effect, one of recent vintage and minor significance in the history of biblical tradition in North America. As such, it brings forth a reaction of "intrigue and alterity" on the part of dominant scholarship. The study is thus meant as a response to such representation and evaluation. Against the charge of novelty, Cuellar argues for the existence of a long-established "cultural archive" for Latino/a criticism—a tradition that not only goes back to the beginnings of the colonial enterprise of the Spanish Empire but also precedes the religious-theological production of the colonies of England to the north. It is in the course of this riposte that the question of nomenclature and purpose are entertained.

The study focuses on the origins of the archive, which are traced to the colonial Mexico of the sixteenth century. He outlines three important facets of this context. First, he points to the development of formal theological education for children of the elite indigenous "Other" in the early sixteenth century, a course of studies that included study of the Bible (1536). This project did not last long, brought to an end by the official prohibition of ordination for natives by the state (1555). Second, he calls attention to the widespread trade in and availability of Bibles throughout the sixteenth century, even after prohibition by the Inquisition (1551, 1554), as shown by the records of those brought to trial for possession, beginning in 1571. Among the latter are to be found the sons of indigenous chiefs, early followers of Luther, and "itinerant crypto-Jews," who were considered as the "primary public enemy." Lastly, he analyzes the situation of the crypto-Jews through the person of Luis de Carvajal, who had arrived from Spain in 1581 and was convicted of owning a copy of the Vulgate in 1589. Following the tradition of crypto-Jews, de Carvajal used the Latin Bible as a means to knowledge of Jewish beliefs and practices. Such behavior amounted to an act of subversion within the empire as well as an exercise in hybrid theology within Christianity. From all three facets, therefore, Cuellar finds hybridity and resistance at the heart of this initial moment of the cultural archive.

Such beginnings yield, in turn, the "residual presence" of a colonial encounter that is full of conquest, bloodshed, repression, but also resistance.

This presence, he argues, lies behind the "hybrid dynamism" of contemporary Latino/a criticism. Such criticism also finds itself inscribed by and resistant to the dominant power—a description of its character. Such criticism must become aware of this cultural archive, this historical trajectory and critical hybridity, so that it can respond in appropriate fashion to colonization and empire—a description of its purpose.

Cuellar thus comes at Latino/a criticism from the outside. He engages in a recovery of the cultural archive of Latino/a criticism—portrayed as going back to colonial times and the encounter of the Spanish Empire and its Others in Mexico—in order to provide contemporary critics with a sense of grounding and mission, in the face of marginalization. Such criticism emerges thereby as a present-day example of a long-lasting tradition of interpretation and called upon to advance the trajectory of hybridity and subversion in the face of alterity imposed by a new imperial power, the United States. His is a pointed exercise in conscientization through expansion of historical boundaries and cultural memory. As such, it is an exercise in cultural studies, with a broad view of what constitutes biblical interpretation, and hence the object of criticism. Its aim is clear: launching a discussion regarding the mission of Latino/a criticism today, in the light of its past and in the face of its present.

Rubén Dupertuis—Foregrounding the Latino/a Critic

Dupertuis readily grants the need for a Latino/a hermeneutics, both in principle and in practice: theoretically, insofar as criticism involves the contextualization of the critic, which includes the dimensions of culture and ethnicity; strategically, insofar as such contextualized criticism creates a space for "Latino/a voices within the academy." Just as readily, however, he problematizes the way in which many have conceived such a movement. The perspective, he argues, tends toward essentialism, advancing a homogenizing view of Latino/a identity and context by flattening the diversity of Latino/a identities and contexts. This problematic he develops in dialogue with Latino/a scholars of religion, such as Michelle González and Rudy Busto, who have offered similar critiques of totalizing impulses in Latino/a theological and religious scholarship. Ultimately, however, the problematic is grounded in the variegations of his own life: the various countries of Latin America in which he has lived or to which he is related; the multiple academic and religious contexts in which he has pursued his education, from the beginning; and his extended life in and relation to the

United States, without any sense of marginalization, given his invisibility as a Latino, insofar as he does not "wear" such identity "in [his] skin color, [his] accent, or even in [his] last name."

Such a path—said to be shared by many others in different ways—leads him to argue for a notion of Latino/a identity that is "complex, fluid, and ambiguous." He is not just "American," therefore, for he is Latino, but being "Latino" for him is multidimensional. As such, his focus emerges as individual rather than group-oriented. His interest lies not in Latino/a hermeneutics or criticism in general, but rather in Latino/a critics, as embodiments of such ambiguity, fluidity, and complexity.

Dupertuis thus eschews any description of Latino/a criticism in terms of distinctive features, while critiquing those that have been put forward, whether in subtle fashion, as in the case of Francisco García-Treto's description of a "new, U.S. Hispanic/Latino consciousness (and culture)" beyond the acknowledged diversity, or in broad strokes, as with Pablo Jiménez's synthesis of the "characteristic traits of Latino hermeneutics" based on the work of two Latino theologians. Any such attempt, he argues, while understandable for and applicable to certain segments of the Latino/a formation, ultimately results in the exclusion of others and works against the diversity of the formation. Consequently, it is the critic as individual, above all, that should be examined, and in this regard he is forthcoming.

Dupertuis lays out a trajectory of conscientization in his process of moving from being a critic to being a Latino critic. Its first phase takes place while in he is in graduate studies in the 1990s. While pursuing historicist studies of early Christian texts within their Greco-Roman context, he becomes aware of an emerging problematic in the field: the role of the social location of the critic in interpretation. This is a development that he accepts without question, up to a point. While both the impact of location on criticism and the contextualization of the critic are accepted as a logical extension of the historicist project of contextualization, they are not pursued, given the perception that one had to decide between analysis of the object or of the subject. In a second phase, as a critic in the academy, he discards this dialectical stance as unwarranted, yet the focus on contextualization remains on the past: the construction of identity in antiquity rather than on "the roles that my social location and my identity might play in any of this." A third phase begins with the present study, in which he addresses his own contextualization as a critic, a Latino critic, and the role that such identity might have played in his scholarship thus far.

What he posits is a possible correspondence between his own sense of identity as a Latino, "messy" and "slippery," and the sense of identity conveyed by Acts in any number of ways, especially in terms of the figure of Paul, just as slippery and messy. The implication is that awareness of the former, even at a noncritical stage, may have influenced the perception of the latter. To what extent and how, however, he is not able to say, much less theorize. What he does affirm is that for anyone, such as himself, who is "interested in what happens when cultures combine, bump, and/or clash," or perhaps "predisposed to think of identity as complex, fluid, and ambiguous," Acts proves fertile territory, suffused as it is with references to cultural and ethnic identity. Such a perception, moreover, is one that goes against traditional ways of dealing with such dimensions of identity in Acts, which are bypassed or relativized in favor of a different, "universalist" category of identity, along religious-theological lines, such as "the new/true Israel." Being a Latino critic, therefore, may have allowed for a different take on context and identity in early Christian texts. The stress throughout, it should be noted, is on the subjunctive.

Dupertuis analyzes Latino/a criticism from the inside, questioning any comprehensive vision of it as inherently incomplete and excluding, in the light of his own sense of overflowing context and identity as a Latino and his extension of such a vision of boundless mixture to the contexts and identities of all Latinos and Latinas. His is a call for attention to the individual at the level of interpretation within the acknowledgment of a social-cultural movement. To what end? The conclusion is to the point: it is imperative for Latino/a critics not to limit "how we name our Latino/a experiences" but to allow for "some messiness" in so doing. It is the diversity of the formation that must be preserved at all cost.

Cristina García-Alfonso—Foregrounding Transnational Engagement

García-Alfonso addresses directly, and through the lens of gender, the problematic of the project, which she phrases as follows: What constitutes being a Latina biblical critic? What one does as a critic, she argues, is grounded on who one is as an individual. To respond properly to the question—to describe her status and role as a critic—requires, therefore, coming to terms with her personal identity. This she does in ethnic and national terms. As a first-generation immigrant to the United States, someone who came as an adult and who has not lived in the country long, she describes her identity as twofold. On the one hand, given her present geographical and academic context within the United States, she views herself as a Latina. On the other hand, given her original geographical and social context, she sees herself as Caribbean, and Cuban in particular. Further, she situates herself in the middle, neither fully American nor fully Cuban. At the same time, however, she points to her identity of origins as prevailing in her life, and hence in her status and role as a critic. To be a Latina therefore signifies, first and foremost, to be Cuban, to be shaped by and to be committed to shaping the "present and future of Cuba"—from within the country of adoption and in conversation with Latino/a theological and critical discourses. This pronounced tilt she describes as her "socio-emotional and existential location."

This overriding sense of relation to origins drives her to begin her quest for a hermeneutical optic not in the United States but in Cuba. Toward this end, she undertakes a critical analysis of the Cuban society and culture that she has experienced, both personally at one time and ongoing through her family, as the "text" with which to approach other texts, social or cultural. This reality, she specifies, has as its setting the "special period" that begins with the collapse of the socialist bloc of nations and the end of subsidies in 1989—a time of deprivation and hardship. Out of such a situation of acute scarcity of and daily quest for the bare necessities of life, García-Alfonso surfaces and forges what she calls a hermeneutics of *resolviendo/resolver* or "making do." This optic reveals three related components and concerns: attention to bodily language and interaction—an emphasis on corporeality; a focus on the material struggles faced by women in the midst of conflict—an option for feminism; and attention to the drive for and ethics of making do—an emphasis on survival as a way of life. Such a "text" is interpreted with the help of literature written by Cuban women and studies of coping in extreme situations.

This feminist optic of making do in extreme situations is brought to bear on all texts, including the biblical writings. While she mentions recourse to ideological and postcolonial criticism as well, she does not pursue their integration into this vision. The study applies the optic to the story of Rahab and the conquest of Jericho in Joshua 6. Two features of making do are identified as particularly relevant to this story: the goal of survival as entailing the preservation of life at any cost, no matter what the circumstances or means; and the use of corporeality as including the selling of the body for sex, if the situation so should warrant.

Her reading of Rahab, which pays particular attention to body language and interactions, presents her as a keen example of a woman—a foreigner and a prostitute to boot—who makes do in a situation of extreme urgency, using whatever power she has at her disposal to her own benefit, and survives. As her city, Jericho, is about to be destroyed by the Israelites, and as she and her family are about to lose their lives, Rahab makes a play for survival. She makes a deal with an advance party from the enemy, whereby she lets them live in exchange for her own life and that of her family upon the conquest, whereupon she is to join the Israelites and their God. Moving against her own people, the Canaanites, among whom she stands as an outsider, she opts for another people in the struggle to survive—and does.

For García-Alfonso, therefore, what Rahab does in effect is not unlike what Cubans in general and Cuban women in particular do every single day of their lives. Their lives of survival under duress are reflected, mutatis mutandis, in the lives of survival under duress led by biblical female characters such as Rahab.

García-Alfonso brings a transnational dimension to Latino/a criticism, insofar as she keeps her eyes on the country of origins and remains fully engaged in and committed to its present and future. She derives a vision of and for life, including life in the country of adoption, from it. This vision she uses to approach the biblical texts, where she finds a similar vision at work in the figure of Rahab: a woman determined to make do, in a context of oppression, in order to survive. This vision García-Alfonso ultimately brings to her status and role as a Latina critic: a determination to make do, to exercise power, as a foreigner, "in new places, in other lands," for the sake of survival and life.

Jacqueline Hidalgo—Embracing Ambivalence and Ambiguity

Hidalgo sees the problematic of Latina/o criticism as a reflection of the problematic of Latino/a identity. She describes this identity as living "at the margins of and in between others' identities"—namely, Latin America and the United States. This space of hybridity and marginalization reveals a twofold dimension: it is a world of "otherness," a "no place" or "no home"; at the same time, it is a world that is real, a place and home in its own right. It is a space marked by ambivalence and ambiguity. For Hidalgo, this real world of otherness both constitutes the context of Latino/a criticism and gives shape to its project. This task she describes as follows: first, preserving ambivalence and ambiguity, the "tensions and pluralities of options," throughout its critical practices; second, focusing on identity and its process of negotiation throughout, especially with respect to spaces of otherness. This task she unpacks for herself, as a Latina critic, in personal terms: materially, through critical engagement with her personal life; discursively, through critical encounter with her scholarly life. The two dimensions are brought together through reflection on and critique of parallel efforts to impose boundaries on identity.

From a personal perspective, Hidalgo invokes a key moment in her life: a tense incident having to do with family life and involving her father, her brother, and herself. In the course of a difficult exchange, her father casts the two siblings into a space of otherness, national and ethnic. In contrast to him, born and at home in Costa Rica, he places them nowhere, neither Costa Rican nor United Statesan (idiolect). This dialectical exercise in homing/no-homing—further reinforced by her own sense of no place among Latino/as, given the rarity of Costa Rican immigration—she uses as a fulcrum for reflection on her identity as a Latina. To be Latina, she argues, is to see ambiguity and ambivalence at all times and in all places. It is to see identity as always in flux: within the life of the family; in the category "Latina" itself; in the concept of identity, as encompassing factors other than ethnicity; in viewing identity in terms of complex and conflicted contexts, involving multiple "webs of power" at work. Such an optic is brought to bear on the family incident as well, through a reading in terms of context and power, especially empire. Her father too had lived as a Latino in the United States and had been cast as an Other in both the United States and Costa Rica. Perhaps, then, in coming to terms with identity, in the face of the United States, he was simply reproducing a similar strategy of inclusion and exclusion. To be Latina, therefore, means to foreground how and why "boundaries of identity and (un)belonging get drawn," especially the "markings and maneuverings of marginalized identities."

From a professional perspective, Hidalgo cites a key text in Revelation, a main area of research for her: the warning at the end about neither adding to nor taking away from what is written. A sharp division is made thereby between those who obey and those who do not, allowing the former to remain within the holy city, while casting the latter outside into a space of otherness, outside the religious community. This dialectical exercise in homing/no-homing she employs as pivot for reflection on her role as a Latina critic. To be a Latina critic means, she proposes, to opt for ambiguity and ambivalence at all levels of criticism. It is to see meaning as in constant flux: arguing for diversity of meaning in texts; allowing for a variety of critical approaches in the field; being interdisciplinary in orientation, engaging in dialogue with other fields of studies, such as Latino/a studies and U.S. religious studies; expanding the scope of the field beyond the analysis of the biblical texts, to include, for example, processes of scripturalization, or how Scriptures are used to set up boundaries of identity and (un)belonging. Such an optic is applied to the warning in Revelation, through a reading in terms of context and power, especially an imperial framework. Perhaps, again, the author had experienced a similar process of othering at the hands of other groups and was now resorting, in dealing with identity, in the face of Rome, to a similar strategy of inclusion and exclusion. To be a Latina critic, consequently, means to highlight hybridity in texts, in readers and readings, in the field, with a view of Scriptures as "sites of struggle."

Hidalgo comes to Latino/a criticism from the outside through the inside. For her, it is imperative, for a conceptualization and formulation of Latino/a biblical criticism, to come to terms with Latino/a identity as a marginalized and hybrid space of otherness. Thus the ambivalence and ambiguity that mark Latino/a identity are to be transferred onto and integrated into the role of the critic. This leads to a driving interest in how identity is negotiated throughout: in the texts of antiquity, in the lives of today, and in the way in which the texts of antiquity, as Scriptures, are invoked and deployed in the processes of identity construction today—above all, in spaces of marginalization and hybridity. As a Latina critic, therefore, her objective is to break down dialectical boundaries of identity by exposing the process of construction, by way of context and power, and bringing out the presence of ambivalence and ambiguity.

Francisco Lozada—Respecting Diversity and Pressing for Representation

For Lozada Latino/a biblical criticism is a given, a movement with a trajectory of scholarship, yet one that is by no means complicated, but rather "quite diverse and particular in its approaches, aims, and principles"—and that is the problematic. It is a movement, therefore, that stands in need of closer scrutiny, which he undertakes to provide by way of discursive configuration as well as personal investment. Thus, on the one hand, he offers a sense of the multiple "issues, objectives, and problematics" at work in the movement, not with a final resolution in mind but rather by way of a broad mapping. On the other hand, then, he accounts for his own role as a Latino critic, and hence for his position, within such a mapping by outlining the principles that underlie his own work. Lozada's modus operandi is to examine the three components that make up the designation for the movement, *Latino/a biblical studies*—the modifier *Latino/a*; the modifier *biblical*; and the substantive *studies*. In each case, he brings out the diversity of options available, a state of affairs that increases exponentially by virtue of the interlocking character of the terms within the same description, foregrounding thereby the multiplicity of approaches within the movement as a whole. In each case, he also situates himself within the given spectrum, while the driving principles locate him within the movement as a whole. The result is an expansive mapping of the movement, its practices and possibilities.

With regard to the adjective *Latino/a*, first of all, Lozada explores the meaning of the signifier as such (alongside *Hispanic*) as well as the question of who actually qualifies as a "Latino/a" critic. In both regards the highly convoluted and conflicted nature of the discussion is brought out, encompassing a spectrum ranging from essentialism to constructivism. His own preference tends clearly toward the latter pole. The specific force of the term *Latino/a*, he argues, depends on any number of social and cultural factors, while it is the foregrounding of such varied identities that is of key importance in assuming the title *Latino/a*.

Second, with respect to the adjective *biblical*, Lozada addresses the issue of the status accorded the Bible as well as the models used for invoking and deploying the Bible among Latino/as. By and large, he argues, Latino/a critics do approach the Bible as "sacred," but only insofar as it is used in "making sense of their reality and marginality." Three major strategies are identified in this regard: the correlational (the experience of the people of God in the Bible as a mirror for the experience of Latino/as), the dialogical (searching the text for light regarding issues of importance to the Latino/a community), and the ideological (analyzing the text in terms of issues of power present in the Latino/a community). He favors the ideological option, since any position, he ventures, must be weighed in terms of ramifications "for the community and toward other minoritized communities."

With regard to the noun *studies*, lastly, Lozada outlines the various critical paradigms at work in the field of studies and subscribed to, to one degree or another, by Latino/a critics (historical, cultural, literary, ideological). His own sympathies lie clearly with the ideological optic, especially because it opens two lines of inquiry that he regards as central to Latino/a identity: postcolonialism, given the legacy of imperialism and colonialism, and liberation, given the legacy of marginalization.

Lozada comes to Latino/a criticism from both the outside, with his emphasis on the enormous diversity of identities, and the inside, with his accent on diversity regarding attitudes toward the Bible and use of critical paradigms. He does so, moreover, in noncombative and nonexclusivistic fashion. He discloses his position, to be sure, but without dismissing the others and calling for critical evaluation of all in terms of consequences, lest any become an excluding master narrative. Two principles underlie such a vision of Latino/a criticism. First, a profound respect for Latino/a "identity(ies), contexts, and conditions"—the "dynamic interaction" of "personal and community" identity(ies), Latino/a "community or communities' histories," "sources" emerging from the community, and relevant "social factors." Second, a political commitment to the transformation of the Latino/a community(ies) from marginalization to representation throughout society and culture.

Rubén Muñoz-Larrondo—Opting for Ecclesial Submission and Resistance

Muñoz-Larrondo approaches Latino/a biblical criticism as a movement both well established, forged over the course of several decades, and in need of ongoing attention, with "fashioning and refining" in mind. For him, this latter task should not, and cannot, have a "single vision" in mind. Two factors would render any such undertaking impossible, both having to do with the character of the Latino/a population: first, its sharp and ever-expanding demographic growth, which has yielded an enormous variety of religious traditions and practices; second, its keen and sustained resistance to integration, which has eschewed assimilation into the religious traditions and practices already in the country, Anglo or Latino/a. The vision offered by Muñoz-Larrondo is thus broad in scope. It is a vision formulated within the religious-theological tradition of reading the Scriptures. It emerges specifically out of his own pastoral-critical perspective within a Protestant tradition of church and interpretation. It responds to a fundamental social-cultural problematic identified at work among Latino/a religious communities: a crisis of identity brought about by the reality and experience of the diaspora—a "sense of in-betweenness, of living between the spaces of a borderland." This optic encompasses five key components, or "hermeneutical criteria," all closely interrelated but also with different foci.

Three of the criteria have to do with the way of life in Latino/a religious-ecclesial communities. The first is fundamental, flowing directly as it does from the foundational problematic presented by life in the diaspora. Such communities invariably identify themselves, first and foremost, not as Christians, but by way of their respective national or regional origins. The first criterion calls for primary identification instead as "citizens of the kin-dom," not apart from but according to their respective ecclesial variations. Its aim is to promote an overriding sense of common identity as "believers and members of the people of God," not only within the country as such but also with similar diasporic communities worldwide. Toward this end, Muñoz-Larrondo argues, a process of material as well as spiritual renewal is imperative, giving rise to self-conception as Christians "with a sense of hope, mission, and character." The second and third criteria expand on this identity as Christians. The second foregrounds a sense of solidarity. It calls on all such communities, as the people of God, to view the Christian way of life as communitarian. Such praxis entails the acceptance of the diversity of gifts in their midst and the sharing of such gifts among one another, with special emphasis on "the powerless and the marginal," not only in the country but also throughout the world. The third criterion highlights the authority of the Bible. It calls on all such communities to value the popular expressions of religion among them, in their exercise of the Christian way of life, but to do so always under the lens of the Scriptures. Such a dialogue between the popular and the biblical demands the subjection of the former to the latter, as part of the envisioned process of material and spiritual transformation.

The fourth criterion turns to the reading of the Bible, as a key element of the Christian way of life, among Latino/a religious-ecclesial communities. It calls on all such communities to follow a balanced approach: to read not in isolation from but in tune with the interpretive tradition of the church, as a whole or in its varied ecclesial representations; to oppose in so doing any attempt at "institutionalism," at domination or imposed interpretation from any ecclesial center, local or global. Such a reading presents as its ideal a "voluntary submission" of the communities to "the tradition of the Christian church," but as "subordinates" or "subalterns" who are in possession of freedom of expression and have the right to dissent "from within" the church.

The final criterion takes up the role of Latino/a critics within the framework of the Latino/a religious-ecclesial communities as outlined. This role is delineated as twofold. Before the world of the academy, the critic should follow the theoretical discourse of scholarship; however, before the world of the church, the critic must follow the vernacular language of the people of God. The criterion calls on critics to take part in the process of material and spiritual transformation, for which it is imperative to speak in terms intelligible to the communities.

For Muñoz-Larrondo, therefore, the critic cannot be conceived apart from the communities of Latino/a Christians, and hence from the call to renewal through material liberation from economic exploitation and spiritual liberation through the optic of "a scriptural Savior and biblical practices." This vision for Latino/a hermeneutics is thus profoundly religious-theological in character, yet one that bears at its core a strong libertarian stance in the face of any ecclesial project of domination. For Muñoz-Larrondo, such a mix of voluntary submission and libertarian opposition to religious-ecclesial authorities is well captured by the representation of the Lukan Paul in Acts 21–23: a hybrid product of the Diaspora, facing evaluation and judgment, jealousy and abandonment, by the Christian Jewish authorities in Jerusalem, for the "different nuances" introduced into the message as part of "the expansion of the people of God." Such is the challenge for Latino/a hermeneutics: looking for "new elements" in diasporic expansion.

Ahida Calderón Pilarski—Opting for the Dignity and Empowerment of Latinas

Pilarski takes on directly the driving problematic of the project, doing so explicitly in the key of gender: What does it mean to be a *Latina* critic? Such analysis of ethnicity, she argues, is "most challenging" as well as "most necessary." It is imperative because it goes to the heart of the question of identity, so much so, in effect, that all critics, not just Latinas and Latinos, should undertake it at some point. In other words, for Pilarski this is a task not only for minoritized groups but also for the dominant formations. It is demanding because it calls for a sophisticated process of conscientization. Such a project has two dimensions, which, though applicable to all critics, she describes from her own perspective as a Latina. First of all, the critic becomes thereby an active subject in history—affirming her own humanity as well as that of one's community and ultimately that of all human beings. Moreover, the critic develops thereby a complex stance of critical engagement—analyzing both the biblical texts and the historical trajectories of Latino/a communities. Such a "hermeneutical platform" allows the critic to construct a "transforming ethnic heritage and discourse" that seeks for Latinas and Latinos the same human dignity claimed by the dominant formations.

Such conscientization turns a Latina woman into a Latina intellectual. For a Latina critic, the process demands attention to four dimensions of identity and hence conversation with four corresponding discursive frameworks—ethnicity, gender, hermeneutics, and faith. The first two deal with society and culture in general, while the last two have to do with criticism as such.

With regard to ethnicity and gender, Pilarski has recourse to racial-ethnic studies and feminist studies, respectively, adopting in each case a constructive view of such concepts. In terms of ethnicity, she defines herself as a Latina, insofar as she is a Latin American who has migrated into the country and now belongs to the Latino/a community within it. This formation, however, can be constructed in any number of ways, given the different material and cultural contexts of the Latino/a groups as well as the context of contestation within which the community finds itself. Consequently, it is necessary, first, to examine closely who is doing the constructing and to what ends, and, second, to appropriate any construction critically, taking into consideration both its positive and negative elements, in order to interact with difference properly. Throughout, the goal should be the preservation of human dignity for all. In terms of gender, she portrays herself as a woman in the Latino/a community and hence as someone who experiences a twofold oppression, both as ethnic and as woman. Therefore, one must subscribe to the project of feminist inquiry, with its foregrounding of the status and role of women in society and culture. At the same time, however, one must identify with recent developments within feminism that take into account the concrete realities of women, and hence any number of other factors of identity that intersect with gender—including ethnicity.

With respect to hermeneutics and faith, Pilarski opts for an expansive view of the critical task in biblical studies. In terms of hermeneutics, she calls for critical reflection on the approach to be deployed toward the text as well as for critical attention to both the context of production and the context of reception. As a Latina critic, therefore, she is keenly interested in the interpretive trajectory of the Latino/a community, going all the way back to the arrival of Christianity in the Americas, but especially so on the part of women. Throughout, she adds, attention must be paid to both the positive and the negative elements of such a history of interpretation. In terms of faith, she calls for consideration of the religious-theological reading of the Bible as Scripture. As a Latina critic, she is interested in the reading of faith practiced by Latino/a communities, whereby they see themselves as in continuity with the reading of faith of the Christian communities in the past, especially as carried out by women.

This transformation of a Latina woman into a Latina intellectual Pilarski further explains by way of an ethnic-racial comparative perspective, drawing on the model of Patricia Hill Collins regarding African American women. To be an intellectual means to embody a program of self-conscious struggle on behalf of Latina women, in whatever context one finds oneself. Such a project situates her within the trajectory established by two path-breaking Latina theologians, Ada María Isasi-Díaz and Pilar Aquino. Both emphasized the concrete realities of Latinas as the point of departure for liberative theological reflection and an agenda of empowerment. Given such a program, to be a Latina intellectual also means being a Latina woman, someone similarly grounded in such concrete realities. As a Latina intellectual, her specific mission is clear: active, critical engagement with the Latino/a communities and the biblical texts with an agenda of empowerment in mind, especially for Latinas.

Pilarski defines Latino/a criticism from the inside, though casting it throughout against a multidimensional theoretical canvas and doing so with self-transformation in mind. A Latina biblical critic, if she is to be a Latina intellectual, must proceed as follows: first, she must insert herself and carve out a position within the trajectories of ethnic studies and gender studies; in addition, she must work from within the concrete realities and experiences of Latinas, which include the pivotal role of popular religion and the Bible among them; further, she must place herself within and advance the path of Latina religious and theological intellectuals; and lastly, she must do so for the sake of Latina women, their conscientization and empowerment for liberation. The mission for Latina biblical critics, therefore, is one writ most broadly.

David Arturo Sánchez—Moving toward Maturity and Engagement

The problematic for Sánchez lies in the very existence of Latino/a biblical criticism within the field of biblical studies. Why, he asks, is there a need for such a "unique hermeneutical barrio," for such a movement and such a discussion? This is a problematic with expansive connotations, given the multiplicity of such barrios. It is signified by the emergence of other racial-ethnic critical movements in the field, like African American or Asian American biblical criticism. It is also evident in the academic world at large, given the presence of racial-ethnic units like African American studies, Asian American studies, and Latin American studies. It is further raised by any number of critical currents based on other differential relations of identity, such as women's studies or queer studies.

Why is this phenomenon a problematic? He adduces two reasons. First, it has to do with the fact of division itself, material as well as discursive, a situation that he finds most ironic. To wit, if the individuals who subscribe to such currents and inhabit such spaces all address the same overarching fields and discourses, should they not do so in the same places and in dialogue with one another, reaping thereby the benefits of "intellectual cross-pollination"? Second, beyond division, there is the fact of hierarchy, which creates and underlies such division.

All such entities, whether in biblical studies or in the academy at large, find themselves where they are not because they wish to be there but rather because they have been confined, "exiled," there. Their discrete existence is thus the result of an exercise in power on the part of the dominant critical approaches, which privilege their own methods and theories while marginalizing those of their Others. The struggle beyond such power moves is clear. All these movements have, from different angles, pronounced the dominant approaches as unable to address properly their realities, experiences, and concerns. In response, they have been relegated to the periphery of academic life by a core that cannot but see itself as core, objective and universal. In such marginalization, however, there is life, and plenty of it. Such critical movements are described as "counter-knowledge systems or intellectual resistance movements" in the face of the dominant approaches.

Latino/a biblical criticism thus emerges as the result of this twofold process: othering by the dominant and overcoming otherness. It is this latter dimension that Sánchez sets out to capture in order to address the "objectives and strategies" of Latino/a critics. For such analysis he appeals to two models, one developed in biblical criticism and the other in social psychology, that he sees as mutually reinforcing.

The first is drawn from the work of Vincent Wimbush, who has studied the process of world-making with respect to sacred texts among African Americans. In constructing a new world, upon violent extraction from the old, African Americans undergo three stages of construction: exiting the old, in utter rejection; forming the new, in dialectical relation to the old; and reforming the new, in dialogical relation to the old and itself. The second model is borrowed from work on the development of minority identity by Donald Atkinson, George Morten, and Derald Wing Sue. In dealing with domination, oppressed groups experience a fivefold development: unquestioned conformity to the representation of self and other imposed by the dominant; a rise of dissonance regarding such representations; the beginning of resistance, with increasing immersion in self and rejection of the dominant other; flowering of introspection, leading to unquestioned immersion in self and rejection of dominant; and synergetic consciousness, involving mature critical appreciation of self and other. Both models, Sánchez argues, can be profitably applied to Latino/a biblical criticism, given its similar origins in trauma and its similar oppression through minoritization.

Such theoretical optics yield a vision for the strategies and objectives of Latino/a biblical criticism. In effect, it is imperative to put behind the dominant interpretations that have relegated us to the periphery and to avoid minority interpretations that would keep us immersed in ourselves in the periphery. Now that the movement and the discourse exist—now that resistance and introspection have flourished; now that we have exited the old and formed the new—we must aim, following the dynamism of the models, toward that stage of mature critical analysis regarding both center and ourselves. In so doing, we move toward a revisioning of our field and our own role in it and reengagement with the dominant with confidence.

Sánchez approaches Latino/a criticism from the outside rather than the inside, doing so in broad comparative perspective and with concientization in mind. The comparative perspective is twofold. First, he casts such criticism as one example of a multitude of academic barrios, all grounded in and shaped by relations of power in society and culture, and in the academy. Its emergence and problematic parallel those of many other movements and discussions. Second, he views it in the light of large-scale social-cultural patterns of development at work in processes of minoritization. Its character and potential again match those of other such movements and discussions. From such a space and with such forces in mind, given the terrain already traversed, he points to the mission ahead: the time has come for critical reengagement, incisive and mature, with and within the core.

Timothy Sandoval—Defending Flexibility in Identity and Scholarship

For Sandoval the problematic of Latino/a criticism consists not so much in the fact that it exists but rather in how it has been configured. This is not to say that the movement as such is not problematic, for it is. Indeed, it raises the complex and controverted question of identity in the world of the twenty-first century and does so in several respects: What does it mean to be "Latino/a in America," to be a "biblical scholar," and, together, to be a "Latino/a biblical scholar"? It is to say, rather, that the construal of this identity in its critical trajectory thus far proves far more problematic. Sandoval approaches the question in personal terms, from the standpoint of his own complicated and conflicted identity as a "person of mixed 'race' or mixed descent"—the child of a Mexican American family on the paternal side and a Norwegian American family on the maternal side. For him, therefore, coming to terms with the professional question involves coming to terms with the personal question. Toward this end, he appeals to critical theory: a view of identity as constructed and fluid; the concept of interpellation, or external calls of placement, adapted from the work of Louis Althusser on ideology; and the call for agency in the face of social scripts, borrowed from the work of Kwame Anthony Appiah on identity.

With respect to personal identity, Sandoval unfolds a threefold process of conscientization through the lens of his educational experience: from grammar school to college ("Mexican maybe, but not yet Latino"); through divinity and graduate school ("not becoming Hispanic"); to the world of the professoriate ("Hey, you, Latino biblical scholar!"). The point of departure is identified as a lack of conscious racial-ethnic identity as a child, given no experience of explicit discrimination and the absence of stereotypical physical traits. Upon this frame of mind come repeated racializing-ethnicizing interruptions—"interpellations"—from the outside. In the first phase, these involve reminders of his "Mexican" ancestry. They provoke ongoing internal ruminations and coping strategies, eventually leading to a crisis of self-worth (fear of privileged treatment as a minority) and self-perception (fear of a fraudulent claim to identity). In the second phase, in the course of theological education, a turning point occurs, when, despite efforts to avoid classification as "Hispanic," he finds himself so labeled. This results in a decision to let institutions have their way in defining his identity. In the third phase, these involve invitations to participate in a variety of projects, ecclesial and academic alike, in his role as a "Latino biblical scholar." This gives way to willing acceptance of such calls, which yields, in turn, a twofold resolution: a constructive coming to terms with the long-standing issue of identity and the eventual adoption of "medio-Chicano" as preferred designation.

With regard to professional identity, Sandoval finds Latino/a biblical criticism, as conceptualized and practiced, too confining in character and scope. In this he follows a constructive critique brought by Benjamín Valentín and Michelle González against Latino/a theological studies in general. Such criticism has been overly concerned—and quite understandably so—with matters of culture and identity, leaving aside as a result other pressing concerns of Latino/a life, such as economics. Such criticism, moreover, has placed undue emphasis—again, quite understandably so—on the role of the reader in interpretation, leaving aside as a result other dimensions of criticism, such as analysis of the text. Such practices, he argues, have come to function as a "too tight script," molding an essentialist view of Latino/a criticism and thus tending toward homogenization. Such practices have further confined the Latino/a critic to marginalization within the field. In response, Sandoval calls for "some legroom," allowing individuals more freedom of choice, more agency. This would allow Latino/as of "mixed heritage," along with second- or third-generation Latino/as, to pursue a larger web of social-cultural concerns as well as a broader set of critical interests. The Latino/a critic would thus function in dialogic fashion, involved at times in matters of Latino/a life, broadly conceived, and at times in issues of criticism, broadly envisioned. The Latino/a critic would thus be, as he puts it, "sometimes more biblical and sometimes more Latina/o." Ultimately, such a vision would give rise to a variety of models regarding Latino/a biblical criticism and ongoing critical conversation.

Sandoval engages Latino/a criticism from the inside, seeking to expand its working parameters by bringing to bear upon it the diversity and complexity of Latino/a life, especially in terms of quarters heretofore unaddressed and untheorized, such as his own, a child of mixed heritage. In his case, the adoption of the term *medio-Chicano* conveys a twofold signification. On the one hand, it involves subscribing to the political goals of the Chicano movement, in terms of justice and well-being for "Latino/a/Mexican American individuals and communities." On the other hand, it entails rejection of the ideological goals of the movement regarding identity, which revolved around essentialist notions of peoplehood. The term is thus meant to serve as both a reminder of the multiplicity of "Mexican American and Latino/a identities" and a marker of resistance in the face of any homogenizing Mexican-Hispanic-Latino/a social script. It stands above all for solidarity around issues of dignity and justice for all Latino/as.

Osvaldo Vena—Bringing the Optic of the South

Latino/a criticism stands for Vena as a given reality, a movement that he describes as engaged in a twofold struggle for "self-identity" and "justice," waged in the face of imperial pressure from the United States, by way of stereotyping and marginalization. Vena readily situates himself within such a project, but in nuanced fashion. The problematic lies for him in its tendency—by no means unique to the movement, but rather lurking in all critical approaches—to homogenize its mode of interpretation. This he sees Latino/a criticism doing in terms of identity and optic, due largely to the geopolitical social-cultural framework within which it finds itself in the country. With regard to critical configuration, Vena specifies that as a Latino—a flattening designation that he views as imposed by the dominant culture—he stands as an immigrant, an "in-between" figure, whose context and perspective have to be distinguished within the movement. With regard to critical lenses, Vena adds that as an immigrant Latino—a position that he sees as providing a distancing eye on the dominant culture—he brings a particular hermeneutical angle to bear on the general tenor of Latino/a criticism. His voice may be described, therefore, as in solidarity and resistance at once.

As an immigrant with an in-between identity, Vena portrays himself as follows: someone who has been in the country for many years, and thus a Latino; and someone who was formed, socially and culturally, in South America (Argentina), and hence a *sudamericano*. This latter dimension accounts, he argues, for a particular variation among the many "social locations" to be found among Latino/as: a rootedness "in the South" rather "in the North." Such grounding carries with it a repertoire of social and cultural markings: a "specific history of colonization (Spain) and neocolonization (United States)," a "specific culture," and a "specific geopolitical orientation." It is this last factor that Vena foregrounds, in the light of the first. Such a social location, he argues, has important ramifications. On the one hand, it provides a measure of distantiation from and autonomy vis-à-vis the "neocolonial influence of the North." On the other hand, it allows for dialogue with any number of global visions, similarly located in the South, in the face of "imperial ideology and theology." It is this edge provided by *el sur* that many Latino/as lack, living as they do within the "belly of the empire," subject to its immediate policies and demands. This edge, he argues, must be maintained and exercised in the struggle against stereotyping and domination.

As a *sudamericano* Latino, Vena portrays the envisioned wielding of this edge in Latino/a criticism. Such criticism, he explains, has largely opted, given its context, for a postmodern approach to interpretation, emphasizing the role of the reader in interpretation and thus the agency and context of the reader, especially in terms of a postcolonial perspective. Vena heartily endorses such a turn to the reader, declaring that there is no such thing as an "isolated reader" and that all readers "belong to some sort of community" (a common identity with common goals, common worldview, and common praxis). At the same time, he qualifies it, as he goes on to define himself as reader.

First, he argues for the incorporation of a critical angle provided by the South, which he identifies with the semiotic work of Severino Croatto and which highlights the text in terms of ongoing rereadings and productions of new meanings, thus bringing both a sense of respect for the text and freedom for the reader in the process of interpretation. His aim in so doing is to introduce a balance, a focus on both texts and readers, correcting thereby not only the keen absence of the text in Latino/a hermeneutics but also the sharp absence of the reader in Croatto. Second, he further argues for the integration of a religious-theological angle, also shaped by the South through the work of Croatto, with a vision criticism as responsible to the academy and the church. His goal is to introduce a "praxis of liberation that arises from a proper understanding of the gospel" in the face of an academy bent on scientific analysis and a church given to spiritual guidance, both in the service of the status quo in the United States. Such liberation entails "solidarity with the oppressed and marginalized of every culture, race, and religion." It is such a liberatory rereading of the biblical texts that he sees as central to Latino/a criticism as envisioned from *el sur*.

Vena approaches Latino/a criticism from the inside by way of the outside. He completely endorses its struggle for identity and justice within the imperial framework of the United States as well as its focus on the voices and contexts of readers as a weapon in this regard. Toward this end, he draws, as an immigrant from South America, on critical weapons from the ideological repertoire of *el sur*. The envisioned task of Latino/a criticism is outlined as follows: first, to pursue a balancing focus on the text, its dynamics and mechanics, in a process of rereading for liberation as contextualized and invested readers; second, to adopt a distinctively religious-theological orientation, avoiding the moralism of the church and the scientism of the academy, with a political-ideological optic of liberation. It is a task, therefore, with liberation from oppression at the core.

Paths in the Making: Rhetorical Strategies

In the preceding close reading of these reflections on the task of Latino/a biblical criticism I have endeavored to bring out the dynamics and mechanics at work in each study along personal and professional, social and cultural, ecclesial and national lines. These aspects I have emphasized in varying fashion, depending upon the particular line of inquiry undertaken in each case. At this point, I should like to move toward a greater sense of the collection as a project. Toward this end, I shall approach the various reflections in terms of the four major rhetorical strategies that I have posited as operative in minoritized criticism. These I have identified as follows: interpretive contextualization, border transgressionism, interruptive stocktaking, and discursive cross-fertilization (Segovia 2009). I hasten to add in this regard that the resultant groupings should not be seen as mutually exclusive. Rather, they are constituted according to what I perceive to be the driving strategy in each reflection; most, if not all, reveal a variety of such strategies, as is to be expected.

Interpretive Contextualization: Puncturing Objectivity and Universality

Agosto brings out both the religious-theological and the social-cultural dimensions of criticism. This he does by drawing guidance from the principles of Latino/a Pentecostal reading of the Bible for the exercise of Latino/a criticism. Working out of poverty and marginalization, Pentecostals seek to empower their members through a reading of the Bible in the Spirit, which involves appealing to personal experience in interpretation, critical sifting of the text, and working for liberation and justice. Criticism must retrieve this impulse of Pentecostalism toward the transformation of the Latino/a community.

Muñoz-Larrondo also links the religious-theological and social-cultural aspects of criticism. Confronting a diasporic situation marked by a profound identity crisis, the Latino/a communities must view themselves, first and foremost, as believers, adopting a sense of solidarity for one another and submitting to a view of Scripture as authoritative, though in guarded fashion—in tune with the tradition of the church, but free to resist institutional domination of any sort. This religious-theological mandate is to be retrieved by criticism: the critic must stand as organically related to the community, working, through the Bible, toward its material and spiritual liberation in the diaspora.

Border Trangressionism: Expanding the Area of Studies

Avalos breaks through the established parameters of Latino/a criticism—and, ultimately, the field of studies—by abandoning two main pillars of such criticism: its traditional religious-theological dimension, its embrace of the Bible as Scripture, and its invariable social-cultural dimension, its commitment to the community. While embracing the cause of liberation for the oppressed, he denies any positive role to the Bible or religion in this regard; all religionism is marked as oppression, including a view of the Bible and Christianity as imperialist. A less oppressive vision of the world, therefore, must involve a thorough deconstruction of religion itself. While identifying himself as a Latino, Avalos denies any influence of ethnic identity upon his work, pointing rather to disability and atheism as key in this regard. In Avalos one finds a radical appeal, as a critic, to the tactic of desacralizing the biblical texts, involving a call to utter honesty regarding religious-theological beliefs and assumptions. Such a call is accompanied by an appeal to contextual enlightenment as a Latino secularist.

Barreto focuses on the theoretical-methodological dimension of criticism in the light of and for the sake of the social-cultural dimension. Latino/as find themselves as a hybrid category within the established racial-ethnic discourse of the nation and should use this category to unsettle the prevailing dialectical framework. This should be done not by reifying the category of hybridity but rather by exploding it, drawing on their own diversity as a formation and mindful of a very different racial-ethnic framework in Latin America. Toward this end, the Latino/a critic must enter into dialogue with racial-ethnic studies, with its emphasis on construction of and ambiguity in categories, thus activating the tactic of heightening the discourse. Such a deconstructive task is to be carried out in the field of studies as well as in U.S. society and culture.

Botta pays close attention to the theoretical-methodological dimension of criticism in the light and for the sake of the social-cultural dimension. The situation of the Latino/a communities is described as one of oppression and discrimination, the result of an economic system based on differential formations and relations of power. Such a system engenders an ideology of racialization whereby the formations in question are characterized by racial and ethnic labels, such as "Latino/as." The Latino/a critic takes on such a designation only as a strategic move, for the sake of solidarity with the community. The critic further adopts a type of historical criticism—derived from the Latin America of the 1970s—that analyzes power, including economics. In appealing to the tactic of heightening the discourse, the critic works toward transformation and justice for the oppressed racial-economic classes, above all the Latino/a communities.

Sánchez's concern lies strictly with the theoretical-methodological dimension of criticism. Having been confined to the periphery by dominant approaches and having flourished in such marginalization, the task of the Latino/a critic ahead is to overcome such otherness by engaging in critical revisioning of both the minoritizing center, the core approaches, and the minoritized movement, the resistance movement. What Sanchez proposes, therefore, is a variation on the tactic of heightening the discourse by breaking down the center-margin binomial.

Interruptive Stocktaking: Problematizing Criticism

Cuellar centers on the social-cultural dimension of criticism. In the face of marginalization within the academic-scholarly world, it is imperative for Latino/a criticism to view itself as but a moment in a long-standing and ever-developing cultural archive of biblical reading, one that reaches back to the beginning of the colonial period and that is very much worth recalling and recovering. Through this appeal to the tactic of taking the cultural turn, the Latino/a critic moves directly against marginalization by placing such work within the expansive trajectory of the Latino/a community in the country. In so doing, the critic further shows how this trajectory has involved and resisted similar dynamics throughout: just as hybridity and resistance to empire (Spain) prevailed then, so must resistance to empire (United States) and hybridity be embraced now.

Dupertuis uses the social-cultural dimension of criticism to shape the theoretical-methodological side. Toward this end, he turns to taking the personal turn as tactic, showing how he comes to Latino/a criticism as the result of a threefold process of conscientization as a critic: first, a historicism that, while realizing the need for interpretive contextualization, views it as in binomial opposition to textual contextualization; second, a historicism that discards this sense of opposition altogether but fails to pursue interpretive contextualization; third, a stance that examines interpretive contextualization and its ramifications for textual contextualization. In so doing, he moves against the traditional essentialism of Latino/a criticism. He foregrounds his own complex and fluid identity and context as a Latino, arguing for similar attention to complexity and fluidity on the part of all other critics. This individualist approach the Latino/a critic brings to bear, in turn, on textual contextualization, avoiding essentialism and emphasizing diversity in Christian antiquity as well.

Hidalgo draws on the social-cultural dimension of criticism to inform and direct the theological-methodological dimension. This she does through the tactic of taking the personal turn. Latino/a identity lies at the margins of other identities. This is a space marked by hybridity, ambivalence, flux at all levels, and engaged in negotiation of boundaries, involving belonging and nonbelonging, at all times. This individualist-collectivist sense of identity the Latina critic is to apply to all components of criticism, foregrounding the problematic of identity construction and bringing out diversity of options throughout.

Lozada's focus remains on the theoretical-methodological dimension of criticism, without losing sight of the social-cultural angle in the process. The intent is to bring out and harp on the diversity at work at all levels of Latino/a biblical criticism—the identity of the critic, the conception of Scripture, the mode of inquiry. The Latino/a critic is to respect and embrace such variety. At the same time, the critic is to take a position, and here Lozada opts, respectively, for a view of identity as constructed, a critique of Scripture, and the appropriation of ideological approaches. The tactic in question here calls for a new category within this strategy, along the lines of taking the discursive turn, that is, examining the Latino/a critical trajectory as such—not in personal, cultural, or global terms. In so doing, the Latino/a critic should remain mindful of the Latino/a community, paying respect for the enormous variety of identities and seeking transformation in the light of sustained colonialism and marginalization.

Sandoval has recourse to the social-cultural dimension of criticism to inform the theoretical-methodological dimension. This he does by way of the tactic of taking the personal turn, foregrounding complexity and ambiguity in his own identity and context as a person of mixed descent. He reveals how he comes to this stance as a result of conscientization as a Latino: from total absence of ethnic identity as Latino; through recurrent reminders from the outside regarding his Latino provenance (Mexican); to acceptance of such categorization and choice of "medio-Chicano" as an appropriate ethnic marker. This individualist approach yields an expansive view of the Latino/a critic, emphasizing variety with respect to critical pursuits as well as ethnic interests. Such an approach also calls for commitment to the goals of dignity and justice for all Latino/as as part of the critical task.

Vena calls upon the social-dimension of criticism to expand the theoretical-methodological angle. Latino/a criticism has developed in reaction to the stereotyping and marginalization encountered within the imperial framework of the United States, waging a struggle for identity and justice. Such a move, an understandable and noble endeavor in its own right, has yielded a stereotyping of critical identity and approach alike. With recourse to the tactics of the personal and the global turn, Vena foregrounds his identity as an immigrant from the South and the critical optic that he bears from the South, both of which can make a decided contribution to Latino/a criticism. Such a Latino/a critic can introduce a measure of distantiation from the North, allowing for dialogue with visions from the South. Such a critic can also bring, through a semiotic approach, a balancing emphasis on texts, in addition to readers, and an insistence on a religious-theological reading of the Bible. Such expansion of Latino/a criticism is advanced with the aim of further sharpening the struggle for liberation in the North itself.

Discursive Cross-Fertilization: Taking the Interdisciplinary Turn

The most important contribution of this collection is signified by the participation of Latina critics. While still quite regrettably a minority in the list of contributors, four in all, such presence breaks what can only be described as a deafening silence and an intolerable absence. Three critics foreground the Latina voice expressly (Alfonso-García, Besançon Spenser, Pilarski), while one (Hidalgo) does so indirectly. Among the former, the discourse of feminist studies is brought thereby into dialogue with Latino/a criticism in various ways.

Pilarski highlights the figure of the Latina critic and the role of Latinas within Latino/a communities in all dimensions of criticism. The social-cultural angle demands attention to the complex and contested character of Latino/a communities alongside a commitment to dignity for all—with Latinas particularly in mind. From a theoretical-methodological perspective, the call is for analysis of production, method, and reception—above all, the trajectory of reception in Latino/a communities, especially by women. The religious-theological angle requires attention to the faith reading of the Latino/a communities, particularly that of Latinas. Toward this end, the Latina critic must function as a Latina intellectual, in critical dialogue with concrete realities, feminist analysis, and interpretive tradition—all for the sake of liberation and empowerment, with Latinas foremost in mind.

Besançon Spenser emphasizes the social-cultural and religious-theological role of criticism, with a focus on women. The Latina critic is related to the reality of Latino/a communities, marked by oppression, and to Latina women in particular, who fare worse in every respect, even within the Christian communities. The Latina critic addresses this situation by appealing to Scripture, the normative Word of God, and its message of hope and liberation for all the oppressed, doing so with Latina women particularly in mind.

García-Alfonso foregrounds the social-cultural dimension of criticism. She turns to the role of women in her country of origins, Cuba, during a specific and ongoing historical period to fashion a hermeneutical tool with a twofold purpose in mind: to analyze the biblical texts that feature women as protagonists and to carve out a role for women as Latinas in her country of adoption. This strategy of taking the cultural turn leads to a twofold vision of survival at all costs in times of travail, including exile, and commitment to transformation, nationally as a Latina as well as transnationally as a Cuban. Toward this end, the biblical texts lend support for the struggles of women.

Critical Mapping for the Future: Ongoing Trajectory

The overview of the reflections as components of a collective project, following the major rhetorical strategies posited for minoritized criticism, shows significant work along all four fronts. Such expansive range of activity is a sign of a critical movement in full development. Within such breadth, two tendencies are worth noting in particular. One is the concern with problematizing criticism, pursued by six critics as a main strategy, which shows pointed preoccupation with matters of method and theory. The other is the recourse to taking the interdisciplinary turn, undertaken by three critics as a main strategy, which reveals the much-needed integration of feminist studies as a discursive partner in a critical movement that has remained predominantly male.

By way of conclusion, I should like to compare the major tendencies or directions exhibited by this collection, the similarities and differences, with those noted in the series of major proposals. This I shall do by invoking the categories deployed in mapping the Latino/a critical trajectory as set out by the major proposals. These involve the religious-theological, theoretical-methodological, and social-cultural dimensions and implications of such proposals. This comparison, I should add, is undertaken in general rather than detailed fashion, given the large and rich amount of material involved. My aim thus is to identify the main tendencies at work in the studies rather than to bring out their multiple interweavings. Such work must remain a task, and desideratum for the future, both for me and for others.

Critical Stance and Mission: Religious-Theological Dimension

In this first category of analysis, a distinct direction is discernible. The set of major proposals were all explicitly rooted in the religious-ecclesial tradition of Christianity. They focused intently on the Latino/a religious communities and openly embraced a religious-theological reading of the Bible, with a view of the texts as Scripture for the communities. This dimension emerges as much reduced in this collection of studies. This is not to say that it is altogether discarded or called into question; it is to say that such a reading is not foregrounded as much.

Only five studies explicitly pursue such an approach, although one does so by way of radical opposition, sharply calling for its elimination. Among those who affirm it, two critics, Besançon Spencer and Muñoz-Larrondo, adopt a heightened view of the Bible as the Word of God, while the other two, Agosto and Pilarski, regard it as a constitutive but problematic component of the Christian tradition. While the former call for critical application of Scripture to the communities, the latter argue for critical engagement with Scripture on the part of the communities. On the other hand, Avalos argues for thoroughgoing secularism and atheism, characterizing any type of religious-theological reading as unliberating and hence detrimental to the communities, insofar as any such reading espouses a thoroughly outdated vision of the world and overlooks the thoroughly oppressive character of the biblical texts.

Critical Stance and Mission: Theoretical-Methodological Dimension

A number of noteworthy tendencies are evident in this second category. The series of major proposals all advanced a way of reading the Bible, although not all expanded on its underlying mechanics or interpretive framework. While some regarded the text as dominant, with a view of readers as active and engaged receivers, others approached the reader as dominant, with a view of texts as indeterminate and potential sources. All further used the Latino/a religious communities as point of entry. This dimension I would describe as much enhanced in this collection.

A majority of the studies, nine in all, take up in direct and substantial fashion either the mechanics or the framework, or both, for the way of reading envisioned. All subscribe as well, in my opinion, to a view of meaning as constructive, some in more explicit or pronounced fashion than others. At the same time, the goals behind such concentration on method and theory exhibit a wide range: informed attention to race and ethnicity (Barreto); integration of the problematic of power, especially economics (Botta); allowing for openness and ambiguity (Dupertuis, Hidalgo, Lozada, Sandoval); comprehensive attention to method as well as production and reception (Pilarski); critical engagement with core discourses (Sánchez); and integration of a perspective from the South, in particular semiotics (Vena). In all cases the particular aims in question flow from the respective social-cultural experience as Latino/as.

Critical Stance and Mission: Social-Cultural Dimension

In this third category of analysis, a clear direction may be detected as well. The set of major proposals all conceived of criticism as both grounded in community and undertaken for the sake of community. Such linkage ranged from the expansive to the circumscribed. This dimension of criticism I would describe as just as vigorous in the collection, and in some respects much enhanced as well.

All studies, in one way or another, adopt such a position—some extensively so, others in more limited measure; some in decidedly personal fashion, others in much general terms. Two critics harp on this dimension, opening new paths for development: marshaling the cultural archive of interpretation (Cuellar) and embracing a transnational commitment (García-Alfonso). Above all, one must also mention in this regard the novel accent on gender, on the lives and practices of Latinas, introduced by Latina critics.

A Concluding Comment

The contrast in similarities and differences between this volume and the set of major proposals is thus noteworthy. The result is greater diversity throughout. First, the collection preserves the religious-theological dimension, following the basic divisions observed in the set of proposals. At the same time, it favors the other dimensions of criticism, while including an argument for the elimination of this particular dimension altogether.

Second, the collection maintains the theoretical-methodological dimension, granting, on the whole, a greater degree of agency to the reader in interpretation. In so doing, it displays a broad range of objectives. Finally, the collection continues the social-cultural dimension, following the basic tenets of the set of proposals. At the same time, it introduces a number of new and significant lines of development in the process. The result is an even more expansive critical mapping for the future of the movement.

As a final observation, I return to a point made in the introduction regarding a fundamental similarity to be noted in the collection: a keen self-awareness regarding the process of minoritization, encompassing both an overriding sense of marginalization and a driving determination of opposition. This vision of Latino/a criticism yields, once again, a vision of the critic as a public figure, not only within the Latino/a community but also beyond it as well—in the religious-ecclesial realm, the academic-scholarly field of studies, and the social-cultural world at large. The influence of liberation on Latino/a critics thus remains unmistakable, yet totally understandable, given the perceived and named ongoing dialectics of minoritization within the country, the academy, and the church. This, however, is a liberation of many, and ever more hues, going in many directions and with many hopes and promises. It is a future that augurs well.

Work Cited

Segovia, Fernando F. 2009. Poetics of Minority Biblical Criticism: Identification and Theorization. Pages 279–311 in *Prejudice and Christian Beginnings: Investigating Race, Gender, and Ethnicity in Early Christian Studies*. Edited by Laura Nasrallah and Elisabeth Schüssler Fiorenza. Minneapolis: Fortress.

Latino/a Biblical Interpretation: A Question of Being and/or Practice?

Francisco Lozada Jr.

This collection of essays on the question of what makes Latino/a biblical interpretation "Latino/a" raises a central and intriguing issue for critics and readers alike: Is identity a matter of being and/or practice? Is the "Latino/a-ness" of an interpretation defined by the personal identity (howsoever defined) of the interpreter? Or is it a matter of how Latino/a biblical interpretation is practiced—that is, are there certain principles, sources, methods (reading strategies), or aims that make some biblical interpretations Latino/a and others not? In this concluding reflection it is not my intention to define Latino/a biblical interpretation in a rigid way, but rather to argue that Latino/a biblical interpretation is a process of becoming, as reflected in this collection of essays. Such a position allows for Latino/a biblical interpretation to include more ways of being (identities) and doing (practices) and suggests a sense of inclusion rather than exclusion. A brief comment on the issue of intersectionality and Latino/a biblical interpretation is introduced as one possible way to move forward.

Factor of Identity

Does one have to be Latino/a to practice Latino/a biblical criticism? This is a question, as I see it, that is centered on whether Latino/a(ness) is assumed to be an essential or a nonessential element (or both) of Latino/a biblical interpretation. Although this question is not directly addressed in the essays, it is surely becoming an important factor and even a guiding principle in the field. However, I would like to move the conversation away from the dichotomous logic of an either/or and toward a both/and. That is, as some of the authors have alluded to, through the foregrounding of their identities, Latino/a identity is not simply fixed but rather both fixed and fluid.

In other words, there is something fixed that identifies one as Latino/a, principally by race/ethnicity (i.e., biologically or genetically connected), a shared language (i.e., Spanish), or a geographical cultural heritage (i.e., cultural home in Latin America). Yet there is also something fluid that identifies one as Latino/a by way of, for example, a shared commitment, experience, or acquired language. The fixity of Latino/a identity varies, but it is often linked to some notion of innateness (full or mixed ethnic/racial identities, birthplace of origins, or language). The fluidity of Latino/a identity may also vary, but it is linked to some notion of purpose (commitment to the Latino/a community, being in a committed relationship with a Latino/a, or agreeing with Latino/a political causes). The interplay of the factors of fixity and fluidity constituting the Latino/a identity is a negotiation. At times, it is not even a negotiation. A fixed or fluid identity is thrown upon one whether one likes it or not. My point here is that both ends of the spectrum (fixity/fluidity) challenge each other and, at the same time, are part of the processual development of Latino/a identity.

This question of what constitutes Latino/a identity has become increasingly important, given the rise of immigration from Latin America to the United States, the developing second- and third-generation Latino/as identifying themselves (or not) as Latino/as, and the growing number of Latino/as of mixed ethnic/racial backgrounds or of nonheterosexual families. The question of identity is particularly important for this project, because it raises another, deeper question—What brings these essays together under the construct *Latino/a*? Is it a sense of commonality or shared identity? Is it a set of shared beliefs and commitments? Is it because all the authors have been identified (by themselves or others) as Latino/a? Or is it because all of the authors share some common political purpose, as some other communities have done in the past (e.g., feminists)? Said another way, is there an underlying sense of oneness that links all of the essays in this volume?

What seems to be certain is that the majority of these essays have at their core a sense of mutuality or commonality for the sake of the good of the Latino/a community. This type of common identity, both fixed and fluid, engenders a sense of community (a safe place to explore) that supports each contributor's identity, but also leaves space for disagreements. Far from being dangerous or destructive, this enables Latino/as to further develop and advance their ideas and conceptualizations in particular, and ultimately the entire field of Latino/a biblical scholarship as well as biblical interpretation in general. Is this shared sense of commitment toward the Latino/a community another possible guiding principle of the field? In my assessment, all of the essays in this volume indicate that it may be.

The question of identity, therefore, is surely a much broader question than simply along fixed lines of identification. The question must extend to issues of purpose and commitment as well. This makes defining Latino/a biblical interpretation a much more complex and nuanced task. Partially, this is also why I prefer not to endorse a fixed definition. Indeed, the danger of endorsing a fixed definition is that it may involve excluding identities that seem to contradict the desired totality of a unified (community) identity—particularly if those identities do not reflect the "normative" views of what constitutes a Latino/a. In other words, to not define is to invite, rather than displace, the outsider. To not define avoids constructing an impermeable border that can often cause fields to become static and exclusive, rather than fluid and open. It also challenges a notion of identity that may be used to define "legitimate" work by deciding who belongs and who does not, who speaks the same language and who does not, who holds the same assumptions and principles and who does not. That said, the danger of not defining, even broadly, is that others outside the community or non-Latino/as will do the defining. The essays in this volume exemplify the process of defining a Latino/a identity in a state of becoming—an engagement that requires and thus is open to constant negotiation.

Factor of Practice

In addition to the question of identity (fixed and/or fluid), some of the essays have focused on the question of practice (or reading strategy) as a strong element that determines what constitutes Latino/a biblical interpretation. In other words, they suggest that what makes Latino/a biblical interpretation "Latino/a" is how it is done. As most of the essays note, one aspect of this reading strategy is the foregrounding of Latino/a identity and its reality. This foregrounding of Latino/a identity challenges normative (Eurocentric) ways of doing biblical interpretation.

The foregrounding or positioning of Latino/a identity carries with it the possibility of discovering new meanings of a text, new ways of thinking about a text, or introducing new knowledge and identities to the text. In addition, the foregrounding of Latino/a identity as a reading strategy does not necessarily restrict the practice of Latino/a biblical interpretation just to Latino/as. Indeed, it implies that using this reading strategy Latino/a interpretations can be conducted by anyone who feels connected or committed to the Latino/a community. However, there is cause for concern in the assumption that Latino/a identity is defined not by identity but rather by practice in that it opens the door for anyone to do Latino/a biblical interpretation. One unfortunate outcome of this assumption could be that concerns, issues, or questions that are particular to the Latino/a community are overlooked or ignored. In addition, it may also lead to the assumption that anyone can be inextricably bound to the Latino/a community by the very fact of producing a Latino/a reading, thus appearing to be a part of the Latino/a community, but not acknowledging that they always have an "out"—not being Latino/a by way of ethnic/racial identification.

Some sense of what Latino/a biblical interpretation is (or is not) is always at work in the decisions one makes during the reading experience. Likewise, publishers, schools, and courses make judgments regarding the nature of Latino/a biblical scholarship. Even in this volume, some essays suggest that Latino/a biblical interpretation is better defined by the practice of it, thus promoting the inclusion of all those empathetic with the Latino/a community or connected directly with the Latino/a community to the practice of Latino/a biblical interpretation. I suggest that perhaps neither being nor practice by itself is the best way to define what Latino/a biblical interpretation is. Instead, a combination of both—something fixed and something fluid—may provide the best fit. In this sense, one could argue that the practice of Latino/a biblical interpretation is not simply the foregrounding of Latino/a identity, that it is also about challenging the idea that there is a "proper" way of doing Latino/a biblical interpretation.

Many essays in this volume support this notion—that there is no single correct way of practicing Latino/a biblical interpretation. Rather, they note that Latino/a biblical interpretation has taken multifarious forms, has focused on different issues and texts, and has drawn from a variety of theoretical positions, sources, methods, and reading strategies. Latino/a biblical reading can and does modify over time as readers, cultures, and politics change. It is a practice that represents the ever-changing relations between readers, texts, and the world. As such, the answer to what Latino/a biblical interpretation is remains open for discussion. What is eminently clear, however, is that Latino/a biblical interpretation is a field that continues to evolve and *become.*

Looking Forward: Intersectionality

In moving forward with Latino/a biblical interpretation, perhaps it would be helpful to shift the focus of inquiry from determining what it is to how it constructs knowledge, which constructs identities and practices. One area that can challenge both of these elements—being and practice—is a focus on the intersectionality of racial/ethnic, sexual, gender, and class identities. A focus in this area presents challenges to any notion of a homogenized identity on which Latino/a biblical interpretation might be perceived to be founded and calls instead for a reading strategy based on intersectional analyses of Latino/a identity and its relation to systems of power/knowledge. Intersectionality also challenges any singular way of doing Latino/a biblical interpretation as canon. The complex interaction between, for example, race and sexuality calls for a variety of ways of doing Latino/a biblical interpretation. Conversely, insisting that there is only one way of doing Latino/a biblical interpretation limits not only the reading strategies but also the way we think about Latino/as.

This is not to say that intersectionality is the only strategy to use in exploring or doing Latino/a biblical interpretation. Intersectionality also has its limitations. For instance, it may lead to a lowered level of vigilance in and commitment to looking at crucial questions of the ethnic/racial formation of Latino/as by turning Latino/as into an abstraction or blurring the differences through the lens of another optic, such as class, sexual orientation, or religion. In other words, race/ethnicity does not circumscribe these other identities, nor do these other identities circumscribe race/ethnicity. They are all intertwined. The same goes with the reading practices.

The issue of intersectionality is one among many other foci that Latino/a biblical interpretation will need to engage head-on in the near future to move away from an assimilationist understanding of sameness (one way of being and doing Latino/a biblical interpretation) toward a liberationist understanding of choice (multiple ways of being and doing Latino/a biblical interpretation). What I would suggest is in order next is a project along these lines.

Contributors

Efrain Agosto
New York Theological Seminary, New York City, New York

Hector Avalos
Department of Religious Studies, Iowa State University, Ames, Iowa

Eric D. Barreto
Luther Seminary, St. Paul, Minnesota

Aída Besançon Spencer
Gordon-Conwell Theological Seminary, South Hamilton, Massachusetts

Alejandro Botta
School of Theology, Boston University, Boston, Massachusetts

Gregory Cuellar
Austin Presbyterian Theological Seminary, Austin, Texas

Ruben R. Dupertuis
Religion Department, Trinity University, San Antonio, Texas

Cristina García-Alfonso
United Hospice Pruitt, Gainesville, Georgia

Jacqueline M. Hidalgo
Department of Religion, Williams College, Williamstown, Massachusetts

Francisco Lozada Jr.
Brite Divinity School, Forth Worth, Texas

Rubén Muñoz-Larrondo
Department of Religious and Biblical Studies, Andrews University,
Berrien Springs, Michigan

Ahida Calderón Pilarski
Theology Department, St. Anselm's College, Manchester,
New Hampshire

David Arturo Sánchez
Department of Theological Studies, Loyola Marymount College,
Los Angeles, California

Timothy J. Sandoval
Brite Divinity School, Fort Worth, Texas

Fernando F. Segovia
The Divinity School, Vanderbilt University, Nashville, Tennessee

Osvaldo D. Venaw
Garrett-Evangelical Theological Seminary, Evanston, Illinois

www.ingramcontent.com/pod-product-compliance
Lightning Source LLC
Chambersburg PA
CBHW030104010526
44116CB00005B/96